Ansett.

Stewart Wilson

CONTENTS

CONTENTS

INTRODUCTION

Welcome to 'Ansett', my attempt to tell the complex story of an Australian business that spanned 66 years from the pioneering days of the airline industry to the recent past. I have tried to present the story in a logical and readable manner which puts the events, people and politics which defined Ansett into context and hopefully goes some way towards explaining its quite remarkable history.

I don't believe there is any such thing as 'definitive' – and this work is certainly not – but the attempt has been made to provide as comprehensive a coverage of Ansett's history as is possible within the constraints of time and cost. The aim has been to provide something with appeal for not only the aviation enthusiast and those involved in the industry, but also for students of corporate history. For them, there is much that can be learned from the Ansett story.

Undertaking such a massive task would not have been possible without the help of many people. Several deserve special mention including airline historians Fred Niven and Gil White who made their comprehensive databases freely available to me (Fred was also responsible for putting together the Ansett family trees in the book); Geoff Wilkes, who lent me his very substantial collection of Ansett photographs and memorabilia; and Mark Brownley, who contributed the 'Ansett Fleet – Guilty as Charged or Just Maligned' chapter.

As for photographs, many people sent in large numbers and we ended up with about ten times the number required. I thank them all and acknowledge their contributions in the photograph captions. Several people's photographs were extensively used and I thank them separately, in particular Eric Allen, Rob Finlayson, George Canciani, Terry Ellis and Geoff Wilkes. As a result of their contributions, most of the photographs in the book have never been published before.

Finally, as always my thanks go to Jim Thorn and all at Aerospace Publications, especially Gerard Frawley for his proofreading and Gayla Wilson, Lee-Anne Simm and Sammi Woodford for taking care of the production aspects of the book. This is the 29th book I've written for Aerospace Publications and quite possibly the most important.

Stewart Wilson
Buckingham
October 2002

Published by Aerospace Publications Pty Ltd (ACN: 001 570 458) PO Box 1777, Fyshwick, ACT 2609, Australia. Phone (02) 6280 0111, fax (02) 6280 0007, email mail@ausaviation.com.au and website www.ausaviation.com.au publishers of monthly *Australian Aviation* magazine. Production Managers: Gayla Wilson and Lee-Anne Simm

ISBN 1 875671 57 9

Proudly Printed in Australia by Pirie Printers Pty Limited, 140 Gladstone St, Fyshwick, ACT 2609. Distributed throughout Australia by Network Distribution Company, 54 Park St, Sydney, 2000. Fax (02) 9264 3278

CHAPTER ONE

ANSETT:

WITH THE BENEFIT OF HINDSIGHT

When the first of the hijacked airliners that would bring terror and destruction to New York City and Washington DC found its target on 11 September 2001 it was at the start of the business day on that Tuesday morning. On Australia's east coast it was late at night on the same Tuesday and as the drama unfolded Tuesday turned into Wednesday the 12th of September.

The terrorist attacks on the USA naturally dominated the news all over the world then and for several days afterwards to the point that almost all other events were largely buried as we all tried to come to terms with what had happened.

In Australia, another major news story broke on 12 September but for the moment had to play second fiddle to New York and Washington. On that day, and following months of speculation and negotiation about its financial health and future ownership, Ansett Holdings Ltd, the parent company of Ansett Australia and its subsidiaries, was put into voluntary administration by owner Air New Zealand.

It wouldn't be correct to say that this story was ignored by the Australian print and electronic mass media but it certainly didn't receive the headlines it would normally have inspired because of what was happening on the other side of the world. As a result, most Australians were unaware of the seriousness of Ansett's situation.

All that changed to two days later, on 14 September. On that day, Ansett ran out of cash and was grounded by the administrator. At the same time, it was revealed that Air New Zealand was also in dire financial straits. The enormity of the situation was suddenly staring us in the face and the emphasis of the local media's headlines changed from the USA to home. At the time it seemed impossible but the facts were plain to see – after more than 65 years of operation, one of Australia's major corporate entities had gone broke and was apparently out of business with the loss of 13,428 jobs.

It was one of three major corporate shocks Australia's business community and the public had to endure at around the same time. Along with Ansett, insurance giant HIH failed as did telecommunications company One.Tel. In all three cases substantial job losses were involved along with enormous amounts of inconvenience for the public. Many other workers also lost their jobs as the effects of the failures filtered down to associated businesses, suppliers and creditors.

For Ansett, 14 September wasn't quite the end. New administrators were appointed the following week, their mission to get at least part of the airline up and running again so there would be a better chance of selling it as a going concern. 'Ansett Mk.II' resumed limited services on 29 September with some help from the Federal Government and the taxpayers of Australia through guaranteed fare protection until the end of January 2002.

In October some potential buyers began showing their faces including an Ansett staff syndicate (ANstaff) and the Tesna syndicate headed by businessmen Solomon Lew (formerly of Coles Myer) and Lindsay Fox, head of the Linfox group of transport and logistics companies. The ANstaff bid was withdrawn in November and on the 8th of that month Tesna's offer was accepted by the administrators. For Ansett and at least some of its staff (about 4,000 people), rescue seemed at hand.

A deadline of 31 January 2002 was set for completion of the deal. Fox and Lew started celebrating their triumph almost immediately, which was a concern for many observers, bearing in mind the adage about 'never counting your chickens before they're hatched'. A deal to lease a fleet of 30 Airbus A320s was announced, new equity partners were introduced to the consortium, executives were appointed and everything looked to be rosy.

The original deadline of 31 January was missed, but on the surface this appeared to be no great problem as the task of getting everything set up was recognised as being enormous. Two days before that a creditors' meeting had formally approved the sale to Tesna and a new deadline of 28 February was announced.

A few cracks started to appear during February: Tesna announced it was reducing its intake of former Ansett staff from 4,000 to 3,000; it was revealed that Ansett Mk.II was not attracting healthy passenger loadings and was losing around $6,000,000 per week; the new frequent flyer scheme was announced but generally dismissed as poor as it appeared to do little to encourage former Global Rewards members who had lost all their points to rejoin; Tesna was attempting to reduce its financial commitment; and finally it was revealed that

The administrators were left with no choice but to wind Ansett up and liquidate its assets. This decision was announced on 27 February to take effect on 4 March, 66 years, two weeks and one day after Fokker Universal VH-UTO operated the inaugural service of the fledgling Ansett Airways Pty Ltd between Hamilton in rural western Victoria and Melbourne's Essendon Airport.

The Ansett era ended at 6.42am on 5 March 2002 when flight AN152 arrived at Sydney after an overnight flight from Perth.

For all involved it was a shattering time, especially the employees who had been offered a job with the new Ansett. For them it had been a double blow. Having suffered the shock of the original failure the previous September, they had had their hopes built up to the point where it seemed establishment of the new Ansett was inevitable, only to have it all come crashing down again.

A Minor Player

Ansett therefore ended as it had begun – strapped for cash. When Ansett Airways flew that inaugural service between Hamilton and Essendon on 17 February 1936 the company's financial position was – like most new enterprises – far from secure. Reg Ansett only kept full control of his airline for just over a year as in April 1937 the company was floated in order to raise the capital required to finance its expansion plans. Ansett's major clients – the farmers of the Hamilton region – purchased most of the shares issue but their investment quickly looked shaky when a £30,000 ($60,000) loss for the first year of operation was announced and the share price halved.

The new capital did allow Ansett to expand its fleet and services. Three Lockheed L.10B Electras were acquired at a cost of £18,000 ($36,000) each, these modern all metal small airliners capable of carrying 10 passengers at

Sir Reginald Myles Ansett (1909-81), founder of Ansett Airways and the driving force behind the business empire that grew into the multi-faceted Ansett Transport Industries.

Tesna had been talking to low cost (and rapidly growing) carrier Virgin Blue on the subject of a merger. Virgin Blue rejected Tesna's overtures.

To many analysts, this was a strong indication that all was not well. Their worst fears were realised on 27 February when Messrs Fox and Lew suddenly announced that Tesna was pulling out of the deal.

Reg Ansett took a huge gamble in 1937 by purchasing three examples of the modern, fast, efficient – but expensive – Lockheed L.10 Electra. The gamble paid off in the longer term, thanks to their extensive use by American forces based in Australia during World War II. VH-UZO still survives.

Ansett Airways began operations in February 1938 with a single Fokker Universal but added this Airspeed Envoy to its fleet eight months later. At that stage – and for a considerable time afterwards – the fledgeling airline was struggling to survive and already recording heavy losses.

up to 200mph (322km/h) and offering operational capabilities far in excess of the airline's original Fokker Universal and the Airspeed Envoy which followed.

The Electra purchase was in some ways indicative of Ansett's financial insecurity at the time in that they were held in bond for a period after arriving in Australia because there was simply insufficient money to pay for them. This was found, but at the cost of Reg Ansett having to hand over more of his personal stake in the airline.

The first Electra entered service at the end of August 1937 and the airline's network expanded over the next year to include Sydney, Adelaide and points in between. The financial position remained precarious, however, and in November 1938 Ansett was approached by the local industry's dominant force – Australian National Airways – on the subject of a takeover. The Ansett board was keen to sell out but Reg Ansett wanted to hang on, putting himself into considerable debt to buy shares in his own airline in order to guarantee its independence.

Ansett Airways carried on as a minor player, surviving a major hangar fire at Essendon which destroyed an Electra, the Fokker and other aircraft. The situation remained basically static after Australia had become embroiled in the war against Germany from September 1939 but it changed in December 1941 when Japan attacked the US naval base at Pearl Harbor in Hawaii. Malaya, Singapore, the Dutch East Indies, New Guinea and other areas immediately to Australia's north quickly fell to the Japanese onslaught and Australia itself came under attack for the first time in February 1942 when Darwin was bombed. The threat of invasion was real.

Pivotal Events

It could be said that three pivotal events spread over a 16 year period prompted the growth of Ansett from a small and struggling airline to a major player on the Australian commercial aviation scene. The first was World War II (and specifically the USA's entry after Pearl

Harbor), the second was the formation of government owned Trans Australia Airlines (TAA) in 1946, and the third was the full implementation of Australia's rigidly controlled Two Airline Policy in 1958.

America's commitment to the fight against Japan resulted in large numbers of its service personnel being based in Australia. A transport infrastructure was necessary to cater for their needs and the airlines benefited greatly from this over a two-and-a-half year period from mid 1942 as the American presence in Australia grew.

Ansett was one of them, despite having only two Electras to devote to the cause. These aircraft were chartered on behalf of the US military and were worked hard, generating regular and useful income. Much more revenue was generated by Ansett's maintenance, engineering and workshop facility at Essendon, this greatly expanding in order to perform contract maintenance, manufacturing and repair work on behalf of the Australian and US military throughout the war.

Once hostilities ended, this work left Ansett in a stronger financial position than it had ever been and allowed it to grow further in the post war environment by purchasing Douglas DC-3s and expanding its route network.

The establishment of TAA at first seemed to signal problems for the still relatively small Ansett as it meant that a second large carrier would be entering the scene as a serious competitor to the industry giant, ANA. TAA started services in September 1946 and although it derived obvious benefits from being a government owned entity, its management quickly proved itself to be competent and progressive. TAA's engineering team was of a very high order and its ability to accurately assess the suitability of a particular type for the airline's operations resulted in some astute purchases, notably the Vickers Viscount.

While TAA was growing, ANA was declining. Poor management had led the airline to a series of heavy financial losses in the first half of the 1950s, this exacerbated

After taking over ANA, Ansett embarked on a concentrated period of 'empire building' during which it acquired several regional airlines in Australia and New Guinea. Butler Air Transport was one of them, rebranded as Airlines of New South Wales in late 1959. DC-3 VH-ANR (photographed here in September 1968) was one of the 19 of its type obtained with ANA. (Eric Allen)

by the death in early 1957 of its chairman and driving force, Sir Ivan Holyman. A merger with TAA had previously been discussed and rejected, while legislative and commercial options designed to save ANA were also looked at.

Politically, the Federal Government had in 1952 introduced the Airlines Agreement Act which was the first stage in establishing a Two Airlines Policy for Australian domestic services. This gave TAA and ANA equal access to mail carriage and government business, and for ANA, government guarantees for the loans necessary to re-equip.

Ansett was not part of this arrangement and was still regarded as a fairly insignificant part of the overall industry. The airline had instigated a major (for it) fleet upgrade program in 1954 with the arrival of its first Convair CV-340 pressurised airliner, this all part of Reg Ansett's plan to continue expanding and survive in the face of the giants TAA and ANA.

When ANA's problems were recognised as becoming terminal in 1957, Ansett offered to take over the much larger airline with money it simply didn't have. It was a clear case of David taking on Goliath and the offer wasn't taken very seriously by anyone. Ansett persisted, and in July 1957 made another offer, this time with financial backing from oil companies Vacuum (now Mobil) and Shell. The offer was accepted the following month

Guinea Airways was another early Ansett-ANA acquisition and was renamed Airlines of South Australia. DC-3 VH-ABR was rare in being a genuine prewar commercial model originally delivered to ANA in 1938. (Eric Allen)

Like hundreds of other airlines all over the world, Ansett chose the ubiquitous Douglas DC-3 as its primary postwar equipment with the first aircraft delivered in 1946. As was the case with most other DC-3s, Ansett's were converted from military C-47s.

and completed on 3 October 1957. On 21 October, the new trading name Ansett-ANA was launched.

Suddenly, Reg Ansett's little airline was playing with the big boys.

The ANA takeover was the first step in an aggressive series of regional airline acquisitions by Ansett-ANA over the next few years including Butler Air Transport (renamed Airlines of New South Wales), Queensland Airlines (which came as part of the Butler deal), Guinea Airways (Airlines of South Australia), New Guinea's Mandated Airlines (Ansett-MAL), MacRobertson Miller Airlines and others. Many more takeovers would be performed in the years ahead.

The Two Airline Policy as applied to Australian domestic trunk route operations was the jewel in the crown for Ansett. This was part of the deal with the Federal Government on the takeover of ANA and was fully implemented via the Airlines Equipment Bill of 1958. It

The government owned Trans Australia Airlines introduced the pressurised Convair CV-240 to service in 1948, this aircraft playing a large part in its early success. Ansett could also see the merits of the Convair and ordered improved CV-340s for delivery from 1954, these later joined by CV-440s. This is CV-440 VH-BZI, delivered in October 1957, the same month that Ansett-ANA was formed.

The Vickers Viscount played a very significant role in the growth of TAA and the demise of ANA, whose piston engined Douglas DC-6s couldn't compete with the turboprop's passenger appeal. The Viscount was also important to Ansett-ANA because under the terms of the Two Airline Policy, TAA was forced to 'lease' three of its Viscounts to Ansett-ANA in exchange for two DC-6Bs. VH-TVF was one of them. Ansett also acquired Viscounts in its own right. (Geoff Wilkes)

introduced heavy regulation covering fleet purchases, routes and fare structures and dominated the industry for the next 30 years.

For Ansett-ANA it virtually guaranteed profits and growth by in effect inhibiting TAA and artificially ensuring that as far as was possible, the market would be shared between the two airlines. For the operator of any business in any field, this was almost fiscal heaven. The only thing better would be a monopoly.

There was an industry joke which had its origins in this period: 'There are two airlines in Australia. One of them operates with government assistance – the other one is TAA!'

Diverse Interests

By the mid 1960s Ansett Transport Industries Ltd – the group's holding company between May 1946 and August 1994 – was established as a major force in the Australian commercial world.

Its airline group was the largest in Australia headed by Ansett-ANA and including regional subsidiaries which operated internal services in all states of Australia except Tasmania plus Papua New Guinea. In addition, Ansett had held a 49% interest in South Pacific Airlines of New Zealand (SPANZ) between 1960 and 1964, flying DC-3s provided by Ansett to over 20 points within both the North and South Islands.

Ansett Flying Boat Services was the first of the Ansett airline subsidiaries to be established, formed in 1952 from the remains of Barrier Reef Airways and joined the following year by the bankrupt Trans Oceanic Airways. AFBS continued flying its Short Sandringham

flying boats from Sydney's Rose Bay to Lord Howe Island until September 1974 when an airstrip was built on the island and the venerable flying boats were given an honourable retirement.

A Helicopter Division was also established and this made history in December 1960 by introducing the world's first airport to city helicopter service between Essendon Airport and a floating heliport on Melbourne's Yarra River using Bell 47s. Reg Ansett was himself an almost daily user of the helicopter to commute from his home at Mount Eliza to Melbourne for a day at the company's office at 489 Swanston Street. Later, in 1980, ATI moved into newly built headquarters at 501 Swanston Street.

But ATI was not just about airline operations, it was a substantial organisation with diverse but often related interests which were purchased or established over the years. These included road transport (both freight and passenger coaches), hotels (the largest operator in Australia with some 40 on the books at one stage), Whitsunday Islands resorts, instrument making, general aviation (distributor of Piper aircraft), insurance, Ford vehicle sales, Avis Rent-A-Car, engineering equipment sales agencies, transport industry insurance, airline catering, television stations (ATV Channel 0 in Melbourne and TVQ Channel 0 in Brisbane), travel agencies, aircraft seat manufacturing, coach and airport bus manufacturing and more.

Many of these businesses had been established in the early post war years when Ansett Airways was still a very small operation. Pioneer Tourist Coaches (later Ansett Roadlines of Australia), for example, had been purchased from its founder as early as 1944 and this was supplemented in 1946 by Ansett Hotels to accommodate passengers using the Pioneer coach services. At the same time, the company's aircraft component manufacturing activities were replaced by building coaches by a new company, Ansair. The result was a self contained series of operations, each one deriving income from the other. Other existing regional road passenger services were purchased in the late 1940s, establishing a substantial network around Australia.

A major and growing part of Ansett Transport Industries' business since 1947 was the development of a chain of hotels and tourist resorts. The luxurious Hayman Island in Queensland's Whitsundays was one of them, for many years serviced by Ansett Sikorsky S-61N helicopters. (George Canciani)

The Lockheed L.188 Electra turboprop served both Ansett-ANA and TAA as their main trunk route airliner from March 1959 until the first Boeing 727 jets arrived 5^1/$_2$ years later. VH-RMA was Ansett's first Electra. (Terence Ellis)

The expansion into the Whitsunday Islands resorts scene began in 1947 when Ansett took over the perpetual lease on Hayman Island which was (and remains) developed as a luxury resort. The island's Royal Hayman Hotel opened in 1950 while interests in Daydream, Heron, Lindeman and South Molle Islands were also established.

ATI's retail division, Ansett Travel Service, sold the tickets for the various other businesses, this in combination with the hotels, coaches and airline resulting in a network of services which could be cross promoted and was in many ways self perpetuating. An Ansett customer could book his or her journey or holiday through Ansett Travel Service, fly to the required destination on Ansett Airways or travel by road on a Pioneer coach, stay at an Ansett Hotel and rent a car from Avis to get around.

This infrastructure stood the overall operation in good stead from 1957 when Ansett-ANA was established because the group finally had a substantial airline at its disposal to help feed the other businesses and vice-versa.

As a side issue, when it came to car rental at Australian airports, customers had no choice but to go to Avis as the company enjoyed a monopoly – by regulation – until June 1979 when competition was finally allowed. In a celebrated example of Australian corporate irony, the man responsible for breaking the Avis monopoly after a sometimes acrimonious battle was the boss of the Budget Rent-A-Car group, Reg Ansett's estranged son, Bob.

The Jet Age

The connection with ANA disappeared from the airline's trading name in November 1968 with Ansett-ANA

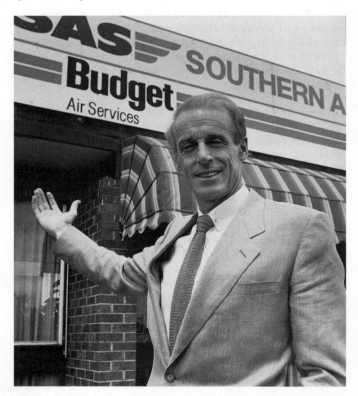

(middle) Dysfunctional families. Ansett owned Avis Rent A Car enjoyed a monopoly at Australia's major airports for some years, but this was vigorously and very publicly challenged by Budget Rent-A-Car, headed by Reg Ansett's estranged son Bob. Bob Ansett was ultimately successful and Avis' monopoly ended in 1979, although Budget later failed. (right) The takeover of the 'giant' Australian National Airways in 1957 by the much smaller Ansett Airlines to create Ansett-ANA was one of the pivotal events in Australian commercial aviation history. Eleven years later, the once great 'ANA' disappeared from the title, replaced by Ansett Airlines of Australia. This pair of Lockheed Electras display both sets of markings. (Terence Ellis)

The jet age came to Australian domestic routes in early November 1964 when Ansett-ANA and TAA simultaneously launched services between Melbourne and Sydney in a carefully choreographed manner which summed up Australia's strict 'two airline' policy. VH-RME was Ansett-ANA's first 727-77, delivered the previous month in an equally stage managed event with TAA's first 727 delivery.

becoming Ansett Airlines of Australia. By then, a whole new era had started in the Australian domestic airline market with the simultaneous introduction of Boeing 727 jets by both airlines in October 1964 for use on major trunk routes, followed by the Douglas DC-9 in April 1967. There was still room for innovation in the less regulated regional airline market, Ansett-MMA introducing Australia's first intrastate jet service in September 1969 when the Fokker F28 Fellowship began plying routes in Western Australia.

The DC-9 purchase sparked a union dispute, courtesy the often militant Australian Federation of Airline Pilots. The AFAP had long been able to get away with just about anything it wanted to achieve by threatening strike action, and had created a situation where, frankly, the airlines (especially Ansett-ANA) were frightened of it. In the case of the DC-9, the union decided it wanted the aircraft ordered by both Ansett-ANA and TAA to have a three crew cockpit – two pilots and a flight engineer – where the aircraft was specifically designed to carry two pilots only.

The DC-9 was not alone in this with all of the new generation of short to medium haul jets – DC-9, Boeing 737 and BAC One-Eleven – designed from the outset with two crew cockpits. The larger, long range intercontinental jets still had a flight engineer's station and would continue to do so for a while yet, but even that would eventually change with the rise of the digital cockpit.

The DC-9 had already been in Australian service for nearly a year when the AFAP demanded that existing two crew DC-9 operations would end at the beginning of March 1968 and the fleet would be grounded. Even though the aircraft had no provision for a flight engineer's station, the union wanted an engineer sitting in the jump seat, with nothing much to do!

Reg Ansett immediately surrendered to the union's demands, while TAA held firm and found its DC-9s

grounded on the appointed day as a result. The AFAP's flight engineer's added to TAA's woes by also forcing the grounding of the airline's 727s and Electras for a couple of days, leaving the market temporarily open to Ansett. After considerable acrimony between the two airlines, the union and a High Court action, the AFAP's demands were formally rejected and the DC-9s carried on operating with a two man crew. TAA's had been out of action for nearly six weeks in the meantime.

Apart from that incident, both Ansett and TAA operated largely in what may be called 'the comfort zone' during the 1970s with the Two Airline Policy ensuring generally good returns and no possibility of further competition on Australia's domestic trunk routes. With parallel scheduling, virtually identical fleets and regulated (and high) fares, there was little incentive for either airline to go out of their way to provide a superior service for passengers.

The term 'Boeing Derby' emerged from this, the derisive joke describing the daily 'races' between Ansett and TAA jets from point to point. If you saw an airliner from one of the operators leave a given city, you could bet your house on the fact that the opposition's flight would follow a few minutes later. For passengers, this meant few if any options as to travel departure and arrival times, but not knowing any better, most of us just accepted this as part of the deal. By an Act of Parliament, the Two Airline System was extended beyond the previously legislated 1977 for an indefinite period.

With one notable exception, Ansett had a fairly quiet period throughout most of the 1970s. Operationally,

From July 1981 there was finally some difference between Ansett and TAA in terms of their fleets when TAA introduced the Airbus A300 widebody to service. Ansett's Boeing 767s would follow two years later. This advertisement at Melbourne Airport in July 1981 was part of a major campaign by TAA to promote its new fleet. Faced with lagging behind TAA in the 'widebody' stakes, Ansett introduced an aggressive campaign of its own, using lines such as 'Why Catch a Bus When You Can Fly A Boeing?' (Rob Finlayson)

Ansett-ANA and (from 1968) Ansett Airlines of Australia operated a total of 28 Boeing 727s of various models between 1964 and 1997, the type playing a significant part in the airline's development over the years. VH-RME was Ansett-ANA's fourth 727-77, delivered in August 1966. (Terence Ellis)

Boeing 727-200s began to replace the earlier models, Ansett Flying Boat Services was closed down following the building of an airstrip on Lord Howe Island, and two familiar types – the Vickers Viscount and Lockheed Electra – were retired from passenger service, although the latter continued as a freighter.

The opening of Melbourne's new Tullamarine Airport in 1971 saw both Ansett and TAA move their operations from Essendon while in 1973 Ansett introduced its innovative Ansamatic (a contraction of 'Ansett' and 'automatic') computerised reservations system. A similar reservations system for ATI's hotels (called 'Ansotel') was introduced in 1977.

Overseas, the granting of independence to Papua New Guinea in 1975 saw both Ansett's and TAA's subsidiaries in the former Australian Territory closed down as such in favour of a new national airline – Air Niugini – in which the initial shareholders were Ansett, TAA, Qantas and the PNG Government.

Non aviation activities continued to develop with ATI purchasing a 50% interest in Diners Club in 1974, Ansett Road Express continued to grow, more hotels were built, a 50% interest in pen manufacturer Biro Bic (Australia)

was purchased as was a minority interest in finance company Associated Securities Ltd, which collapsed two years later causing ATI considerable financial distress. Avis Rent-A-Car became a wholly owned ATI subsidiary in 1978.

The exception to what was mostly a fairly routine period occurred in 1972 with the beginning of the battle for control of Ansett Transport Industries that would eventually lead to the company being jointly owned by Peter Abeles' TNT and Rupert Murdoch's News Corporation.

TNT wanted to make a bid for Ansett as part of Peter Abeles' plans to broaden his company's business base and eventually expand it into the global market. In March 1972 TNT acquired a minority shareholding in ATI by purchasing shares held by W R Carpenter Holdings and Boral, but not before an extraordinary act of political interference by long serving Victorian Premier Sir Henry Bolte on behalf of his friend Reg Ansett.

Sir Reginald (who had been knighted in 1969) was strongly opposed to TNT's move on the company, prompting Sir Henry to invoke an ancient piece of legislation which prevented a company registered outside Victoria (TNT was incorporated in New South Wales) gaining control of a local organisation. This restricted TNT's shareholding to 23.5%, its voting rights to 10%, and its representation on the board of directors to two, with Peter Abeles one of them.

It was to no-one's great surprise that on his retirement from politics in 1973 Sir Henry Bolte was appointed to the Ansett board. However, when a further battle for control of Ansett by TNT, News Corp and Robert Holmes a Court's Bell Group erupted later in the decade there was no benevolent Victorian Premier to help Sir Reginald out.

Ansett-ANA's second jet was the Douglas DC-9-30, once again introduced to service simultaneously with TAA's aircraft in April 1967. There was considerable controversy surrounding the DC-9's introduction when the pilots' union insisted that a third crewmember – a flight engineer – be carried despite there being no provision for one. (Eric Allen)

A New Regime

With the benefit of hindsight it can be seen that by the late 1970s Ansett Transport Industries was probably ripe for takeover. The company had grown into a very substantial organisation with assets in the region of $300,000,000 and about 14,000 employees. Its interests were diverse and in the main profitable but the company was also very conservative – too conservative in the eyes of some. Peter Abeles and TNT could see its potential if managed with a little more vigour in a changing, increasingly global business environment. Abeles had already made his intentions towards Ansett clear and despite Sir Henry Bolte's interference in 1972 had his toe in the door through TNT's 23.5% shareholding.

The Australian domestic airline industry was also starting to change, almost imperceptibly at first. Some cracks were starting to appear in the solidity of the Two Airline Policy and there was a feeling that sooner or later it would be dismantled.

The system was soon to be challenged, notably by former New South Wales intrastate operator East-West Airlines, by the early 1980s under the control of Bryan Grey, who had ambitions to make his airline into a third trunk route carrier despite the limitations imposed by the Two Airline Policy. Grey's East-West flew cut price services to some of the capital cities using Fokker F28s but got around the rules by making an intermediate stop en route. Sydney-Melbourne flights, for example, included a stop at Albury. Grey also challenged the system in court and later went on to form Australia's first post deregulation domestic carrier, the short-lived Compass Airlines.

As for Ansett, the battle for control began in earnest in mid 1979 with the Bell Group, Ampol and TNT the major early players. Rupert Murdoch's News Corporation entered the fray later in the year, initially prompted not by any interest in ATI's airlines or other transport busi-

It all changed at Ansett Transport Industries in January 1980 when control of the company was jointly acquired by News Corp and TNT, headed by powerful businessmen Rupert Murdoch (left) and Peter Abeles, respectively. Murdoch and Abeles became joint managing directors while Sir Reginald Ansett stepped away from that position but remained as chairman until his death the following year.

nesses but by its television stations in Melbourne and Brisbane. A now ageing Reg Ansett tried to prevent these attempts to take over 'his' company by doing a deal with Bell which would remove TNT and News from the equation.

As detailed in a following chapter, this ploy failed and after much movement and more than a little back stabbing, the issue was settled in January 1980 when ATI's shareholding was settled at 50% each for TNT and News with Sir Peter Abeles and Rupert Murdoch as joint managing directors. A disappointed Reg Ansett resigned as managing director but stayed on as chairman until his death in December 1981 at the age of 72.

The arrival of News Corp and TNT as Ansett's owners brought with it a spate of new aircraft orders during the first half of the 1980s. The first was in March 1980 when the company's largest order to date was placed, a $600m contract to purchase 12 Boeing 737-200s, four 727-200LRs and five 767-200s. A new livery was introduced along with the new era, and the first 737-200 (VH-CZM) was delivered in June 1981.

Ansett's first widebody (or 'semi widebody') airliner was the Boeing 767-200 which entered service in June 1983. This event was delayed by seven months partly due to Ansett requesting a deferral of deliveries thanks to the economic downturn in Australia at the time, and partly because of union demands which resulted in Ansett's early 767s being the only ones in the world built with a three man cockpit which included a flight engineer. (Julian Green)

Party Time

The TNT-News takeover certainly breathed new life into the organisation, especially over the first decade when considerable amounts were spent on fleet upgrades and other acquisitions.

Under the stewardship of TNT-News, the regional subsidiaries and affiliates were reorganised and rebranded (sometimes more than once); the Ansett Golden Wing Club for business travellers was established; business class was introduced; Ansett Australia Air Cargo was renamed Ansett Air Freight and operated as a separate entity which worked in conjunction with the company's road freight businesses; ATI's Whitsunday Islands interests were expanded to include half ownership of the airport on Hamilton Island plus taking over the operating lease of South Molle; management contracts were established with South Pacific operators Air Vanuatu and Polynesian Airlines; and a brief foray into the trans-Tasman market was made following several attempts to gain approval.

As for the main game, Ansett's fleet re-equipment program got underway in March 1980 when its largest ever aircraft order was placed with Boeing, the $400m contract covering 12 737-200s, four 727-200LRs and five 'semi widebody' twin aisle 767-200s.

The 737-200s were ordered to replace the similar number of DC-9s then in service, a move which many passengers saw as being a backwards one as the DC-9 – although now getting a few years old – was popular with the travelling public. Compared with its successor, the DC-9 had wider seats and a quieter cabin, but the decision to purchase the 737s was as much a result of doing a very good deal with Boeing as much as anything else.

The arrival of the first 737-200s in June 1981 occurred shortly after the company's branding was given a revamp. Gone was the now familiar predominantly red livery with the stylised 'A' tail markings – in its place came a thoroughly modern overall 'Eurowhite' scheme with a colourful Southern Cross and Star of Federation tail logo. Gone, too was the trading name Ansett Airlines of Australia and in its place came simply the word 'Ansett.' – complete with the full stop, this apparently something to do with making a 'statement', according to the hyperbole experts who conceived it.

The 767 order caused Ansett some problems which would be ongoing. As it had done 16 years earlier with the DC-9, the AFAP once again flexed its muscles and demanded the new Boeing have a flightdeck crew of three – two pilots and a flight engineer. The airline's management bowed to union pressure and allowed the aircraft to be built with a flight engineer's station.

The 767 was designed to have a two crew cockpit at a time when the flight engineer was clearly becoming an unnecessary anachronism, just as the coal shovelling fireman had become as the age of steam trains passed into history several decades earlier. The result was a fleet of 767s which were unique in having a flight engineer on board, with the additional manufacturing and operating costs it entailed.

Ansett's 767 order was also important in the wider context in that it represented the first significant separation of the two airlines when it came to major equipment purchases. TAA had ordered the Airbus A300 widebody and put it into service in July 1981, just at a time when the industry was undergoing one of its regular 'early decade bust' parts of the economic cycle. The airline found itself with excess capacity as a result, forcing the immediate leasing out of one of the five A300s it had ordered and the deferred delivery for a year of another.

The delivery of Ansett's first 767s was delayed by seven months, partly due to the crewing dispute and partly at the airline's request so as to avoid an overcapacity problem. The first one – complete with three crew cockpit – entered service in June 1983, two years after TAA introduced widebody airliners to the Australian market and at a time when the worst of the downturn was over.

Ansett's ordering spree continued into the 1980s, with the Paris Air Show in June 1985 representing the high point. Australian aviation journalists at the show will

Ansett's spending spree continued into the mid 1980s, two of its most important orders being for the Boeing 737-300 (below) and Airbus A320 (above), the latter the world's first fly-by-wire airliner. Even though both are properly regarded as being fine airliners, the wisdom of Ansett acquiring two different types for essentially the same role was questioned then and remained a subject of discussion for many years. (Julian Green/Bill Lines)

(AWAS) – which quickly became a major player on the world stage – and for TNT, which signed a 'commitment' for up to 72 BAe 146 freighters for its expanding European air express business. The 146 in both passenger and freighter forms was also ordered for Ansett and the TNT contract encouraged British Aerospace to open a second assembly line at the old Avro works in Manchester.

The 737-300 entered service with Ansett in September 1986, followed by the A320 in January 1989, this event delayed by more than a month while union problems involving flight attendants, flight engineers and pilots were dealt with. Once again the AFAP tried to tell Ansett that the A320 required a third cockpit crew member – a flight engineer – even though there was no provision for him or her. This was eventually sorted out, but later in the 1989 it became clear that this skirmish was only the AFAP warming up for the main event!

The second half of the 1980s saw the Ansett group continue to expand its interests. Offshore, there was the establishment of AWAS as noted above; Ansett New Zealand in October 1986 after ATI acquired a 50% interest in domestic operator Newmans Air (later 100%); and Ansett took an initial 20% stake in US carrier America West in June 1987.

In Australia, some of the regional subsidiaries were reorganised and renamed. For example, Ansett Airlines of New South Wales became Air NSW in May 1985, Ansett NSW in March 1990 and Ansett Express in November 1990; and in July 1987 it was announced that Ansett would take over Perth based Skywest Holdings which had previously acquired the former New South Wales intrastate operator East-West. East-West and Skywest had joined forces largely in an attempt to break away from the constraints imposed by the Two Airline Policy on interstate routes.

The purchase gave Ansett an additional small operation in Western Australia through Skywest Airlines and new options on the east coast through East-West. The latter was restyled as 'Eastwest' and developed into the 'tourist' arm of the Ansett network, serving ports such as Queensland's Gold Coast using a fleet of BAe 146s.

Eastwest was given a young, 'hip' and 'with it' image in a bid to attract the younger tourist market but it didn't work very well and the airline failed to make money in the newly deregulated world of Australian skies. A more upmarket image was applied in early 1993 but by the end of that year the airline had disappeared from the scene.

Changing Times

The Australian airline scene entered a period of constant change in the mid 1980s, most of it resulting from

remember it well, with Sir Peter Abeles in 'a buying mood'. He was followed around the show by a herd of journalists and airliner manufacturer representatives, all of them hanging on his next move as he visited chalets and spoke to industry heavyweights, notably those from Boeing and Airbus.

And Sir Peter didn't disappoint. At the show he announced a $US380m order for eight of the new and as yet unflown Airbus A320 airliners, the world's first with fly-by-wire flight controls.

Three weeks later, 12 second generation Boeing 737-300s were ordered to replace the relatively noisy and thirsty 737-200s which had only entered service in 1981. These were smaller than the A320 and available two years earlier. The stretched 737-400 with about the same passenger capacity as the A320 was ignored as it would not be available until after the A320, leaving Ansett with two different narrowbody aircraft types to fill its future trunk route needs. Although both the A320 and 737 were and remain perfectly fine aircraft, many questioned the wisdom of this duplication of types in the Ansett fleet.

Sir Peter's buying spree continued into 1987 with substantial orders for the 737 for the newly established leasing company Ansett Worldwide Aviation Services

the recognition that deregulation was not an issue of 'if', but 'when'. The ball started rolling in earnest in 1985 when the Federal Government commissioned its Independent Review of Economic Regulation of Domestic Aviation, chaired by Tom May. Submissions were taken from the airlines, state governments, unions and the public over the next two years.

The report was presented in January 1987 and was critical of the Two Airline System, saying it did not serve the travelling public well. Five options were presented for consideration, ranging from maintaining the status quo to full deregulation.

The decision was made and it was announced that from 1 November 1990, Australian domestic airline operations would be deregulated. No longer would fares, fleets and schedules be determined by regulation. The airlines could now set their own agenda and make their own progress (or mistakes) based on their own decisions. The new rules meant that anyone with the financial and infrastructure wherewithal could start an airline and compete in the Australian domestic market against the 'big two'.

By the second half of the 1980s and for a time afterwards Ansett commanded the majority of the Australian domestic market. Government owned TAA was suffering by comparison, especially in the business market which Ansett had come to dominate. Initiatives such as the Golden Wing Club had been very successful and even though total passenger numbers were split pretty much 50/50 in the early and mid part of the decade, Ansett had the edge when it came to the higher yield end of the market. After that, Ansett began to edge ahead overall.

TAA, with James Strong at the helm, reinvented itself as Australian Airlines from August 1986 ahead of major changes. Many of these were to do with the now seemingly inevitable coming of deregulation but others were part of the greater overall plan, when the government owned carrier would merge with the also government owned Qantas to create a very substantial force in both the domestic and international markets.

Qantas eventually took over Australian in September 1992 and the Australian Airlines name disappeared, ahead of the planned privatisation of the combined operation. The public float of 75% of Qantas was successfully launched in July 1995, the remaining 25% already having been acquired by British Airways.

Pilots in Dispute

But before any of that happened, both Ansett and Australian had to endure one of the most disruptive events in the history of the Australian airline industry – the pilots' dispute which started in August 1989 and lasted some five months.

This was another example of the AFAP flexing its muscles and assuming it would once more get away with it. Ostensibly, the dispute was over a massive 27% pay claim but the real reason was consolidation of the union's power in the forthcoming deregulated era. The AFAP had assumed the airlines would quickly surrender to its demands but this time they held firm with the support of the Federal Government under Prime Minister Bob Hawke.

What the AFAP didn't properly appreciate was the fact that it was not just taking on the airlines per se, but in the case of Ansett, its owners, two of the world's most powerful and influential businessmen in Peter Abeles and Rupert Murdoch. For the Australian Government, there was considerable vested interest in the ongoing viability of Australian Airlines, bearing in mind its planned privatisation.

Six days into the dispute, the AFAP dramatically demonstrated its poor, greedy and tactically inept leadership when it convinced its 1,647 members to resign en masse, leaving the country with in effect no domestic air services. This action at a stroke lost the union any support it may have had from the government and the public and forced the airlines to bring in foreign aircraft and their crews to help restore a semblance of service. At least the dispute occurred during the northern hemisphere 'off' season, so there were aircraft and crews available. Even the RAAF chipped in, flying passengers in C-130 Hercules and HS.748 transports and doing its public image no harm at all as a result.

It took nearly five months for the dispute to resolve itself, in which time the airlines suffered massive revenue drops and many areas of the nation's economy which depend on reliable air services to survive had to cut down by putting off staff.

At the end of the day, the AFAP completely failed in its aims and was beaten into submission with little or no remaining power base, no sympathy from the industry, government or public and no credibility whatsoever with any of them. 'It's about time', was a common thought expressed throughout the industry – and it was.

Gradual Decline

It's impossible to tell exactly when the decline of Ansett began. Some say it started with the pilots' dispute which contributed to the group's pre tax profit dropping

A320 at rest – a sight temporarily symbolic of Ansett on 14 September 2001 and permanently from 4 March 2002. (Theo Van Loon)

Deregulation of the Australian domestic airline industry finally came in November 1990, this allowing new entrants into the market. The first of them was the low fare Compass Airlines and its Airbus A300-600s in December 1990 – it failed a year later. (Airbus)

from \$67.33m in 1988-90 to just \$2.58m in 1989-90. This was only part of the problem, however, as Eastwest and Ansett New Zealand in particular were both losing substantial amounts.

Others suggest it was the deregulation of the industry which started the ball rolling downhill, as Ansett no longer had the cosy protection of the Two Airline Policy, while there is also a case to suggest the real damage started when it became apparent that both TNT and News Corp were not as interested in Ansett as they had once been.

Both companies were having their own problems in the early 1990s when the latest 'down' part of the economic cycle hit. This time the worldwide downturn was more marked than usual largely due to the effects of the Gulf War, and both Peter Abeles and Rupert Murdoch were facing difficulties with their primary businesses. TNT alone had lost nearly \$400m between 1990 and 1992.

Speculation that both TNT and News were considering selling at least a part of their interest in Ansett began in early 1991, and at the time it was thought that News was the most likely candidate to bail out first. The speculation grew during the course of 1991 when problems arose with several operations. Eastwest and Ansett NZ both continued to lose heavily while overseas, America West – in which TNT-News held a 26% interest – went into Chapter 11 Bankruptcy protection. Overall, analysts estimated Ansett's 1990-91 loss at around \$50m and considered the company needed a \$200m capital injection. This amount of money was not easily available from the company's owners at the time.

It is really from this point that Ansett began to lose its way as it was more often than not unprofitable over the next few years and its domestic market share continued to gradually decline. Management restructures, the sale of non core assets, staff redundancies and wage deals became more common as the decade progressed, all this at a time when the global airline industry was going through further major changes. Ansett Transport Industries lost \$92.1m in the 1991-92 financial year.

This was also the era of commercial agreements between individual airlines, codesharing and the eventual establishment of large global alliances formally linking a number of airlines and their frequent flyer rewards programs. The announcement of codeshare agreements on various routes became an almost daily occurrence all

over the world for several years until it seemed that every operator was in some way hooked up with someone else.

Ansett was no exception, having put in place commercial agreements with international carriers Lufthansa, United, Northwest, Alitalia, All Nippon, Garuda, Singapore, Swissair and Malaysian by early 1993. Ansett even had a codeshare arrangement with British Airways for a while, but this lapsed when BA bought into Qantas. Others were later added and it all culminated in March 1999 when Ansett was admitted to the Star Alliance as a full member, this group led by United Airlines and Lufthansa and eventually adding several other major carriers to its books including Singapore Airlines.

The year leading to deregulation was interesting and underscored the relatively comfortable existence enjoyed by both Ansett and TAA/Australian under the Two Airline Policy. Suddenly, a few more discount air fares became available – albeit usually with restrictive conditions attached – as both airlines sought to gain an advantage over each other.

When the first post deregulation startup – the low fare Compass Airlines – began operations in December 1990 a price war was immediately triggered with the major airlines starting to offer fares which were only a fraction of what was previously charged. The idea, of course, was to squeeze out Compass wherever possible, although it was naturally impossible to get executives from either Ansett or Australian to admit that!

The deep discounts offered by Compass and the major airlines stimulated new traffic as people who could not afford to fly before were now able to. But this was to prove Compass' undoing. It doesn't matter how many tickets an airline sells, if they are sold for a price less than their cost, the airline is going to fail. And Compass failed in December 1991, blaming everyone but itself for its troubles. Yes, the major airlines had contributed by matching Compass' fares in some areas, but in a free and deregulated market they were entirely within their rights to do so providing there was no collusion.

Compass also had the wrong aircraft in service. The widebody Airbus A300s it leased were simply too large. What was needed was a larger fleet of smaller airliners of 737/A320/MD-90 size so that higher frequencies and greater scheduling flexibility could be offered.

A second new cut price operator launched services in August 1992. Southern Cross Airlines traded as

The launch of Ansett International in September 1994 brought with it a new corporate image for the airline and its last livery. Ansett International operated to various ports in Asia using Boeing 747-300s (and later -400s) leased from Singapore Airlines but was badly hit by the Asian economic crisis of 1997-98. This is 747-300 VH-INH, one of the original pair of aircraft used by Ansett International. (Craig Fraser)

Compass, the management hoping to cash in on the goodwill it thought the name had with the general public. 'Compass II' – as it was dubbed – only lasted seven months before it also failed under a cloud of financial impropriety, this later proven and resulting in a jail sentence for its chairman.

So far, deregulation of the Australian domestic airline system had been something of a fizzer with two new airlines starting and both failing quickly. It would be another seven years before further attempts would be made to take on the 'Big Two'.

Australia in the meantime reverted to another Two Airline System, but this time an unofficial one and largely by default. The question as to whether or not the local domestic market was large enough to support more than two trunk route carriers was starting to be asked, and it still is.

Changing of the Guard

A significant event in the history of Ansett occurred in September 1992 when both Rupert Murdoch and Sir Peter Abeles stood down as joint chairmen and chief executives of ATI. News Corp CEO Ken Cowley took over as chairman and TNT CEO David Mortimer as deputy chairman. Sir Peter stated at the time that he would continue working to rejuvenate Ansett's financial fortunes but ill health forced him to resign most of his positions both with TNT and Ansett shortly afterwards.

The time was ripe for a 'changing of the guard' and some progress was made with Ansett. A strong indication that a sale was looming appeared in 1993 when for the first time since becoming a private company under TNT-News Control, ATI's full results for the 1992-93 financial year were published. As a private company there was no obligation to do this but the figures showed a profit of $59.5m before tax and abnormals compared with a $91.2m loss the previous year. Even though the net result was a deficit of $181.2m after foreign exchange losses were taken into account, publishing the operating profit was seen as a message to potential buyers that the business was viable.

The 1993-94 result was even better with a gross profit of $209.2m recorded, the highest in Ansett's history. But this was the peak; after that, there was a mixture of losses and modest profits.

Ansett's operational history had one more significant event up its sleeve. That was the inauguration of services in September 1994 of Ansett International, established to operate from Australia to various points in Asia using Boeing 747s leased from Singapore Airlines. These were supplemented by a 767 later on.

Ansett International immediately established a reputation for a high level of service – its 747s were called 'Spaceships' to promote generous legroom in all classes – but the airline was a consistent money loser. It suffered badly during the Asian economic crisis of 1997-98 and was forced to drop several routes as the Asian market dramatically collapsed.

Ansett International was never able to properly develop due to financial constraints within the Ansett organisation. It was certainly unlucky to be hit by the Asian economic crisis when it was and as this market was its sole area of operation, the effects are obvious. Like the rest of the airline, Ansett International needed a big influx of money and some proper direction, and this could really only be provided by a new owner with the best of connections in the global airline industry.

The launch of Ansett International brought with it a new livery – Ansett's last – featuring a stylised gold 'A', the Southern Cross and the Federation Star, plus an advertising campaign based around the slogan 'One of the World's Great Airlines'. Ansett was picking up a raft of awards from the travel industry and others at the time, so on the surface at least, it was.

Meanwhile, back in the boardroom, things were starting to move on the ownership front by May 1995 when Air New Zealand began serious discussions about purchasing half of Ansett. At first it was thought to be the News Corp shareholding that was up for sale but by the end of the year it was confirmed that it was TNT's half that would be purchased by Air NZ for $425m.

The deal was consummated in October 1996 and required some other shuffling of the various shareholdings including News Corp obtaining a 100% interest in Ansett New Zealand by purchasing TNT's half. Air NZ pledged $150m to recapitalise Ansett.

Ansett carried on under its new regime but the signs continued to be less than encouraging. Domestic market share continued to drop as the 1990s progressed, the

The Boeing 767-200, flagship of Ansett's domestic mainline fleet at the end and the centre of many of the airline's troubles in its final months. (Rob Finlayson)

airline's financial position was not as strong as it could be and further restructures, new business plans and disposal of non core assets were implemented. This stage of the story would be to most observers the beginning of the end.

Kiwi Kapers

The period between March 1999 and February 2000 was a remarkable one, not just for Ansett but for many airlines in the region. For a while it seemed that just about everyone was looking at purchasing an interest in everyone else: Singapore Airlines in Ansett and Air NZ, Air NZ in Ansett, Qantas in Air NZ, Ansett employees in their own airline and so on.

For Ansett, the main game centred around Singapore Airlines and Air NZ. SIA first publicly expressed an interest in acquiring a stake in Ansett in January 1999, initially 25%. This was increased to 50% in March 1999 when it made a formal offer to purchase News Corps' shareholding. To most, this was a godsend because SIA was exactly the tonic required to boost Ansett's fortunes. It was large, profitable, cashed up and a major player in the global airline industry.

Unfortunately for Ansett, SIA and the Australian airline industry, Air NZ decided to spoil the party. As an existing half owner, it had the pre-emptive right to purchase the other half providing the price was matched, and that's the direction it took. Air NZ lacked all the virtues (for Ansett) held by SIA but despite serious misgivings by almost the entire industry, continued its quest to gain full control of Ansett.

Not surprisingly, SIA backed down from what had seemed to be a done deal with News, and the industry let out a collective groan. For many, the moment Air New Zealand completed its deal to take control of Ansett (on 23 June 2000 for $680m) was the moment the airline began its death throes.

SIA stayed in the game, however, by purchasing an 8.3% stake in Air NZ in April 2000. This was increased to 25% a few days later, the maximum allowed by New Zealand's foreign ownership laws.

Most observers were concerned that Air New Zealand's ambitions were not matched by its ability to pay the entry fee, and they were correct. On the day after Ansett was put into voluntary administration the New Zealand flag carrier announced a $NZ1.42 billion loss (after write down provisions for Ansett) for the 2000-2001 financial year and the financially crippled airline had to be bailed out by the taxpayers of the land to the tune of an initial $NZ885m. It reverted to majority state ownership as a result.

Other shareholdings had to be adjusted when Air NZ took control of Ansett. News Corp had previously announced it was selling its 100% interest in Ansett NZ to a consortium of investors. This happened in September 2000, the new operating company called South Pacific Airlines but operating as Qantas New Zealand under a franchise agreement. The new operator's fleet of Dash 8s and BAe 146s remained as before with the aircraft still owned by Ansett but repainted in Qantas colours.

Qantas New Zealand only lasted until April 2001 before collapsing. The airline had rarely got within light years of being profitable in its 13 years of operation as an Ansett subsidiary and nothing changed with the new owner. Ansett NZ's own pilots had in reality applied the final nail to the airline's coffin in August 1999 when they staged a series of strikes over employment contracts, the dispute dragging on for some time and worsening the airline's already precarious financial position.

Downhill Slide

The beginning of the end for Ansett – at least publicly – was two days before Christmas in 2000 when the first of a series of maintenance disasters to the airline's Boeing 767 fleet appeared. These involved missed scheduled maintenance, non compliance with manufacturer's Alert Service Bulletins, the fitting of incorrect parts and operating aircraft with no-go unserviceabilities.

The situation was a disaster for Ansett financially, operationally and in the public relations sense as the litany of problems just kept on coming between December 2000 and April 2001. Most of the 767 fleet was temporarily grounded over the busy Christmas-New Year period and again over Easter when the Civil Aviation Safety Authority finally ran out of patience with Ansett and formally grounded the 767s pending inspections and audits of their maintenance history. Aircraft had to be leased in from other operators to cover the capacity shortfall.

CASA also threatened to withdraw Ansett's operating licences and the airline can consider itself lucky this didn't happen. The regulatory authority was at the time cracking down on exactly this sort of thing throughout the industry but seemed content to pick on small operators who were easier targets. The general feeling was that if it had been 'Fred Bloggs Airlines' operating a couple of Piper Navajos out of a country town its Air Operators' Certificate would have been withdrawn months earlier. But this was Ansett, Australia's second largest airline....

Ansett tried to counter the enormous amount of adverse publicity it was receiving by launching a 'touchy feely' advertising campaign featuring various minor celebrities telling the world how they love to fly Ansett. The word 'absolutely' was the campaign's hook, and staff were told that when dealing with the public they had to answer 'absolutely' to questions which would normally be answered with the affirmative 'yes'. 'Do you have a flight to Melbourne today?' – 'Absolutely.'

Ansett didn't reveal what staff were told to say if a 'no' answer was required – 'absolutely not', perhaps?

Even though the agency responsible for the advertising campaign could probably produce graphs, charts, demographics and computer simulations proving how successful it was, the fact is that the public wasn't fooled. One non aviation person (but a regular air traveller) told this writer: 'I can't for the life of me see how an ad featuring Bernard King [a sometime television chef and talent quest judge] asleep in a business class seat is going to inspire thousands of passengers to rush out and buy Ansett tickets.'

The public did not need hyperbole and tricky marketing ploys. What it needed was for someone from very senior management – like Air NZ-Ansett group managing director/CEO Gary Toomey – to get up and say something like, 'Okay, we've stuffed up badly but these are the measures we're taking to make sure nothing like this ever happens again and that our passengers will receive a safe and reliable service.....'

By mid 2001 most knew that Ansett and Air New Zealand were in big trouble, although that trouble turned out to be even worse than expected. Both Qantas and Singapore Airlines made offers to buy into Air NZ, with the Australian carrier's offer quickly rejected. Shortly afterwards, Air NZ would be approaching Qantas with cap in hand and asking it to buy Ansett.

SIA was stymied by the New Zealand Government, which dithered irresponsibly on the issue of raising foreign ownership levels and the moment was lost. This was probably Air NZ's and Ansett's last chance.

The Australian domestic airline scene had changed considerably a year earlier with the launch of services by low fare startups Impulse and Virgin Blue. Both airlines stimulated substantial increases in passenger traffic but they also took some traffic away from the major carriers and the vast majority of these were from Ansett. Not helped by its maintenance problems in 2001, Ansett's share of the now larger Australian domestic market had dropped to not much more than 40% by the time the airline collapsed.

Impulse lasted only until May 2001 when it was absorbed into Qantas under bizarre circumstances. Impulse's owners were trumpeting its profitability one minute and saying the airline was going broke the next while doing the deal with Qantas. It was strange to see the bosses of these two airlines – who had previously been at each other's throats as savage competitors – sitting together, smiling for the cameras and telling the world how wonderful each thought the other one was. It seemed all very convenient and for Qantas meant the removal of one competitor from the market.

Of course Ansett in effect subsequently removed itself from the market giving a Qantas massive dominance, but Virgin Blue was showing signs of being here to stay, albeit on a small scale as it gradually built up its fleet and network. Virgin Blue chairman Sir Richard Branson may be the master of the seemingly inconsequential publicity stunt guaranteed to get a spot on the evening news, but underneath the public image of the joker lies a very hard nosed businessman with the runs on the board to prove it.

Virgin Blue played a role in what turned out to be Ansett's penultimate roll of the dice before it went under. In August 2001 Air NZ-Ansett offered Sir Richard $250m for his airline, an offer very publicly turned down when a piece of paper purporting to be a cheque for that amount was torn up – in front of the television cameras, of course!

The very last roll of the dice was in the second week of September 2001 when a desperate Air New Zealand offered Ansett to Qantas. The offer was rejected two days later. The date was September the 12th.....

Storm clouds over an Ansett Airbus A320 – an omen that hit hard in 2001. (Rob Finlayson)

CHAPTER TWO

ANSETT CHRONOLOGY 1936-2002

What follows is a summary of some of the milestones achieved and significant events recorded during Ansett's 66 years of operation. Included is information on the fleet, the company and its subsidiaries, its corporate history and other items of general interest which tell the story of Reg Ansett's airline.

Many of the items mentioned here – and others – are expanded upon in the main text, this chronology intended to put the long and complicated Ansett story into some kind of perspective.

January 1936: Ansett Airways Pty Ltd established, based in the sheep farming rural centre of Hamilton, western Victoria.

11 January 1936: Delivery of Ansett Airways' first aircraft, Fokker F.XI Universal VH-UTO purchased from Messrs G H Purvis and R A Savage of Sydney NSW for £1000 ($2000).

17 February 1936: Ansett Airways' first service, from Hamilton to Melbourne's Essendon Aerodrome. The service was conducted five days a week (Monday-Friday) and the aircraft used for joyflights on weekends.

25 May 1936: Ansett begins carrying mail between Melbourne and Hamilton.

22 October 1936: Delivery of Ansett Airways' second aircraft, Airspeed Envoy VH-UXM.

October 1936 – Airspeed Envoy VH-UXM delivered.

8 December 1936: Delivery of two seater Porterfield 35/70 Flyabout VH-UVH, to be used for joyflights.

16-18 December 1936: Reg Ansett flies the Porterfield 35/70 in the South Australian Centenary Air Race between Brisbane and Adelaide via Sydney and other centres. After successfully protesting a revised handicap allowance, Ansett was awarded first place in the handicap section and won £500 ($1,000) prize money.

14 April 1937: Privately owned Ansett Airways Pty Ltd converted into a public company as Ansett Airways Ltd with a nominal capital of £250,000 ($500,000) comprising £1 shares. The move ensures sufficient backing for Ansett's expansion plans which included the purchase of new aircraft and the introduction of new routes. Four new Lockheed L.10B Electras were ordered of which three were delivered.

Shortly afterwards, the airline announced a £30,000 ($60,000) loss for the previous year and the share price halved. At the same time, the airline moved its headquarters to Essendon.

26 August 1937: Delivery of the first of three Lockheed L.10B Electras at a price of £18,000 ($36,000) each. VH-UZO *Ansertes* was followed by VH-UZN *Ansirius* in September and VH-UZP *Ansalanta* in October. VH-UZO entered service on 30 August. Difficulties in paying for the aircraft when they arrived in Australia meant the Lockheeds were held in bond for a time until financial backing was found, but at the price of Ansett having to hand over a large part of his personal stake in the airline.

August 1937 – first L.10 Electra delivered.

5 September 1937: Ansett launches Melbourne-Mildura-Broken Hill services with the new Lockheeds followed by Melbourne-Sydney (via Narrandera) in early October. Sydney-Narrandera-Mildura-Adelaide and Melbourne-Adelaide were also subsequently added, these routes in direct competition with the large Australian National Airways (ANA) which had been formed in May 1936 by amalgamating Holyman Airways, Adelaide Airways, West Australian Airways and various shipping interests.

15 August 1938: Ansett further expands its network by introducing a Sydney-Cootamundra-Narrandera shuttle service which connected with flights travelling to and from Melbourne, Adelaide, Broken Hill and Mildura. In September, Hay was added to some Adelaide flights.

November 1938: ANA's policy of attempting to remove competing airlines from the market extends to financially vulnerable Ansett with ANA boss Ivan Holyman approaching Reg Ansett on the subject of a takeover. Ansett's directors (who were not aviation people) were keen to sell out but Reg Ansett was not. He went into considerable debt to buy up shares and keep his airline as an independent operation. The matter was resolved by April 1939.

28 February 1939: A significant fire in the Ansett hangar at Essendon destroys the Lockheed L.10B Electra VH-UZN and Fokker Universal VH-UTO while the Porterfield VH-UVH was badly damaged. Three other aircraft in the hangar were destroyed along with a quantity of spares. With its Electra fleet reduced to two, Ansett was forced to cut some services.

December 1939: By the end of 1939 Ansett's primary routes were Melbourne-Mildura-Renmark-Adelaide; Melbourne-Narrandera-Sydney; Melbourne-Hamilton; and Sydney-Mildura-Broken Hill-Adelaide.

1940-41: Normal operations continued after Australia's declaration of war on Germany, but Ansett expanded its presence at Melbourne's Essendon Airport including building an engineering facility. This allowed it to take advantage of the rapidly growing US military presence in Australia from 1942.

May 1942: Ansett acquires the flying training school Airflite Pty Ltd.

June 1942: With Australia now embroiled in the war against Japan as well as Germany, Ansett ceases airline services, except for Melbourne-Hamilton flights using the Airspeed Envoy. The two Lockheed L.10Bs are instead operated under lucrative contract to the USAAF for flights within Australia over the next two-and-a-half years. The aircraft also assisted in the evacuations of Darwin and Broome.

Along with other airlines, Ansett also greatly expanded its engineering, maintenance and workshop facilities as a result of contracts forged with the US military. Contracts with the Australian Department of Aircraft Production and US Service of Supply were won covering maintenance and also the repair of damaged RAAF and USAAF aircraft.

By 1945 Ansett employed 2000 people. ANA took over Ansett's profitable Sydney-Adelaide route on 29 June 1942, operating a daily each way service using Douglas DC-2s.

1 February 1945: After its wartime hiatus, Ansett resumes interstate services with daily Melbourne-Wagga Wagga-Canberra and Melbourne-Mount Gambier-Adelaide flights.

31 May 1946: The Ansett holding company's name becomes Ansett Transport Industries Ltd (ATI) with a nominal capital of £1,000,000 ($2m) of which £360,000 ($720,000) was issued. At the same time, the airline's operating name reverts to Ansett Airways Pty Ltd, a division of ATI.

17 May 1946: Electra VH-UZP crashes near Parafield, Adelaide during an attempted night landing in poor weather. Amazingly, all 12 on board survive and injuries are few and very minor.

June 1946: Ansett obtains three ex USAAF C-47s through the US Foreign Liquidation Commission, these converted to civil DC-3C standards at Essendon. They were VH-AMJ *Anselina*, VH-AMK *Anstratus* and VH-AML *Ansaga*. Three others joined the fleet between July 1948 and November 1951 plus another briefly leased from TAA for two months in 1950 while *Anstratus* was being repaired following a ground accident at Mascot.

June 1946 – first DC-3 delivered.

29 July 1946: Ansett resumes Melbourne-Sydney flights (six per week initially) using Douglas DC-3s.

September 1946: A fundamental change in the Australian airline industry with the start of services by government owned Trans Australia Airlines (TAA). The appearance of the efficient and progressive TAA marked the beginning of the end for the once dominant ANA and eventually led to its decline and takeover by the much smaller Ansett.

March 1948: Ansett introduces tourist or economy class to its DC-3s with lower fares in an attempt to stimulate business. This was a first for Australia and involved reconfiguring the DC-3s from three to four abreast seating, increasing capacity from 21 to 28 passengers. The move was a test of the regulations as the Commonwealth Government had been attempting to force Ansett to increase fares. Legal opinion supported Ansett and the lower fares remained. Four abreast seating soon became the norm in DC-3s.

12 January 1950: Ansett applies to operate a service between Melbourne and Christchurch (New Zealand). The application is rejected and approval given to TEAL.

April 1950: Ansett purchases a controlling interest in flying boat operator Barrier Reef Airways in exchange for financing two Sandringhams which are used for services to Southport and Rose Bay on Sydney Harbour. The first Sandringham was delivered the following month – VH-BRC *Beachcomber*, the former TEAL ZK-AMH *Auckland*.

22 August 1950: Ansett attempts to purchase the trunk routes operated by New Zealand National Airways Corporation (NZNAC) and a subsidiary, Ansett Industries (NZ) is established. The New Zealand Government was looking to dispose of NZNAC at the time but Ansett's and others' offers were rejected and NZNAC was retained.

5 January 1951: After more than 13 years' service, Ansett's last Lockheed L.10B Electra (VH-UZO) is sold to South Coast Airways based at Wollongong.

1 May 1952: Barrier Reef Airways fully absorbed by Ansett Airways and Ansett Flying Boat Services established to take over its routes. The Barrier Reef Airways name continues to be used until March 1953.

May 1952 – Ansett Flying Boat Services established.

October 1952: Introduction of the Airlines Agreement Act, the first stage of what would become Australia's highly regulated Two Airline Policy and intended mainly to help an ailing ANA.

20 May 1953: Ansett Flying Boat Services takes over Trans Oceanic Airways which had ceased operations the month before. This plus the earlier Barrier Reef Airways takeover allows Ansett to consolidate its flying boat operations at Rose Bay, Sydney, from which it flew to initially Hobart, Grafton, Southport, Brisbane, Hayman Island, Townsville, Cairns and Lord Howe Island. From 1959, control of Ansett Flying Boat Services was handed over to Airlines of New South Wales.

17 August 1954: The start of a major fleet update for the still relatively small Ansett with the arrival in Australia of its first Convair CV-340 pressurised piston engined airliner. VH-BZD was purchased second hand from Braniff and was followed by a second, new aircraft in April 1955. A third CV-340 was leased from Hawaiian Airlines for seven moths from November 1956.

August 1954 – first Convair CV-340 delivered.

4 October 1954: Convair CV-340 VH-BZD enters service on the Melbourne-Sydney-Brisbane service. Hobart was added to the Convair network in March 1955, in both cases competing with ANA and TAA.

May 1955: Ansett wins a legal battle with ANA and the Victorian Railways over the right to operate a Melbourne-Mildura service.

18 January 1957: The death, in Honolulu, of ANA chairman Sir Ivan Holyman at a time when his airline was in dire financial straits. A merger with TAA had previously been discussed and rejected by the Government owned airline, as were various other commercial and legislative options designed to save ANA.

8 June 1957: Ansett increases competition with ANA

and TAA with the delivery of the first of six new Convair CV-440s (VH-BZF), the others arriving between September and December.

24 June 1957: Ansett offers £3m ($6m) to take over ANA. At this stage nobody was taking Ansett's overtures very seriously as it was a relatively small operator. ANA's directors also considered the airline to be worth considerably more than what was offered. There was also the fact that Ansett had nowhere near the financial resources to consummate the deal had it been accepted!

30 July 1957: With ANA's position rapidly deteriorating, Ansett makes a further takeover offer of £3.3m ($6.6m). This time the offer was backed with financial support from oil companies Vacuum (now Mobil) and Shell.

23 August 1957: Ansett's takeover offer for ANA accepted.

23 September 1957: Reg Ansett announces he has signed a contract with Lockheed for the purchase of four Electra turboprop airliners.

3 October 1957: The sale of ANA to Ansett Transport Industries is formally completed.

21 October 1957: With the takeover of Australian National Airlines completed, the new trading name Ansett-ANA is established. The parent company's operating name is changed from Ansett Transport Industries Ltd to Ansett Transport Industries (Operations) Pty Ltd, this the umbrella organisation for all Ansett airline operations.

October 1957 – Ansett-ANA created. (Eric Allen)

5 February 1958: After a sometimes messy and acrimonious battle, Butler Air Transport is taken over by Ansett Transport Industries. Queensland Airlines (QAL) came under Ansett control at the same time as Butler had itself taken over what was originally Aircrafts Pty Ltd in 1948 and renamed it QAL in January 1949. Butler and QAL not only provided Ansett-ANA with new routes but also some important new equipment, notably a pair of Vickers Viscounts. Butler was renamed Airlines of New South Wales in December 1959.

27 March 1958: The Federal Government refuses Ansett-ANA an import licence for the four Lockheed Electras it had ordered the previous September. It also refuses a licence for TAA to import two Sud Caravelle jets but approves the import of Vickers Viscount 810s. Later, three Electras were approved but TAA was forced to order the same aircraft instead of Caravelles.

24 September 1958: The Airlines Equipment Bill introduced to Federal Parliament, this part of the deal involving Ansett's takeover of ANA. Australia's Two Airline Policy on trunk routes comes into full effect with the passing of the Airlines Equipment Act, a move which dictated the course of mainline operations for the next three decades. It was hugely beneficial to Ansett-ANA because it virtually guaranteed profits and was – ironically – detrimental to the government owned TAA.

It forced parallel equipment choices, fares and schedules on both airlines, inhibited several of TAA's plans, nullified much of TAA's astute judgement when it came to aircraft selection, and the notorious cross-charter element of the Act forced TAA to hand over some of its highly successful and popular Vickers Viscount turboprops in exchange for Ansett-ANA's less appealing Douglas DC-6B piston engined airliners.

22 December 1958: Ansett acquires the shares and route licences held by Southern Airlines Ltd which had ceased operations the previous month. The routes from Melbourne included points in Victoria extending to Adelaide, the Bass Strait islands and Launceston.

10 March 1959: Ansett-ANA's first Lockheed Electra (VH-RMA) arrives in Melbourne. It enters service eight days later on the Melbourne-Sydney route.

17 March 1959: Delivery of Ansett-ANA's first new Vickers Viscount V.832 (VH-RMG). Three others were delivered over the next month and two more second hand Viscount 810 models were subsequently acquired along with three TAA Viscount 700s. These were swapped for DC-6Bs under the Two Airline Policy rules. Another Viscount was purchased from TAA in 1962. Ansett-ANA already had two Viscount 700s acquired through the Butler takeover.

March 1959 – first Lockheed Electra delivered. (Eric Allen)

April 1959: Ansett-ANA captures more than half of the Australian domestic market for the first time, carrying 53.3% of passengers compared to TAA's 46.7%.

1 July 1959: South Australia based Guinea Airways Ltd taken over by Ansett Transport Industries, five months after the first offer had been made. It is renamed Airlines of South Australia in December.

March 1959 – first Vickers Viscount delivered. (Eric Allen)

5 October 1959: Delivery of Ansett's first Fokker F27 Friendship, Srs 200 VH-FNA which was initially operated by Ansett-ANA. Between them, Ansett and its regional affiliates received 42 F27s over the years.

19 December 1959: Butler Air Transport (which was taken over by Ansett in February 1958) is renamed Airlines of New South Wales.

October 1959 – first Fokker F27 delivered.

21 December 1959: Guinea Airways renamed Airlines of South Australia.

18 January 1960: Airlines of South Australia starts operations.

March 1960: Ansett Transport Industries purchases the routes from Melbourne to points in Victoria, Tasmania, South Australia and the Bass Strait islands formerly operated by Southern Airlines. Southern had ceased operations in November 1958.

11 July 1960: Ansett-ANA inaugurates its Sydney-Brisbane-Port Moresby 'Golden Orchid' service using a Douglas DC-6B. From now, both TAA and Ansett were able to operate to PNG, having taken over from Qantas.

December 1959 – Airlines of NSW formed out of Butler Air Transport. (Geoff Wilkes)

19 October 1960: ATI enters the New Zealand market by acquiring 49% of South Pacific Airlines of New Zealand's (SPANZ) shareholding and supplies two Douglas DC-3s for operations from December.

21 December 1960: Ansett-ANA inaugurates Australia's first airport to city helicopter service between Essendon and a floating helipad on Melbourne's Yarra River, using a Bell 47J. The service remained in place until February 1980. Reg Ansett had himself had been using a helicopter to commute from his home in Mount Eliza to the Yarra Heliport since early 1959.

12 January 1961: Papua New Guinea's Mandated Airlines Ltd (MAL) acquired by Ansett Transport Industries from W R Carpenter & Co and renamed Ansett-MAL. The deal included light aircraft charter operator Madang Air Services, which had recently been taken over by MAL.

August 1961: Ansett-ANA purchases two Bristol Freighter Mk.31Ms from the Pakistan Air Force (plus another for spares) as VH-BFA and BFB. The former entered service on the Melbourne-Hobart-Melbourne freight run on 21 October and both were transferred to Ansett-MAL in May 1964. Three other Freighter Mk.21s (VH-INJ, INK and INL) were inherited from ANA with the takeover, these previously used on the famous Air Beef scheme in 1949-54. All were retired 1958-61 and scrapped.

October 1961: After many years of trying to gain approval to compete with TAA on services to Darwin,

Ansett-ANA operates its first 'Golden Boomerang' services to the Northern Territory capital.

17 December 1961: Ansett Transport Industries subsidiary Victorian Air Coach Services begins operations with DC-3s from Melbourne to centres in Victoria, South Australia and Tasmania, these mainly the routes formerly operated by Southern Airlines (see March 1960, above).

February 1963: Airlines of South Australia introduces its first Piaggio P.166 light transport (VH-ASA).

19 April 1963: Western Australia's MacRobertson-Miller Airlines (MMA) partially taken over by Ansett Transport Industries which acquires an initial 70% of the shareholding. The remainder is purchased in June 1969.

19 August 1964: Ansett bails out of South Pacific Airlines of New Zealand.

16 October 1964: The jet age begins for Australia's domestic airlines with the carefully stage managed and simultaneous arrival at Essendon of the first Boeing 727-100s for Ansett-ANA (VH-RME) and TAA after their delivery flights from the USA. Boeing allocated customer designation suffixes to its commercial aircraft, this retained regardless of the aircraft type. Ansett's suffix was '77', the new jets were therefore 727-77s. They were later joined by 727-277s, 737-277s, 737-377s and 767-277s. A new Ansett – ANA colour scheme with a large 'swept A' on the tail was introduced with the 727.

October 1964 – first Boeing 727 delivered. (Geoff Wilkes)

2 November 1964: The start of jet operations on Australian domestic routes when both Ansett-ANA and TAA operate their first Boeing 727 revenue services between Melbourne and Sydney. Ansett's VH-RME covered the 380nm (704km) distance in 47min 55sec, about seven minutes faster than the previous domestic airliner record established by a TAA Lockheed Electra.

7 March 1965: Ansett-ANA introduces the 26-30 passenger Sikorsky S-61N helicopter (VH-BRI *Coral Islander*) to service, operating to the Whitsunday Islands resorts.

March 1965 – Sikorsky S-61N services to Whitsundays resorts start.

21 August 1965: The final Ansett-ANA Douglas DC-6B service to New Guinea, the route taken over by the Lockheed Electra turboprop.

17 September 1965: Delivery of the sole DHC Caribou operated by Ansett-MAL in New Guinea. It was sold in January 1969.

24 September 1965: Redelivery of the first of three Ansett-ANA Douglas DC-4s (VH-INJ) converted to Aviation Traders Carvair freighters. VH-INK and INM followed in November 1965 and July 1968, respectively.

1965 – first of three Carvair conversions redelivered. (Terence Ellis)

29 August 1966: Ansett subsidiary Victorian Air Coach Services ceases operations, its services absorbed into Ansett-ANA's network.

13 September 1966: An Ansett-ANA Boeing 727 sets a new speed record between Perth and Adelaide, covering the 1,165nm (2158km) distance in 1hr 53min 30sec with the aid of a 191kt (354km/h) tailwind. The aircraft achieved a maximum ground speed of 665kt (1232km/h).

4 December 1966: Ansett subsidiary Queensland Airlines (QAL) ceases operations; from the next day services are operated by Ansett-ANA.

13 April 1967: The first Ansett-ANA Douglas DC-9-31 (VH-CZB) arrives in Australia. The numerically first aircraft (VH-CZA) temporarily remained in the USA for crew training and was delivered 11 days later. Services began on 17 April.

The DC-9s ordered by Ansett-ANA (and TAA) were subject to some controversy before delivery thanks to the militant and aggressive pilots' union, the AFAP. Even though the DC-9 was specifically designed for operation by two pilots only, the AFAP tried to insist that a flight engineer's station be built into the cockpit. This would have resulted in substantial redesign, enormous expense and delays. Happily, the dispute was resolved and the DC-9s were flown by two people, but the AFAP would successfully try the same tactic later when Ansett ordered Boeing 767s.

December 1966 – QAL ceases operations. (Eric Allen)

9 May 1967: The final Ansett-ANA scheduled Douglas DC-3 service, VH-ANH operating Essendon-Warracknabeel-Horsham.

April 1967 – first Douglas DC-9 delivered. (Geoff Wilkes)

11 May 1967: Ansett-ANA's last two Douglas DC-6Bs (VH-INS/INU) withdrawn from service.

26 May 1967: Delivery of the first of two Sikorsky S-62As for Ansett-ANA (VH-AND), these purchased to service the Bass Strait oil rigs. VH-ANE followed shortly afterwards. VH-AND's life was short – it crashed into the sea after suffering engine failure in August 1967.

May 1967 – Ansett-ANA ceases scheduled DC-3 services. (Terence Ellis)

November 1967: Ansett's last two Bristol Freighters (Mk.31s VH-BFA and BFB of Ansett-MAL) sold to New Zealand's SAFE Air for spares.

22 December 1967: Delivery of the Ansett group's first De Havilland Canada Twin Otter, Srs 100 VH-MMY *Yampi* for MacRobertson Miller. Ansett Airlines of New Guinea received two Twin Otter 300s in December 1969 (VH-PGS and PGT).

14 March 1968: The Ansett Helicopter Division (including the Bass Strait oil rig servicing contract with Esso-BHP and most of the aircraft) sold to Airfast Services for operation by Helicopter Utilities.

June 1968: Airlines of New South Wales renamed Ansett Airlines of New South Wales.

24 June 1968: Ansett-MAL renamed Ansett Airlines of Papua New Guinea, although the name was not used publicly until the following December.

1967 – Douglas DC-6B withdrawn from service. (George Canciani)

September 1968: Ansett-ANA Douglas DC-4 passenger operations draw to a close with the Lockheed Electra replacing the venerable DC-4 on the Cocos Island run.

1 November 1968: Airlines of South Australia renamed Ansett Airlines of South Australia.

November 1968: Ansett Transport Industries acquires the remaining 30% shareholding in MacRobertson Miller Airlines to become sole owner. Name changed to MacRobertson Miller Airline Services Pty Ltd in June 1969.

1 November 1968: The ANA connection is dropped from the airline's trading name, Ansett-ANA becoming Ansett Airlines of Australia on this date, a division of Ansett Transport Industries (Operations) Pty Ltd. With this came a new red and white livery for the airline and its subsidiaries, based around a stylised 'A' on the tail – the 'Alpha' scheme as it was known.

1968 – new name (Ansett Airlines of Australia) and livery. (Geoff Wilkes)

1 June 1969: MacRobertson Miller Airlines renamed MMA Airline Services.

14 August 1969: Delivery of Ansett's first Fokker F28 Fellowship regional jet (VH-MMJ *Pilbara*), leased from the manufacturer and operated by Ansett-MMA until June 1970 when the airline's own F28s began arriving.

2 September 1969: Australia's first intrastate jet airliner service when Ansett-MMA Fokker F28-1000 Fellowship VH-MMJ flies Perth-Port Hedland and return.

14 May 1970: A man forces his way into the cockpit of Ansett DC-9 VH-CZG at Sydney Airport shortly before departure to Brisbane. The passengers were evacuated as the man spoke with the pilots. He left the aircraft after about 30 minutes and was arrested.

1 July 1970: Ansett acquires Papuan Airlines (formerly

August 1969 – Australian Fokker F28 operations begin with Ansett-MMA.

Papuan Air Transport – Patair). The airline is renamed Ansett (P&NG) in July 1972 but reverts to local control in December 1973.

6 August 1970: The final Ansett-ANA Vickers Viscount service, flown by V.832 VH-RMH.

1 December 1970: Ansett Airlines of New South Wales inaugurates intrastate jet services in that state when F28-1000 VH-FKD flies Sydney-Dubbo. Flights from Sydney to Wagga Wagga and Broken Hill were soon added to the network, but jet services are suspended in April 1971 due to unsatisfactory loadings. The F28s were then transferred to Ansett-MMA.

6 May 1971: The last Ansett-ANA Lockheed Electra passenger service. All three of the airline's Electras were then converted to freighters in the USA and returned to service the following year. An additional Electra freighter was acquired from the USA in 1975.

19 June 1971: Ansett-ANA's final services from Melbourne's Essendon Airport. From the next day, all flights operated from the new Tullamarine Airport.

14 February 1972: The end of the Ansett Convair era when the last two CV-440s (VH-BZF and BZN) are withdrawn from service with Airlines of South Australia and ferried to Essendon for storage and resale.

February 1972 – last Convairs withdrawn. (Terence Ellis)

21 March 1972: Thomas Nationwide Transport (TNT) acquires 23.5% of Ansett Transport Industries' shares from W R Carpenter Holdings and Boral. TNT managing director Sir Peter Abeles joins the Ansett board of directors in June 1972. TNT's voting rights are limited to 10%.

31 May 1972: The first Lockheed Electra freighter conversion (VH-RMC) is redelivered for service with Ansett Air Freight.

15 November 1972: An attempted hijack aboard Ansett Fokker F27 VH-FNI on approach to Alice Springs when a passenger entered the cockpit and threatened the crew. The aircraft landed safely and negotiations with the man were undertaken. An attempt to overpower the man by a Northern Territory policeman ended with the hijacker being shot and the policemen seriously injured during the scuffle. The incident hastened the introduction of increased security arrangements at several major Australian airports.

19 February 1973: Delivery to Australia of Ansett's first stretched Boeing 727-277 Advanced (VH-RMU). The first revenue flight was on February 26. The aircraft had been handed over to Ansett in the USA the previous November but it was temporarily leased to United Airlines for use in a NASA contract. Both Ansett and TAA had requested a delivery deferment of their first 727-200s due to a downturn of passenger traffic in Australia.

1 November 1973: Ansett Airlines of Papua New Guinea and Ansett (P&NG) cease operations, their

February 1973 – first Boeing 727-200 delivered. (Geoff Wilkes)

routes taken over by new local flag carrier Air Niugini which has Ansett, Qantas and TAA as its initial shareholders.

10 September 1974: The final Ansett Flying Boat Services flight, from Sydney to Lord Howe Island by Short Sandringham VH-BRC *Beachcomber*. Its stablemate, VH-BRF *Islander*, had undertaken its final visit to Lord Howe on August 15.

September 1974 – final Ansett flying boat service. (Geoff Wilkes)

4 July 1979: The start of a series of major acquisitions of Ansett Transport Industries shares as a prelude to eventual takeover. The major players at this stage were Robert Holmes a Court's Bell Group and Sir Peter Abeles' TNT, both of which already had an interest in the company.

5 November 1979: Ansett employs its first female airline pilot, Mrs Debbie Wardley, after a series of court actions which ruled the airline must employ her. In June, the Victorian Equal Opportunity Board had ruled that she must be employed by Ansett and that the airline should pay damages for discrimination against her on the grounds of her gender.

10 December 1979: In a major departure from the fleet purchase stringency of the Two Airlines Policy, TAA orders four Airbus A300B widebody airliners without Ansett having to place a similar order. Its first widebody would be the Boeing 767, ordered in March 1980.

11 January 1980: After several months of Ansett Transport Industries shares movement involving several major players, the company's shareholding is settled at 50% each for TNT and News Ltd, the latter having completed acquisition of its half share the previous month. On this day it was recommended that smaller shareholders accept TNT's offer for their shares.

22 January 1980: Sir Peter Abeles (TNT) and Mr Rupert Murdoch (News Ltd) confirmed as joint managing directors of ATI. Sir Reginald Ansett remained as chairman (after standing down as managing director).

29 January 1980: The last Ansett Boeing 727-100 service when VH-RMS operates flight AN213 from Adelaide to Melbourne.

17 March 1980: Ansett places its largest ever aircraft order so far, a $400m contract covering the purchase of 12 Boeing 737-200 Advanced (to replace the DC-9s), four 727-200LRs and five 767-200s. The order was also the sixth largest placed with the Boeing Commercial Airplane Company to that point.

18 April 1980: Ansett Boeing 727-200 VH-RMO operates a charter flight from Townsville to Singapore via Darwin, this seen as a challenge to the Qantas monopoly as Australia's international carrier. Attempts to gain approval to make this a regular service failed.

1 July 1980: Ansett Airlines of Australia Air Cargo renamed Ansett Air Freight.

July 1980 – Aeropelican joins the Ansett family. (SW Collection)

3 December 1980: After making several attempts to gain approval, Ansett inaugurates trans-Tasman flights with Boeing 727-200 VH-RML, Hobart-Christchurch. TAA's first service on the same route was three days later and both airlines had to use Qantas flight numbers. Ansett withdrew from the route in March 1982.

21 January 1981: Air Vanuatu established, owned 60% by the Vanuatu Government and 40% by Ansett Transport Industries. Initial equipment was a Douglas DC-9-30 from the Ansett fleet and management was also handled by Ansett. Ansett disposed of its Air Vanuatu shareholding in March 1986.

13 April 1981: Another trading name change, the airline now known simply as 'Ansett.' (with the full stop). A new 'southern cross' livery accompanies the change.

April 1981 – another new name (Ansett.) and livery. (George Canciani)

29 April 1981: Airlines of Northern Australia established as a division of Ansett Transport Industries (Operations) Ltd.

14 June 1981: Delivery of the first of four Boeing 727-277LRs (VH-ANA), these longer range models purchased for their ability to carry a full passenger load from Sydney to Perth against the prevailing westerly wind. Services began on 20 June (between Melbourne and Brisbane) and all four had been delivered by the end of June. Sydney-Perth services started on 29 June.

June 1981 – first Boeing 727-200LR delivered.

20 June 1981: Delivery of Ansett's first Boeing 737-277 (VH-CZM). Its first revenue flight was AN088 Melbourne-Coolangatta on 1 July. Seven of the 12 aircraft on order had been delivered by the end of 1981 with the others following between January and June 1982.

June 1981: Ansett Airlines of New South Wales renamed as simply Airlines of New South Wales.

1 July 1981: MMA Airline Services renamed Airlines of Western Australia.

13 July 1981: TAA's first Airbus A300 arrives in Australia, ushering in a new era for the Australian airline industry.

17 July 1981: Ansett Airlines of South Australia is renamed without the 'Ansett' prefix after a reorganisation of its management structure.

31 July 1981: NSW regional carrier Aeropelican Inter-City Commuter Air Service (which flies commuter services between Newcastle/Belmont and Sydney) becomes part of the Ansett fold when 80% of owner Masling Commuter Services is purchased by TNT-News subsidiary Bodas Pty Ltd. Masling had itself acquired Aeropelican a year earlier. The company was renamed Aeropelican Air Services in 1982.

September 1981: Queensland based Bush Pilots Airways signs an interline agreement with Ansett; name changed to Air Queensland in December 1981.

23 December 1981: The death of Sir Reginald Ansett, aged 72.

16 February 1982: The launch of Ansett's Golden Wing Club, the first of its kind in Australian domestic airline operations. Lounges are initally established at Sydney, Melbourne and Brisbane airports.

17 June 1982: The last Ansett DC-9 revenue service when VH-CZA operates flight AN056 between Launceston and Melbourne. The aircraft was then sold to the US Navy. Up to the time of its final flight, VH-CZA's 15 year career had seen it log 39,190 flight hours and 42,731 landings; travel 26,332,338km; carry 2,795,804 passengers; consume 134 million litres of fuel; and require 744,610 maintenance man-hours to keep it in the air.

5 April 1983: Ansett Air Freight introduces Boeing 727-200 VH-RMX to service, operating between Perth and Melbourne in basically standard trim. The aircraft

June 1981 – first Boeing 737-200 delivered. (Geoff Wilkes)

went to the USA later in the year to be converted to full freight configuration by Hayes Aircraft in Alabama and re-entered service in January 1984.

10 June 1983: The arrival in Australia of Ansett's first Boeing 767-277 (VH-RMD). The delivery had been delayed by seven months partly at Ansett's request due to a downturn in Australian domestic traffic and partly due to the interference of the AFAP pilots' union which – as it had done with the DC-9 16 years earlier – insisted on the installation of a flight engineer's station in an aircraft designed specifically for two crew operation. Where it had failed with the DC-9 the AFAP succeeded with the Ansett 767s, resulting in the initial five aircraft being the only 767s in the world with a three crew cockpit.

The first Ansett 767 revenue service was flown by VH-RMD on 27 June, operating Melbourne-Sydney.

June 1983 – first Boeing 767 delivered. (Rob Finlayson)

January 1984: Redelivery to Ansett Air Freight of Boeing 727-277F VH-RMX after conversion to full freighter configuration in the USA.

31 January-1 February 1984: The last Ansett Lockheed Electra flight when freighter VH-RMC operates a Cairns-Brisbane-Melbourne overnight service.

September 1984: Ansett launches jet services to Hamilton Island's newly completed airport using Boeing 737s

1983 – Boeing 727-200F joins Ansett Air Freight. (Geoff Wilkes)

and simultaneously ends the Sikorsky S-61N helicopter service from Proserpine to the Whitsunday Islands resorts. Hamilton Island is half owned by Ansett and it has exclusive rights to providing air services.

26 November 1984: Ansett Airlines of Western Australia renamed Ansett WA.

26 April 1985: Arrival in Australia of the first BAe 146-200 regional jetliner (VH-JJP) for Ansett WA. The first service was conducted two days later, flights MV352/353 Perth-Kalgoorlie and return. The 146 was subsequently purchased in substantial numbers for use by various Ansett operators and by TNT as freighters.

April 1985 – first BAe 146 delivered for Ansett WA.

1 May 1985: Ansett Airlines of New South Wales renamed Air NSW.

2 June 1985: At the Paris Air Show, Ansett joint managing director Sir Peter Abeles announces a $US380m order for eight of the new and as yet unflown Airbus A320 150 seat airliners. Nine more A320s were optioned. In order to placate the unions, Ansett subsequently announced that its A320s would be fitted with a flight engineers' station, despite the aircraft being designed specifically for two crew operation. As it happened, all were delivered with the standard arrangement. Ansett was indulging in a buying spree at the time – less than three weeks later the airline also ordered 12 Boeing 737-300s (see below), despite the two aircraft types filling a similar part of the market.

21 June 1985: Ansett announces an order for 12 'second generation' Boeing 737-300s to replace the 737-200s which had only been in service since mid 1981.

July 1985: Ansett Transport Industries records a $64.7m net profit for the 1984-85 financial year, up 46% on the 1983-84 figure of $44.2m. Revenue in 1984-85 was $1.22bn, up 16%.

16 August 1985: Airlines of Northern Australia renamed Ansett NT.

September 1985: Responding to TAA's successful introduction of business class, Ansett follows suit, initially only on Sydney-Melbourne flights on Boeing 727s and 737s. The existing four abreast first class is retained, business class combining first's greater seat pitch and service standards with economy's six abreast configuration. The fare is set at 20% above economy class and 20% below first.

3 December 1985: Ansett Transport Industries purchases a 51% interest in newly established Perth based freight operator Transcorp. Transcorp initially operated a single Boeing 707 freighter mainly on services to ports including Sydney, Perth, Singapore, Melbourne and Brunei.

16 December 1985: Ansett half owner Thomas Nationwide Transport Ltd changes its name to TNT Ltd, this better reflecting the company's ambitions in the global marketplace.

March 1986: Announcement of the formation of Ansett Worldwide Aviation Services (AWAS), established to offer fleet leasing and management services to the world's airlines. Early orders were for 12 Boeing 737-300s, six McDonnell Douglas MD-83s (plus six options) and options on nine Airbus A320s, these originally placed by Ansett the previous year. AWAS will also have access to 22 Fokker 50s through its US associate Corsair.

12 June 1986: Announced that ATI and the Bond Corporation have teamed in a 50/50 joint marketing and development venture to promote the Skyship series of airships in the Asia-Pacific region. A new company – Asian Pacific Airships – is formed.

Ansett Fifty.

1 9 3 6 - 1 9 8 6.

27 June 1986: Airlines of South Australia ceases operations due to cost pressures; most of its routes are taken over by Kendell Airlines. ASA's country network had been subsidised for many years by firstly charters to Woomera and then to the Moomba oil fields. Lloyd Aviation won the Moomba charters contract in 1985.

1 July 1986: Ansett and Qantas sign a commercial agreement that will promote both carriers in areas where one or the other is inadequately represented.

August 1986: Ansett purchases Traveland, Australia's largest tour package holiday wholesale chain.

4 August 1986: A corporate change for the government owned Trans Australia Airlines (TAA). From this date it is known as Australian Airlines and is the first step towards a merger of it with Qantas and eventual privatisation of the combined entity. The airline became an incorporated public company on 30 April 1988, resulting in the removal of direct government control.

22 August 1986: The first of 12 Boeing 737-377s for Ansett delivered (VH-CZA). The aircraft entered service on 15 September, its first sector between Melbourne and Sydney. All 12 were in service by January 1987 by which time a further four had been ordered for delivery in late 1988.

1986 – Airlines of South Australia ceases operations. (Geoff Wilkes)

17 August 1986: After accepting a contract to manage the newly established Cook Islands International Airlines on behalf of the Cook Islands Government, Ansett introduces a Boeing 767 service between Sydney and Rarotonga.

August 1986 – first Boeing 737-300 delivered.

October 1986: New Zealand's Newmans Air becomes Ansett New Zealand, owned 50% by ATI, 27.5% by Brierley Investments and 22.5% by Newmans.

January 1987: Release of the Report of the Independent Review of Economic Regulation of Domestic Aviation – the Two Airline Policy. The Review basically says that the policy which has existed for three decades is not serving the Australian travelling public well and presents five options for the future ranging from retaining the *status quo* to full deregulation. At least partial deregulation is clearly favoured.

1 February 1987: Ansett New Zealand (formerly Newmans Air and now half owned by Ansett Transport Industries) operates its first trunk service between Christchurch and Auckland with one of two DHC Dash 8s previously used by Newmans. Four Boeing 737-100s were also being obtained from AWAS, these formerly America West (and originally Lufthansa) aircraft from the very start of the 737 production run. They entered service in July.

1 February 1987: Ansett's Boeing 737-200 fleet remained in service for only about six years, replaced in service by quieter and more fuel efficient 737-300s. The last Ansett 737-200 service was flown on this day, Sydney-Melbourne by VH-CZR. The highest time member of the fleet (VH-CZN) had only 12,700 hours logged when it was withdrawn from service in December 1986. All 12 were sold to America West.

1987 – Ansett New Zealand launches operations. (Brian Chidlow)

5 May 1987: TNT's European Division takes delivery of its first BAe 146-200QT freighter for its air express business.

May 1987: Ansett wins a 10 year management contract for Polynesian Airlines (Air New Zealand also bid for the contract) and supplies a leased Boeing 767 to the airline.

18 June 1987: Ansett (through owners TNT/News) announces it is taking a 20% stake in America West Airlines at a cost of $US31.8m. America West already had a

strong association with Ansett having purchased its 12 737-200s, leased other 737s from AWAS and sold 737-100s to Ansett New Zealand.

July 1987: Ansett companies continue the buying spree instigated after the TNT-News takeover with a $400m order for 15 Boeing 737-300s for AWAS and up to 72 BAe 146s, most of them QT freighters for TNT's European air express business. The $1.5bn deal with British Aerospace persuaded it to open a second BAe 146 production line at Manchester, but TNT eventually acquired only 13 146-200QTs and 10 146-300QTs for its European operations.

31 July 1987: Announced that TNT-News Corp will take over Skywest Holdings, which also owns former NSW regional carrier East-West Airlines. The intention is to operate East-West as a leisure airline. The deal included the acquisition of Skywest Airlines and charter associate Skywest Aviation. Skywest and East-West had started to combine operations in 1983 as part of an attempt to break away from Australia's Two Airline Policy on interstate routes.

10 September 1987: Delivery of the first Fokker 50 (VH-FNA) initially for service with Air NSW. The aircraft entered service on 16 November on a Sydney-Dubbo flight. Three more were delivered before the end of the year.

October 1987: Yet another major order from Ansett companies, this time six Boeing 757-200s and 12 737-300s for AWAS plus four 737-300s for Ansett and five 737-500s, reportedly for Ansett New Zealand.

7 October 1987: Announced by the Federal Government that Australia's Two Airline Policy will be terminated and that the domestic airline industry will be fully deregulated.

November 1987: Ansett New Zealand orders two BAe 146-200s, the aircraft to be used mainly to develop new traffic through the South Island tourist port of Queenstown.

10 November 1987: The Trade Practices Commission rules that Ansett's acquisition of the Skywest/East-West

group requires disposal of part of its interest and its shareholdings on competition grounds. Ansett's association with regional operators Kendell Airlines and Lloyds were also part of the problem. An attempt was made to sell Skywest without success, resulting in the TPC reversing its decision a year later.

18 March 1988: Air NSW operates its last official Fokker F27 service (Brisbane-Coolangatta-Newcastle-Sydney) after 29 years with the airline and its predecessors. Several F27s were temporarily returned to service in July when the airline's new Fokker 50 fleet was grounded after a spate of power losses.

15 April 1988: Following New Zealand Government approval, Newmans (22.5%) and Brierley Investments (27.5%) sell their stakes in Ansett New Zealand to half owner, the Ansett group, giving it 100% of the shares.

7 August 1988: Bodas Pty Ltd – a TNT-News company – purchases a major shareholding in Adelaide based Lloyd Aviation which operates regional airline Lloyd Air and charter activities.

30 October 1988: Former Lufthansa Boeing 707-330C purchased by Ansett Air Freight from Transcorp after it ceased operations and was wholly taken over by Ansett Transport Industries five days earlier. As VH-HTC *Brisbane* the 707 flew in TNT colours mainly on freight flights within Australia until December 1990 when it was withdrawn from use and sold to Global Air.

26 November 1988: The first Ansett Airbus A320-200 (VH-HYB) arrives in Australia, followed by VH-HYA and HYC the following month. Named 'Skystar' by the airline, the A320's service entry was delayed while union problems involving flight attendants, flight engineers (for which the A320 had no provision), pilots and ground engineers were sorted out.

The inaugural service was flown by VH-HYB on 2 January 1989, flight AN12 from Melbourne to Sydney. Ansett's A320 orders were modified several times over the next few years but by the time of the airline's collapse in September 2001, 20 were in service.

8 May 1989: Delivery of the first BAe 146-200QT freighter (VH-JJY) to Ansett Air Freight.

July 1989: East-West Airlines orders eight BAe 146-300s (plus four options).

17 July 1989: Ansett introduces business class across its fleet, finally fully matching the initiative introduced by TAA in 1984. Fares are set at 15% above standard economy. First class is retained for the moment.

November 1988 – first Airbus A320 delivered. (Geoff Wilkes)

18 August 1989: The start of the most damaging airline pilots' dispute in Australian commercial aviation history when the Australian Federation of Airline Pilots (AFAP) begins a campaign which sees all of its 1,647 members resign en masse six days later. The dispute was ostensibly over a massive (27%) pay claim but it was really about consolidation of the power of the union in the lead-up to airline deregulation in late 1990.

The AFAP expected the airlines to quickly capitulate (as they had always done in the past) but this time they held firm with the support of the Federal Government, eventually forcing the badly led and tactically inept AFAP into submission and leaving it with little or no power base. The result was chaos in Australia's domestic airline system for nearly five months with revenues slashed and jobs lost in the many areas of the economy that rely on air travel. The situation was alleviated to some extent with the chartering of aircraft and crews from overseas airlines – happily, the dispute largely coincided with the northern hemisphere 'off season' – and the use of some RAAF and RAN transport aircraft.

August 1989 – start of the crippling pilots' dispute. (Wally Civitico)

1 March 1990: Air NSW renamed Ansett NSW.

June 1990: Ansett takes over Wagga Wagga (NSW) based regional carrier Kendell Airlines, the Kendell family selling its remaining shares to TNT-News company Bodas Pty Ltd.

June 1990: Ansett Air Freight introduces its first two BAe 146-200QT freighters (VH-JJY and JJZ) into service, the aircraft operating nightly 'crossover' services from Cairns to Hobart via the major east coast ports.

June 1990 – Ansett takes over Kendell Airlines.

July 1990: Ansett recorded a modest $2.58m pretax profit for the 1989-90 financial year compared with $67.33m the previous year, much of this reduction attributable to the pilots' dispute and despite strong traffic growth. East-West Airlines lost $7.22m over the 12 months.

July 1990: Ansett NZ lost $NZ29.3m in the year to June 1990.

29 August 1990: Delivery of the first two BAe 146-300s (VH-EWI and EWJ) to Eastwest (previously East-West) Airlines, the slightly revised name reflecting the airline's new corporate identity. The first scheduled service was on 5 September with VH-EWI operating the appropriately numbered flight EW146 from Sydney to Coolangatta.

September 1990: As deregulation approaches, both Ansett and Australian Airlines begin offering an increasing number of discounted fares on most routes, some of them slashing 50% off the standard tariff.

September 1990: Ansett orders 10 Airbus A321s for delivery from late 1995 but these are never delivered.

30 September 1990: Lloyd Aviation (owned by TNT-News company Bodas Pty Ltd) ceases scheduled services and the company is merged into Skywest.

4 October 1990: A revised corporate image for Ansett with the unveiling of a new livery based on the Australian flag and a new marketing name – Ansett Australia. The livery is gradually applied to all aircraft in Ansett associated airlines' fleets.

October 1990 – new Australian flag livery and Ansett Australia name.

1 November 1990: The Australian domestic airline industry is formally deregulated – the Two Airline Policy is no more.

28 November 1990: Ansett NSW (formerly Airlines of New South, Air NSW etc) is renamed Ansett Express and introduces a 'hub bypassing' philosophy with more direct flights. The airline moves its base of operations from Sydney to Brisbane as part of the restructure. Initial fleet is nine Fokker F28 jets and seven Fokker 50 turboprops.

November 1990 – Ansett NSW renamed Ansett Express. (Bill Lines)

December 1990: Ansett Air Freight withdraws its Boeing 707-320C freighter (VH-HTC) from service. It remained grounded at Perth until sold and ferried to the USA in January 1992.

1 December 1990: Australia's first post deregulation domestic startup – Compass Airlines – begins low fare operations on major trunk routes. Headed by former East-West boss Bryan Grey, it operates a small fleet of leased Airbus A300-600s. Both Ansett and Australian Airlines begin offering remarkably similar cut price fares. Unfortunately, Compass had a short life – it collapsed in December 1991.

6 December 1990: The British Aerospace-Ansett Flying College is formally launched, the professional flying training facility to be located at Tamworth NSW. The first courses are scheduled to commence in September 1991 with a fleet of new CT-4B Airtrainers, Piper Warriors and Piper Senecas. With Piper unable to supply the Warriors due to its bankruptcy, the Socata Tobago was substituted instead.

January 1991: Ansett NZ's total losses since beginning operations in July 1987 are estimated at close to $NZ100m.

February 1991: Speculation that Ansett owners News Corp and TNT are considering selling at least some of their interest in the airline. News Corp was known to be in need of a cash injection (and Ansett was not one of its core businesses) while TNT was also having difficulties.

April 1991: Ansett increases its stake in financially troubled America West from 20% to 26% in a debt-for-equity deal resulting from the airline's exposure to AWAS.

April 1991: Ansett withdraws from service the first of five Fokker 50s it will put into storage over the next three months.

4 May 1991: Ansett NT ceases operations as a result of losing its primary money making route (Darwin-Ayer's Rock) to regular Ansett Boeing 737 flights. The airline's Darwin-Katherine-Tennant Creek-Alice Springs 'milk run' was unprofitable and in effect subsidised by the other service.

May 1991: Ansett Express takes delivery of the first of three Fokker F28-4000s (VH-EWA) transferred from Eastwest.

July 1991: US carrier America West – in which TNT-News has a 26% interest – goes into Chapter 11 bankruptcy protection due to a serious liquidity and debt problem. A further worry for the part owners is the fact that the airline has 11 Boeing 737-300s leased from AWAS.

25 August 1991: Ansett and Australian Airlines simultaneously announce frequent flyer 'loyalty' programs, with points accumulated able to be exchanged for either goods (like kitchen knives and computers) to free flights. The schemes were subsequently modified, cutting out the 'free set of steak knives' aspects.

September 1991: Further speculation that TNT and News Corp may start selling some of their interest in Ansett which has estimated losses of $50m for the 1990-91 financial year and is in need of a $200m capital injection in the short term. Both Ansett partners have their own financial problems to solve.

October 1991: Ansett begins installing inflight video screens to its Boeing 767 and Airbus A320 fleet, this now

standard practice pioneered in Australia in late 1990 by new entrant Compass.

18 January 1992: Eastwest introduces the Boeing 727-200 to service (VH-ANE) on the Sydney-Coolangatta route, the aircraft taken from the Ansett fleet and repainted in Eastwest colours. Two other 727s (VH-ANF and RMN) subsequently flew in Eastwest markings before reverting to Ansett operations and livery in 1993. In Eastwest service they were configured in an all economy class, 164 seat layout.

January 1992 – Eastwest introduces the Boeing 727-200 to service.

March 1992: With business class proving to be increasingly popular and the patronage of first class dropping, Australian Airlines abandons it and starts reconfiguring its aircraft with business and economy classes only. Ansett had only recently upgraded its first class cabin and responded by abolishing the first class fare, moving business class passengers up to first and full fare economy up to business. Three months later it changed again, with first and business classes reinstated in their own right. Ansett dumped first class on domestic services altogether in 1997.

11 May 1992: The Hamilton Island resort is placed into receivership. Its airport is half owned by Ansett and the airline (along with subsidiary Eastwest) has exclusive rights to operate there. The resort continues to trade under receivership.

July 1992: Despite substantial traffic growth and high load factors, Australia's domestic airlines lose money in the 1991-92 financial year. Ansett lost $66.4m and subsidiary Eastwest a staggering $142.6m. The overall figure for ATI was a $92.1m loss. Australian Airlines lost $38.5m while Ansett co-owner TNT had lost nearly $400m over the previous two years. Ansett New Zealand lost $NZ33m in 1991-92.

July 1992: Ansett enters into a codeshare arrangement with the USA's Northwest Airlines on services from Australia to Los Angeles via Honolulu. In return, Northwest buys seats on Ansett domestic connecting flights.

17 July 1992: Rupert Murdoch steps down as Ansett Transport Industries' joint chairman and joint chief executive. News Corp chief executive Ken Cowley replaces him. After Sir Peter Abeles also steps down two months later, Mr Cowley becomes sole chairman and TNT chief executive David Mortimer deputy chairman.

August 1992: Ansett and Queensland regional operator Flight West sign a commercial agreement covering codesharing on Queensland coastal routes; integrated ground handling, catering and interline/oncarriage; and participation in Ansett's frequent flyer program.

31 August 1992: Southern Cross Airlines – trading as Compass – begins operations as Australia's second post deregulation low cost startup. Reviving the name Compass was done for what were thought to be positive marketing reasons. Dubbed 'Compass II' by the media, the new airline uses McDonnell Douglas MD-80s but has an even shorter life than its predecessor – it collapsed in March 1993 with financial impropriety by chairman Doug Reid later proven.

September 1992: Sir Peter Abeles resigns as managing director and chief executive of TNT. He remains director and deputy chairman and says he will concentrate his efforts on rejuvenating the financial fortunes of Ansett Transport Industries. However, he also resigned from those positions the next month following illness.

14 September 1992: Qantas formally acquires Australian Airlines for $400m, the latter's livery beginning to disappear from the fleet by mid 1993 and the Qantas brand covering both international and domestic operations. Privatisation is the next step.

January 1993: By the beginning of the year Ansett has commercial (including frequent flyer) alliances with international carriers Lufthansa, United, Northwest, Alitalia, All Nippon, Garuda and Malaysian. The existing frequent flyer agreement with British Airways will be terminated as it takes a 25% stake in the privatised Qantas. Singapore Airlines and Swissair were added to the list in the first few months of 1993.

January 1993: Ansett Transport Industries reports a profit of $37.4m for the six months July-December 1992, its first since 1989-90.

February 1993: Loss making Eastwest Airlines changes its image from a 'cheap and cheerful' holiday airline to something more upmarket in an attempt to improve yields.

18 April 1993: NSW regional operator Hazelton Airlines switches allegiances from Australian Airlines to Ansett by signing a commercial agreement. The agreement covers access to Ansett's reservations systems, terminal facilities and baggage handling/tarmac services. Hazelton retains its own facilities and remains independent.

July 1994 – new and final livery. (Craig Murray)

April 1993: Although not officially announced, Ansett Express operations begin to wind down with its three Fokker 50s withdrawn over the next month or so for lease to an Indian operator. Some confusion follows as two of the aircraft return to Ansett service later in the year, temporarily in Ansett Express livery.

April-June 1993: Loss making Eastwest Airlines is wound down with its fleet of two Boeing 727-200s and four BAe 146-300s repainted in Ansett Australia colours.

May 1993: Reported that Singapore Airlines is looking at acquiring an equity stake in Ansett.

1 July 1993: Ansett WA ceases operations under that name, operations now conducted under the Ansett Australia banner with aircraft carrying normal Ansett livery. At the same time, loss making Eastwest quietly disappears as an entity and is absorbed into the general Ansett fold.

July 1993: For the first time, Ansett Transport Industries releases full details of its financial performance,

statistics covering the 1992-93 financial year. Highlights included an operating profit of $59.5m before tax and abnormals (compared to a loss of $91.2m the previous year) but a net deficit of $181.2m after foreign exchange losses were taken into account. Ansett New Zealand posted its sixth consecutive operating loss in 1992-93 – $NZ37.2m ($A31m).

11 September 1993: Ansett Australia begins services to Denpasar, Indonesia, from Darwin, Melbourne, Perth and Sydney using aircraft from its normal domestic fleet. The airline's true international arm – Ansett International – would start operations a year later.

1 January 1994: Eastwest Airlines formally ceases to exist.

March 1994: Ansett orders five additional Airbus A320s, these substituting for five of the 10 A321s which were ordered in September 1990.

3 May 1994: Announcement of the establishment of Ansett International, operating services to ports mainly in Asia. Initial equipment is two Boeing 747-300s leased from Singapore Airlines. Services started in September.

July 1994: Ansett Australia Holdings – which replaces Ansett Transport Industries as the group's umbrella company – records an after tax (but before abnormals) profit of $139.9m for the 1993-94 financial year. Gross profit was $209.2m, the highest ever recorded by the airline.

12 July 1994: Ansett Air Freight puts Douglas DC-8-62F N1804 (leased from Arrow Air) into service on the Sydney-Auckland route.

28 July 1994: The unveiling of Ansett's new corporate livery, timed to coincide with the launch of Ansett International. The new livery – which is applied to the whole Ansett fleet – comprises a blue fin with a stylised gold 'A' encompassing the Federation Star in white (this to be the airline's new logo) plus the stars of the Southern Cross. The design proved to be Ansett's final livery.

23 August 1994: America West – in which Ansett has a 26% interest – emerges from Chapter 11 bankruptcy protection just over three years after entering it.

29 August 1994: Reorganisation of the Ansett companies sees Ansett Australia Holdings Ltd replacing Ansett Transport Industries Ltd as the umbrella company, and Ansett Australia Ltd replacing Ansett Transport Industries (Operations) Pty Ltd as the airline operations part of the organisation. On the same day, Ansett International's first Boeing 747-300 (VH-INJ, leased from Singapore Airlines) arrives in Australia.

4 September 1994: After conducting a scheduled domestic Sydney-Perth flight on 31 August, Ansett International operates its first 'proper' service, flight AN881 from Sydney to Osaka using Boeing 747-312 VH-INJ. The first service from Sydney to Hong Kong (AN887 with VH-INH) was operated on 10 September.

September 1994 – Ansett International launches services.

Ansett Australia had started flying to Denpasar, Indonesia the previous September using aircraft from its normal fleet.

5 October 1994: Skywest Airlines takes delivery of Fokker 50 VH-FNH, the first of an initial three aircraft transferred from Ansett Australia.

19 October 1994: Ansett International Boeing 747-312 VH-INH suffers minor damage at Sydney when it is forced to land with its nosewheel retracted following a mechanical problem. The aircraft returned to service on 11 December, the temporary gap in Ansett International's capacity filled by a 747-400 leased from Qantas and a 747-300 Combi leased from Malaysian Airlines.

October 1994 – Skywest receives first Fokker 50. Keith Anderson)

May 1995: The first serious possibility that Air New Zealand is negotiating to purchase a half share in Ansett, although at this time the seller is thought to be News Ltd. It is reported that discussions have been going on since October 1994. The talks were over by July 1995 with News reportedly frustrated by Air NZ's delays in agreeing to a figure. A price of between $400m and $600m was rumoured.

30 June 1995: Ansett Holdings Ltd formed as the holding company, replacing Ansett Australia Holdings Ltd.

July 1995: Ansett Australia Holdings records a net profit of $51m for the 1994-95 financial year, including a $13m loss in the second half.

31 July 1995: The float of 75% of Qantas is launched, the remaining 25% already owned by British Airways.

September 1995: News Ltd and Air New Zealand resume talks about the sale of News' 50% stake in Ansett.

November 1995: Air New Zealand's plans to invest in Ansett take a different turn, the airline now talking to TNT about purchasing its half share.

December 1995: Confirmed that Air New Zealand will purchase TNT's 50% stake in Ansett for $425m. At the same time it is announced that Ansett has disposed of its own relatively small stake in TNT, 23 million shares worth about $44m.

February 1996: The New Zealand Commerce Commission issues a draft ruling vetoing Air NZ's purchase of TNT's Ansett share on competition grounds. Ansett New Zealand is the main stumbling block, the NZCC concerned about having two domestic airlines owned by the same organisation. Another complication is the fact that Qantas owns 19.9% of Air New Zealand.

February 1996: Ansett orders two Airbus A320s (an additional four aircraft are already on order), two Boeing 767-200s for domestic services, one 767-300 for international services and one 737-300. All will be leased. The domestic orders will allow Ansett to retire its remaining Boeing 727s and Fokker F28s. The new 767-200s will be able to operate with a two man crew following agreement by Ansett's flight engineers.

March 1996: First reports of fumes entering the cabins of Ansett BAe 146s, causing discomfort for passengers and crew. The issue became a contentious one over the next few years.

27 March 1996: Ansett International takes delivery of its first Boeing 767-300 (VH-BZF), the aircraft to be used on services to Jakarta and Kuala Lumpur. It joins three 747-300s in the Ansett International fleet.

31 March 1996: Ansett launches its high frequency Capital Shuttle service between Sydney and Canberra using Kendell Airlines and its Saab 340s.

June 1996: The New Zealand Commerce Commission approves Air NZ's purchase of TNT's 50% interest in Ansett after the airline's other shareholder, News Ltd, agrees to take over full control of Ansett NZ.

July 1996: Ansett Holdings records an operating loss of $18.6m for the 1995-96 financial year, although this was artificially increased to a net profit of $57.3m after unrealised foreign exchange gains and tax benefits were taken into account. Ansett International recorded a small profit. The airline continues to lose domestic market share to Qantas (47.6% in 1995-96) and announces an extensive cost cutting program.

2 July 1996: Ansett and Korean Air start a codeshare arrangement on each other's flights between Seoul, Sydney and Brisbane. Ansett International launched services to Seoul on the same day.

July 1996: Ansett sells charter operator Skywest Aviation to Darwin's Paspaley Pearling Group and the operation is renamed Pearl Aviation. Skywest Aviation is separate from Skywest Airlines which is also owned by Ansett and not for sale. The move is part of Ansett's recent disposal of non core businesses including bus and coach builder Ansair, road transport company Ansett-Ridgeways and general aviation firm Pacific Aviation.

August 1996: Ansett sells its half share in the Australian Air Academy (formerly BAe-Ansett Flying College) to co-owner British Aerospace. The facility is subsequently renamed British Aerospace Flight Training.

30 August 1996: The Fokker 50 flies its last service with Ansett Australia, the occasion also the final time a propeller driven aircraft flew an Ansett service. The last flight was performed by VH-FNI which operated the AN538/539 services from Sydney to Ballina and return. The Fokker 50 remained in service with regional subsidiary Skywest.

September 1996: Ansett Australia introduces electronic (allegedly 'paperless') ticketing to the Australian domestic market.

1 October 1996: Following shareholder and regulatory approval, Air New Zealand formally acquires TNT's 50% share of Ansett Australia Holdings for $A325m. Part of the deal is that Air NZ will inject a further $150m into undercapitalised Ansett. News Ltd takes over Ansett NZ at the same time.

October-December 1996: The shares roundabout – 51% of Ansett International sold by Ansett Holdings to Australian institutional investors including insurance giant AMP (so as to meet Foreign Investment Review Board requirements); Ansett Holdings sells its Ansett New Zealand shares to News Ltd; and Ansett Holdings acquires 100% of Bodas Pty Ltd, formerly owned by TNT-News and responsible for most of the airline acquisitions over the last few years.

13 December 1996: Ansett announces the sale of its last six Boeing 727-200s – five passenger aircraft and a freighter – to Tennessee based Intrepid Aviation. Four departed for the USA almost immediately, leaving two in service until April 1997.

January 1997: Former Cathay Pacific managing director Rod Eddington takes up his appointment as Ansett's executive chairman. He replaces Ken Cowley, who remains a director of the airline.

January 1997: Ansett International launches its first around the world fare. Called World Adventure, the package includes sectors with allied operators Malaysia Airlines, Singapore Airlines and Lufthansa.

January 1997: Ansett appointed the official carrier for the Sydney 2000 Olympics, its successful bid consortium including international carriers Air New Zealand, Lufthansa, Malaysia Airlines, South African Airways, Thai Airways International and United Airlines. As the official carrier, Ansett and its partners will carry members of the Australian Olympic committee, the Games organising committee, many of the competing athletes and others travelling on Olympics business before and during the event. Ansett subsidiary Traveland was appointed the official Olympics travel agent.

January 1997: Ansett announces its revamped 'Global Rewards' frequent flyer program in association with international partners Air New Zealand, All Nippon Airways, Cathay Pacific, Malaysia Airlines, South African Airways, Swissair, Thai and United. Lufthansa and Lauda Air were quickly added to the list.

March 1997: Qantas sells its shareholding in Air New Zealand.

2 April 1997: Shortly after removing first class from its domestic fleet,

April 1997 – the Boeing 727 is retired from Ansett service. (Rob Finlayson)

Ansett launches its enhanced business class. Called BusinessFirst, it is close to the standards of the old first class. Economy class was upgraded at the same time.

23 April 1997: After 33 years, the Boeing 727 bows out of Ansett service when 727-200 VH-ANB flies the type's last commercial sector, flight AN36 from Hobart to Melbourne. Ansett operated a total of 23 727s over the years. VH-ANB was also the last 727 delivered to Ansett, in August 1981 as part of an order four long range 727-200s acquired for nonstop operations from the east coast to Perth. It was also the 4,000th jet airliner built by Boeing.

26 April 1997: The Boeing 727's absolutely last hurrah with Ansett when five special flights over Melbourne are put on for staff and enthusiasts. Between them, 727-200LRs VH-ANA and ANB took 700 people up during the day.

May 1997: Announcement of the formation of the Star Alliance, initially comprising United, Lufthansa, Thai International, SAS and Air Canada. Others – including Ansett and Air New Zealand – would also subsequently join. Between them, the five founding airlines serve 584 international destinations including 340 in the USA.

20 June 1997: Ansett, Air New Zealand and Singapore Airlines sign a Memorandum of Understanding covering plans to form the largest commercial alliance of airlines in the Asia-Pacific region. The agreement was subject to regulatory approval, this forthcoming (from the Australian Competition and Consumer Commission) in June 1998. The association with SIA further fuels speculation of a possible investment in Ansett.

July 1997: Ansett Holdings records a modest $7.7m operating profit for the 1996-97 financial year, but after taking into account restructuring costs, tax writeoffs and foreign exchange losses the bottom line was a $35m net loss. Ansett International lost $46m while the regional subsidiaries between them made a profit of $10m.

November 1997: Ansett International drops Shanghai from its schedules, the first of many services into Asia suspended over the next few months as the region's economic crisis takes its toll.

January 1998: Ansett International drops first class from its fleet and replaces it with the enhanced

Sydney 2000

Official Airline of the Sydney 2000 Olympic Games

'BusinessFirst' introduced to domestic services in April 1997.

11 February 1998: In what seems to be something of an anomaly, Ansett New Zealand (now owned 100% by News Ltd) joins the Qantas frequent flyer program, fuelling speculation that Qantas is looking to take over the former Ansett/TNT/News company. The airline operates in direct competition with Air New Zealand on domestic services, despite News Ltd still owning half of Ansett along with Air NZ.

May 1998: Ansett disposes of its Whitsunday Islands resorts, selling its 100% interest in Hayman Island and its half share in Hamilton Island Airport to the BT Hotel Group for a total of $94m. BT already has a majority share of Hamilton Island plus a minority interest in the airport. Hayman's sale price was a bargain basement $61.5m – the resort cost over $300m to develop. The sale of Hamilton Island Airport ends Ansett's exclusive rights to the facility.

July 1998: Ansett Holdings returns a modest trading profit of $27.8m for the 1997-98 financial year. Before tax operating profit was $82.2m after taking into account abnormals such as the sale of fixed assets and other items like Hayman Island and its 50% share of Hamilton Island Airport plus foreign exchange gains. Domestic airline operations made a gross profit of $54m and regional subsidiaries contributed $15m but Ansett International lost $57.2m, this operation badly hit by the Asian economic crisis which started in late 1997.

September 1998: Ansett launches its 'Great Business Plan', designed to make the company more efficient and increase profitability to 10% of revenue. The plan results from the Business Review Program conducted with consultants Bain & Co over the previous 10 months, this intended to identify short term cost savings and longer term operating strategies.

21 October 1998: Ansett regional subsidiary Kendell Airlines orders 12 Bombardier CRJ200 regional jets and options 12 more. The aircraft will see a major expansion of Kendell's fleet and route network, taking over many services now operated by Ansett and resulting from Great Business Plan initiatives.

December 1998-January 1999: More non core asset disposals by Ansett – its 68% stake in Diners Club Australia (to Diners Club International); and wholly owned subsidiary Transport Industries Insurance. TII was established in 1960 as a captive insurer to manage Ansett's requirements and became a general insurer in 1975, offering travel and general insurance products.

January 1999: Ansett introduces direct internet bookings for domestic services, bypassing the previous internet links to agents Traveland or Jetset.

January 1999: After months of speculation, Singapore Airlines confirms it is interested in acquiring a 25% equity stake in Ansett.

12 March 1999: Skywest operates its last Jetstream 31 service when VH-ESW flies Karratha-Port Hedland-Broome.

22 March 1999: Ansett Worldwide Aviation Services takes delivery of the first of seven Next Generation Boeing 737-700s it has on order.

28 March 1999: Ansett is admitted to the Star Alliance as a full member. Half owner Air New Zealand is admitted on the same day.

29 March 1999: Singapore Airlines announced it has offered to purchase News Ltd's 50% holding in Ansett for $A500m. The offer is greeted with enthusiasm by most observers and for a time it appears that consummating the deal is certain. However, as owner of the other 50%, Air NZ has pre-emptive rights to the first option on Ansett, providing its bid at least matches SIA's. Despite this, it looks as if the SIA deal will go ahead, SIA officially announcing the purchase.

April 1999: Ansett and leading regional carrier Hazelton Airlines sign a five year agreement under which Hazelton will be the sole preferred NSW carrier for Ansett other than on routes also operated by Ansett. Ansett also secured first right of refusal on 20% of Hazelton's shares.

15 June 1999: Ansett sells its door-to-door express road freight business to TNT; Ansett Air Freight renamed Ansett Australia Cargo.

June 1999: Sale discussions between SIA and Ansett discontinued due to uncertainties created by Air NZ's position on its pre-emptive rights to purchase the 50% share owned by News Ltd. Air NZ had approved the sale to SIA but major shareholder Brierley Investments Limited increased its stake in the airline and then attempted to get SIA to buy Ansett through Air NZ directly or through BIL. The result was an impasse.

June 1999 – Ansett Air Freight renamed Ansett Air Cargo. (Brian Wilkes)

July 1999: Ansett recorded greatly improved profits for the 1998-99 financial year, Ansett Australia reporting a before tax operating profit of $163m, including a $15.9m profit by the regionals and a much reduced loss of just under $10m by Ansett International. As for parent company Ansett Holdings Ltd, its before tax profit was $200.4m including $52.8m worth of abnormals mainly involving the sale of non core assets. Ansett Australia staff numbers fell by 450 to 11,920.

August 1999: Ansett New Zealand's pilots stage a series of 24 hour strikes in protest against new employment contracts proposed by the airline. Many saw the action as foolhardy as it worsened Ansett NZ's already precarious financial position. The dispute dragged on and got to the stage where the airline locked out 125 of its 146 pilots in September.

August 1999 – Ansett International receives its first Boeing 747-400. (Gerard Williamson)

August 1999: Ansett sells its catering arm to Gate Gourmet, part of the SAir Group (Swissair).

11 August 1999: Ansett International's first Boeing 747-400 (VH-ANA, leased from Singapore Airlines) is delivered. VH-ANB follows in September.

30 September 1999: The first of Kendell Airlines' 12 Bombardier CRJ200 regional jets (VH-KJF) is delivered to the company's Wagga Wagga base.

September 1999 – Kendell Airlines' first CRJ200 delivered. (Rob Finlayson)

28 December 1999: The last Ansett Fokker F28 service when VH-FKI flies AN335 from Mount Newman to Perth.

December 1999: Further complicating the Ansett ownership issue, plans are formulated for an employee buy out of News Ltd's share in the airline.

18 February 2000: Announced that Air NZ has exercised its pre-emptive rights and will purchase News Ltd's 50% of Ansett Holdings for around $A680m. Industry reaction is subdued, many analysts predicting problems and ruing the opportunity Ansett may have missed by not being taken over by the larger, cashed up, prestigious and more dynamic Singapore Airlines.

March 2000: Further confusion in the ownership saga of the region's airlines when it is revealed that Qantas is looking at purchasing the 47% of Air New Zealand owned by Brierley Investments.

March 2000: Announced that News Corp is selling its 100% interest in Ansett New Zealand to a group of investors which includes Australian bush clothing manufacturer R M Williams.

April 2000: Singapore Airlines acquires an 8.3% stake in Air New Zealand and a few days later increases that shareholding to 25%, the maximum allowed by New Zealand's foreign ownership laws.

April 2000: Ansett Worldwide Aviation Services (AWAS) sold by TNT-News Corp to US based aircraft lessor MSDW Aircraft Holdings. The new merged entity was renamed Ansett Worldwide in July 2001 but has no association with the airline or its owners.

5 June 2000: NSW regional operator Impulse Airlines expands onto the trunk routes (initially Sydney-Melbourne), offering low fares using Boeing 717s. Impulse was absorbed into the Qantas fold in May 2001.

23 June 2000: Air New Zealand's acquisition of Ansett is formally completed following finalisation of the necessary regulatory details.

July 2000: Ansett Australia posted an operating profit of $96.7m for the 1999-2000 financial year, down 40.5% on the previous 12 months. By comparison, Qantas' domestic operations posted a record operating profit of $272m, up 5.9%. Ansett International turned around to record an $8.1m profit while the regionals' profit dropped by two-thirds to $5.2m. Overall, Ansett Holdings reported a before tax profit of $121.7m, down 36.6%. Parent Air NZ posted an after tax loss of $NZ600m after taking substantial abnormals into account.

31 August 2000: Sir Richard Branson's Virgin Blue Airlines launches operations on Australian trunk routes using a fleet of Boeing 737s. Initial services were on the Brisbane-Sydney route but the low fare airline's network quickly expanded.

4 September 2000: Ansett New Zealand becomes Tasman Pacific Airlines, operating as Qantas New Zealand under a franchise agreement. It lasts only until April 2001 before collapsing

September 2000 – Ansett New Zealand sold. (Peter Clark)

October 2000: Ansett-Air New Zealand acquires a 20% stake in regional carrier Hazelton Airlines and announces its intention to gain full control. It is the opening shot in a protracted bidding war for the airline which eventually sees Ansett prevail over Qantas.

29 October 2000: Kendell Airlines introduces the Bombardier CRJ200 regional jet to service, initially on the Canberra-Adelaide route.

December 2000: Former Qantas deputy chief executive Gary Toomey is appointed the new managing director/chief executive officer of the Air NZ-Ansett group, just in time for the airline's major problems to publicly emerge.

23 December 2000: Ansett's terminal problems (at least in the public's eyes) begin when seven of its Boeing 767-200s are temporarily grounded after it is discovered they had not undergone mandatory structural inspections. In some cases, the aircraft are well past the due dates. The groundings occur over the busy Christmas period, costing the airline dearly.

Further maintenance oversights are discovered over the next couple of weeks (including the fitting of incorrect leading edge slats to a 767) along with cracks in the tail surfaces of one of the grounded 767s. Investigations by CASA into Ansett's maintenance and records keeping practices begin.

February 2001: The Air NZ-Ansett Group announces its first financial results since integration. It made a net profit of just $NZ3.8m for six months to December 2000 and then only after a large tax credit is taken into account.

March 2001: Ansett-Air NZ gains control of Hazelton Airlines by acquiring over 90% of the shareholding.

March 2001 – Ansett-Air NZ gains control of Hazelton Airlines.

10 April 2001: While undergoing engine pylon inspections which should have been carried out months earlier (Boeing issued an Alert Service Bulletin in March 2000), it is discovered that four of the seven Boeing 767-200s being examined have cracks in the pylons. The cracks require grounding and repair.

12 April 2001: It is discovered that an Ansett 767 had flown with an incorrectly stowed emergency exit slide, this a 'no go' item. CASA finally loses patience and grounds Ansett's entire fleet of ten 767s – or one-third of the airline's capacity – on the day before the busy Easter holiday period. CASA also threatens to issue a 'show cause' notice as to why Ansett's Air Operators' Certificate should not be withdrawn. All the 767s have to undergo detailed inspection and their maintenance paperwork examined in detail. The first of the grounded 767s returns to service on 20 April and the remainder are back by the first week of May. Several aircraft are leased in from other operators to help cover the capacity shortfall.

27 April 2001: Ansett announces it is selling early model 767-200s and replacing them with newer (but still second hand) leased 767-300s.

2 May 2001: Faced with a PR disaster, Ansett launches its 'absolutely' advertising campaign which completely fails to convince the public that Ansett is safe and reliable.

8 May 2001: Ansett Australia Holdings acquires the remaining Hazelton shareholding and now has 100% ownership.

May 2001: Rumours abound about Air New Zealand's financial position and speculation about changes of ownership are rife. Qantas and Singapore Airlines at the forefront of them. Both made offers, Qantas' rejected in June and SIA's stymied by the New Zealand Government's dithering on the issue of raising foreign ownership limits from the current 25%. Air NZ's share price plummets as news of its financial position leaks out and SIA later withdraws its offer.

5 August 2001: Delivery of the first Boeing 767-300 (VH-BZL) intended for domestic services as part of the program to replace the troublesome and ageing 767-200s. Leased from Air Canada, this was the only one to (briefly) enter service before the airline's collapse. Two other leased 767-300s (VH-BZI and BZM) were delivered in September, but too late.

August 2001: The last throw of the Air NZ-Ansett dice? The group offers $250m to take over Virgin Blue, an offer publicly rejected by Sir Richard Branson.

6 September 2001: Singapore Airlines withdraws its share purchase offer.

10 September 2001: Air NZ offers Ansett to Qantas.

12 September 2001: Qantas decides against taking up Air New Zealand's offer to purchase Ansett. Ansett is put into voluntary administration with PriceWaterhouseCoopers.

13 September 2001: Air New Zealand reports a $NZ1.42bn loss for the 2000-2001 financial year including substantial provisions and write-downs associated with Ansett.

14 September 2001: Ansett, Ansett International and the airline's regional subsidiaries are grounded by the administrator when they run out of cash.

17 September 2001: Union pressure results in the appointment of new administrators, Mark Korda and Mark Mentha of Andersen. They immediately set about finding a buyer for the airline as a going concern.

27 September 2001: Ansett Kick-Start (or Ansett Mk.II) launched, getting the airline back into the air in a limited way. The subsidiaries were also able to restart limited operations at around the same time.

29 September 2001: Ansett Mk.II begins flying between Sydney and Melbourne with five A320s. Brisbane, Perth and Adelaide are subsequently added to the list and 16 A320s return to service, although passenger loads are poor despite the Federal Government guaranteeing fares protection until 31 January 2002.

3 October 2001: Air NZ reverts to majority state ownership when the NZ Government announces it will recapitalise the airline to the tune of $NZ885m (about $A725m). This leaves it with an 83% interest and substantially reduces the level of holding by SIA and Brierley Investments.

12 October 2001: The Federal Court accepts Air New Zealand's offer of a $150m payment from it to Ansett, in settlement of any financial claims Ansett may have against its former owner. The money is to be used by the administrators as working capital for Ansett Mk.II, but the Australian Government wants it to go towards paying workers' entitlements. The payout effectively means that Air NZ is able to absolve itself from any further interest in, or responsibility for Ansett.

15 October 2001: ANstaff, an Ansett staff syndicate led by former CEO Graeme McMahon announces a bid for the airline. The bid is withdrawn in mid November.

19 October 2001: Businessmen Solomon Lew (formerly of Coles Myer) and Lindsay Fox (road transport company Linfox) announce a $3.6bn bid for Ansett's mainline assets, under the Tesna syndicate name. Of that, $270m is for the purchase of the Ansett assets necessary to restart the airline. Tesna says it will lease 30 new Airbus A320s, re-employ 4,000 Ansett workers, take over the liability of workers' entitlements for re-employed staff and finance the new aircraft.

8 November 2001: The Tesna bid for Ansett is accepted by the administrators and a deadline of 31 January 2002 is set to finalise the deal.

14 December 2001: Skywest Airlines is sold to Airline Investments Limited (AIL), a consortium of West Australian businessmen, for $6.5m. The airline subsequently signed reservations, ground handling, co-branding and cargo handling agreements with Tesna for the new Ansett, but the collapse of those left Skywest to fend on its own without a direct passenger feed from a major domestic carrier.

18 December 2001: Tesna announces the involvement of financier and Ryanair chairman David Bonderman and former America West chief executive Bill Franke as equity partners.

1 January 2002: Former BMI (British Midland) executive James Hogan is appointed the new Ansett's chief executive.

29 January 2002: An Ansett creditors' meeting approves the sale of Ansett to Tesna. A new deadline of 28 February is set.

March 2002 – farewell Ansett. (Theo Van Loon)

February 2002: A few cracks start to appear in the Tesna bid: the number of Ansett staff to be re-employed is reduced from 4,000 to 3,000; estimates that Ansett Mk.II is losing $6m per week emerge (some put it even higher than that); it becomes clear that public confidence in Ansett Mk.II is not great; and the announcement of the proposed frequent flyer scheme (on 19 February) is greeted less than enthusiastically as it does nothing to encourage previous Global Rewards members who have lost all their points to rejoin.

11 February 2002: Many observers' fears that all is not well with the Tesna bid seem to be confirmed when it is revealed that the consortium is having talks with Sir Richard Branson about merging the new Ansett with Virgin Blue. Branson is not interested.

21 February 2002: Reports that Tesna is trying to reduce its $270m Ansett purchase price commitment by 10%. The administrators reject the plan.

27 February 2002: One day before the deadline, Fox and Lew announce they are not going ahead with the deal to resurrect Ansett. The pair blame the Australian Government, the airports and others but it is revealed that a large part of the Tesna plan involved what were in effect subsidies from Australian taxpayers which virtually guaranteed profits. The administrators have no choice but to shut the airline down and announce that it will take effect from midnight on 4 March. Ansett will be wound up and its assets liquidated.

5 March 2002: Ansett's final revenue flight (AN152) arrives in Sydney at 6.42am after flying the overnight 'red eye' service from Perth. It departed the Western Australia capital at about 11.45pm the previous night. The aircraft involved is A320 VH-HYI.

7 March 2002: Announced that Aeropelican is to be sold to the IAP Group, the southern hemisphere's largest supplier of airliner spare parts and owner of Horizon Airlines. The sale was completed on 26 April.

8 March 2002: Ansett Airbus A320 VH-HYB (leased from Ansett Worldwide) departs Melbourne for storage at Mojave, California. Others soon follow. The administrators have 94 Ansett owned aircraft to sell – A320s, 737s, 767s and BAe 146s.

2 May 2002: The administrators announce the sale of Ansett's Sydney terminal to Sydney Airports Corporation Limited for $192m and on the following day announce the sale of Ansett's interests in the Melbourne domestic terminal to the airport's owners. A week earlier, the Canberra Airport terminal had been sold to the airport's owner and the Cairns facility to the Cairns Port Authority.

7 May 2002: The Australiawide consortium – led by former ANstaff consortium advisor Michael Jones – is named as preferred tenderer to purchase both Hazelton and Kendell Airlines, which had been operating under administration since the previous September. It was revealed at the same time that Kendell had lost about $10m since then. The sale was scheduled to be finalised in the first week of June but after some delays due to contractual and administrative issues not being resolved the contract was finally signed on 28 June. Some more delays resulted in settlement finally occurring in late July and the new airline began operations as Regional Express (Rex) on August 6, using former Kendell and Hazelton Saab 340s and Fairchild Metros.

4 June 2002: The last Ansett flight out of Sydney Airport when Boeing 737-377 VH-CZM is ferried to Melbourne for storage pending its sale.

23 June 2002: Announced that Virgin Blue has agreed to purchase the former Ansett jet base facility at Melbourne Airport for a reported $7m.

July 2002: The Australian Securities and Investment Commission (ASIC) decides not to initiate action against Air New Zealand and its former directors in the wake of the Ansett collapse, despite a belief that Air NZ may have engaged in 'misleading and deceptive' conduct. ASIC decided not to proceed because it would be too expensive, logistically difficult and risky.

16 September 2002: The administrators release their third report to creditors, revealing assets worth $630m had been sold with another $98.1m pending. Also noted is the difficulty in selling Ansett's aircraft in a severely depressed world market. Forty three Boeing 767s, Airbus A320s and BAe 146s remain unsold with a further 13 under negotiation.

CHAPTER THREE

FROM STUDEBAKERS TO ELECTRAS

The town of Hamilton, about 250 kilometres west – as the crow flies – of the Victorian capital Melbourne lies in the heart of some of the best sheep and cattle grazing country in Australia. Promoted as the 'Wool Capital of the World', it is one of the most intensely grazed wool growing regions on the planet.

The area was first settled in 1837 after the New South Wales Surveyor-General, Major Thomas Mitchell passed through on his journey of exploration which traced the courses of several major rivers including the Murrumbidgee, Murray and Darling. In doing so he found substantial areas of top quality grazing land in both NSW and Victoria. The area's population quickly grew as the graziers moved in and was further boosted in the 1850s with the discovery of gold.

These days Hamilton and the area surrounding it has a population of around 12,000 and contains tourists attractions intended to celebrate its history. One of them is the 'Big Woolbales', five linked buildings that look like oversized wool bales, each containing displays relating to the town's rural past – shearing and farming equipment, wool samples and other items.

Another attraction is the Sir Reginald Ansett Transport Museum, celebrating the airline that started operations in Hamilton 99 years after the first white settlers went to the area, and the man who established that airline. It was 17 February 1936 that one of the great occasions in Australia's aviation history occurred – the inaugural Ansett Airways Pty Ltd service between Hamilton and Melbourne's Essendon Airport.

Eight passengers boarded the newly acquired Fokker F.XI Universal VH-UTO for the 12.30pm departure – Mr K E Barr, Mr H E Heine, Miss E T Lascelles, Mrs W R Pearson, Miss A Shields, Mr J R Simpson, Mr K M Wilson and Reg Ansett himself. The aircraft was flown by Vern Cerche and the one-way fare was £2 ($4). The scheduled arrival time at Essendon was 2.15pm and the return flight left Melbourne at 2.45pm for a 4.30pm return to Hamilton.

The inaugural service was big news for the local community, the *Hamilton Spectator* reporting: 'Amid great public interest the new daily air service to Melbourne and return was inaugurated by Ansett Airways Pty Ltd yesterday. More than 200 people gathered at the Hamilton aerodrome to see the giant Fokker depart on its initial journey. Precisely at 12.30pm the graceful metal bird took to the air and in a very few minutes was winging swiftly away....'

Use of the term 'giant' to describe the Fokker seems amusing with the benefit of hindsight while the 'airfield' from which the inaugural flight departed was simply a suitably large paddock which had been leased from the Hamilton Water Board. Facilities were therefore minimal at that stage but the departure of VH-UTO was the start of something big.

'RM'

Reginald Myles Ansett was born at Inglewood, a small town near Bendigo, Victoria on 13 February 1909. One of six children, his father operated a bicycle repair shop but when he enlisted in the Australian Imperial Force (AIF) in 1915 and went off to fight in France during the Great War, Mrs Ansett took her brood to Melbourne.

On Mr Ansett's return to Australia after the conflict, the family purchased a small woollen knitting business in the Melbourne suburb of Camberwell. Renamed Ansett Knitting Mills, the business was successful and retained its name until as late as 1992 despite having been sold 18 years earlier. It had been relocated to Seymour in central Victoria during the 1940s.

The young Reginald left school when he was 14 years old to work in the family business and displaying an aptitude for things mechanical, studied at Melbourne's Swinburne Technical College to emerge a qualified knitting and sewing machine mechanic.

But sewing machines held little fascination for 'RM' as he was already known by friends and family, an appellation which remained throughout his life, later extending to employees of his airline and business associates. Like many other young men of his time, Ansett became fascinated by the exploits of pioneer airmen such as Charles Kingsford Smith and resolved he would learn to fly.

Ansett was able to achieve this aim in 1929, the lessons paid for by cashing in an insurance policy his parents had taken out for him some years earlier. Armed with his new licence (number 419 in Australia), he realised there was much more to the world than his local area and wanted to see more of it. Attempts to find a job in the fledgling aviation industry failed, so he travelled to Darwin by ship and instead found work as an axeman with a survey party operating in the Northern Territory.

The idea of establishing a peanut growing plantation in the Territory was briefly considered but rejected. With the Great Depression in full swing by 1931, Ansett was forced to return to Melbourne after the

The start of it all in December 1931 with Reg Ansett standing beside his Ansett Roadways Studebaker. Initial 'service car' operations were between the Victorian regional centres of Maryborough and Ballarat. (Ansett)

Federal Government withdrew funding for the survey work he was involved in.

On The Road

Reg Ansett's time in the Northern Territory had one lasting effect on him – the realisation of the vastness of Australia and the resultant importance of transport, especially in rural and regional areas.

Ansett therefore saw an opportunity and despite having only £50 ($100) in his pocket, some ideas in his head and well developed work ethic in his soul, he decided to establish a road service initially covering the 290 kilometres between the gold mining centre of Ballarat and Maryborough in the western district of Victoria and later to other centres including Melbourne. Scraping up a bit more cash he purchased a second hand Studebaker sedan for £70 ($140) on hire purchase and launched his Ansett Roadways 'service car' business in December 1931 as a one man operation carrying passengers and small items of freight. With no employees apart from himself, Ansett acted not only as the new venture's driver but also its mechanic, business manager, marketing manager and chief cook and bottlewash!

Small newspaper advertisements were run to announce the arrival of the new venture: 'Be In Melbourne By 1.30pm', said the heading; 'An entirely new car service will start operations Monday, 7th December. Cars will leave J Strangio's National Café, 7.30am daily. Book early. R Ansett, Prop.'

Despite attracting clientele from local farmers and the generally wealthy graziers of the area, Ansett Roadways was losing money at an alarming rate for such a small operation. A change of headquarters to Hamilton in October 1932 brought with it a change of fortune and the business began to pick up as the Hamilton-Ballarat route was well patronised. A second Studebaker was quickly added to the fleet as was the company's first employee, 23 years old driver Colin MacDonald, who remained with Ansett until his retirement in the mid 1970s.

Once established in Hamilton, Ansett Roadways grew with Colin MacDonald responsible for opening up new services using Hamilton as the hub. More vehicles and routes were added and the motor garage Ansett Motors was formed in the town to service the company's vehicles and to take on outside work.

Government Interference

By 1935 Ansett Roadways had a dozen vehicles at its disposal including larger coaches capable of carrying economic loads. The time had come to expand beyond rural Victoria and start servicing the potentially lucrative routes to Melbourne.

This was easier said than done, because the Victorian Government intervened on behalf of the Victorian Railways. Like most railways around the world before, then and since, VR was largely inefficient and was looking for protection from the increasingly popular road transport operators such as Ansett Roadways in order to maintain profits, or at least minimise losses.

As VR was owned by the Victorian Government, this protection was willingly forthcoming in 1935 through the introduction of a Bill which would regulate the road operators and restrict their operations. The Bill was introduced by the then Victorian Attorney-General, Robert Menzies. Mr Menzies, of course, later went on to become Australia's longest serving Prime Minister, was knighted and as PM had substantial dealings with Reg Ansett as his airline grew into a major operator in the 1950s and 1960s.

For Ansett, the new regulations resulted in him being denied a licence to operate his coaches to Melbourne as they stated that such licences would only be issued for routes which did not compete directly with the railways.

Some skullduggery was engaged in to get around the restrictions. Colin MacDonald explains: 'We couldn't take passengers beyond Ballarat, so we had to get up to all sorts of lurks. We used to send out a scout car. We would discover the police were in Bacchus Marsh, so we would send forth our scout car loaded with bags on the roof, all dummies. The passengers would be cousins of the driver, so no fares. The police would zip after them. Meanwhile we used to skid down the other road through Geelong and back into Melbourne that way.'

This kind of chicanery was all very well but it had no future. Unable to expand his road passenger transport business in the way he wanted, Ansett's thoughts therefore turned to air transport, an area he had long been interested in anyway. Besides, the state governments had no control over air services!

The experience was a good learning one for Reg Ansett and taught him that the best way to deal with governments was to have them on your side as much as possible, a philosophy that would later pay dividends.

Reg Ansett certainly quickly learnt how to exploit a given situation to his own advantage and was always keen to do so. Many of those who knew him mention two sides to his character – the sometimes generous and always down to earth 'shirt sleeves' man who involved himself in all aspects of his business and who could be

Ansett Airways' first aircraft, Fokker F.XI Universal VH-UTO which inaugurated services for the new airline between Hamilton and Melbourne on 17 February 1936. (Ansett)

'just one of the blokes' adored by most of his employees; and the hard nosed businessman who would take no prisoners when it came down to it.

The former head of Ansett's engineering section, John Bibo, commented on his boss at the time of the airline's 50th anniversary in 1986, reflecting on when he first became part of the newly merged Ansett-ANA in 1957 having previously been part of the defunct larger operator: 'There were all sorts of rumours about Reg Ansett's attitudes; he was to some extent an ogre to us'. But he turned out to be good to work for and was a genuine aviation enthusiast: 'He knew every phase of the operation and had a magnificent overall grasp of things.'

Although the new road transport regulations introduced to Victoria in 1935 stymied Ansett Roadways' immediate plans, they did not mean the end of the operation. The name carried on for many more years as one of the several road passenger and freight businesses owned by the Ansett Transport Industries group over

Ansett Airways added Airspeed Envoy VH-UXM to its fleet – if that's the word for an airline with two aircraft! – in October 1936. Reg Ansett's de Havilland Moth can be seen in the background of this shot taken at Hamilton. Ansett had purchased the Moth for business use in 1934 and it was used by the Ansett Flying School as a trainer and for joyflights.

The two seat Porterfield 35/70 Flyabout purchased by Ansett Airways in December 1936 for use by the flying school and for joyflights. The Porterfield immediately earned its keep, Reg Ansett flying it in the South Australia Centenary Air Race and winning the handicap section. The then substantial £500 ($1,000) prize was desperately needed by Ansett Airways, which was losing money at an alarming rate. (Ansett)

nearly five decades. If nothing else, the situation directly led to the formation of the first Ansett Airways in early 1936.

Into The Air

Despite his business being very much a land-bound one up to this point, Reg Ansett maintained his passion for flying and in 1934 purchased de Havilland DH.60M Moth VH-UNF which he used as a business aircraft, flying to the various parts of Victoria served by his road vehicles.

Preparations for the establishment of his airline began in late 1935, these including gaining the appropriate licences, organising the necessary finance – largely through the wealthy graziers of the Hamilton district – and obtaining a suitable aircraft. This was found in the form of Fokker F.XI Universal VH-UTO owned by Harry Purvis and used mainly for joyflights over the New South Wales mid-north coast town of Coffs Harbour. Ansett and Colin MacDonald flew to Sydney to inspect the aircraft and although Purvis was away at the time it was decided to purchase it. The deal was done by telephone on Boxing Day 1935, Ansett paying £1,000 ($2,000) for the Fokker. A spare engine was an additional £250 ($500), money that Ansett didn't have, so a promissory note was issued.

Ansett Airways Pty Ltd was formally established in January 1936 and its first two key employees taken on – pilot Vern Cerche and engineer John Davies. A couple of other engineers sourced from Essendon were also hired. Everything was now just about in place for the new airline to start operations, a move considered by most outsiders to be a very brave one which was doomed to failure. Events over the next few years probably should have proved the doubters correct, but their opinion didn't take into account Reg Ansett's determination, his ability to make things happen, and his willingness to risk everything in order to save his airline.

The initial Hamilton-Essendon service operated five days a week with the Fokker used for joyflights on the weekend in an attempt to generate more income. Passengers paid 10 shillings ($1) for these flights or if they required a little more excitement, aerobatic flights in the Moth were offered for £1/10/- ($3). The Ansett Flying School was also established at Hamilton using the Moth. There was also some help from the Federal Government with the awarding of a contract to carry mail at the rate of eight shillings ($0.80) per pound of weight, this coming into effect on 25 May 1936.

Reg Ansett always had great ambitions for his airline with expansion of routes and the fleet part of the plan from the start. The operational fleet doubled in October 1936 with the delivery of Airspeed Envoy VH-UXM, this an aircraft with a bit of history behind it as it had previously been the personal aircraft of Lord Nuffield, founder of the famed Morris Motors company in England. The Envoy was considered a luxurious 'business aircraft' for its day, even featuring a 'water closet' in the rear of the cabin!

In early December 1936 Ansett Airways purchased a Porterfield 35/70 Flyabout VH-UVH, a two seat high winged cabin monoplane which was put to work on joyriding flights and for use by the flying school. The Porterfield was soon to earn its keep by generating some much needed cash and publicity for Reg Ansett.

Air Race Victory

Despite Ansett Airways indulging in a variety of activities it was losing money at a substantial rate, the extent of which would be revealed the following year. A chance to help replenish the coffers arose in March 1936 with the announcement of an air race between Brisbane's Archerfield airfield and Adelaide's Parafield as part of South Australia's centenary celebrations. The Centenary Air Race would be held the following December and total prizemoney of £1,000 ($2,000) was on offer, half of which was allocated to the winner of the handicap section.

The race was conducted in over three days, starting on December 16 and travelling Archerfield-Coffs Harbour-Mascot; Mascot-Cootamundra-Essendon; and finally Essendon-Nhill-Parafield, arriving on the 18th. Reg Ansett entered the newly delivered Porterfield in the handicap section and went on to win it ahead of a British Klemm Eagle and a Klemm L.27a.

The win was not without its dramas for Ansett. Immediately before the last stage from Nhill to Parafield he was informed by the organisers that his handicap allowance had been incorrectly calculated and would be changed, dropping the Porterfield from first to second place. Upon his arrival at Parafield Ansett lodged a protest which was supported by most of his fellow competitors and five days later he was confirmed as the winner and recipient of the £500 ($1,000) prizemoney.

Onwards and Upwards

By the beginning of 1937 Reg Ansett realised that in order for his airline to expand further and establish the desired route network, a substantial infusion of cash was needed. The only way this was going to be achieved was by reconstituting the airline as a public company and issuing large numbers of new shares.

This fundamental change to the company's existence occurred on 14 April 1937 when privately owned Ansett Airways Pty Ltd was converted to the listed Ansett

Airways Ltd with a nominal capital of £250,000 ($500,000) comprising £1 shares. The new entity's initial issued capital was a modest £8,303 (16,606), this subsequently increasing by a further £135,000 ($270,000).

The float was not easy to sell as potential shareholders needed considerable convincing that the airline industry was a sound one in which to invest their money, given its generally shaky history. The usual underwriters and financiers refused to have anything to do with the float of a small and relatively insignificant airline led by a man whose ideas and plans were thought to be rather greater than his ability to deliver. As a result, Reg Ansett had to do most of the selling himself to a less than enthusiastic market. The fact that he succeeded illustrates the tenacity and determination of the man, and not for the last time.

At the time of the listing Ansett Airlines also moved its headquarters from Hamilton to Melbourne's Essendon Airport, a sensible move in view of the expansion plans that were in place including the purchase of new aircraft.

There were some major obstacles to overcome first, not the least of which was the announcement shortly after the float that the airline had lost £30,000 ($60,000) over the previous 12 months, a period in which it carried 12,624 passengers on its single route and on joyflights. The financial result had the predictable effect on Ansett's share price – it halved overnight.

Undaunted, Ansett pressed on with his plans and took the highly risky – but necessary – step of ordering the Lockheed L.10B Electra all metal, retractable undercarriage, fast, ten passenger and thoroughly modern airliner. At a price of £18,000 ($36,000) each plus taxes, spares and associated infrastructure they were extremely expensive. Three L.10s were delivered to Ansett later in 1937 but only after Reg Ansett had to perform another set of financial acrobatics in order to raise the money to pay for them.

The fact that Ansett was able to purchase the Electras at all was largely as a result of a November 1935 Federal Government decision to lift import restrictions on US built civil aircraft, these restrictions intended to help protect the British industry as Australia's ties to the 'Mother Country' were still very strong at the time. Even so, hefty import duties were still payable on aircraft imported from the USA if they were purchased instead of a comparable British type.

The first two Electras (VH-UZN *Ansirius* and VH-UZO *Ansertes*) arrived at Port Melbourne aboard the SS *Mirrabooka* in August 1937, followed by VH-UZP *Ansalanta* in early October. They were held in bond at the docks for a short time while the money to pay for them was found, Reg Ansett having started this process earlier and initially with little success. The money market was not interested, especially after the airline's financial results for the previous year

had been announced; the banks refused to issue funds in advance of shareholders taking up more of the company's uncalled capital; and the shareholders themselves were unwilling to invest further.

One of the battles Ansett had to fight was over the £14,000 import duty imposed on the Lockheeds. He eventually convinced the powers-that-be there was no comparable British aircraft – which there wasn't – and the crippling duty was dropped.

New investors were equally difficult to convince. Reg Ansett even placed advertisements in newspapers in an attempt to sell some of his own shares to pay for the Lockheeds and eventually he prevailed, but only after being forced to hand over a large chunk of his own interest in Ansett Airways along with other personal assets.

Ansett took possession of the first of the three Electras in late August 1937 and following assembly at Essendon, launched its Melbourne-Mildura-Broken Hill service on 5 September, followed by Sydney-Narrandera-Mildura-Adelaide, Melbourne-Narrandera-Sydney, Sydney-Mildura-Adelaide; Melbourne-Sydney direct and Melbourne-Adelaide over the next the next few months. These were operated by the Lockheeds, the Envoy was used on the Essendon-Hamilton service and the Fokker was retained for backup and joyflights.

Later – in February 1938 – Ansett launched evening joyflights over Melbourne using Electra VH-UZP. The flights operated on Tuesday and Thursday nights, passengers paying £1 ($2) for 15 minutes. Four such flights were normally conducted each evening but in what could well have been a first – certainly in Australia – some Melbourne residents began complaining about the noise and how it prevented them from sleeping.

Ansett Airlines thus became a more significant player with modern aircraft and a true route network in three states. With the expansion came competition with other airlines on some routes, especially the industry giant

A general view of Ansett Electra VH-UZP Ansalanta, *this the third of the trio and delivered in October 1937. Note the open luggage locker door behind the engine nacelle.*

The cockpit of a Lockheed L.10 Electra, by the standards of the day the very latest in civil aircraft technology. (Lockheed)

been established by pioneer aviators and national heroes Charles Kingsford Smith and Charles Ulm in October 1928 but it was January 1930 before operations began using a fleet of four Avro Tens (licence built Fokker F.VII/3m) initially linking Sydney with Brisbane and Melbourne. Hobart was subsequently added but the airline was short-lived, suffering an enormous setback with the loss its aircraft *Southern Cloud* in March 1931 on a flight between Sydney and Melbourne (the wreckage was not found until 27 years later) and financial problems. ANA folded in June 1931.

The second Australian National Airways was a rather more substantial affair. Formed in Melbourne in May 1936, just three months after Ansett Airways had begun operations, the new ANA resulted from a merger between Holymans Airways and Adelaide Airways. Holymans had been formed by Ivan and Victor Holyman, members of the Holyman shipping family in Launceston. Victor was killed in a flying accident in 1934 while Ivan went on to become one of the dominant forces on the Australian aviation scene, remaining ANA's chairman until his death in early 1957.

Holymans Airways had been founded in July 1934 as an outgrowth of Tasmanian Aerial Services, while Adelaide

Australian National Airways. The Lockheeds quickly established a reputation for reliability and punctuality but even those attributes were insufficient to stem the airline's losses to a major degree. By mid 1938 Ansett's share price had dropped further to only eight shillings ($0.80) each and the graziers who still constituted the majority shareholding were nervous.

It appeared the airline was ripe for a takeover attempt, and so it proved to be with ANA making the move.

ANA versus Ansett

There had been two Australian National Airways in the country's brief commercial aviation history. The first had

Ansett on the Road

Considering how Reg Ansett started in business – by establishing Ansett Roadways in 1931 – it's not surprising that the company had a long association with road transport over many years, eventually operating large fleets of passenger coaches and trucks. These businesses contributed a very substantial amount to Ansett Transport Industries' bottom line.

The expansion of Ansett's road transport interests began in 1944 when the company purchased Pioneer Tourist Coaches Pty Ltd, a business founded by A A Withers in 1905. Also in 1944, Ansett bought Provincial Motors (formerly the Provincial Roadways passenger service) which operated a service station and Ford car agency in Bendigo, Victoria.

Further expansion followed in the postwar years with Ansett Transport Industries acquiring Liberty Motors (Australia) with franchises to sell Kaiser-Frazer, Jowett, Allard and Stacatruck products. Several regional road services were purchased at around the same time – White Cars based in Cairns, Healesville Road Services near Melbourne, Eastern Roadlines (Bairnsdale and Albury) and Tasmania's Webster Romtech Astor Motors. Liberty Motors was sold in 1954.

There was further expansion in 1955-56 when Pioneer launched daily express services between Melbourne and Sydney and also added Pioneer Express to its tour operation which by now was operating some 250 coaches. The company was renamed Ansett Roadlines of Australia in 1958. Road freight operations were also boosted in 1955 when Road Express (NSW) was purchased and renamed Ansett Road Express, this in turn retitled as Ansett Freight Express in 1960.

Expansion continued into the 1970s by the purchase of well known furniture removals business Ridgeways in December 1972, the original company having been formed by Ernest Wridgeway in Melbourne in 1882. Others were subsequently added to the list including Albury Border Transport in 1975.

By the mid 1970s, ATI's road transport interests were dominant players on the Australian market. Of the group's total income of $327.8m in the 1974-75 financial year, $15.1m came from road passenger operations and $31.6m from road freight. The road passenger fleet comprised 210 vehicles and more than 450,000 passengers were carried over 15.3 million kilometres. The road freight business was even larger with 1,011 vehicles in the fleet by 1975 including 263 prime movers and 180 furniture removal trucks.

Ansett Pioneer was sold to Trailways in 1986 and after 63 years, the Ansett road transport era ended in 1994 when Ansett Freight Express and Ansett Wridgeways were both disposed of.

The decision in 1937 to purchase three expensive but efficient Lockheed L.10B Electras was a highly risky but very necessary one. Ansett Airways was by then a listed company but Reg Ansett had to sell more shares in his own airline in order to raise the cash to pay for the Lockheeds. VH-UZN Ansirius *was the second of the Electras to enter Ansett service, in September 1937. (Ansett)*

Airways dated back to 1935. Others were subsequently taken into the ANA fold, including Airlines of Australia in 1938 which in turn had absorbed several other pioneer operators including New England Airways, Rockhampton Aerial Services and North Queensland Airways. Airlines of Australia was purchased through ANA subsidiary Bungana Investments, a company which also subsequently gained a controlling interest in New South Wales intrastate operator Butler Air Transport and by association, its subsidiary Queensland Airlines.

ANA's financial backing came from Huddart Parker, Union Steam Ships, the Adelaide Steamship Co, the Orient Line and Holymans, all of these shipping interests. The result was a substantial organisation from the word go and one which remained the dominant force in the Australian airline industry until the early 1950s.

ANA launched its first services in November 1936 with a fleet of 23 aircraft including two examples of the new generation of airliner, the Douglas DC-2. The first DC-3s arrived in 1937 and as a result the airline was largely responsible for the development of a modern air transport system in Australia. Initial services used Holymans and Adelaide Airways timetables. From there, ANA grew with a policy of taking over the competition wherever possible in order to strengthen its own position.

Ansett Airways became the target in November 1938 when Ivan Holyman approached Ansett's directors on the subject of a takeover. This was the time when Ansett shares were at a low ebb – only eight shillings ($0.80) each or 40% of their issue price – and the company was vulnerable. Holyman offered just under nine shillings ($0.90) per share, an amount that was very attractive to the major shareholders. Ansett Airways was still losing

money and there appeared little hope for the share value to improve, at least in the foreseeable future.

The offer provoked yet another major battle for Reg Ansett and once more he had to put everything on the line to save his airline. Ansett Airways' chairman Ernest O'Sullivan was a banker whose sole concern was profits and dividends for the shareholders. He and most of his fellow directors had little or no interest in aviation per se and were keen to accept ANA's offer because in the cold hard light of day, the airline was not exactly a financial success.

Reg Ansett saw it differently and tried to convince the directors and other shareholders to look ahead, consider the potential of commercial air transport in Australia and of Ansett Airways in particular. He called an extraordinary general meeting of shareholders to put his case. Delivered with much passion, his words convinced the important ordinary shareholders that they should hang on and all but one of the directors eventually agreed with him and also decided to stick it out. The other director would not be moved, so once more Reg Ansett had to go into substantial debt to buy him out. Ernest O'Sullivan resigned there and then.

Disaster at Essendon

It now seemed that Ansett Airways might have a chance to settle down and get on with the business of doing business, but there was still one more disaster to overcome. On the morning of 28 February 1939, a fire broke out in the Ansett Airways hangar at Essendon, apparently in the rear fuselage area of Electra VH-UZN *Ansirius*. It quickly spread through the rear part of the hangar, and although the office area was saved, six aircraft were not including the Electra, the Fokker

Ansett at War

On 1 September 1939 Germany began its invasion of Poland, prompting Britain to declare war two days later.

As expected, Australia immediately followed and ANA quickly found four of its new Douglas DC-3s impressed into military service. Other airlines also had to give up some aircraft but for the moment Ansett carried on as before and continued to lose money despite the subsidies. There was some expansion of the airline's maintenance and engineering facility at Essendon in 1940-41, this bringing in valuable military work from the Royal Australian Air Force and others. Although still unprofitable, Ansett Airways paid its shareholders a dividend for the first time in 1941.

The situation for both Australia and Ansett changed completely after Japan's attack on the US Naval base at Pearl Harbour on 7 December 1941. The USA was now involved in the war and would shortly start building up a very substantial presence in Australia, the country used as a major base for American aircraft, ships, troops, logistics centres and command headquarters. This presence was responsible for completely turning Ansett around.

Disaster at Ansett's Essendon headquarters in February 1939 when a fire in the hangar destroyed one of the Electras and the Fokker Universal along with three other aircraft and spare parts. The Porterfield was also badly damaged. This was the last in the long line of financial and other setbacks which had inflicted Ansett Airways since its formation three years earlier – things would shortly start to look up. (Ansett)

Universal, the Moth and the Porterfield (which was later rebuilt) plus privately owned Avro Avian VH-UGA and Percival Vega Gull VH-ABS owned by Shell. The damage bill was estimated at around £40,000 ($80,000).

Services were temporarily disrupted and despite now having a fleet comprising just two Electras and the Envoy, some semblance of normalcy was restored and most services were still able to be flown.

By early 1939 Ansett's major routes were Melbourne-Mildura-Renmark-Adelaide, Sydney-Mildura-Broken Hill-Adelaide, Melbourne-Narrandera-Sydney and Melbourne-Hamilton, several of these in direct competition with ANA. The airline's financial position continued to worsen with heavy losses still being recorded. From a purely business point view, the attitude taken by the previous chairman and the directors was undoubtedly correct – Ansett Airways was very much a financial basket case.

ANA again approached Ansett on the subject of a takeover shortly after the fire but talks were discontinued in April only to be revived again two months later when an offer of £56,000 ($112,000) was made for the whole airline. No resolution was achieved but it appeared it was going to be only a matter of time before Ansett Airlines either went out of business or was absorbed into ANA.

Then, two things happened which turned the company's fortunes around – the threat of war and war itself.

The worsening situation in Europe and the seeming inevitability of Britain (and therefore Australia) being involved in the fight against Nazi Germany led the Australian Government to think ahead to the time when the nation's commercial transport aircraft might be needed to assist in the war effort. The government reasoned that the airlines needed to be strong to deal with this eventually, which is precisely what happened. Subsidies were put in place with ANA the main beneficiary, while Ansett got some much needed financial relief from July 1939 via subsidies to the tune of £33,000 ($66,000) per annum.

Due to the ever increasing amount of war related work, Ansett ceased operating its scheduled airline routes (except Hamilton-Melbourne) in June 1942, ANA taking over the only one which had been consistently profitable, Melbourne-Adelaide. The two surviving Electras (VH-UZO and UZP) were dedicated exclusively to transport flights on behalf of the US military for the next two-and-a-half years, logging sometimes extraordinary utilisation including up to 20 hours per day in some cases. Eleven hours a day, seven days a week was typical. At Essendon, Ansett's engineering and maintenance facility was greatly expanded.

Before that, both Electras had come close to the action. Following the first Japanese air attacks on Darwin on 19 February 1942, the Electras were flown to the Northern Territory capital to assist in the evacuation, the aircraft also taking part in the evacuation of wounded civil and military personnel from Broome, WA after it had also been bombed in March. In May 1942 Ansett added another string to its bow when it purchased the assets of Mascot based flying training organisation Airflite, this having in late 1940 won a government contract to service the training aircraft which operated from the airport.

From June 1942, both Electras were leased to the US military for transport and communications work within Australia, operated by the US Army Services of Supply (USASOS), initially flying from Melbourne to Cairns and Darwin. By late 1942 they were based at Sydney's Mascot Airport for use on a shuttle service between there and Townsville. The aircraft were given a temporary camouflage paint scheme in 1942 but still carried their normal civil registrations. Ansett's advertising at the time emphasised its contribution to the war effort and

World War II transformed Ansett from a struggling operation sustaining consistent heavy losses to a profitable and expanding organisation. A large part of the transformation was due to the company's overhaul, repair, engineering and manufacturing activities at Essendon. This photograph was taken at the end of the war and shows a happy Ansett workforce in front of an Avro Anson which has just been through the workshop. Note the B-25 Mitchell and two Dakotas in the background. (Ted Melton)

the need for sacrificing peacetime services for the common good – 'You've Given Your Seat To A Soldier', it said.

Control of the Ansett aircraft passed to the Directorate of Air Transport, Army Air Force, South-West Pacific Area in March 1943, the two Electras continuing to ply the Sydney-Townsville shuttle throughout 1943 and 1944.

VH-UZP was out of action for a short time following an accident in November 1944. After takeoff from Sydney with a high ranking US Army officer on board, the aircraft suffered engine problems, resulting in pilot Captain Jimmy Broadbent making a forced landing on Narrabeen Beach in Sydney's northern suburbs. None of the 10 people aboard the aircraft was injured, but the Electra was damaged during the subsequent salvage operation when the tailwheel was pulled out of the rear fuselage as attempts were made to drag the aircraft to safety ahead of the rising tide.

Another Lockheed was added to the Ansett fleet from January 1943 when L.14 Super Electra VH-ADT was leased from W R Carpenter Airlines for just over a year. The aircraft was flown by Carpenter crews but suffered from constant problems with its engines, these not fully solved until a shipment of spare parts arrived from the USA. An 'orphan' in the Ansett fleet, the Super Electra was transferred to ANA in 1944 and then purchased by Qantas later in the same year when it took over Carpenters.

The Directorate of Air Transport was disbanded in October 1944 and reorganised as the 5298th Troop Carrier Wing (Provisional), its assets at the time comprising two USAAF Troop Carrier Squadrons (the 22nd and 33rd),

seven RAAF transport squadrons (Nos 33-41), two air cargo control squadrons and the aircraft contributed by ANA (five Douglas C-49s and two DC-3s), Qantas (three Douglas C-53s), Guinea Airways (two Douglas C-50s) and Ansett Airways (two Lockheed L.10s).

Despite the intensive flying that was being carried out by Ansett's Electras, it was back at the company's Essendon base where the most lucrative activities were taking place. Under contract to the Australian Department of Aircraft Production, the expanded maintenance, repair and modification facility was kept busy looking after RAAF and USAAF aircraft.

The facility's activities were wide ranging – the routine maintenance of aircraft and engines, repairing battle or accident damage sustained in battle or through accidents and modification programs which included everything from installing dual control systems in some aircraft to fitting radar to B-24 Liberators.

Manufacturing work was also undertaken including that of airframe and operational equipment components and spare parts for engines. To cope with the workload, streamlined assembly and modification procedures were introduced to increase efficiency and profitability. The extra work saw Ansett's workforce increase tenfold to some 2,000 people by 1945 and commensurate with that was the introduction of a feature hitherto unknown by the previously perennially struggling company – profits!

For the first time Ansett Airways was 'cashed up' and was able to enter the postwar world of commercial aviation with new confidence.

CHAPTER FOUR

PLAYING THIRD FIDDLE

The postwar Australian airline industry witnessed considerable change very soon after the fighting had stopped, almost entirely due to the political climate of the time and the philosophies of the first peacetime government.

The wartime leader, John Curtin, was a Labor Party man but the circumstances of his time in office meant he had no opportunity to impose traditional Labor/socialist concepts on the nation. Indeed, Curtin was forced by those circumstances to subjugate several of his beliefs including those involving compulsory military service for young men.

Curtin became Prime Minister in 1941 (replacing the conservative Robert Menzies) and rose to the task he was confronted with during World War II. He is properly regarded as being a very good Prime Minister at a difficult time. Unfortunately, he died while in office just a month before Japan was finally defeated and therefore never saw his work completed.

Curtin was replaced by Ben Chifley, who had been Treasurer and Minister for Postwar Reconstruction during the conflict. Unhindered by the constraints imposed by war, Chifley's socialist ideals were able to be more fully expressed after 1945. Industry and business were prime targets with nationalisation high on the agenda in association with attempts to reduce the influence of the private enterprise capitalists.

The airlines did not escape his attentions, Chifley's government acquiring Qantas in June 1946 (it was owned half by private interests and half by BOAC before then) and looking at nationalising Australian National Airways which was owned by members of the 'big end of town', people who were anathema to his government's doctrines. For its part, ANA made no secret of the fact that it wanted to monopolise the industry by taking over whichever of the smaller operators it could and was also looking at expanding its operations to include international routes

As part of his duties as Minister for Postwar Reconstruction, Chifley had established in 1944 a committee with the task of investigating the Australian commercial aviation industry and what could be done with it after the war. Chifley wanted complete nationalisation but the committee's compromise recommendations were still quite extraordinary in their own way: that all airline operations should come under the control of a single, enormous public company with a diverse list of shareholders including the Commonwealth Government.

This concept was rejected by Chifley, who set about trying to implement a no-compromise situation where all of Australia's airlines would be absorbed into a single, government owned entity.

This ideologically driven concept was, of course, ridiculous and also legally doubtful. Advised of this fact, Chifley was forced to back down, but in November 1944 the government announced that a wholly state owned airline would be established to provide domestic air services after the war. This in conjunction with planned nationalisation of Qantas resulted in the government owning airlines for both international and domestic services. The concept was a real threat to the privately owned airlines, especially ANA.

The protests were loud and long with – not surprisingly – ANA leading the charge against the government's plans. But it was not alone as many in Australia's general business community could see that their own industries might also come under the control of Chifley's government if its plans were allowed to be developed unchecked.

On 16 August 1945 – two days after Japan laid down its arms – the Australian National Airlines Bill was passed by the Australian parliament, this setting up the legislative framework under which the new nationalised 'super airline' could be established. Several of the privately owned airlines immediately challenged the legality of the Bill in the High Court, ANA, Guinea Airways and MacRobertson Miller Aviation (under the collective title the Airline Operators Secretariat) arguing that the government's plan to have a monopoly on interstate air services was contrary to Section 92 of the Constitution, which states: 'On the imposition of uniform duties of customs, trade, commerce, and intercourse among the states, whether by means of internal carriage or ocean navigation, shall be absolutely free....'

The High Court judges agreed with the airlines, ruling that the Bill's monopoly provisions were invalid, although they also ruled that the Commonwealth did have the right to a monopoly on air services within Australia's territories. The government subsequently removed any references to monopolies as they applied to interstate operations in the Act but also added provision for only a government owned airline to operate to the Australian Capital Territory (which meant ANA and others could not fly to Canberra), the Northern Territory (which excluded Darwin) and Papua New Guinea.

Ansett's two surviving and very hard worked Lockheed L.10B Electras continued in service after the war until VH-UZP crashed in May 1946 and VH-UZO was sold in January 1951. (Terence Ellis)

TAA Formed

As a natural progression from the revised Australian National Airlines Bill, the Commonwealth Government established the Australian National Airlines Commission in 1946, this being the umbrella organisation for the 100% government owned Trans Australia Airlines. TAA operated its first service between Laverton (near Melbourne) and Sydney with a DC-3 on 9 September 1946, this significant event setting in motion the chain of events which eventually led to radical changes within the industry.

As will be discussed in greater detail in the 'David Versus Goliath' chapter, ANA was not as financially sound as its directors wanted everyone to believe and the establishment of TAA was the primary factor which ultimately led to its demise 11 years later. Far from realising its plans to dominate the postwar airline scene, ANA now found itself struggling against a well funded and well organised competitor which enjoyed all the advantages of being backed by the taxpayers of Australia.

In that sense Ben Chifley achieved his objective and put the knife into ANA further by directing that TAA should have exclusive access to government business (which included large numbers of public servants travelling around the country) and air mail on those routes which TAA contested.

★

2,500,000 MILES
WITHOUT MISHAP

★

ANSETT AIRWAYS IS THE SAFEST WAY TO TRAVEL

Ansett Airway Lockheed Electra Airliners have flown 2,500,000 miles without a single mishap . . . . . . a magnificent safety record.

Regular Services between

Sydney	Melbourne
Adelaide	Mildura
Broken Hill	Swan Hill
Wagga	Narrandera
	Hamilton

ANSETT AIRWAYS

25 MARTIN PLACE, SYDNEY. Phone **BW4607** (2 lines)
AFTER HOURS, Mr. DODSON, UL 1376.
Bookings at all Leading Travel Agencies

No. 7 of a series: Passengers disembarking from an Ansett Douglas airliner.

TAA enjoyed this sort of advantage for the crucial first three years of its existence, backed up by a high level of expertise within its ranks, especially in the areas of commercial management and engineering. It was also proving adept at making correct equipment choices and its standard of passenger service was generally regarded as superior to ANA's. For its part, ANA embarked on a lengthy political and public campaign designed to undermine TAA, but with little success.

Ben Chifley's government was short lived, removed from office in 1949 by an electorate which was disturbed by attempts to nationalise just about anything that moved – including, crucially, the banks – and his insistence that wartime petrol rationing should remain in place. Both of these policies were hugely unpopular with the general public which was only prepared to tolerate Chifley's socialist ideals up to a point. When it came to their money and their ability to freely travel in that increasingly important symbol of postwar prosperity – the motor car – Australians were not so benevolent.

The new Prime Minister was the conservative former Victorian Attorney-General Robert Menzies, in the top job for the third time after two brief previous terms between April 1939 and August 1941, at which

time he was forced to resign by his own party. Two months later John Curtin won the general election and became Prime Minister. This time Menzies (later Sir Robert) would last somewhat longer, the Liberal Party leader remaining in power until 1966 before retiring.

The arrival of Menzies caused ANA to briefly believe that TAA would be dismantled as the Liberals' philosophy was in favour of private enterprise and against nationalisation. But Menzies knew a good thing when he saw it and TAA was certainly a good thing. It was starting to make money and gaining a reputation for excellence in most areas. The thought of TAA being closed down was probably based more on wishful thinking by ANA's directors than anything else but they were nevertheless disappointed when it didn't happen. They also knew they had a problem.

Instead of dismantling TAA and causing more disruption to the industry, Menzies' government decided to attempt to stabilise it by introducing a high degree of regulation based around two major interstate carriers – TAA and ANA. This began to come into effect from 1952 under the Airlines Agreement Act as a prelude to full implementation of the Two Airline Policy and was initially introduced largely to help an ailing ANA. As for Ansett Airways, it remained a minor factor in the overall scheme of things, at least for the moment.

On the international scene, the June 1946 takeover of Qantas by the Australian Government was done more in the normal commercial sense than by 'nationalisation' as such – although the result was the same – but the waters were muddied slightly by the formation of British Commonwealth Pacific Airlines in the same month.

BCPA grew out of a 1944 meeting in Montreal which discussed the possibility of establishing a postwar Australia-USA-Canada service intended mainly to break Pan

DC-3 VH-ABR was an ANA aircraft until October 1957 when it became part of the merged Ansett-ANA fleet. As such, it never flew operationally in this immediate postwar Ansett Airways livery but has been preserved in airworthy condition and repainted to represent a DC-3 of that period. (Terence Ellis)

Two views of Ansett Airways' first DC-3 (VH-AMK Anstratus), delivered in June 1946 and converted by the airline at Essendon from the former USAAF C-47A 42-93449. An ANA DC-3 is in the background.

American's monopoly on Pacific routes. The Australian, Canadian, New Zealand and British governments were involved in the discussions, although when the time came to establish the new airline, Canada pulled out. This left BCPA's ownership at Australia 50%, New Zealand 30% and Britain 20%.

The new carrier was at first a 'paper' airline only, with no aircraft of its own. ANA operated BCPA's Sydney-Auckland-Fiji-Canton Island-Honolulu-San Francisco-Vancouver service under contract using Douglas DC-4s. This arrangement continued until 1948 when BCPA obtained its own DC-4s and then pressurised DC-6s the following year. BCPA and its Australia-USA-Canada service was absorbed into Qantas in 1954. ANA partially fulfilled its own international aspirations by purchasing a 33% stake in Cathay Pacific and 49% of Air Ceylon.

Ansett Looks Ahead

It was against this background that Ansett Airways set about establishing itself in the postwar world of the Australian domestic aviation market. The end of the wartime contracts saw the company's employee numbers drop from 2,000 to 300 but there had been a good build up of cash reserves and the establishment of a solid reputation over the previous three years.

Ansett had already taken advantage of its relatively healthy financial position to establish interests in other areas outside aviation. Continuing the road transport theme which was the foundation of the company, Pioneer Tourist Coaches Ltd was purchased in 1944 along with Provincial Motors, a service station and Ford car dealership in Bendigo. The company's manufacturing division was renamed Ansair Pty Ltd in 1945 and began building coach bodies for the rapidly expanding Pioneer operation.

Ansett Hotels was established in 1946, this growing to became Australia's largest hotel operator through either building or purchasing some 40 facilities in five Australian states, the Northern Territory, Australian Capital Territory and Papua New Guinea. In combination with the airline, these hotels and the coaches provided Ansett with the opportunity to market a package of travel and accommodation options to the tourist industry. This concept was further expanded in 1947 when Ansett took over the perpetual leases on Hayman and Daydream Islands in the Whitsundays and developed them as tourist resorts.

All of this activity led to a reorganisation of the Ansett group of companies. On 31 May 1946 a new

The Australian airline industry changed forever on 9 September 1946 with the inaugural service (between Melbourne and Sydney) of the government owned Trans Australia Airlines. This photograph captures the scene at Sydney's Mascot Airport immediately after the arrival of the DC-3 used on that first flight.

umbrella entity was established – Ansett Transport Industries Ltd (ATI) – with a nominal share capital of £1,000,000 ($2m) of which £360,000 ($720,000) was initially issued. ATI's subsidiaries at the time of its formation were Ansett Airways Pty Ltd, Pioneer Tourist Coaches Pty Ltd, Pioneer Tourist Hotels Pty Ltd, Ansair Pty Ltd and Air Express Pty Ltd. Another operating division would be added in May 1952 – Ansett Flying Boat Services, established by the takeover of Barrier Reef Airways and Trans Oceanic Airways (TOA) a year later. AFBS's history is discussed in the following chapter.

Postwar Rebuilding

Ansett Airways had resumed flying some commercial services before the war had ended, restarting daily interstate flights on the Melbourne-Wagga Wagga-Canberra and Melbourne-Mount Gambier-Adelaide routes in February 1945 with its two Lockheed L.10B Electras when they had finished operating on behalf of the US military.

Winning approval to operate these routes took some doing, the Department of Civil Aviation initially refusing to do so. Ansett, it will be remembered, had ceased all commercial activities (except on the Melbourne-Hamilton route) in June 1942 with most of its services taken over by ANA. Not surprisingly, ANA was reluctant to hand the more profitable ones back and the issue wasn't resolved for several months.

With the coming of peace and the threat of a seemingly strong ANA and potentially even stronger government owned TAA to contend with, it was imperative that Ansett Airways get itself organised as quickly as possible. By the end of 1945 Ansett was an even smaller operator than it had been before the war with a fleet of just two hard worked Electras on strength. The Airspeed Envoy was now retired, having been damaged beyond repair in a forced landing during a Hamilton-Essendon flight in August.

New routes, new aircraft and greater capacity were

urgently needed, Reg Ansett joining just about every other airline in the world in deciding to purchase Douglas DC-3s for his postwar operations. Luckily for everyone there were thousands of surplus C-47 military versions becoming available as the needs of the war effort disappeared, and after some delays caused by a shortage of US dollars, Ansett ordered three C-47s from the United States Foreign Liquidation Commission in the Philippines in late 1945.

Other Australian airlines obtained C-47s from the same source at the time including ANA (12), Butler Air Transport (3), Qantas (3), Guinea Airways (2). The Department of Civil Aviation also purchased two for pilot examination flights. These C-47s were sold for an average $US20,000 each.

Ansett For Sale

The establishment of TAA had stymied most of Reg Ansett's plans for his airline in the postwar world because until the government owned entity was announced, the assumption had been that there would only be the large ANA and a growing Ansett to contest Australian domestic routes. The plan was for Ansett to gradually duplicate ANA's route network and become one of the 'big two', but TAA's formation saw an end to that.

In fact TAA posed a direct threat to Ansett's very existence. After the Australian National Airlines Commission had been established and before TAA launched services, Reg Ansett had approached the Commission on the subject of it purchasing his airline for use as the basis for the forthcoming new operator.

Considering the numerous trials and tribulations Reg Ansett had to endure in his operation's formative years and the personal sacrifices he had made to ensure its survival, this action surprised many who knew him. Some say that for a brief period he was quite depressed about his airline's prospects and could see no other way. Others were a little more cynical, suggesting the money raised from the sale would be used to start another airline, but as the deal wasn't done, we will never know.

The price Ansett Airways put on itself for sale to the ANAC was £20,000 ($40,000) plus £102,476 ($204,952) for the book value of assets which included the three C-47s on order, the two Electras and various vehicles and other items of equipment associated with the airline. The profitable road transport operations were not included in the package.

After commissioning an independent valuation of Ansett Airways (which concluded it was worth substantially less than had been claimed), the ANAC made a counter offer based on those figures. The offer was rejected and the airline continued on its way.

Getting On With It

Faced with a large amount of uncertainty over its future and the effects the launch of TAA would have on the industry generally, Ansett Airways set about shoring up its position as much as possible.

After conversion to civil DC-3C standards at Ansett's Essendon facility, the first C-47 (VH-AMK *Anstratus*) entered service in June 1946 followed by VH-AML in November and VH-AMJ in June 1947. Three more C-47/DC-3s were added to the fleet between then and 1950 while VH-TAG was leased from TAA between June and August 1950.

VH-TAG was leased to cover the temporary loss of VH-BZK (the former VH-AMK) while it was being repaired following an accident at Sydney's Mascot Airport. The incident involved a collision with a train at the airport while the DC-3 was preparing to leave for Coffs Harbour and Brisbane, damaging its starboard wing, nose and undercarriage and tearing the starboard engine away. The Department of Civil Aviation paid Ansett £27,000 ($54,000) compensation to cover the damage and losses.

As for the two Electras, VH-UZP crashed on approach to Adelaide's Parafield Airport in May 1946 and was written off while VH-UZO was sold to South Coast Airways in January 1951. This ended a nearly 14 years association with the Lockheed L.10 by Ansett, an aircraft had which proved to be both durable and cost effective. Reg Ansett's decision to risk everything by purchasing Electras in 1937 had proved to be a sound one.

Ansett Airways grew slowly, restricted by its small size and the might of its competitors. Melbourne-Sydney flights were resumed in July 1946 at the rate of six per week using the newly delivered DC-3. Flights to Adelaide and Brisbane were added as more capacity became available. Each of these services from Melbourne included an intermediate stop on the way while ANA and TAA flew direct.

The introduction of the DC-3 into Ansett service

Two views of the demise of Electra VH-UZP on the night of 17 May 1946. The aircraft flew into the ground during an attempted instrument approach to Adelaide's Parafield aerodrome in darkness and heavy rain. Amazingly, all 12 people on board escaped with only one passenger slightly hurt.

brought with it another innovation for the airline – its first air hostesses. Miss Eve Saxton was the trailblazer for Ansett, joining the airline in May 1946 with Margaret Reid, Olive Sims and Ivy Allan quickly following. This quartet formed the entire Ansett Hostess Department at the time and their training was minimal – a tour of Essendon Airport, a quick lecture on the DC-3, and that was it!

Setting Lower Fares

The Commonwealth Government inadvertently provided Ansett with the opportunity to offer something different to its larger competitors in 1947 when the Department of Civil Aviation (DCA) introduced aeronautical charges to airlines using government owned aerodromes and navigation aids. All three lodged protests against this citing an unacceptable increase in costs. The only option for the airlines – or so it seemed – was to increase fares by as much as 20%. Both ANA and TAA agreed to this, but Ansett – thinking outside the square – went a different direction.

There was no such thing as economy class as such in those days, aircraft such as the DC-3 normally carrying 21 passengers in a spacious three abreast arrangement. Ansett decided that increasing the capacity of his DC-3s to 28 passengers four abreast was the way to go, this improving seat-mile operating costs, providing greater revenue opportunities and removing the need for fare

Business partners. Ansett's passenger coach, airline (and hotel) activities complimented each other well, each creating business for the others. Ansett took over Pioneer Tourist Coaches in 1944 and established its Hotels division two years later. The DC-3 in the photograph is VH-AMJ Anselina, *one of the original trio purchased from the USAAF. (Anthony McGee)*

increases. Ansett in fact wanted to go further than that and proposed fare *reductions* on some routes. These were substantial – up to 20% – the economic reasoning being that they were more than made up for by the 33% increase in potential passenger capacity resulting from the cabin reconfiguration.

It was radical thinking at the time, designed to stimulate demand and in effect a precursor to today's no frills airlines because the fare reductions were combined with a lower standard of cabin service. As so many of Ansett Airways' passengers were tourists heading off for a holiday somewhere (hopefully at one of Ansett's expanding number of hotels or on a Pioneer coach tour), this was not as important as it was to the business travellers who used TAA and ANA.

The government attempted to force Ansett to raise its fares along with everyone else but Reg Ansett argued that neither it nor the DCA had any jurisdiction over the control of fares on interstate operations. The Commonwealth Attorney-General offered advice to the government that this was probably correct and no further action was taken.

Ansett introduced the first of its lower fares in March 1948 on the Sydney-Coffs Harbour-Brisbane route at a rate 20% lower than before. TAA matched the lower fare on its Melbourne-Brisbane direct service while ANA didn't budge. Three months later, Ansett cut the fare on its tourist flights to Tasmania.

A feature of Ansett's early postwar operations was an effort to increase revenues by placing a greater emphasis on air freight operations. Average passenger load factors on its DC-3s was a modest 54% (or 15 passengers per flight) in 1948 so there was ample opportunity for improvement. An agreement with large road freight company Colliers Interstate Transport was therefore struck, this seeing Ansett's average weekly freight uplift increase from around 16 tonnes in 1948 to 57 tonnes a year later.

The arrangement made much better use of the aircraft and increased their revenue earning utilisation substantially. The DC-3s were used for passenger transportation during the day, had their interiors stripped for freight operations at night and were reconfigured for passengers early each morning.

By 1952 Ansett Airways had about 5% of the nation's domestic passenger traffic and was slowly growing, but the introduction of the Airlines Agreement Act the following year ensured – for the moment – that it would not be able to grow sufficiently to offer a genuine challenge to ANA and TAA as a substantial third domestic trunk route airline. There were still opportunities for modest network growth, however, new services introduced including a daily one from Brisbane to Cairns (via points in between) using DC-3s and introduced in 1954.

This precursor of the definitive Two Airline Policy of 1958 has been described as 'a kind of 2¼ Airline Policy, with the quarter causing more trouble as time passed', especially to ANA which in many ways seemed to have lost the plot. On the other hand, TAA was getting stronger, boosted by some astute equipment choices such as the

Australian National Airways (ANA) was the 'giant' of the Australian airline industry and was expected by its owners to dominate the scene after World War II. But the socialist Chifley government had other ideas. Pictured here are two of the airline's DC-3s at Melbourne's Essendon Airport.

pressurised Convair CV-240 from 1948 and the Vickers Viscount turboprop from late 1954.

Looking Overseas

Reg Ansett was never known to stand still for long during his career, always looking for new opportunities and chances to expand his airline and other business interests.

Possible opportunities in the New Zealand market came to his attention in 1950, one of them involving international services from Australia and the other New Zealand domestic operations. Both attempts failed this time, but the lure of competing in the New Zealand market remained strong and would be readdressed a decade later.

The first attempt was in January 1950 when Ansett Airways applied for approval to operate a service between Melbourne and Christchurch using Douglas DC-4s. The idea was to initially fly from Sydney and then transfer to Melbourne after it gained status as an international port of departure. Ansett's proposal was rejected by the Australian and New Zealand governments and the route awarded to Tasman Empire Airways Ltd (TEAL) instead, this international operator was established in 1940 and at that time owned jointly by the governments of Australia, New Zealand and Britain. In 1965 it was renamed Air New Zealand.

In August 1950, the New Zealand Government was tout-

ANA DC-3 freighter VH-ANU Lemana *was purchased by the airline in December 1945. ANA operated more than 40 DC-3s over the years, starting in late 1937. Of these, nearly half ended up with Ansett-ANA after the merger but VH-ANU was not one of them as it was sold to New Zealand's Mount Cook Airlines in June 1955.*

Ansett Airways began its postwar fleet upgrade with an initial three ex USAAF C-47s upgraded to civil DC-3 standards, the first one entering service in June 1946. VH-BZA Ancirrus *photographed here was Ansett's fourth DC-3, delivered in July 1948. (John Gates)*

Hotels and Resorts

Ansett Transport Industry's hotels and resorts business represented a substantial part of the company's operations over the years, growing through acquisitions and building to become Australia's largest hotel operator.

ATI established the Ansett Hotels division in 1946 and launched its chain of tourist hotels the following year with the acquisition of Hobart's Imperial Hotel. The Lufra Hotel at Eaglehawk Neck in Tasmania was opened in the same year as the first new hotel built in Australia after World War II.

From, there the chain grew to encompass more than 40 establishments in Australia, New Zealand and Papua New Guinea. Three Gateway Inns were built between 1971 and 1977 in Perth, Brisbane and Adelaide, these high rise complexes including the inns, Ansett offices and airport bus terminals.

Disposal of some of the Hotels began as early as the late 1950s but others were established after that. Ansett finally left the hotel and resort business in May 1998 with the sale of the Hayman Island resort and its half share of Hamilton Island Airport to the BT Group.

The hotels operated by Ansett over the years include:

New South Wales: Australia Hotel (Ballina); Bayview Hotel (Bateman's Bay); Black Dolphin Motel (Merimbula); Coffs Harbour Hotel (Coffs Harbour); Eden Hotel (Eden); Fitzroy Hotel (Coffs Harbour); Fotheringham's Hotel (Taree); Marlborough Hotel (Cooma); Marlin Hotel (Ulladulla); Queanbeyan Hotel (Queanbeyan); Railway Hotel (Tamworth); Ryan's Hotel (Albury); Telegraph Hotel (Tenterfield); Victoria Hotel (Nambucca Heads).

Victoria: Bull & Mount Hotel (Stawell); Commercial Hotel (Camperdown); Gordon Hotel (Portland); Kalimna Hotel (Lakes Entrance); Mac's Hotel (Portland); Manyung Hotel (Mount Eliza); Murray Hotel (Mildura).

Queensland: Cecil Hotel (Brisbane); Gateway Inn (Brisbane); Hides Hotel (Cairns); Queens Hotel (Townsville); Royal Hayman Hotel (Hayman Island); Pacific International Hotel (Cairns, joint venture with the Kamsler family); Strand Hotel (Cairns).

Australian Capital Territory: Wellington Hotel (Canberra).

South Australia: Blue Lake Motel (Mount Gambier); Crown Hotel (Kingston); Gateway Inn (Adelaide); Jens Hotel (Mount Gambier).

Tasmania: Club Hotel (Burnie); Imperial Hotel (Hobart); Lufra Hotel (Eaglehawk Neck); Metropole Hotel (Launceston).

Western Australia: Gateway Inn (Perth).

Northern Territory: Ayer's Rock Chalet; Glen Helen Hotel; Mount Gillen Hotel-Motel (Alice Springs); Palm Valley Lodge; Serpentine Lodge.

Papua New Guinea: Gateway Hotel (Port Moresby); Huon Gulf Hotel (Lae).

In 1947 ATI decided to develop resorts in the Whitsunday Islands off the coast of Queensland and took over the perpetual lease of Hayman Island (where the building of a luxury resort was planned) and Daydream Island. To administer these businesses a new subsidiary – Barrier Reef Islands Ltd – was established.

The Royal Hayman Hotel on the island opened in 1950 and from 1964 was serviced by a scheduled helicopter service using a 26 passenger Sikorsky S-61N. The helicopter service also linked Proserpine, Mackay, Happy Bay, South Molle Island and Daydream Island. The Hayman resort had to be largely rebuilt in 1970 after it sustained damage from cyclone 'Ada' and went on to become widely recognised as Australia's premier resort.

TAA caused a minor revolution in the Australian domestic airline market in 1948 when it introduced the pressurised Convair CV-240 to service. It was a big hit with passengers and took business away from ANA. Six years later, TAA would introduce the turboprop Vickers Viscount with even greater effect. (Convair)

ing the sale of New Zealand National Airways Corporation (NZNAC) and received a proposal from Ansett covering the acquisition of NZNAC's primary trunk routes, these to be operated in conjunction with a road transport system similar to that established by Ansett Transport Industries in Australia. Ansett Industries (NZ) Ltd was registered with a capital of £10,000 ($20,000) to administer any operations established in the country.

Tenders for the sale of all or part of NZNAC were invited in November 1950, the New Zealand Government looking for potential purchasers only from its own country, Australia or Britain. Bids were duly received – including from Ansett – but after more than 18 months of negotiation and discussion with the interested parties, the New Zealand Government announced in July 1952 that none of the offers received

Ansett's CV-440 fleet was delivered in the second half of 1957 at the time negotiations for the takeover of ANA were underway and being completed. VH-BZH arrived in mid September 1957, just over two weeks before the ANA purchase was completed. This shot was taken at Essendon in October 1957, the month ANA was absorbed. Note the Scottish Aviation Twin Pioneer parked behind.

Ansett followed its CV-240s with six examples of the upgraded CV-440 Metropolitan. VH-BZF was the first of them, delivered in June 1957.

were considered reasonable and that NZNAC would be retained.

Over The Weather

By 1954, Ansett Airways had reached a point where some important decisions had to be made. With only a handful of DC-3s in its fleet it was still a small operator but had nevertheless carved out a niche market for itself and had proved to be a constant annoyance to ANA by taking passengers away from the larger carrier.

TAA had been going from strength to strength – also at a cost to ANA – and the former giant of the Australian airline scene was in rapid decline, partly due to the quality of its opposition and partly because of its own management's failings.

Ansett's DC-3s were no longer suitable for mainline services as they were relatively slow, had limited carrying capacity and were unpressurised. The travelling public was starting to become used to the greater comfort offered by a pressurised airliner's ability to fly 'over the weather' and would soon expect this feature to be a regular part of their journeys.

TAA introduced the 40 passenger Convair CV-240 pressurised twin piston engined airliner to Australian skies

Compared to TAA and ANA, Ansett Airways was a very minor player on the Australian domestic airline market in the 1950s but it upped the ante in August 1954 when the Convair CV-340 was introduced to service. Ansett's Convairs took some traffic away from ANA, just as TAA's had done six years earlier. VH-BZD was the first of three CV-340s used by the airline and was a former Braniff aircraft. The shot was taken at Sydney Airport in 1955. (Brian Reed via Eric Allen)

ANA introduced the four engined but unpressurised Douglas DC-4 to service in 1946 and eventually operated 12 of them. VH-ANA Amana was the first and was one of five new production and purely civil DC-4-1009s delivered to the airline in that year. The others were converted ex USAAF C-54 Skymasters.

in 1948 with great success as it was popular with passengers and reliable. Ansett had observed this and realised a similar move was necessary, especially since TAA would shortly be upping the ante even further with the introduction of the Vickers Viscount pressurised turboprop.

On 17 August 1954 Ansett Airways announced it had been granted approval to import a single 44-52 seat Convair CV-340 (an upgraded 240); three months later it was announced that a further four aircraft had been ordered. Ansett eventually took delivery of two CV-340s (plus one temporarily leased from Hawaiian Airlines) and six examples of the next version, the further improved CV-440 Metropolitan.

The first CV-340 (VH-BZD) was purchased second hand from Braniff and arrived in Australia on 17 August 1954 after being ferried from the USA. The aircraft cost ₤400,000 ($800,000) including spare parts and entered service on the Melbourne-Sydney-Brisbane route on 4 October 1954. A second CV-340 (VH-BZE) arrived in April 1955 allowing an extension of services on which the aircraft operated, the fleet supplemented between November 1956 and June 1957 by a third CV-340 (VH-BZG) leased from Hawaiian Airlines to cover the expected increase in traffic generated by the Melbourne Olympics. The Convairs were as successful for Ansett as they had been for TAA and moved the airline onto a 'higher plane' (so to speak) it terms of operational capability and passenger appeal.

The CV-340 had a relatively brief career with Ansett with the type out of service by April 1959 following its replacement by the CV-440. Six of these were ordered to become the airline's primary equipment on inter-capital city services. The first one (VH-BZF) arrived on 8 June 1957 and was followed by the remaining five before the end of the year.

The first CV-440 was delivered just two weeks before Reg Ansett made his first offer to take over the bankrupt ANA. The others were therefore taken into the fleet largely during that frantic period between then and early October when the ANA deal was being negotiated and finalised. As a result of the establishment of Ansett-ANA and the fleet of higher capacity former ANA DC-4s and DC-6s that came with it, the new CV-440s spent little time plying the intended trunk routes but more with the regional airline subsidiaries that the new force in the Australian airline industry would acquire or establish over the next few years.

The Convairs had one lasting effect on the domestic airline scene because in combination with Ansett's budget fares policy, they took a little more business away from both TAA and ANA. This forced the larger carriers to respond by offering cheaper fares and a lower standard of service on some routes using unpressurised Douglas DC-4s.

FLEET SUMMARY – May 1954

Ansett Airways: 1 Convair CV-340; 6 Douglas DC-3.
On order: 1 Convair CV-340.
Ansett Flying Boat Services: 1 Short Sandringham; 1 Short Hythe.

Another Ansett Airways collector's card, this one a bit scratchy but of interest because it shows a retouched 'colourised' view of the airline's first Convair CV-340, VH-BZD. (via Geoff Wilkes)

CHAPTER FIVE

BOATS WITH WINGS

The era of the big flying boats is one of the more romantic episodes in the history of civil aviation and is largely confined to the 1930s when the Shorts boats linked the far reaches of the British Empire and Pan Am's Clippers explored the Caribbean, the Far East and the North Atlantic. It was a Pan Am Boeing 314 Clipper that performed the world's first trans-Atlantic passenger service in June 1939. Passengers on these flights were transported in hitherto unheard of levels of luxury and comfort.

World War II rudely interrupted these services, but flying boats went on to give sterling service in the maritime patrol, anti submarine and minelaying roles during the conflict. The Short Sunderland and Consolidated Catalina were foremost in the military role, and both types also saw service in the early years of peace.

The war was largely responsible for the demise of the flying boat as a major commercial influence because between 1939 and 1945 literally thousands of new airfields were built all over the world to service the land based air forces. The result was that when commercial aviation resumed after 1945 there was plethora of airfields available to accommodate the industry and therefore a greatly reduced need for flying boat services.

Some pockets of flying boat activity remained in place after the war, but by 1950 they were few and far between. The Pacific was one region which continued to see flying boat services for a few years, but it was Australia which retained a scheduled commercial flying boat service until 1974, and as part of a major airline.

That airline was Ansett and Ansett Flying Boat Services (AFBS) was the subsidiary which kept the age of the big flying boat alive in Australia for many years after others had closed down.

PBY-5A Catalina VH-BRI The Golden Islander *operated the AFBS Proserpine-Hayman Island service for nearly three years from October 1959 before sinking at its moorings at the island after a heavy landing caused damage and allowed water into the hull. Just discernable forward of the blister is the legend 'Ansett-ANA'. (David Thollar)*

The Sandringham

The mainstay of the AFBS fleet was the Short Sandringham, a civil conversion of the famous wartime Sunderland and an airliner which found favour with several operators after hostilities had ended. The Sandringham could carry up to 45 passengers in a (relatively) high density day layout, although some were operated with accommodation for as few as 16 passengers in a long range 'night' configuration complete with sleeping berths for all of them. The AFBS aircraft had 41 seats including 16 on the upper deck.

The Sunderland's cavernous interior made it an obvious candidate for conversion to civil passenger and freight carrying duties. The first conversion program was conducted between 1942 and 1944 when 25 Bristol Pegasus powered Sunderland IIIs were modified for BOAC on the production line. Utilitarian bench seats were fitted, the guns and military equipment removed and the turrets replaced by fairings.

After VE Day, 18 of these Sunderlands were further modified for civil operations as the *Hythe* class with accommodation for 24 day or 16 night passengers plus a 2,948kg (6,500lb) mail load. They plied the Empire routes to India, Singapore, Australia and New Zealand and were joined by two new conversions postwar plus two for Uruguay's CAUSA.

A more comprehensive conversion for civil use resulted in the Sandringham, the sole Sandringham 1 prototype (converted from a Pegasus powered Sunderland III) first flying in November 1945. The conversion was extensive with reshaped nose and tailcone plus rectangular windows and a remodelled interior with two decks and spacious accommodation for 16-24 passengers, complete with dining room and cocktail bar. All other Sandringhams converted between 1945 and 1948 were powered by Pratt & Whitney Twin Wasp engines regardless of the Sunderland mark (either III or V) from which they were derived.

Designations were applied to versions developed for specific operators: Mk.2 (Argentina's Dodero with accommodation for 45 passengers); Mk.3 (also for Dodero); Mk.4 (New Zealand's Tasman Empire Airways Ltd – TEAL); Mk.5 – (BOAC 16-22 seaters); Mk.6 (Norway's DNL, radar equipped 37 seaters); and Mk.7 (BOAC *Bermuda* class as 30 seaters). The total number of Sandringham conversions performed was 27.

BOAC began replacing its boats with Constellations and Canadair Fours in 1949 and ended flying boat operations completely in November 1950. Its fleet of Sandringhams and Sunderlands was dispersed to operators such as Aquila Airways, CAUSA and Qantas.

The final conversion was carried out long after the others, in 1963 when Ansett Flying Boat Services modified a former RNZAF Sunderland GR.5 to near Sandringham standards at its flying boat base in Sydney.

BRA+TOA=AFBS

Ansett Flying Boat Services was formed out of the amalgamation of two other postwar Australian flying boat operators, Barrier Reef Airways (BRA) and Trans Oceanic Airways (TOA), both of them established by former Royal Australian Air Force flying boat pilots.

BRA launched operations in July 1947 between Brisbane and the Heron Island resort on Queensland's Great Barrier Reef. Its co-founders were Stewart Middlemiss, who had flown Catalinas during the war including as Commanding Officer of No 11 Squadron, and Chris Poulson, the owner of Heron Island.

BRA began operations with two ex RAAF Boeing built P2B2-2 Catalinas. Operations were soon expanded to include Daydream, Lindeman, South Molle and Hayman Islands (the latter owned by Ansett) plus Gladstone on the Queensland coast. BRA acquired five other Catalinas for use as a source of spares.

The Catalinas were replaced by a pair of ex TEAL Short Sandringhams in 1950-51, these becoming VH-BRC *Beachcomber* and VH-BRD *Princess of Cairns*. It was through these purchases that Ansett became involved with flying boats. Unable to raise the necessary finance from the banks, Stewart Middlemiss approached Reg Ansett who saw an opportunity and agreed to help out. In exchange for a 51% interest in the company, BRA gained two Sandringhams and Ansett gained a flying boat operation.

In May 1952 Ansett took over full control of Barrier Reef Airways and established Ansett Flying Boat Services, although BRA continued operating under its original name until March 1953. Stewart Middlemiss was appointed the new company's managing director.

Trans Oceanic Airways began operations in May 1947 and was formed by Bryan Monkton, another RAAF Catalina pilot during the war and one who had flown covert 'Black Cat' minelaying operations. Monkton purchased five ex RAAF Sunderlands from the Commonwealth Disposals Commission in October 1946, three of which were converted to Hythe standards and put into service. The first of them – VH-AKO *Australis* – was first flown in its new guise in March 1947.

Operating from the flying boat base at Rose Bay on Sydney Harbour, TOA conducted flights to various points in the Pacific including Fiji, the New Hebrides,

Sandringham VH-BRE *Pacific Chieftain was a former Qantas aircraft which entered service with AFBS in December 1954. It was written off at Lord Howe Island in July 1963 and is photographed here at Evans Bay, Wellington, during an October 1955 trip to New Zealand. (via Geoff Wilkes)*

Noumea and New Caledonia and the first service to Lord Howe Island in August 1947. Charter flights to other parts of the world were also flown including migrant flights from Europe. More locally, services to Grafton, Hobart, Townsville and other points were also undertaken. Famed pilot and navigator P G Taylor joined the firm as a director in late 1948 and four of the larger Short Solent flying boats were added to the fleet in 1951. The first Solent flew in 1944 and 22 were built for BOAC and TEAL.

TOA always had a difficult existence as it was continually arguing with the authorities over the issue of rights to fly to various overseas ports. As government owned Qantas was Australia's designated international carrier, it could prevent TOA from conducting these flights, even though it had no intention of servicing most of them itself. As a result, approval for flights was often only given the day before they were scheduled to depart and sometimes denied completely. As far as Bryan Monkton was concerned, Qantas was deliberately trying to put his airline out of business and the Australian Government was helping it.

A couple of well publicised accidents also damaged TOA. One of them – involving Solent VH-TOC in October 1951 – saw the aircraft collide with a dredge just after a night takeoff from the Brisbane River. Despite losing a substantial section of a wing in the collision, the pilots were able to perform a successful emergency landing without injury to anyone on board. The accident resulted from the flarepath which had been laid on the water drifting away from its proper location into the path of the dredge. Flying boat operations from the base at Hamilton Reach on the Brisbane River were shut down after the accident and moved to Redland Bay, 40 kilometres from Brisbane.

Continually short of cash, TOA struggled throughout its life, Bryan Monkton admitting to the author many years later that he was no businessman and that the thought of conducting normal business management practices – like going to the bank to borrow some money for urgently needed capital – 'never entered his head'. Personal problems within the business also caused problems and TOA was put into liquidation in July 1952 with all services except Sydney-Lord Howe Island suspended.

TOA finally ceased all operations in April 1953 and was absorbed into AFBS the following month at the suggestion of Stewart Middlemiss. The purchase included all of TOA's assets including its maintenance facilities at Rose Bay. This became AFBS's headquarters for the remainder of its existence.

The flying boat base at Rose Bay on Sydney Harbour – or Sydney Water Airport to use its proper name – saw commercial operations by Qantas, TEAL and Trans Oceanic Airways in the immediate postwar years, and then Ansett Flying Boat Services. By 1954 only AFBS remained and continued operations from there over two more decades. This shot shows the base as it was more than 40 years ago with a Sandringham (possibly Beachcomber) undergoing refuelling and maintenance.

Diminishing Network

With the takeovers completed, AFBS in mid 1953 found itself with a fleet of one operational Catalina, three Sandringhams and one Hythe. Its network included Grafton, Southport (Gold Coast), Brisbane, Hobart, Hayman Island, Townsville, Cairns and Lord Howe Island. The network gradually diminished as the land based airliners of TAA and Ansett began to predominate and by 1959 – when Airlines of NSW took over the management of AFBS – regular services were flown only to Hobart, Hayman and Lord Howe. Within another year Lord Howe was AFBS's sole destination and would remain so until 1974.

The Catalina remained in the fleet only until April 1953, a three week charter flight around the Pacific by VH-BRA under the command of Stewart Middlemiss its last journey. Flying from Rose Bay, the sojourn visited Noumea, Suva, Samoa, Itatake and Papeete before returning to Sydney. VH-BRA was scrapped shortly afterwards.

One other Catalina later flew with AFBS. VH-BRI *The Golden Islander* (a PBY-5A) was purchased from the USA and delivered in October 1959. It operated a Proserpine-Hayman Island service for nearly three years before sinking at Hayman after a heavy landing in July 1962. The landing had popped some rivets in the hull, allowing water in. The Catalina gradually filled up overnight and was found sunk at her moorings the following morning.

But it was the Sandringham which did the bulk of AFBS's work over two decades. VH-BRD *Princess of Cairns* only lasted until October 1952 when it sank at its moorings in the Brisbane River. VH-BRC *Beachcomber* was used to maintain services until a replacement was found, this arriving in the form of VH-BRE *Pacific Chieftain*, a former

Right at the end of her Australian career, Beachcomber *almost came a cropper in June 1974 when a gale blew her ashore at Lord Howe Island. Damage was minimal and the Sandringham was able to be flown back to Sydney after temporary repairs. (David Daw)*

VH-BRC *Beachcomber* in Ansett Airways colours on Sydney Harbour in the mid 1950s.

Qantas aircraft. The ex TOA Hythe VH-AKP *Tahiti Star* was also in service at the time before it was retired in March 1954.

Beachcomber and *Pacific Chieftain* operated together for the next decade on the Lord Howe service and also for charters around the Pacific. It was near the start of one of these – a flight to Polynesia – in July 1963 that *Pacific Chieftain* was lost during an overnight stay at Lord Howe after completing the first leg of its journey from Sydney. A cyclone hit the island during the night, causing the Sandringham to break free of its moorings and be damaged beyond repair.

Down to only one Sandringham, AFBS needed to find a replacement quickly if services were to be maintained.

Rescue came in the form of an ex Royal New Zealand Air Force Sunderland GR.5 which was purchased and extensively modified to near Sandringham specifications at Rose Bay. As VH-BRF *Islander*, this 'Sandringham' was identifiable by its more bulbous nose and entered service in early October 1963.

By then, AFBS and its Sandringhams had become an established part of the Sydney scene and a familiar – if somewhat old fashioned – sight over the city skyline as they flew into and out of Rose Bay. The airline itself was never the greatest money spinner within the Ansett group but performed a vital service in being the only air link with Lord Howe Island, which had no conventional airport. There had long been plans to

Beachcomber at Rose Bay in May 1964, sporting the 'old' Airlines of NSW boomerang and spears logo. (Geoff Wilkes)

VH-BRF Islander *was the last flying boat delivered to AFBS, in September 1964. Not a true Sandringham,* Islander *was converted from an RNZAF Sunderland to replace VH-BRE* Pacific Chieftain, *which was damaged beyond repair when a cyclone hit Lord Howe Island the previous year. VH-BRF is photographed at its moorings at Lord Howe in June 1973. (Eric Allen)*

build such a facility, but the prohibitive cost meant the decision had been deferred on several occasions.

AFBS carried 7,705 passengers in 1965 at an average load factor of 74%; flew 119,536 statute miles (192,369km) – the equivalent of 124 round trips from Sydney to Lord Howe – and flew 856 hours uplifting 136 tonnes of freight and 26.5 tonnes of mail. These figures varied little over the years.

Final Fling

It was left to *Islander* and *Beachcomber* to see out Ansett Flying Boat Service's final years. Finally, after eight years of procrastination, a decision was made in May 1968 to construct an airstrip on Lord Howe Island. It was to be 4,200 feet (1,280m) in length and suitable for use by a Fokker F27. More procrastination followed. In

October 1970 the runway's planned length was reduced to 4,000 feet (1,220m) in order to save some money, the estimated cost of $1.5 million to be shared between the Federal and NSW State Governments.

A further increase in estimated costs to $2.5 million caused another delay and another reduction in runway length – to 3,000 feet (915m) – and this was agreed to in May 1973. Construction finally got underway in March 1974 and the first aircraft to land on the still incomplete airfield was an RAAF Caribou conducting a medical emergency mission on 4 August 1974. The runway was officially opened a week later.

The original intention was to conduct the last flying boat service to Lord Howe on 31 May 1974 but delays in completing the new runway saw this extended to September. There was still some drama to come for the Sandringhams when on 9 June 1974 *Beachcomber* was blown ashore during a gale and *Islander* – which was being prepared for sale – had to fly to the island four days later to rescue 75 stranded passengers who were taken back to Sydney in two trips over two days.

Damage to *Beachcomber* was confined to a torn off float and a damaged wing and after temporary repairs on site it was flown back to Sydney on 20 August. *Islander* made its final journey to Lord Howe on 15 August

On the step. The Sandringhams were a magnificent sight as they departed. This dramatic shot captures VH-BRC Beachcomber *at the point of liftoff as it thunders down Sydney Harbour in November 1973. (Eric Allen)*

AFBS occasionally put on special flights for enthusiast groups and others, including several for the Aviation Historical Society of Australia. It was during one of these that VH-BRF Islander was photographed on Lake Eucumbene in November 1971. (Eric Allen)

VH-BRC Beachcomber on its beaching trolleys at Rose Bay in April 1974. Less than two months later the Sandringham was damaged in a gale at Lord Howe Island but was able to be repaired on site and flown back to Sydney. (Eric Allen)

The upper deck passenger cabin of Beachcomber, *taken in 1974 immediately before delivery to new owner Antilles Air Boats. (Geoff Wilkes)*

but *Beachcomber* had the honour of performing the very last flying boat service to the island on 10 September, returning to Sydney the next day.

Both Sandringhams were sold to Antilles Air Boats in the US Virgin Islands (West Indies). Owned by the flamboyant Captain Charles Blair and his wife, the movie actress Maureen O'Hara, Antilles Air Boats operated a fleet of amphibians and smaller flying boats in the area. Trans Oceanic Airways founder Bryan Monkton had worked for the company a few years earlier.

Now carrying the US registration N158J and the name *Excalibur VIII, Islander* was the first to depart for its new home on 25 September 1974 with Ansett's Captain Lloyd Maundrell and Charles Blair at the controls. Maureen O'Hara was also aboard. *Beachcomber* departed on 28 November as N158C *Southern Cross*, creating a significant piece of history in the process as the last four engined flying boat to leave not only Rose Bay but also Australia.

Beachcomber now resides in England's Southampton Hall of Aviation while *Islander* eventually found its way into Kermit Weeks' Fantasy of Flight collection at Miami, Florida in the USA.

(left) The end of an era. Captain Lloyd Maundrell and his crew with Beachcomber *in September 1974. Ansett Flying Boat Services ceased to exist in the same month. (right) A great view of Sydney and the Opera House from* Beachcomber *in September 1974 as it departs the city on the final flight to Lord Howe Island. As a completely irrelevant sidelight, the author was working at the Opera House at the time and has been able to identify his car in the car park below! (Geoff Wilkes)*

CHAPTER SIX

DAVID VERSUS GOLIATH

When Australian National Airways chairman and driving force Sir Ivan Holyman died in Hawaii on 18 January 1957, so did the airline behind which he had been the prime mover since its formation in 1936. ANA had been facing difficulties for several years and was on the verge of collapse before Sir Ivan's death, but his departure was both symbolically and practically the final nail in the coffin.

Several factors contributed to ANA's decline and fall, the most significant of which were the establishment of government owned Trans Australia Airlines, and the inadequacies of ANA's own management, including Ivan Holyman himself. Holyman had a romantic rather than hard nosed businessman attitude to ANA with the ruthless quest for profits not his first priority. He enjoyed the lifestyle associated with being the chairman of ANA and sometimes his heart ruled more than his head.

This kind of attitude would have been fine if ANA had little or no substantial competition – the situation the airline thought it would be in the postwar years – but the reality was that the Australian Government established TAA and ANA failed to properly deal with it, preferring instead to hope it would go away and assume it would when the conservative Liberal government came to power in 1949. Although the new government was much more sympathetic to the private sector generally than the socialist Chifley Labor administration had been – and subsequently introduced legislation to help ANA – it was never going to dismantle TAA, especially since it began returning a profit only three years after being established. One of ANA's main arguments in its anti TAA campaign was that the government owned airline was going to be a substantial drain on the public purse, but this quickly proved to be not the case.

ANA was also guilty of ignoring the gentle rise of Ansett Airways and failing to see that despite its modest stature, the 'upstart' operator created a niche for itself in the postwar years, introduced some innovation (like 'no frills' services and lower fares), and took some business away from ANA, especially after the introduction of its small fleet of pressurised Convair CV-340s in 1954.

Further, Reg Ansett *was* hard nosed when it came to business, was always looking for opportunities to increase his company's revenues and profits, was ambitious, ruthless when necessary, and perhaps most

importantly, had already been through several periods of considerable personal and professional sacrifice in order to keep Ansett Airways afloat.

The final result was one of the great ironies of Australian commercial history in any field – the small Ansett taking control of its much larger competitor – the irony complete when ANA's earlier attempts to take over Ansett are remembered. It was very definitely a case of David defeating Goliath.

Fleet Foibles

One of the problems which faced ANA during most of its final decade of existence was that of not having a fleet which was competitive with the opposition's. By 1948 ANA used DC-4s on main trunk routes and DC-3s on secondary services, both of these unpressurised and becoming 'second string' against more modern types.

TAA had set a new standard in passenger comfort in the second half of 1948 when it introduced the Convair CV-240 to service. A true postwar airliner incorporating the latest piston engined technology, the Convair was pressurised and quickly found favour among the travelling public for the more comfortable journey it provided for them. Such was the success of the Convair, it would not be unreasonable to say that this was the aircraft upon which TAA's early success – and therefore platform for the future – was built.

It wasn't until 1953 that ANA was able to offer pressurised airliners to the market in the form of two second hand Douglas DC-6s purchased from National Airlines in the USA. ANA did try to get some DC-6s earlier, but it was foiled by a combination of factors including its own weak financial position and the refusal of the Chifley Labor government to release sufficient of the necessary scarce and tightly controlled US dollar licences. That is why ANA was so keen to see the conservative and pro private enterprise Liberal party come to power at the 1949 election and with it the hope that TAA would be dismantled. The Liberals won, but TAA stayed.

ANA found itself behind the fleet equipment game once again from October 1954 when TAA took delivery of its first Vickers Viscount pressurised turboprop. Even though that first aircraft was lost only three weeks later when an attempted three engined takeoff during a crew training flight went wrong, TAA was still able to launch Viscount services before the end of the year.

By the time of the Ansett takeover, ANA had 20 DC-3s in service. VH-ANT was one of them and remained in the Ansett fleet until late 1968, by which time it was operating as a dedicated freighter.

The Viscount was an airliner which can be truly regarded as having caused a revolution in the Australian airline industry and elsewhere. A phenomenon known as 'The Viscount Jump' occurred almost wherever it was introduced and Australia was no exception. This involved an immediate and substantial jump in traffic on many routes, passengers switching to the smooth newcomer in large numbers in preference to airlines operating piston engined types.

The reasons behind ANA's failure to obtain Viscounts has long been the subject of much heated discussion, with various opinions and versions of the story offered by leading aviation writers since then. The popular version is that when ANA could not be offered the favourable Viscount delivery positions it sought, Ivan Holyman had a 'dummy spit', cancelled the options his airline had placed on six aircraft and ordered piston engined DC-6Bs from Douglas in their place.

Other writers more sympathetic to ANA discount this and although agreeing that the airline did in fact cancel its Viscount options in late 1952, offer no explanation as to why. It is known that ANA then looked at a proposed turboprop version of the Handley Page Hermes before requesting approval to order the two second hand DC-6s mentioned above and two new DC-6Bs under the terms of the Airlines Agreement Act which had just come into force. ANA received its first DC-6B in early 1955 and eventually took delivery of four between then and late 1956.

Whatever the real truth behind the decision not to go with the Viscount, it was a bad one. The DC-6 was certainly a fine aircraft with an admirable record behind it and a long future ahead. It was larger, had longer range and certainly greater structural integrity than the Viscount – which was at best a short-medium range aircraft in its early versions – but the passenger appeal and operating economics of the turboprop were a formidable combination with which the DC-6 could not compete. The DC-6B was the last new aircraft type to enter ANA service before the Ansett takeover.

Corporate Capers

The years 1946-49 were undoubtedly extremely difficult for ANA, faced with an openly hostile Australian Government and an increasingly strong competitor in the form of TAA. Modest profits began to turn into substantial losses from the 1948-49 financial year, this trend continuing until 1954-56 when profits were again recorded, although these were tempered by the large amount of debt the airline was carrying due to its acquisition of the DC-6s and DC-6Bs. The losses returned in

A group of happy passengers in a DC-4, the scene posed by the Douglas publicity department. This might have been appropriate in the late 1940s but not nearly a decade later when passengers expected pressurisation, less vibration and less noise in the cabin. (Douglas)

On 3 October 1957 Ansett Transport Industries achieved what had only months earlier seemed impossible – it took over the once mighty Australian National Airways to establish Ansett-ANA. DC-6B VH-INS was one of more than 30 largely obsolescent piston engined types inherited as a result of the takeover. (Eric Allen)

1956-57 and by mid 1957 these were in excess of £40,000 ($80,000) each month

ANA had attempted to raise some much needed capital in 1949 through a shares float, the idea revolving around converting ANA into a public company by increasing nominal capital from £1,000,000 ($2m) to £1,500,000 ($3m) through the issue of £1 ($2) shares. Of the total shares, 350,000 would be offered to the public.

Unfortunately, ANA's timing was poor. The airline had suffered three fatal accidents the previous year and these were still fresh in the minds of many; while investment in the airline industry generally was considered as risky by most 'serious' investors at the time. More than five decades on, nothing much has changed! There was also the constantly strengthening position of TAA, this causing many industry and business analysts to think that perhaps ANA's days were numbered.

The result was that the share offer was largely ignored and had to be withdrawn, leaving ANA as a private company still in the hands of its original five shipping company owners.

Towards Regulation

As 1952 progressed, it became clear to the Australian Government that some 'tidying up' of the local airline industry had to be done. There had been constant bickering over the imposition of airways charges over the previous two years and the level at which they were set. This combined with a temporarily high inflation rate, a substantial increase in the cost of fuel and a general economic downturn contributed to ANA losing over £500,000 ($1m) in the 1951-52 financial year, while even TAA's progress was momentarily halted when it lost £75,000 ($150,000) in the same period.

The government and the airlines – notably ANA, which was trying to reverse its own misfortunes – looked at various schemes to improve the situation. Several were proposed, promoted and examined including amalgamating TAA and ANA into a single entity.

The airlines also sought and won a 66.7% reduction in the airways fees owed between July 1947 and June 1952. This deal resulted from a court challenge to the Air Navigation Act by the airlines, the litigation dropped in return for the discounts which saved ANA some £600,000 ($1.2m). Further assistance was received in April 1952 when the government broke TAA's monopoly on air mail carriage by allowing ANA to transport mail on the Tasmania-Melbourne and Melbourne-Adelaide-Perth routes.

These and other revisions and discussions eventually led to the October 1952 introduction to parliament of the

There were many factors which contributed to ANA's downfall including its fleet, which could not compete with TAA's Vickers Viscount turboprops. The Viscount caused a revolution on the Australian domestic market – as it did in other parts of the world – through its enormous passenger appeal.

A Butler Ambassador and an East West Airlines DC-3 at Sydney Airport in 1958, shortly after Ansett gained full control of Butler. The airline (renamed as Airlines of NSW) and East West would soon be sharing the highly regulated New South Wales intrastate market. (Vance Ingham)

Civil Aviation Agreement Bill, the first step in the eventual implementation of the tightly regulated Two Airline Policy. Three subsidiary pieces of legislation were associated with the main Bill: the Air Navigation (Charges) Bill; the Income Tax Social Services Assessment (Air Navigation) Bill; and the Australian National Airlines Bill.

For ANA the Civil Aviation Agreement Bill was significant in that it threw several potential lifelines to the struggling operator, this a deliberate act by the government to assist the cause of private enterprise. Among the Bill's provisions were guarantees for the loans ANA needed to re-equip (these worth £6,000,000) and the granting of ANA equal access to mail carriage, government business and the lease of government equipment.

The new situation certainly helped ANA and allowed it to modernise its fleet by ordering Douglas DC-6s, but only it and TAA were covered by the legislation. Two carriers which would have some significance in the years that followed were not; Ansett Airways and Butler Air Transport.

As already noted, Ansett introduced the Convair to service in 1954 and made further inroads into ANA's market, while Butler had ambitions which would also see it attempt to enter the interstate market.

Butler Air Transport was basically a New South Wales intrastate operator but was also the owner of Queensland Air Lines, which flew the Brisbane-Gladstone route, stopping at several other towns on the way. ANA had a 49.5% interest in Butler through its Bungana Investments subsidiary, but this did not stop company founder Arthur Butler from pursuing ambitions to expand his airline to some trunk routes and therefore compete with his airline's half owner.

Servicing the Sydney-Melbourne route was Butler's main aim, and to achieve that it placed an order for two Vickers Viscounts in June 1954. Services with the new turboprop began in November 1955, initially between Sydney and Dubbo NSW. A Sydney-Melbourne via Wagga Wagga service was launched the following month, in defiance of ANA's instructions to its 'associate' that it should not operate into Victoria. As Butler's operations were not covered by the Airlines Agreement Act it could legally operate on routes in competition with TAA and ANA – as could Ansett – but the fact that it was partially owned by ANA created an interesting situation which further damaged the larger carrier.

Death Throes

Ivan Holyman was knighted in 1956, probably the only highlight in a year that witnessed ANA's fortunes further decline to the point that various proposals put to the government seemed to have more than a hint of desperation about them.

These included the establishment of a kind of national 'communal' airline based around the fleet and routes assets of TAA and ANA, rationalising them into more or less a single entity for greater efficiency; further variations on pooling resources; and even introducing a system whereby TAA and ANA would each operate in specific zones at the exclusion of the other.

None of these schemes held any appeal for the government as they all involved bolstering ANA's fortunes at the expense of TAA, so they were quickly rejected.

When Sir Ivan Holyman died in January 1957 it immediately became clear that ANA's days were numbered. It was unable to meet the payments due for the loans acquired to purchase the DC-6 fleet, shareholders were getting very nervous and some strange and ineffective appointments were made to the airline's board. The most notable of these was probably the appointment of Adelaide Steamships' Percy Haddy as the new chairman.

ANA had two pressurised Douglas DC-6s and four DC-6Bs in service by the second half of 1957 as the airline's 'flagship' aircraft. All four DC-6Bs remained in Ansett-ANA's fleet until the mid 1960s, VH-INU going to TAA as part of the 'cross charter' fleet swap agreement between 1960 and 1966. The aircraft is photographed here at Brisbane in early 1958, still wearing the final ANA livery. (Geoff Wilkes)

He knew nothing about the airline business, had no track record of effectively dealing with government, and no concept of the need for good public and media relations. Haddy was therefore exactly the wrong man to have in charge at this crucial point in ANA's history.

More proposals from ANA to the Federal Government followed Holyman's death, each one of them clearly made out of desperation and mainly revolving around the concept of a merger between TAA and ANA. In June 1957 the ANA board offered to sell the airline to the government for £12,000,000 ($24m), probably four times what the airline was actually worth. The proposal was quickly rejected. There was a certain arrogance about ANA's dealings with government at this point, the chairman and board members often adopting the attitude that they were somehow immune from criticism and that the government would immediately agree to whatever proposals, demands and threats were made.

Sir Ivan Holyman's son Ian (who had been appointed to the ANA board after his father's death) made an offer for the airline on 22 July 1957 through a new company called Holymans Holdings Pty Ltd, the consortium offering £3,250,000 ($6.5m). This bid was eventually withdrawn as one of only two formally received by the ANA board, despite persistent stories that just about everyone in the aviation industry was interested in acquiring ANA.

The only other genuine bid on the table was from that 'upstart', that constant thorn in the side of ANA – Ansett.

Enter Ansett

Ansett Transport Industry's involvement with the ANA sale discussions began as early as March 1957 when Reg Ansett and Ian Holyman held a meeting on the subject of a takeover and the continued involvement of the Holyman family in such a venture. These petered out but the matter briefly resurfaced four months later.

As part of the ANA takeover deal, Ansett also acquired an interest in New South Wales based carrier Butler Air Transport. Butler had previously acquired two Viscounts and had ambitions to expand into interstate operations. It used DC-3s and Airspeed Ambassadors (briefly) on its regional routes. This is DC-3 VH-IND photographed at Sydney's Mascot Airport in 1959, after the takeover and just before repainting in Airlines of NSW colours. VH-IND was a former ANA aircraft. (Eric Allen)

DC-6B VH-INS in interim Ansett-ANA livery and photographed outside the airline's terminal at Melbourne's Essendon Airport.

Reg Ansett formally broached the subject of his company taking over ANA on 24 June 1957 when it offered – in writing – £2 ($4) per share or about £3,000,000 ($6.0m) in total. The offer was summarily rejected by the ANA board in what could be described as insulting terms. Percy Haddy's written reply had an arrogant and condescending tone very much along the lines of 'go way little boy, you can talk to the adults when you grow up'. As had always been the case, ANA did not take Ansett seriously.

Despite this – and obviously realising it was running out of time and options – ANA responded a little more positively a few days later and approached Ansett about buying the airline but not ANA's properties, investments or other assets. This time it was Reg Ansett who did the rejecting, stating that it wanted the lot or nothing including – significantly – Bungana Investments and its shares in Butler Air Transport.

In one way Percy Haddy's dismissive rejection of Ansett's offer had some basis, even if the ANA chairman wasn't aware of it. In truth, Ansett Transport Industries was at that time in no position to make an offer for ANA because it simply didn't have the money available to complete the deal.

From July 1957, the pendulum began to swing towards Ansett as ANA slipped further into the mire. The Holyman bid was faltering, others expressed an interest or claimed they were going to bid but didn't, and the Federal Government decided to wash its hands of ANA. A Cabinet meeting on the 25th of the month was a major turning point when it was decided that all future demands, proposals and threats from ANA would be ignored and/or refused.

Ansett had meanwhile been working hard towards making a second formal bid for ANA, but this time with the financial backing to make it become a reality. Equally importantly, the Federal Government was by now on side and supported Ansett's plans. Much of the credit for this must be given to Reg Ansett himself through meetings with the relevant ministers and the Prime Minister, Robert Menzies, the same man who more than two decades earlier had tried to kill off Ansett's road transport service when he was Victorian Attorney-General.

RM played the political game well, telling the politicians what they wanted to hear as regards his plans for what would become Ansett-ANA and ensuring them that any such takeover would fit the government's 'two airline' policies.

In return for this, Reg Ansett was able to negotiate amendments to the Airlines Agreement Act which brought the full implementation of the Two Airline Policy into play and established a scenario which virtually guaranteed profits for the new Ansett-controlled airline.... and for TAA.

In For The Kill

By the end of July 1957, Ansett Transport Industries was in a position to make a genuine and funded offer to take over ANA thanks to the support of two major fuel companies, Vacuum (now Mobil) and Shell. In what was a beautiful bit of manoeuvring by Reg Ansett, he approached Shell and asked for money in exchange for a long term contract to supply fuel for Ansett-ANA. Shell readily agreed, because until now Vacuum had been ANA's exclusive supplier of fuel.

When Vacuum heard of this it immediately tried to counter the Shell deal because it obviously didn't want to lose the business. Discussions followed and at the end of the day both agreed to directly finance Ansett's takeover of ANA to the tune of a £1,000,000 ($2m) loan with extremely generous repayment terms, *and* share the subsequent supply of fuel to the airline, *and* between them provide another £1,000,000 in the form of very extended credit for the supply of aviation fuel and related products. This was a truly remarkable deal by any standards, and of course both companies became substantial shareholders in the new airline.

Ansett Transport Industries made its second formal bid for ANA on 30 July 1957. The offer was £3,300,000 ($6.6m): £1,000,000 ($2m) payable on the signing of contracts; £1,250,000 ($2.5m) 12 months after the signing contracts; and the balance of £1,050,000 ($2.1m) 24 months after the signing of contracts. Interest on the outstanding balance would be paid at the rate of 6% per annum and a further £133,000 ($266,000) was offered to secure an option on the shares in Butler Air Transport held by ANA's Bungana Investments.

Faced with no choice, Ansett's offer was accepted by the ANA board on 23 August 1957 and formally completed on 3 October. The new entity – Ansett-ANA – operated its first services on 21 October and carried more than 4,000 passengers on that day, a record for the Australian airline industry.

Douglas DC-6B VH-INS in ANA markings. This aircraft was originally delivered new to the carrier in August 1956, by which time the airline was already in serious financial trouble.

The New Regime

The Ansett takeover of ANA went remarkably smoothly considering some of the potential difficulties, not the least of which was the relative inexperience of the Ansett executives who were appointed to the top jobs within Ansett-ANA, and the inevitable resentment some ANA people had towards their new 'masters'.

Two actions had to be taken quickly: the removal of many of the most senior ANA executives from positions of responsibility and influence; and the retrenchment of excess staff. Many of ANA's senior executives had already proved themselves to be inadequate in some areas and simply had to go, Ansett instead preferring to promote people from lower on the ladder and let them develop with the new airline. This proved to be a good move and many of these remained with the Ansett organisation for many years and made a substantial contribution to the company's growth. Others from this 'second level' of ANA management went to TAA or Qantas and most of them went on to make their marks with those operators.

As for employee numbers, Ansett-ANA had about 3,500 at the time of the takeover, about 1,000 more than TAA. Of these about 500 were retrenched over the next few months.

If the establishment of Ansett-ANA was a pivotal moment in the history of the Australian airline industry, so was the legislative effort which followed – the full establishment of the Two Airline System.

During his discussions with the Federal Government during the period which led up to the takeover, Reg Ansett had been able to acquire the government's agreement to establish a scenario that would restrict competition on trunk routes to just two carriers – TAA and Ansett-ANA. Everything was regulated, from fleet acquisitions to routes and fares, this establishing a situation which virtually guaranteed profits for both airlines and also provided them with the financial guarantees necessary to purchase new aircraft.

This was especially important for Ansett-ANA which inherited obsolescent piston engined DC-6s, DC-6Bs, DC-4s and DC-3s from ANA as its main fleet along with the Convairs and DC-3s used by Ansett Airways. If ANA couldn't make money from this fleet mix and compete successfully with TAA's Viscounts (and forthcoming Fokker F27 Friendship turboprops on regional routes), then neither could Ansett-ANA. As discussed in the next chapter, Ansett had already ordered Lockheed Electras before the takeover to form the basis of its future main trunk route fleet.

The Airlines Equipment Bill was introduced to parliament in September 1958 and quickly passed. Several amendments followed over the years and it was this piece of legislation that created the shape and destiny of the Australian domestic airline industry over the next three decades.

FLEET SUMMARY – November 1957

Ansett-ANA: 2 Convair CV-340; 4 Convair CV-440; 18 Douglas DC-3; 8 Douglas DC-4; 2 Douglas DC-6; 4 Douglas DC-6B; 3 Bristol Freighter; 1 Bristol Sycamore.
Ansett Flying Boat Services: 2 Short Sandringham.

ANA Douglas DC-4 VH-INY, one of eight in the fleet at the time of the Ansett takeover. Unpressurised, the DC-4 was starting to show its age as a main trunk line aircraft by the mid 1950s. This particular DC-4 remained in Ansett-ANA service for only five months after the takeover. (Ellis Collection)

CHAPTER SEVEN

BUILDING AN EMPIRE

Even though the October 1957 acquisition of Australian National Airways was undoubtedly a triumph for Reg Ansett and his company, it brought with it certain operational, logistical and potential financial problems.

The main fleet of Douglas DC-6s, DC-4s and DC-3s (plus Ansett's own Convairs and DC-3s) was rapidly approaching obsolescence and needed replacing; the route network which covered the capital cities (except Darwin) plus local operations in New South Wales, Victoria, Tasmania and Queensland was extensive but incomplete and in some ways fragmented; most of ANA's senior management had proved itself to be ineffective and had to go; and on top of that the airline was overstaffed.

The senior positions at Ansett-ANA were largely taken over by Ansett people with others from the 'second tier' of ANA management promoted to more senior roles, while staff numbers were cut by about 500 to 3,000 in the first few months.

Fleet renewal was of vital importance and would be quickly addressed through the auspices of the Airlines Equipment Bill of September 1958, this representing full implementation of the government's highly regulated Two Airline Policy. Highly advantageous to Ansett-ANA and usually to TAA's cost, agreement to implement this had been a crucial part of Reg Ansett's strategies and

negotiations with the government before the final offer to purchase ANA was made

Of equal significance were Reg Ansett's own plans for his airline, these revolving around enormous expansion over the next decade based on the acquisition of existing smaller operators to create a network covering most of Australia plus Papua New Guinea and even New Zealand for a time.

In the six years after the Ansett-ANA merger, the airline acquired outright ownership or a majority interest in several pioneering Australian airlines – Butler Air Transport in New South Wales, Guinea Airways in South Australia, Mandated Airlines in New Guinea, MacRobertson Miller Aviation in Western Australia, Queensland Airlines and South Pacific Airlines of New Zealand.

Others would be added in later years and there was also Ansett Flying Boat Services, established in 1952 by absorbing Barrier Reef Airways initially and then the bankrupt Trans Oceanic Airways the following year. Most of these were owned by Ansett Transport Industries (Operations) Pty Ltd, the ATI subsidiary established as the umbrella organisation for Ansett's airlines.

Reg Ansett's philosophy behind this considerable expansion was initially quite simple.... he wanted to ensure that his airline would not be put in the same position that

Two of the Ansett-ANA Helicopter Division's float equipped Bell 47J-2A Rangers at Essendon in 1966. VH-IND in the foreground was delivered in March 1965 and VH-INW (behind) in May 1964. Both went to Helicopter Utilities in 1968. (Geoff Wilkes)

ROTARY WINGS

Ansett-ANA was a pioneer in the commercial use of helicopters in Australia, its Helicopter Division established in October 1957 when the first of two Bristol Sycamores were received. The first Bell 47J Ranger was taken into service in early 1959 and the fleet built up over the next few years to eventually total three Bell 47Gs, 10 47J Rangers, one JetRanger and two Sikorsky S-62s. The two Sycamores were both written off in 1960 and 1961.

There was also the separate Barrier Reef operation which started in March 1965 linking the Queensland coast with the Whitsunday Islands resorts using two Sikorsky S-61Ns. This continued until September 1984 when jet operations to Hamilton Island began.

Reg Ansett was an early user of helicopters for business and private transportation, commuting daily from his home at Mount Eliza to the floating Melbourne City Heliport on the Yarra River in central Melbourne. The heliport was also the scene of Australia's first airport-to-city helicopter service, launched by Ansett-ANA using a Bell 47J linking Essendon Airport to the Melbourne central business district in December 1961.

Ansett's helicopters were put to work on a variety of jobs ranging from charter, transport and utility roles to powerline patrol, survey and servicing Esso-BHP's oil exploration ships off the Gippsland coast. Operations were also flown in Papua New Guinea but the attrition rate among the Bell 47s was high, with four written off in accidents over the years.

The discovery of natural gas in Bass Strait in April 1965 by Esso-BHP led to the establishment of extensive drilling operations in the area. Ansett-ANA won the contract to service the drilling rigs and ordered two Sikorsky S-62s for the job. Both were delivered in May 1967 but one of them (VH-AND) was lost just three months later when it suffered engine problems while approaching to land on the *Glomar III* rig and was forced to ditch. The pilot and eight passengers escaped serious injury.

The other S-62 (VH-ANE) continued working the contract with support from a Bell 47J until March 1968 when the Ansett Helicopter Division, most of its remaining aircraft and the Esso-BHP contract were sold to Airfast Services for operation by subsidiary Helicopter Utilities.

The Bell JetRanger (VH-ANC) was retained mainly for the use of Reg Ansett until 1970 when it was replaced by a new machine (VH-AND). This was sold in early 1980 after the takeover of Ansett by TNT-News.

ANA found itself and that it would not be vulnerable to exactly the same pressures that Ansett had applied to the once mighty carrier. His moves on the various intrastate carriers ensured any threats were removed and also provided a virtual monopoly in most of the states in which they operated. All this in combination with the provisions of the Airlines Equipment Act ensured Ansett's financial and operational security as much as was possible.

ATI also expanded its non airline activities in the years following the ANA takeover including the establishment of a Helicopter Division in 1959 – and introduced Australia's first airport to city helicopter service between Melbourne and Essendon in December 1960 – and in 1965 established Ansett General Aviation which distributed the Piper light aircraft range in Australia. Other existing areas of operation were also expanded – hotels and resorts, road freight and road passenger services – while even television stations were added to the portfolio through Brisbane's TVQ Channel 0 and Melbourne's ATV Channel 0.

Ansett Transport Industries operated from the old ANA offices in William Street Melbourne until 1961 when it moved into its own building – Ansett House – at 489 Swanston Street. A new and larger headquarters next door at 501 Swanston Street was opened in 1980, the older building remaining and several other properties in the same block added over the years.

(left) Sikorsky S-62A VH-ANE, one of two delivered in May 1967 to service the Bass Strait oil rigs contract. (right) Bell JetRanger VH-AND on the Melbourne City Heliport in April 1979. This was the last helicopter used by Sir Reginald Ansett for commuting from his home to the office and was disposed of in February 1980. Built as a Model 206A, it had been upgraded to 206B standards. (Eric Allen & Geoff Wilkes)

Ansett's first helicopter, the former British European Airways Bristol Sycamore VH-INO. It was delivered in October 1957 and written off just over two years later. It is seen here carrying an underslung trigonometry station.

The Electra Saga

Ansett Airways was looking at introducing new aircraft types to service well before it took over ANA. As early as February 1957 the airline announced it was considering purchasing the as yet unflown Lockheed L.188 Electra turboprop for use on main trunk routes. The Electra would fly in December 1957 and had already attracted orders from several operators included US majors Eastern and American.

Reg Ansett visited Lockheed in the USA in June 1957 and on his return announced that Electra delivery positions had been reserved. A $US10m firm order for four aircraft was placed the following September. TAA, meanwhile, had evaluated and selected the French Sud Aviation Caravelle, the West's first short-medium range jet airliner and the aircraft which pioneered the fashion of mounting the engines on the rear fuselage.

These fleet re-equipment decisions resulted in the first real test of the Two Airline Policy and the Federal Government's resolve to enforce it, because to the industry's great surprise, Cabinet refused import applications by both TAA and Ansett-ANA for their new aircraft. In the case of TAA's Caravelles, this was partly because the Department of Civil Aviation was concerned that Essendon Airport's facilities were not up to the standards appropriate for jet operations.

Reg Ansett immediately met with the Minister for Civil Aviation (Senator Shane Paltridge) to discuss the matter and request the decision be reconsidered. TAA also made representations to its government owners, but to no avail.

Both airlines were given approval to order Vickers Viscount 800 series aircraft – which Ansett didn't really want – but issues surrounding the Electra continued to be subject to negotiation and discussion. Qantas also wanted Electras to service its shorter routes in the Pacific and to Asia, while New Zealand's TEAL – half owned by Qantas – would also get Electras even though it really wanted the de Havilland Comet 4.

The end result was that TAA and TEAL were denied the jets they wanted and Ansett-ANA and Qantas got their Electras. On 22 May 1958 the Australian Government announced that the purchase of 21 new aircraft worth more than £20,000,000 ($40m) had been approved for Ansett-ANA, Qantas, TAA and TEAL. Of these, only two were Electras for Ansett-ANA instead of the four it requested (and a similar number for TAA) along with four Electras for Qantas and three for TEAL plus four Viscount 800s and six Fokker F27 Friendship regional turboprops for TAA.

The government's decision was also significant because it established the criteria on which future requests for fleet re-equipment by the airlines would be judged. In return for any restrictions it might impose on re-equipment choices and their entry to service, the Australian Government agreed to release sufficient overseas funds to cover the full cost of the new aircraft; provide capital support to TAA, Qantas and TEAL; guarantee loans to Ansett-ANA under the terms of the Airlines Agreement Act; and spend money on upgrading airports and airways facilities.

The philosophies behind these decisions were enshrined in the Airlines Equipment Bill which went before parliament in September 1958 and set the scene for the very high level of regulation which remained in place for

An evocative night shot of Ansett-ANA Electra VH-RMA at Essendon Airport in August 1968. The Electra had been the main trunk route aircraft for both Ansett and TNT until the Boeing 727 jet came along. RMA was Ansett-ANA's first Electra, delivered in February 1959. (Terence Ellis)

The Electra survived its early troubles to become a reliable airliner which was popular with both passengers and crew. VH-RMB is shown here in January 1967, five years before it was converted to a freighter. (George Canciani)

the next 32 years. The re-equipment situation which had developed in 1957-58 around the Electra and Caravelle – especially that TAA was not able to take delivery of its first Electra until three months after Ansett-ANA due to its late reservation of delivery positions – led to a further piece of legislation in 1961, the Airlines Agreement Act.

In fact, TAA would have received its first Electras even later than it did if Ansett-ANA had not been forced to give up two of its delivery positions in favour of the government owned carrier in a rare example of the political decisions then being made working to Ansett's disadvantage. It could be argued that this merely helped balance the disadvantage TAA felt had been imposed on it by not being allowed to order Caravelles in the first place.

The Airlines Agreement Act extended the Two Airlines Agreement until 1977 and introduced strict rules covering

Ansett Airways had ordered four Electras shortly before the ANA takeover but was refused an import licence by the Federal Government, as was TAA for the Caravelle jets it wanted. This first test of the Two Airline Policy's fleet procurement rules resulted in Ansett-ANA eventually getting Electras but TAA also had to acquire them. VH-RMB is shown here at Sydney in April 1961, two years after it was delivered. (Eric Allen)

Ansett gained a majority shareholding in Western Australia's MacRobertson Miller Airlines (MMA) in April 1963 and full control the following year. Unlike most other Ansett subsidiaries, MMA was allowed to retain its name, this not changing (to Airlines of WA) until 1981. Viscount V.720 VH-RMQ (a former TAA aircraft) briefly flew in MMA's attractive 'Jetstream Service' colours but was involved in a fatal crash in December 1968, just days after this photograph was taken at Perth. (Eric Allen)

new aircraft orders by Ansett-ANA and TAA: any new aircraft should be ordered by both airlines simultaneously, arrive in Australia simultaneously and enter service simultaneously; neither airline could place an order for jet airliners before 18 November 1962; neither airline could introduce a jet airliner to service before 1 July 1964; and both airlines would offer equal capacity on trunk routes, calculations which resulted in the 'equal capacity' figure based on the assumption of 68% average load factors.

Those routes were defined as being Melbourne-Sydney-Brisbane, Melbourne-Brisbane, Melbourne-Coolangatta, Melbourne-Adelaide-Perth, Melbourne-Perth, Melbourne-Hobart, Melbourne-Launceston-Hobart, Sydney-Adelaide, Sydney-Launceston-Hobart, and Sydney-Coolangatta.

The Airlines Equipment Bill brought with it some revisions to the airliner purchases previously approved by the government. For Ansett-ANA, this resulted in the ordering of two Electras, four Viscount 800s and six Fokker F27s for regional services.

Ansett-ANA's Electras were initially fitted with 78 passenger seats (60 first class and 18 economy, the reverse of today's normal configuration) and the first example (VH-RMA) arrived in Australia on 10 March 1959 – three months ahead of TAA – entering service on the Melbourne-Sydney route eight days later. VH-RMB entered service the following month, allowing an extension of services to Brisbane and also Melbourne-Perth non stop flights. By then, Ansett-ANA had applied for the importation of a third Electra. This was initially refused by the government but was finally approved in November 1959

V.818 Viscount VH-RML was purchased by Ansett-ANA from Cubana in February 1962. Despite its initial reluctance to operate the Viscount, the airline found it an ideal compliment to the larger Electra and flew them side-by-side under 'The System of the Golden Jets'. (Terence Ellis)

A very rare colour shot of Butler Air Transport V.747 Viscount VH-BAT, photographed at Sydney in December 1957. Before the Ansett takeover of ANA, Butler was part owned by the larger carrier but despite this purchased Viscounts to challenge ANA (and TAA) on some trunk routes. Ansett also gained a share of Butler with the ANA takeover but the battle for full control was acrimonious, controversial and according to many, legally marginal. (Eric Allen)

with VH-RMC being delivered in March 1960. TAA also acquired a third Electra.

The Lockheed Electra proved to be successful in Australian and overseas service but not before having to overcome some significant problems in its early days. The first of these manifested itself as soon as the aircraft entered service when a high level of noise and vibration was noted in the forward cabin. The problem was fixed by modifying the engine mounts through a kit supplied by Lockheed, the work able to be performed locally under the manufacturer's supervision. This 'Electra Refinement Program' took six days to complete per aircraft.

More serious were several fatal crashes in the USA during 1959 and 1960, two of which involved the aircraft breaking up in flight. Speed restrictions were imposed on the aircraft and a painstaking investigation revealed a design defect in the engine mountings which allowed a potentially disastrous engine/propeller oscillation (called 'whirl mode') to develop, resulting in the wing eventually shaking itself to pieces.

A major and hugely expensive modification program (which was borne by the manufacturer) followed which solved the problem but inhibited further Electra sales. What was called the Lockheed Electra Achievement Program (LEAP) required that aircraft be flown back to the factory for modification, keeping each of them out of service for a month or so including ferrying and testing in the first half of 1961. The actual modification process at the factory took 22 days.

Despite this the Electra was hugely successful for Ansett-ANA, that three month advantage in delivery dates it held over TAA's aircraft proving crucial. Operating in conjunction with the airline's new Viscount 800s under the 'System of the Golden Jets' promotional banner, the new Lockheeds immediately began attracting strong passenger loadings and materially contributed to Ansett-ANA winning more than half of the total Australian domestic market in mid

1959. At the beginning of the year Ansett-ANA held 45.8% of the market and TAA 54.2%. In April – the month the Electra entered service – Ansett-ANA recorded a majority market share (53.3%) for the first time and maintained that advantage over the next few months.

The System of the Golden Jets concept in combination with the two new turboprop airliners was successful for Ansett-ANA. The aircraft were furnished in a gold decor and the Golden Supper Club was offered on late night flights between Sydney and Melbourne, complete with hostesses attired in gold lamé outfits.

Viscounts and the Cross-Charter

Considering the very substantial impact TAA's Vickers Viscounts had had on the Australian domestic airline market earlier in the 1950s – they were a very large nail in ANA's coffin – it's perhaps surprising to learn that Reg

Ansett-ANA didn't really want Vickers Viscounts in its fleet but eventually operated 12 of them including two inherited from Butler and three leased from TAA as part of the controversial Cross-Charter Agreement. This is the former Butler V.747 Viscount VH-RMO on approach to Sydney in July 1967. (Eric Allen)

Air freight became an increasingly important part of Ansett-ANA's activities during the 1960s, leading to the conversion of three Douglas DC-4s to Aviation Traders Carvair configuration with a redesigned forward fuselage allowing straight-in loading. VH-INK was the second conversion, redelivered to Ansett-ANA in November 1965. (Terence Ellis/Eric Allen)

Ansett wasn't all that keen on acquiring the British airliner once Ansett-ANA had been established. Ansett wanted more Electras but the government's 'equal fleets' and services policies left him with little choice but to order it.

As it turned out, this was probably just as well as when each of Ansett's Electras had to return to the USA for modification there were sufficient Viscounts to cover the capacity loss. The Electra and Viscount complemented each other well and were the front line main route equipment for both Ansett-ANA and TAA until the Boeing 727 and then Douglas DC-9 jets entered service.

The first four Viscounts ordered by Ansett-ANA in its own right were four V.832s under the provisions of the Airlines Equipment Bill. The first of these (VH-RMG) was delivered in March 1959 (just a week after the first Electra had arrived) and entered service on 20 April. The other three V.832s were delivered within a few weeks and all were originally fitted with 52 passenger seats.

These weren't the first Viscounts to be taken into the Ansett-ANA fleet. Two earlier model V.700s had come with the takeover of Butler Air Transport in February 1958 while two V.810s were later obtained second hand from Continental Airlines (1960) and Cubana (1962).

By far the most controversial of Ansett-ANA's Viscount fleet were the three TAA V.720s that were taken into the fleet in March 1960. These were very reluctantly forced out of TAA's hands into Ansett-ANA's by the Federal Government under the 'fleet equality' aspects of the Airlines Equipment Bill. Under what was called the 'Cross-Charter Agreement', TAA had to give up three of its Viscounts in exchange for two Ansett-ANA Douglas DC-6Bs. The DC-6Bs were no match for the Viscounts in terms of passenger appeal and TAA was not at all happy about the arrangement! Further, by getting three aircraft in exchange for two, Ansett-ANA had the opportunity for additional flexibility in its scheduling.

The Cross-Charter was a formal arrangement involving an exchange of money, Ansett-ANA paying TAA £160/18/- ($321.80) per day for the Viscounts while the DC-6Bs cost TAA £199/12/- ($399.20) per day. The controversy surrounding the Cross-Charter Agreement reached all levels of politics, the public and TAA's employees, many seeing it as a deliberate attempt to help boost Ansett-ANA's fortunes at the expense of TAA – which it most certainly was.

Traffic figures indicate that it served to increase Ansett-ANA's load factors by six or seven points on the major trunk routes while TAA's remained static due to the capacity limitations which had been imposed on it. On many flights, the unavailability of seats on TAA services led to passengers switching to Ansett-ANA as there was no alternative. Overall, the agreement probably cost TAA two percentage points of market share.

The arrangement also helped other aspects of Ansett-ANA's bottom line. The airline had inherited four DC-6Bs from ANA and by 1960 they were all worth considerably

VH-TVC, one of the three TAA Viscounts operated by Ansett-ANA from March 1960 under the Cross-Charter Agreement. This aircraft crashed into Botany Bay after departing Sydney Airport in November 1961. (Eric Allen)

Ansett-ANA acquired four Douglas DC-4s from Japan Air Lines in 1963-65, three of them genuine commercial models built after World War II. VH-INJ was the first of them (received in August 1963), initially serving with Airlines of NSW for a short time. This shot was taken at Sydney in November 1963. (Eric Allen)

less than what was still owing on them. Selling them would have resulted in a substantial capital loss, while retaining them in service would also have been financially doubtful as passengers were not keen to use them when they could fly in the much smoother and faster Electra or Viscount. To get rid of half of its DC-6B fleet in this way – and get Viscounts in exchange – was a big boost for Ansett-ANA in several ways. When the time came to sell the DC-6Bs, Ansett-ANA's debt-to-equity ratio in them was much more attractive.

The Cross-Charter Agreement formally ended in late August 1966 when the last of the four DC-6Bs still operated jointly by the two airlines was retired. Ansett-ANA kept two of the three TAA Viscounts (one had crashed in 1961) until October 1966 and April 1967, respectively, when they were returned, while another had been purchased from TAA in 1962. This brought the total number of Viscounts operated by Ansett-ANA to 12.

From a safety point of view, the Viscount's time with Ansett-ANA was not a happy one with three lost in fatal accidents during the 1960s. The first occurred on 30 November 1961 when V.720 VH-TVC – on cross-charter from TAA – broke up over Botany Bay a few minutes after departing Sydney-Kingsford Smith Airport on a flight to Canberra. The wreckage was found in the bay the following morning, examination of it leading investigators to conclude the starboard wing and tailplane had separated, probably due to extreme turbulence.

The next accident was on 22 September 1966 involving V.832 VH-RMI when it suffered a fire in the port inner (No 2) Dart and failure of the adjacent engine in a flight between Mount Isa and Longreach in Queensland. The pilots were unable to feather the engines' propellers and during an attempted diversion to Winton the Viscount's port wing failed due to being weakened by the fire raging within it.

The original cause of the fire was found to be a faulty cabin pressurisation blower mounted on the port inner (No 2) engine, a loose oil metering unit allowing metal on metal

contact, the generation of heat, a healthy amount of oil still being delivered and subsequent ignition. The fire spread into a wing compartment housing a fuel tank, at which point a tragic outcome became almost inevitable.

The final Ansett Viscount accident was on 31 December 1968, less than two months after the 'ANA' suffix was dropped from the airline's name to become Ansett Airlines of Australia. V.720 VH-RMQ went down while on descent into Port Hedland (WA) after a flight from Perth, this also a former TAA Viscount but one that had been purchased by Ansett-ANA in 1962 to replace VH-TVC. As the former VH-TVB, this aircraft was the longest serving and highest time Australian Viscount, delivered in November 1954 and with 31,747 flight hours and 25,336 cycles in its log books. At the time of the crash it was being operated by MacRobertson Miller Airlines which was partly owned by Ansett.

The age of the aircraft was significant because the cause of the crash was found to be separation of the

An interesting part of Ansett-MAL's fleet was its four Cessna 336 Skymasters, one of which was modified to allow the whole rear fuselage engine/propeller section to swing to one side for loading freight directly into the cabin. VH-CMY is captured here at Bankstown in June 1965. (Eric Allen)

One of the most significant types introduced to Australia in the late 1950s was the Fokker F27 Friendship, the aircraft which brought smooth turboprops and cabin pressurisation to rural and regional centres around the country. Ansett and its regional subsidiaries eventually operated more than 40 F27s of which Srs.200 VH-FNA was the first, delivered in October 1959.

starboard wing due to a fatigue failure. By that stage there were only five Viscount 700 models still operating in Australia (including VH-RMQ), three with Ansett and two with TAA which had only recently withdrawn most of its fleet. All Australian Viscount 700s were immediately grounded when the crash occurred, its Australian career effectively ending then. Question marks over the structural integrity of the Viscount's wing – which due to the zinc bearing light alloys used was prone to stress corrosion and had a relatively poor fatigue life – were unfortunately proven to be justified.

Fokkers For The Regionals

The third significant new type introduced to Ansett-ANA shortly after the merger was the Fokker F27 Friendship regional airliner. As the most successful of the turboprop 'DC-3 replacements' to be developed in the 1950s, the F27 was found to be ideal for operations on Australian intrastate and regional routes and did indeed become a true replacement for the venerable Douglas airliner. Some 80 eventually found their way onto the Australian civil register over the years including 42 with Ansett and its associated airlines.

For regional and rural communities, the pressurised F27 offered new standards of service for passengers who had lived with rattly and unpressurised piston engined types for many years.

As it had done with the Viscount, TAA pioneered the Friendship in Australia by placing an order for six in March 1956 with the first one delivered in April 1959. Ansett-ANA selected the aircraft for use on its country services in July 1958 and an initial order for six was approved by the Federal Government the following September. Like TAA, Ansett placed many more follow-up orders over the following years.

Ansett-ANA's first F27 (Series 200 VH-FNA) was delivered in October 1959 and although originally intended for Queensland Airlines, first flew in Ansett-ANA colours. Nine were in service by the end of 1961 flying with Ansett-ANA and Airlines of New South Wales, the latter operating in a highly regulated environment in the state, where it was licenced to fly on some routes and Tamworth based East-West Airlines on others, with no crossover. Each therefore had a monopoly on the routes it served, which was good for the airlines' bottom lines but not so good for passengers, who had no competitive options from which to choose.

(left) F27-200 VH-FNE, fifth of the original batch of six Friendships delivered to Ansett-ANA in late 1959-early 1960. This aircraft went into service with Queensland Airlines (QAL) immediately after delivery. Note the revised nose profile compared with VH-FNA, this resulting from the fitting of weather radar. (right) Butler Air Transport became Airlines of NSW in December 1959, operating on the heavily regulated New South Wales intrastate market. F27-200 VH-FNB was part of the new airline's initial fleet.

Eventually, F27s flew with all of Ansett's subsidiary and associated airlines and the type remained in service until the end of 1990 when Eastwest (now part of Ansett) sold its last four aircraft.

Butler Air Transport

Ansett Transport Industry's policy of acquiring regional airlines to shore up the group's position in the Australian market began in earnest immediately after the deal to take over ANA had been completed in October 1957.

New South Wales based Butler Air Transport – which was partly owned by ANA subsidiary Bungana Investments – was the first of them, the result of a highly controversial series of events which eventually saw Ansett gain full control of the airline, but only after Reg Ansett's methods were brought into question. Even today, the circumstances of the takeover rankle many who remember it.

Arthur Butler was regarded by many as one of the aviation industry's gentlemen, but he was also ambitious and an astute businessman. What was called the Butler Air Transport Company began operations in December 1934 – more than a year before Ansett Airways – after having won a tender to operate the Charleville (Queensland) to Cootamundra (NSW) section of the England-Australia air mail route. Cootamundra was a major rail centre at the time and from there the mail was transported to Sydney by train.

Butler used a pair of de Havilland Dragons for this service but it ended in 1938 when Qantas took over, operating flying boats between Sydney and Brisbane on the mail operations. Butler was forced to reorganise, relocating to Sydney and establishing a network of services within New South Wales. After the war, Butler obtained three ex USAAF Douglas C-47s and after conversion to civil DC-3 standards used them on services from Sydney to Bathurst, Coffs Harbour, Evans Head and Parkes. By 1948 Butler served 20 points in New South Wales and further expanded its operations in December of that year when it acquired a controlling interest in Queensland Airlines.

The Australian Government then played a hand in Butler's future by trying to transfer its route network to the newly established and government owned TAA. This plan was thwarted by a High Court ruling and Butler continued operating intrastate services in New South Wales.

ANA – through Bungana Investments – made an offer to take over Butler Air Transport in 1948 but this was rejected by the shareholders. Undaunted, it and ANA's Holyman family began buying Butler shares on the open

MMA already had one Fokker F27 in service by the time of the Ansett takeover, VH-MMS, delivered in December 1959. It remained with the airline afterwards and by 1966 four were in the fleet along with eight DC-3s, a DC-4 freighter, a Dove and a Piaggio P.166. (Geoff Wilkes)

market, between them gaining 51% of the stock but not a majority of voting shares. Despite this, Butler continued to expand with ambitions to compete with ANA on some trunk routes. In the 1950s the Butler fleet continued to mainly comprise DC-3s with de Havilland Herons introduced on some country services and then Airspeed Ambassadors obtained from British European Airways pending the arrival of two Vickers Viscounts which had been ordered.

The Viscount order threw out a direct challenge not only to part owner ANA but also to the Two Airline Policy which was starting to come into play in Australia. The first Butler Viscount arrived in Australia in September 1955 followed by the second a year later. Sydney-Melbourne services were launched in December 1955, much to the displeasure of ANA.

Arthur Butler was a man who believed in looking after his employees and encouraging them to become directly involved in their company. In what later proved to be a critical move, Butler issued an additional 100,000 shares at the end of 1956 which were made available to employees on a time payment plan, the idea being to reduce the Bungana/ANA/Holyman shareholding to below 50%.

By now ANA was in serious trouble and on the verge of collapse, but this didn't prevent considerable legal wrangling occurring between then and early 1957. In November 1956 Bungana Investments was granted an injunction over the allotment of shares by Butler; there were wrangles and meetings over the appointment of new company directors; Bungana applied for a writ to prevent a Butler board meeting from allotting shares, and so on. Finally, in January 1957, Arthur Butler resigned as chairman of the company

(left) F27-200 VH-FNI in Ansett-ANA colours on approach to Sydney Airport in April 1966. This aircraft later flew with Airlines of South Australia. (right) Like most other Ansett regional subsidiaries, Airlines of South Australia operated Fokker F27s at some stage, four of them eventually flying in ASA colours. (Eric Allen)

Butler Air Transport also operated three Airspeed Ambassadors, these remaining in service only until August 1958 when they were returned to original operator British European Airways for resale. This is VH-BUJ at Sydney in December 1957, when the battle for full control of Butler was approaching its climax. (Eric Allen)

he had formed, handing over temporarily to Mr R Nash and then Sir John Northcott. Nash moved to the chair of Butler subsidiary Queensland Airlines (QAL).

Battle for Butler

When Ansett took over ANA in October 1957 it also acquired Bungana Investments and its minority shareholding in Butler. Obtaining a majority of Butler's shares was important for the newly established Ansett-ANA for several reasons: it removed Butler from competing on trunk routes with its Viscounts; provided a carrier to operate NSW intrastate services; and also gave Ansett an operator in Queensland through Butler's ownership of QAL.

Ansett Transport Industries therefore made an offer to Butler's employee shareholders but it was rejected by the Butler board which discouraged them from selling by announcing plans to issue 80,000 more shares for the airline's workers. This was contested by Ansett and resulted in a court injunction being issued to prevent it happening.

Recently delivered Convair CV-440 VH-BZH briefly flew in hybrid Ansett/Butler markings in 1958 before the airline's name changed to Airlines of NSW. (Brian Reed via Eric Allen)

More very rare colour. Queensland Airlines was part of the Butler Air Transport group when control was gained by Ansett. Among its fleet was Douglas DC-3 VH-AVL, photographed here at Sydney in February 1956. QAL was wound up in 1966. (Eric Allen)

Then all hell broke loose, Reg Ansett engineering a 'fiddle' of Butler's shareholding by in effect giving hundreds of his employees Butler shares and then flying them – as nominee shareholders – from all over Australia to load Butler's annual general meeting in Sydney on 21 January 1958 with pro Ansett voters. The idea was to ensure a majority of Ansett people were elected to Butler's board of directors and has been likened to the 'branch stacking' activities that occurred at many Australian Labor Party meetings over the years when candidates for seats were being selected.

It is well known that the Federal Government favoured Ansett's quest to take control of Butler and QAL, but answers to the many questions surrounding just how much the government was involved in the scheme have never been answered and probably never will be.

The manoeuvring was in full flight well before the infamous Butler AGM. The original meeting had been scheduled for 31 December 1957 but was adjourned due to the conflict between ATI and Butler. On 20 January 1958 the Equity Court extended the restraining order on Butler to prevent the issue of the new shares, while the controversial AGM the following day was itself adjourned before the vitally important election of new directors could be held. However, an Ansett backed resolution that no new shares

could be issued without the approval of an extraordinary general meeting of shareholders was approved.

Another meeting on 28 January saw the director's ballot held but with no result due to a formal challenge over the validity of many of the proxy votes. Ansett claimed it had 19,039 votes to 17,634 but Butler chairman Sir John Northcott needed to obtain legal advice on the situation and declined to declare the poll for a further week. The final meeting was held on 5 February, at which Northcott declared the Ansett employees' proxy votes invalid. Ansett challenged this in the Equity Court and won – Sir John's decision was overruled and Ansett gained control of Butler Air Transport and QAL.

New elections were held with Sir John Northcott temporarily remaining as chairman and Arthur Butler as managing director. Both would resign within a couple of months and Ansett set about purchasing the 100,000 employee shares that had been issued, offering twice their paid up price. It was an offer too good to refuse and by the end of April 1959 Ansett Transport Industries held 99.8% of Butler's shares and the company's stock exchange listing was removed.

The whole episode was an extraordinary one in Australian corporate history, in any field. What it did show was more proof of Reg Ansett's tenacity in business and his

Two examples of the venerable Bristol Freighter remained in Ansett service until November 1967, albeit for the last three years or so with Ansett-MAL in Papua New Guinea. Freighter Mk.31 VH-BFA was one of them, photographed here before being transferred to MAL in May 1964.

One of the more unusual types to carry Ansett-ANA livery was this Czechoslovakian Let L.200A Morava four seat light twin, the only one of its kind in Australia. Purchased from Coastal Airways in August 1964, it was used for feeder services out of Mackay (Qld) until February 1967. It was popularly known as 'eggs, meat and vegetables' due to its VH-EMV registration. (David Thollar)

determination that Ansett-ANA would grow and survive. The Butler takeover also showed a ruthless streak and a willingness to stretch the limits of the law. Many still think those limits were exceeded on this occasion with – according to some – the tacit approval of the Australian Government.

Butler Air Transport continued operating under its own name flying DC-3s, three Ambassadors (temporarily) and the two Viscounts until December 1959 when it was renamed Airlines of New South Wales. The Ambassadors had been returned to BEA a year earlier for resale on Ansett's behalf (they eventually went to Dan-Air) and the new airline's fleet was built up around the DC-3 and Fokker Friendship. Further name changes were introduced over the years: Ansett Airlines of New South Wales (June 1969), Air New South Wales (June 1981), Air NSW (May 1985), Ansett NSW (March 1990) and finally Ansett Express in November 1990. The airline was absorbed into the mainstream Ansett Australia system in October 1993.

As noted earlier, New South Wales intrastate operations were tightly regulated with Airlines of New South Wales and East-West Airlines sharing the traffic, operating only to designated ports and never in competition. This policy took Ansett to the courts once again when the NSW State Government ordered a reshuffling of routes which Ansett claimed favoured East-West. The High Court ruled against Ansett's assertion that the State did not have the right to make these changes, this decision

A typical scene at Melbourne-Essendon Airport's terminal in the early 1960s with Ansett-ANA and TAA Electras and Viscounts parked on the apron. (postcard via Geoff Wilkes)

backed up later on appeal to the Privy Council. It would be nearly four decades later that air services in New South Wales would finally be fully deregulated.

Queensland Airlines had a much shorter life, lasting only until December 1966 when it was absorbed into the mainstream Ansett-ANA operation. By then it was operating a single Fokker F27, two DC-3s and a Piaggio P.166B for local services. QAL was not a good money spinner for its owner and only ever achieved average passenger load factors of 40-43%.

Guinea Airways

Guinea Airways was at one stage a major force on the Australian civil aviation scene, established in 1927 out of the Guinea Gold company which was set up in the then Australian Territory of Papua New Guinea to exploit its extensive gold resources. As there were few proper roads, transporting men, gold and equipment to and from the mining areas was a time consuming and expensive business. The solution was to use air transport to carry all of this and the result was a successful and profitable operation probably unique in the world.

Some of the equipment which needed to be transported was bulky and heavy, Guinea Airways eventually purchasing a number of Junkers W34 and larger G31 aircraft to perform the tasks, these all metal transports regarded as highly advanced for their day. Operating as a separate company to Guinea Gold, Guinea Airways quickly established itself, carrying substantial amounts of freight and passengers not only for its associate company's operations but also for others.

If there was ever a place that needed the aeroplane and benefited from it, Papua New Guinea was surely near the top of the list, air transport opening up parts of the Territory which had not been readily accessible before. One extraordinary statistic illustrates the scope and success of Guinea Airways' operation – in just one month in 1930 the airline carried more air freight than the entire world airline industry in the whole of the year!

Guinea Airways expanded its operations to mainland Australia in early 1937, initially using a Lockheed L.10 Electra flying Adelaide-Darwin and then Adelaide-Sydney, although as this route was in competition with ANA, financial returns were poor. The Adelaide-Darwin service's profitability subsequently improved when it became part of the

Guinea Airways became a wholly owned Ansett Transport Industries subsidiary in July 1959 and was renamed Airlines of South Australia shortly after. Included in its early fleet was DC-3 VH-ANZ, the former ANA Largana. *(Terence Ellis)*

subsidised Empire Air Mail Scheme, while from 1939 Guinea Airways also operated on several other subsidised routes within South Australia. Lockheed L.14 Super Electras were purchased to service these.

Everything changed for Guinea Airways in December 1941 when Japan entered the war and quickly began its march through the south-west Pacific area, including Papua New Guinea. The airline lost 10 of its fleet of 15 aircraft during the early battles of the invasion and the others were impressed into RAAF service. Worse, Guinea Airways was forced to abandon the Territory and was never to return.

Now permanently based in Adelaide, the airline suddenly found the substantial profits it was making in Papua New Guinea were reduced to very modest figures. It survived the war by flying on behalf of the American forces based in Australia. Postwar, Guinea Airways' hopes of returning to PNG were dashed by the Chifley government and its aims of nationalising all Australian air services. This it wasn't permitted to do (see chapter 4, 'Playing Third Fiddle') but it did establish the government owned Trans Australia Airlines in 1946 and also took control of international carrier Qantas. Guinea Airways therefore lost its right to operate to and within PNG (to Qantas) and also its Adelaide-Darwin service to TAA.

Court challenges failed and Guinea Airways was left as a small basically intrastate operator flying from Adelaide to seven points in South Australia plus Broken Hill in New South Wales. Privately owned Australian National Airways had made two attempts to take over Guinea Airways during the war years and this had created considerable division between the directors (who were in favour of such an arrangement) and ordinary shareholders, who were not.

Finally, in August 1945 and without the approval of the shareholders, Guinea Airways' directors turned the airline into a *defacto* ANA subsidiary by allowing the larger carrier to take over all of its operations, staffing, maintenance and day to day operations without a penny changing hands.

Guinea Airways continued as an ANA 'associate' airline operating DC-3s as its primary equipment until Ansett took over ANA in October 1957. It then struck a deal with TAA, turning all the aspects of the business previously handled by ANA over to the government owned carrier.

This situation sat uncomfortably with Reg Ansett, who had his own expansion plans in mind and knew that losing Guinea Airways' South Australian feeder traffic to TAA was not desirable. In March 1959 Ansett Transport Industries offered £200,000 ($400,000) to buy Guinea Holdings Ltd's aviation interests – Guinea Airways in

Airlines of South Australia was the last Ansett subsidiary to operate Convairs, the final CV-440 service not taking place until May 1973. VH-BZN was one of the pair which survived in service until then. *(Terence Ellis)*

Papua New Guinea's Mandated Airlines became an Ansett subsidiary in January 1961. As Ansett-MAL, it continued to operate its varied fleet within the Australian Territory. The Douglas DC-3 was Ansett-MAL's mainstay with 11 in service by the mid 1960s including VH-AOI, a former Butler aircraft. (Eric Allen)

effect – but this was rejected. A further offer was then made for the whole of Guinea Holdings which included a very substantial blue chip shares portfolio.

The offer was 17s 6d ($1.75) per share or about £1,700,000 ($3.4m) in total, this in reality reflecting only the value of Guinea's shares portfolio. Once again the Guinea Holdings board recommended rejection of the offer but the shareholders disagreed and voted to sell. On 1 July 1959 Guinea Airways became a wholly owned subsidiary of Ansett Transport Industries.

The name Guinea Airways did not last for long. The airline was renamed Airlines of South Australia in December 1959 and continued flying intrastate services as well as the Broken Hill route. The DC-3s were gradually replaced by Convairs (the last two remaining in service

until 1973) and Fokker Friendships. Piaggio P.166s were also used on some local services.

Airlines of South Australia was never hugely profitable for ATI but one route was a good money-spinner. The service from Adelaide to the Woomera Rocket Range was heavily utilised and subsidised and at its peak in the 1950s and 1960s, ASA was the only airline flying it. When Woomera's activities began to scale down so did the airline's profitability.

The final nail in the coffin came in 1986 when the South Australian Government deregulated air services in the state. Ansett Transport Industries therefore closed Airlines of South Australia down on 27 June 1986 and most of its routes were taken over by Kendell Airlines. At the time, ASA's fleet comprised three Fokker F27s.

Also in Ansett-MAL's fleet in the 1960s was a pair of Bristol Freighters which were transferred from Ansett-ANA in May 1964. Both were former Pakistan Air Force aircraft. (Eric Allen)

Ansett-MAL operated a DHC Caribou on freight services in New Guinea between September 1965 and January 1969, hoping to use the aircraft's exceptional STOL capabilities to advantage in a difficult operating environment. (Terence Ellis)

New Zealand Foray

Ansett Transport Industries had made two unsuccessful attempts to expand its airline operations into the New Zealand market in 1950. The first was a rejected application to fly between Melbourne and Christchurch and the second a bid to purchase the trunk routes operated by state owned New Zealand National Airways Corporation. After reconsidering its position, the New Zealand Government decided to keep NZNAC and Ansett would have to wait another ten years before it could operate on the other side of the Tasman Sea.

The opportunity arose in October 1960 when ATI announced it had acquired a 49% interest in South Pacific Airlines Ltd, which had been established by local interests the previous year. Under the revised name South Pacific Airlines of New Zealand (SPANZ) the airline began operations on 14 December 1960 initially using two DC-3s supplied by Ansett – ZK-BYD (formerly VH-AVL) and ZK-BYE (VH-IND). Both DC-3s were modified to 'Viewmaster' configuration with enlarged cabin windows.

The airline's first services were from Auckland to Christchurch via Alexandra. The network gradually expanded to cover 18 other ports in New Zealand when two more DC-3s were added to the fleet in 1961.

SPANZ quickly proved not to be the financial success Ansett had hoped and withdrew from the company in October 1964 citing an 'unhelpful' New Zealand Government and ongoing losses. Ansett's shareholding in SPANZ was not sold but presented to its employees. The shares quickly became worthless as SPANZ was placed in receivership in November 1965 and flew its last service (Invercargill-Auckland) in February 1966.

Two decades later, Ansett would once again tackle the New Zealand domestic market on a larger scale but with similar results – financial losses and an 'unhelpful' government!

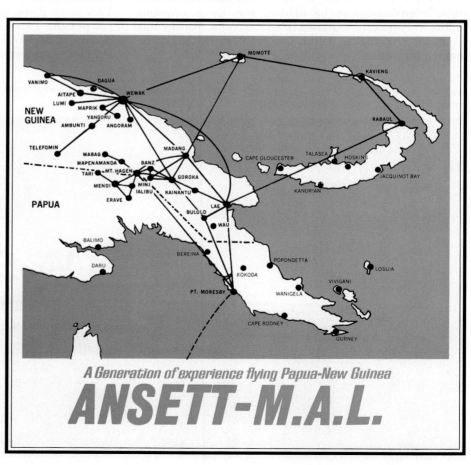

A Generation of experience flying Papua-New Guinea
ANSETT-M.A.L.

Victorian Air Coach began operations in December 1961 following purchase of the intrastate routes previously flown by Southern Airlines. It survived until August 1966 when its services were absorbed into Ansett-ANA's network. Six DC-3s were operated at various times including VH-ANQ, shown here at Swan Hill in March 1965. (Eric Allen)

Ansett-MAL

Even though the Australian National Airlines Bill of August 1945 promoted by the Chifley Labor government had many of its aspects ruled illegal by the High Court (see chapter 4 'Playing Third Fiddle') it was ruled that the Commonwealth did have the right to a monopoly on air services within Australia's territories, notably the Australian Capital Territory, the Northern Territory and Papua New Guinea.

Approval for Ansett-ANA to operate into Darwin and Canberra did eventually come many years later (October 1961 in the case of the NT capital) but the first of these conventions to be broken was those covering flights to Papua New Guinea from Australia. For the moment, internal flights within the Territory by Ansett remained forbidden.

The PNG market was potentially lucrative, especially those services relating to transporting personnel and freight to and from Australia. As an Australian territory, PNG witnessed a large and constant stream of public servants passing through it as they either started or completed their periods of service with the administration or came home on leave.

Until July 1960 Qantas had the rights to operate services from Australia and PNG and within it but this was rescinded following investigations into the overall subject of PNG air services and numerous complaints about Qantas. As a result both Ansett-ANA and TAA were given approval to operate regulated flights (as per the Two Airline Policy guidelines) to and from Australia and TAA took over domestic services alongside local operators.

VH-RMF was the second Ansett-ANA Boeing 727-77 to arrive in Australia, in November 1964. Like the others in the initial order for four, it remained in service until the second half of the 1970s. (Eric Allen)

The toss off a coin decided which airline would operate the first post-Qantas service from Brisbane to Port Moresby. TAA won and conducted its first flight with one of the Douglas DC-6Bs leased from Ansett-ANA under the cross-charter agreement on 9 July; Ansett-ANA launched its 'Golden Orchid' service two days later, also using a DC-6B.

Ansett-ANA then began looking for a way to operate domestic services within Papua New Guinea without directly encroaching on TAA's rights in this area. A well organised domestic operation would itself have considerable profit potential as well as providing a very significant 'feed' for the Golden Orchid flights to Australia.

The solution was found in Mandated Airlines, a long established and large operation which had been founded in 1936 by the merger of PNG pioneers W R Carpenter Aerial Service and Pacific Aerial Transport, both of which could trace their pedigrees back to the early 1930s. By 1960 Mandated Airlines had also absorbed several other PNG operators including Island Airways, Madang Air Services and Gibbes Sepik Airways, the operation founded by Australian World War II fighter ace Wing Commander Bobby Gibbes. W R Carpenter and Co remained Mandated's major shareholder.

Mandated operated eight DC-3s as its main fleet but also a variety of smaller and light aircraft types including Cessna, Norseman, Dragon and Junkers aircraft with two Piaggio P.166 feederliners on order. This diverse fleet reflected the different types of operation the airline had to undertake, many of them to remote areas with short, undulating airstrips hewn out of the forests and often in precarious locations.

Ansett-ANA applied for approval to operate PNG internal services in December 1960 under the name Guinea Airways but on 12 January 1961 it announced it was purchasing Mandated Airlines and its subsidiaries from W R Carpenter Ltd for £950,000 ($1.9m). About half of this was financed via a transfer of Ansett Transport Industries shares to Carpenter, thus providing it with a substantial stake in ATI. At this stage there was no attempt to take over PNG's other major local operator, Papuan Airlines (Patair), and the idea of reviving the old Guinea Airways name was shelved.

Now renamed Ansett-MAL, the 'new' airline had its own independent administration and operated under PNG laws and corporate regulations which included a lower tax rate than mainland Australia. New aircraft types were introduced including Twin Otters, Bristol Freighters and even a DHC Caribou between 1965 and 1969, the airline looking to take advantage of its extraordinary short field performance. Light aircraft types continued to be used including four Cessna 336 Skymaster 'push-pull' light twins, one of which was modified by Sydney based Aerostructures so that the rear fuselage – including the engine and propeller – could be swung to one side to provide easy access to the cabin for bulky loads.

By early 1966 Ansett-MAL's fleet comprised 11 DC-3s, four P.166s, two Bristol Freighters, one Caribou, seven Cessna 185 Skywagons, four Cessna Skymasters, one Cessna 182 Skylane and one Cessna 206 Skywagon.

Ansett-MAL's name was changed to Ansett Airlines of Papua New Guinea in June 1968 and in July 1970 Patair was acquired, becoming Ansett (P&NG) Ltd two years later. With the coming of independence to Papua New Guinea, all of Ansett's interests in the country were absorbed into the new national carrier Air Niugini in November 1973. Ansett, Qantas and TAA were Air Niugini's initial shareholders.

Victorian Air Coach

In order to establish intrastate services in Victoria, ATI in March 1960 purchased the route network previously operated by Southern Airlines and established its own new operator, Victorian Air Coach.

Southern Airlines had been incorporated in late 1954 as an offshoot of Goulburn Valley Air Services and after a battle to gain the necessary operating licences (due to objections from the Victorian Railways) began serving the Melbourne-Balranald (NSW) route in May 1955 using Avro Ansons and subsequently de Havilland Doves. Services within Victoria were added along with flights to Flinders Island, King Island, Launceston and Adelaide.

Two de Havilland Herons were added to the fleet in 1958, these mainly to counter strong opposition from Ansett-ANA which had decided to compete on some routes. Despite attempts to raise capital through shares issues and to attract subsidies, Southern was losing heavily and in financial trouble by the second half of 1958. Staff were put off and services cut until finally, in November 1958, the airline stopped flying.

Negotiations for the sale of Southern Airlines and its route licences to Ansett Transport Industries were immediately started and on 22 December 1958 Southern's shareholders agreed to accept the £30,000 ($60,000) that was offered. The deal was not completed until March 1960.

Ansett's Victorian Air Coach began operations in December 1961 using DC-3s, six of which flew with the airline at various times over the next few years. Operations ceased in August 1966 and the airline's services were absorbed into Ansett-ANA's network.

MacRobertson Miller

Another of the pioneering regional operators to fall into Ansett's hands in the years after the ANA takeover was Western Australia's MacRobertson Miller Airlines, a direct descendent of the Commercial Aviation Co established in South Australia in 1919 by former Australian Flying Corps pilot Horrie Miller and his business partner Arthur Kennedy. Commercial operated a variety of types including the Armstrong Whitworth FK.8, Avro 504K, de Havilland DH.9 and Bristol Fighter, the aircraft used mainly for joyflights and charters. Some scheduled airline services were briefly flown from Adelaide to towns in the St Vincent's Gulf and Spencer Gulf areas using the FK.8 and a Curtiss seaplane.

Looking to expand his operation, Miller in 1927 made contact with MacPherson Robertson – known as 'Mac' Robertson – of the famous MacRobertson confectionary empire. Miller proposed the formation of an airline with Robertson's financial assistance and he agreed, MacRobertson Miller Aviation (MMA) starting operations from Adelaide in May 1928 using a de Havilland DH.9 and flying to several points in South Australia.

The need to generate more cashflow in the depressed early 1930s prompted the company to tender for the Perth-Daly Waters section of the newly established Empire Air Mail route. To the industry's great surprise it won, defeating the highly fancied and well established West Australian Airways by severely undercutting its prices.

MacRobertson Miller Aviation therefore became a Western Australian operator from October 1934, its fleet of three de Havilland Dragons flying from Perth to Daly Waters via 13 points in between. De Havilland DH.86s

How can both airlines be the same?

We've got Susan Jones

Twenty-two-years-old Susan is an Ansett-ANA air hostess, 1967 model. She's the result of everything we've learned in over 30 years about the gentle art of caring for people who fly.
It's her charm and know-how that win people. She knows how to serve a gin and tonic, stop a nose-bleed, massage a bruised ego, distract children, quietly put a pillow under your head,

light your cigarette, hand you your paper — and how to say the word that cheers after you've had one hell of a day.
Susan knows how to make flying time fly. Will she be on your flight? We have lots of Susan Joneses. No matter which one is watching over you, you'll get the message:

ANSETT-ANA
CARES FOR YOU ALL THE WAY

The 'We've Got Susan Jones' advertising campaign of the late 1960s was a very successful one for Ansett-ANA, although in truth, there was very little difference between the two domestic airlines as the heavy regulation under which they operated was intended to keep them the same. We like the bit where it says: 'She knows how to.... light your cigarette'. How times have thankfully changed!

and Lockheed L.10 Electras were later added, the latter serving the airline throughout World War II before DC-3s were obtained in late 1945. Eight DC-3s eventually joined the airline along with Avro Ansons.

MacRobertson Miller teamed up with ANA to establish the Air Beef Scheme in November 1948, an innovative and successful concept designed reduce the time taken to move beef carcasses from remote parts of the state to the markets in major towns. Subsidised by both the Federal and State Governments, the scheme was successful and profitable for all concerned – the airlines, the cattle growers and the market operators. The Air Beef Scheme continued until 1960, by which time ANA had been taken over by Ansett. MMA would shortly follow.

MMA continued to grow in the 1950s and 1960s, gradually establishing a vast network across Australia's biggest state with contracts to provide air services to mines and other outback locations a substantial part of the business. By 1960 MMA's fleet comprised one Fokker Friendship, six DC-3s and a de Havilland Dove and services had expanded into the Northern Territory.

Some corporate reorganisation and expansion had also occurred in the interim with the formation of MacRobertson Miller Airlines in August 1955, the slightly revised name resulting from the merger of the original MMA and Perth based Airlines (WA) Ltd which was itself a pioneer operator dating back to 1935.

By the early 1960s MMA was in need of a capital injection for expansion and a fleet upgrade. The MacRobertson company (which held 62% of MMA's shares) was also looking to raise some extra cash at the time and wanted to sell its holding in the airline. It firstly approached the Commonwealth Government with a proposal that TAA take it over. As TAA was not allowed to operate intrastate services this left Ansett Transport Industries as the only viable alternative. After a period of negotiation it was announced in April 1963 that ATI had acquired 70% of MMA's shares and therefore had control of the company.

MMA's fleet further expanded after the Ansett takeover and by 1966 comprised four Friendships, eight DC-3s, one Douglas DC-4 freighter, one Dove and one Piaggio P.166. Two Viscounts were used in 1968-69 under the 'MMA Jetstream Service' banner.

Ansett took full control of MMA in November 1968 and its name was changed again to MacRobertson Miller Airline Services. The airline made some history in September of the following year when it introduced Australia's first intrastate jet airliner service with the Fokker F28 Fellowship, VH-MMJ flying Perth-Port Hedland and return. The F28 became an important part of the MMA fleet for many years and was joined by the BAe 146 from April 1985.

Unlike most of Ansett's regional subsidiaries, MMA was allowed to keep its famous old name for some time after being

The Piaggio P.166 served as a feederliner with several Ansett regional subsidiaries. P.166B Portofino VH-ASA is shown here in May 1968 in Airlines of South Australia colours. (Terence Ellis)

taken over but that changed in July 1981 when it became the far less evocative Airlines of Western Australia. This change was wholly unacceptable to most 'Westralians' who had become rather attached to 'their' MMA. The name changed again to Ansett WA in November 1984. That was the final incarnation of an airline that even then could trace its lineage back over more than six decades because in July 1993 it was absorbed into the overall operations of Ansett Australia.

Into The Jet Age

The next step in the growth of both Ansett-ANA and TAA was inevitably the transition to jets. Under the terms of the 1961 Airlines Agreement Act they had been barred from ordering jets before 18 November 1962 and operating them before 1 July 1964. These limitations were imposed partly in the interests of ensuring the airlines had the necessary traffic and infrastructure to support jet operations and partly due to concerns about Melbourne's Essendon Airport, which had not been developed at a pace suitable for modern air transport operations.

When Ansett-ANA and TAA did order their first jets an upgrade of Essendon had to be undertaken, this involving extending the east-west runway by 60 metres (200 feet) – which left it still barely adequate – and strengthening it as well as widening and strengthening taxiways plus smoothing out some bumpy parts of the north-south

runway. By then, Essendon's days as Melbourne's main airport were running out because plans for the construction of a new Melbourne Airport at Tullamarine were well underway. Approval to start work on the new airport was given in November 1962 and both Ansett and TAA formally transferred their operations to 'Tulla' in June 1971.

On 19 November 1962 – the day after the jets ordering restriction expired – the Federal Government announced that Ansett-ANA and TAA had been given approval to order an initial two Boeing 727-100s each for delivery in the second half of 1964. All of the available short-medium range jets available to the market had been evaluated including the smaller Sud Caravelle and BAC One-Eleven. Eventually, the choice came down to the 727 or de Havilland (Hawker Siddeley) Trident, both of these medium sized trijets capable of seating (typically) 114 passengers in two classes in the case of the 727 and about 90 in the Trident.

There is no doubt that the 727 was the better choice for Australian operations as it carried more payload than the Trident, had greater development potential, comparable operating economics and more modest airfield requirements.

It is one of the great tragedies of the British aircraft industry that the Trident was not built as it had been originally intended, and that is as a direct competitor

A nice Boeing portrait of Ansett-ANA 727-77 VH-RME before its delivery to Australia. The Seattle manufacturer did very well out of Australia's domestic airlines in the decades that followed, selling them more 727s, 737s and 767s. (Boeing)

ANSETT GENERAL AVIATION

One of Ansett Transport Industries' most successful businesses was Ansett General Aviation (AGA), the Australian distributor for the Piper range of light aircraft. AGA operated during the boom years of light aircraft deliveries from the mid 1960s through to the late 1970s, and was responsible for increasing Piper's presence and sales penetration in the Australian market during that time.

Brisbane based Commerce International was the Piper agent until February 1965 when the newly established Ansett General Aviation Ltd was appointed the new distributor. The appointment prompted litigation, Commerce International instigating legal action against Piper and ATI while the Association of Commercial Flying Organisations of Australia (ACFO) criticised the move on the grounds it would lead to greater use of light aircraft on third level and supplementary airline routes.

The ACFO claims were easily refuted and Reg Ansett eliminated the Commerce International problem by buying the company! Ansett General Aviation formally began business from its Bankstown Airport (Sydney) headquarters on 3 May 1965 and the Piper brand never looked back in Australia.

Apart from selling its South Australian division to Williams Refrigeration in April 1973 (which traded as Williams General Aviation with the Piper dealership for South Australia and the Northern Territory), AGA continued largely unchanged until 1983. In that year and after a series of ownership moves, Pacific Aviation was established to take over the general aviation interests of Ansett, Stillwell Aviation, Consolidated Press and Aviall Australia.

The new company continued to sell Piper aircraft as well as conduct charter and corporate operations, provide maintenance, engineering and spare parts services and operate general aviation terminals at Essendon, Sydney and Brisbane Airports through its Flight Facilities division.

Pacific Aviation became a wholly owned subsidiary of Ansett Transport Industries in December 1992 but was later disposed of.

Ansett General Aviation established a Helicopter Division in the late 1970s to distribute the Aerospatiale range, especially the new AS.350 Ecureuil (Squirrel) 5-6 seater, a serious contender for the market hitherto dominated by the Bell JetRanger. This part of AGA didn't last long – it was dismantled after the TNT-News takeover of Ansett in early 1980 and the Aerospatiale distributorship disposed of. According to industry legend, this happened because Sir Peter Abeles didn't like helicopters!

From a business point of view it was a shame, because the move out of helicopters coincided with the massive and long lasting worldwide slump in light aircraft sales which affected all manufacturers including Piper. At the same time, sales of the Squirrel were growing....

to the 727 but with the advantage of being ready for service earlier. Even as metal was being cut on the first aircraft, launch customer British European Airways insisted on a smaller, less flexible aircraft with lower weights and reduced range. To its later regret, De Havilland's board acquiesced to BEA's demands and the resulting aircraft was considerably less capable than had been intended.

At a stroke, a huge market was handed to Boeing and the 727, that aircraft going on to become the most commercially successful jet airliner of all time until surpassed by Boeing's own 737. The irony was that – entirely predictably – when it put the Trident into service BEA immediately began complaining that it was too small and had insufficient range!

The 727 had one other advantage as far as an Australian purchase was concerned, the fact that Boeing already had a strong and expanding presence in Australia through Qantas, which had been flying 707s since 1959.

In line with Boeing practice, the 727s for Ansett-ANA and TAA had their own customer identification designation suffixes, this number applying to all Boeings purchased by a given customer over the years regardless of type. In the case of Ansett-ANA, its new jets were 727-77s (TAA's were -76s) while subsequent examples include the 727-277, 737-277, 737-377 and 767-277.

Delays and Extra Costs

Even though approval to purchase the 727s was given in November 1962, it was February 1963 before contracts were signed with Boeing.

Delays were caused by the Department of Civil Aviation and its requirement that an upper limit of 109 passengers be imposed on the aircraft in Australian service (due to emergency exit limitations) and that they be accommodated in seats capable of absorbing 12g rather than the standard 9g. The DCA had one other rather extraordinary requirement – that the seats be facing backwards! Other required and requested modifications mainly related to operational equipment.

The airlines agreed to install the 12g seats but not to the direction in which they were pointing. As for the seating limitation, additional emergency exits were incorporated and the 727s' seating limit was raised to 140 in an all economy, high density configuration. All these modifications (including those specified by the airlines themselves) added more than 25% to the price of a standard 727.

Another additional cost the airlines had to bear with the 727 was an archaic tax, a 7.5% import duty which applied to all non British aircraft under the terms of the British-Australia Trade Agreement of 1957. This stated that the duty had to be paid if an aircraft was purchased instead of an equivalent British type, and the influential pro British forces within Federal Cabinet led to the decree that the Trident constituted an equivalent British type. The duty therefore had to be paid on the 727s, adding about £155,000 ($310,000) to the price of each one. One Minister – James Killen – even went as far as saying that the airlines should be compelled to buy British! And this was 1962, not 100, 50 or even 25 years earlier....

The jet age finally arrived on the Australian domestic airline scene in October 1964 with the simultaneous and carefully orchestrated delivery of the first Boeing 727-100s to both Ansett-ANA and TAA. 727-77 VH-RME was Ansett's first and flew its inaugural revenue service between Melbourne and Sydney on 2 November 1964. (Terence Ellis)

The government applied the same duty to Ansett – ANA's and TAA's Douglas DC-9s when the first of the them arrived in 1967, citing the BAC One-Eleven as an 'equivalent British type', but sensibly, that decision was reversed.

727 Into Service

Under the terms of the Airlines Agreement Act, any new aircraft purchased by Ansett-ANA and TAA should be ordered by both airlines simultaneously, arrive in Australia simultaneously and enter service simultaneously. The arrival and entry to service of the Boeing 727 adhered to these dictums.

The big day was 16 October 1964 and the place Essendon Airport. As it was impossible to have the first new 727s for both airlines arrive *exactly* simultaneously they touched

down at Essendon a few minutes apart after their delivery flights from Seattle with Ansett-ANA's VH-RME having the honour of leading the way ahead of TAA's VH-TJA.

After conducting demonstration flights to Adelaide, Brisbane, Canberra, Perth and Sydney both airlines began revenue services with their new jets on 2 November 1964, operating Melbourne-Sydney initially and then expanding services to Adelaide, Brisbane and Perth within a few days.

Ansett-ANA's second 727 (VH-RMF) entered service in November 1964 and approval was given to buy two more, these arriving in August 1965 (VH-RMD) and August 1966 (VH-RMR). Two other 727-100s – both of them 727-77C convertibles – were added to the fleet in 1969-70.

The Boeing 727 was a substantial success in Australian service, providing many air travellers with their

The second phase of Australia's transition to jets on its mainline domestic routes started in April 1967 with the delivery of the first Douglas DC-9s, once again for both Ansett-ANA and TAA. The first Ansett DC-9-31 was VH-CZB, 11 more followed between then and November 1971. (Eric Allen)

An Ansett-ANA DC-9 at a soggy Essendon, this photograph taken shortly after the first aircraft arrived in 1967. (George Canciani)

Comparing Ansett-ANA's performance in 1965 (excluding the regional subsidiaries) with TAA in the same period reveals some interesting figures and also underlines the importance of regional operations to the overall picture. The TAA figures (in parenthesis) do, however, include operations in Papua New Guinea except where noted: passengers flown 1,582,827 (TAA 1,786,436); hours flown 93,103 (96,640); miles flown 21,500,496 (22,042,555); average passenger load factor 65.3% (66.4%, mainland services only); and freight carried 37,306 tonnes (28,247 tonnes).

More Jets

With orders for the Boeing 727 placed, the time had come for both Ansett-ANA and TAA to consider the purchase of a second, smaller jet airliner type to supplement the 727 and replace the Vickers Viscount for use on 'thinner' routes and at times of lower passenger numbers on the main trunk routes. The introduction of such an aircraft would allow jet services to destinations such as Alice Springs, Launceston, Mount Isa and others, places which couldn't handle 727s because of runway restrictions.

Serious investigations began in 1963 and covered the BAC One-Eleven (which first flew in August 1963) and the Douglas DC-9 which was scheduled to fly in early 1965. The Caravelle was not seriously considered, nor was the forthcoming Boeing 737 which was not launched until February 1965.

The One-Eleven and DC-9 were both twinjets with their engines mounted at the rear, following the trend established by the Caravelle. The One-Eleven was able to seat about 65 passengers in two classes or 74-89 in an all economy class arrangement. The DC-9 was originally offered in two models: the basic Series 10 and the Series 20 with more powerful engines, increased weights and improved payload-range performance. Both had seating capacities similar to the One-Eleven.

Even though the One-Eleven would be available earlier than the DC-9, the American aircraft had one notable advantage and that was its powerplant – the same Pratt & Whitney JT8D turbofan that was fitted to the Boeing 727. From an engineering point of view both aircraft were regarded as equally proficient and operating economics were much of a muchness, but the DC-9-20 held the advantage when it came to operational parameters, especially payload-range and airfield performance.

Neither really had the passenger capacity that would be needed but in March 1964 Ansett-ANA announced a letter of intent to purchase six DC-9-20s. TAA didn't announce its order until April 1965 for the same model but within a few weeks both revealed they had changed their order to cover six of the stretched DC-9-30 which could carry up to 25 more passengers than the Series 10 and 20.

first taste of flying by jet and giving the airlines reliability, speed and profitability. Both Ansett and TAA went on to buy many more later model 727s to ply the major trunk routes. Ansett eventually operated 27, including freighters and short term leases and did not retire its last example until April 1997.

A Powerful Force

By the mid 1960s Ansett Transport Industries was a very large Australian corporation with a wide range of interests and activities. The group owned seven separate airline operations, had 59,000 shareholders and generated revenues of £46,500,000 ($93.0m) in the 1964-65 financial year. Apart from its airline interests, ATI had continued to expand its other businesses including road transport, hotels and resorts, manufacturing, trading and television stations.

Airline operations were the biggest part of ATI with 60% of the total investment in the company tied up in that area. In return, they earned 65% of ATI's total revenue in the 1964-65 financial year. The Ansett airlines served about 270 centres in Australia and Papua New Guinea and the combined networks covered some 92,000 kilometres or approximately 60% of Australia's total domestic network. The combined fleet totalled 118 aircraft ranging from the single engined Cessnas operated by Ansett-MAL to Ansett-ANA's 727s.

In 1965 the Ansett group of airlines carried 2.3 million or 53.5% of the 4.3 million passengers who flew on scheduled Australian domestic flights and uplifted 47,700 tonnes of freight, or 58.7% of the domestic total. Air freight had become an increasingly important part of Ansett-ANA's activities to the point where several Douglas DC-4s and DC-3s were dedicated to that task and two DC-4s had been converted to Carvair configuration with an entirely new nose section which incorporated a large swinging door at the front to allow straight-in loading. A third Carvair would be converted in 1968.

The Australian DC-9s incorporated some modifications to make them more suitable for local operations – low pressure tyres, an auxiliary power unit etc – while both airlines went to considerable trouble to ensure the DC-9s were readily compatible with the 727's cabin styles and equipment so as to create as far as was possible a 'seamless' transition from one type to the other for passengers and cabin crews.

Deliveries were originally scheduled to start in late 1966 but Ansett-ANA wanted this delayed due to a downturn in traffic. As it happened, the inability of Pratt & Whitney to sustain the planned delivery rate of its civil engines as the needs of the Vietnam War grew and demanded more military powerplants resulted in the JT8D program falling behind schedule and delaying the delivery of all DC-9s at the time.

DC-9-31 VH-CZB at Essendon in November 1969, immediately before its livery changed from 'Ansett-ANA' to 'Ansett Airlines of Australia'. The change had officially occurred a year earlier but aircraft had to wait for heavy maintenance before they were repainted. (Terence Ellis)

Delivery and Problems

The first DC-9s for TAA (VH-TJJ) and Ansett-ANA (VH-CZB) arrived at Essendon Airport on 13 April 1967, touching down in that order because it was TAA's turn, remembering Ansett had the honour when the 727s arrived. Such were the petty details of the Two Airlines Policy! Unfortunately for both, this arrival date precluded putting the new airliners into service for the Easter holiday period, as had been hoped.

Both Ansett-ANA and TAA inaugurated DC-9 services on 17 April 1967 between Sydney and Melbourne, the list of destinations expanding as more aircraft arrived. The first order for six aircraft had been filled by July 1969 by which time the purchase of a further six for each airline had been approved. These were delivered between February 1970 and November 1971.

Unfortunately, the DC-9's early Australian service was marred by a union dispute, courtesy the militant Australian Federation of Airline Pilots. The union decided it wanted the aircraft ordered by both Ansett-ANA and TAA to have a three crew cockpit – two pilots and flight engineer – where the aircraft was specifically designed to carry two pilots only, standard practice on the new generation of short-medium range jets.

The DC-9 had already been in Australian service for nearly a year when the AFAP demanded that existing two crew DC-9 operations would end at the beginning of March 1968 and the fleet would be grounded. Even though the aircraft had no provision for a third cockpit crew member, the union wanted an engineer sitting in the jump seat, along for the ride as a passenger with no duties to perform.

Continuing the great Australian airline tradition of being intimidated by the union, Ansett-ANA immediately surrendered to its demands, while TAA held firm and found its DC-9s grounded on the appointed day as a result and remaining so for six weeks. The AFAP added to TAA's woes by also forcing the grounding of the airline's 727s and Electras for a couple of days, leaving the market temporarily open to Ansett. After considerable acrimony between the two airlines, the union and a High Court action, the AFAP's demands were formally rejected and the DC-9s carried on operating with a two man crew just as they did everywhere else in the world.

The DC-9 was another good choice for the Australian market and complemented the Boeing 727 nicely. It proved to highly reliable with a very low proportion of delayed departures caused by mechanical problems. Ansett kept its DC-9s in service until June 1982 when they were replaced by the Boeing 737-200, while TAA's last aircraft wasn't retired until late 1989, replaced by 737-300s.

FLEET SUMMARY – March 1961

Ansett-ANA: 3 Lockheed L.188A Electra; 5 Vickers Viscount 810; 5 Vickers Viscount 700; 9 Fokker F27 Friendship; 2 Douglas DC-6B; 2 Douglas DC-4; 12 Douglas DC-3; 1 Convair CV-440.
Airlines of New South Wales: 3 Fokker F27 Friendship; 8 Douglas DC-3.
Ansett Flying Boat Services: 2 Short Sandringham.
Airlines of South Australia: 2 Convair CV-440; 4 Douglas DC-3.
Ansett-MAL: 5 Douglas DC-3.
Queensland Airlines: 1 Fokker F27 Friendship; 3 Douglas DC-3.
Helicopter Division: 1 Bristol Sycamore, 4 Bell 47J Ranger.

FLEET SUMMARY – January 1966

Ansett-ANA: 3 Boeing 727-100; 3 Lockheed L.188A Electra; 6 Vickers Viscount 810; 5 Vickers Viscount 700; 3 Douglas DC-6B; 5 Douglas DC-4; 4 Fokker F27 Friendship; 2 ATEL Carvair; 10 Douglas DC-3; 1 Piaggio P.166. On order: 1 Boeing 727-100; 3 Douglas DC-9-30.
Airlines of New South Wales: 4 Fokker F27 Friendship; 4 Douglas DC-3.
Ansett Flying Boat Services: 2 Short Sandringham.
Queensland Airlines: 1 Fokker F27 Friendship; 2 Douglas DC-3; 1 Piaggio P.166B.
Airlines of South Australia: 2 Convair CV-440; 4 Douglas DC-3; 1 Piaggio P.166B.
MacRobertson Miller Airlines: 4 Fokker F27 Friendship; 8 Douglas DC-3; 1 Douglas DC-4; 1 DH Dove; 1 Piaggio P.166.
Ansett-MAL: 11 Douglas DC-3; 4 Piaggio P.166; 2 Bristol Freighter; 1 DHC Caribou; 7 Cessna 185 Skywagon; 4 Cessna 336 Skymaster; 1 Cessna 206; 1 Cessna 182.
Helicopter Division: 1 Bell 47G; 7 Bell 47J Ranger; 1 Sikorsky S-61N.

CHAPTER EIGHT

LIFE IN THE COMFORT ZONE

On 1 November 1968, Reg Ansett extracted his final revenge on Australian National Airways when the 'ANA' suffix was dropped from his airline's name. From that date, the airline's trading name became Ansett Airlines of Australia, a division of Ansett Transport Industries (Operations) Pty Ltd.

A new livery accompanied the change, this featuring a red and black cheatline, white fuselage top and red tail with a stylised 'A' logo within a white circle. Ansett's subsidiary airlines adopted the same livery, creating uniformity of image and colour which was used on all their literature, ticketing, advertising and promotional material in what was an early Australian example of what would these days be called corporate 'branding'.

By the end of the 1960s Ansett Transport Industries was one of Australia's largest and best known privately owned industrial conglomerates with its wide range of activities. Reg Ansett had himself become a very famous Australian with a high profile through the activities of his companies. Despite this, the general public got to see very little of the man himself as he generally shunned media attention.

He was knighted in 1969 to become Sir Reginald Ansett KBE and would preside over ATI for another decade before the winds of change inevitably came to what was a very conservative company in the old style. ATI's reluctance to adopt the more dynamic and higher risk approach to business which began to emerge in the corporate world from the mid 1970s would eventually cost Reg Ansett control of his airline. Whether or not this new way of doing business was better than the old methods is a matter for debate....

'His' airline? By the early 1970s Sir Reg's personal stake in ATI was down to about 1% but Ansett Airlines was very firmly seen to be his company by employees, the public and Sir Reg himself. His influence was all pervading and would remain so for some years yet.

A threat would appear in 1972 when TNT's Peter Abeles attempted a takeover which was thwarted by the interference of Victorian Premier Henry Bolte (see below) TNT emerged from that with a substantial

shareholding nevertheless, setting the scene for a complete takeover in conjunction with Rupert Murdoch's News Corp later in the decade. By then, Ansett Airlines was ripe for change, as was the whole Australian airline industry.

Both Ansett and TAA operated in largely comfortable circumstances throughout the 1970s with the Two Airline Policy ensuring generally good returns and no possibility of further competition on Australia's domestic trunk routes. With parallel scheduling, virtually identical fleets and regulated high fares, there was little incentive for either airline to go out of their way to provide a superior service for passengers. The airlines were happy to leave well enough alone.

For passengers there was little chance to seek out lower fares. The high prices of domestic tickets became more obvious from the early 1970s as international fares began to come down, largely as a result of the Boeing 747 coming into service. The 747's high seating capacity resulted in lower seat-mile costs for international airlines and therefore the opportunity to offer lower fares. This in turn stimulated substantial growth in passenger numbers on international services.

For Australian domestic passengers there was no such incentive and if they wanted to fly they had no choice but to pay the high fares. It was often noted at the time that it was considerably cheaper to fly to an overseas destination like Hong Kong than it was to travel from Sydney to Perth.

The Two Airline Policy's long term future seemed officially assured in August 1972 when the Minister for Civil Aviation (Senator Robert Cotton) announced the government had decided to extend it for a further five years until November 1977 with five years notice of termination. This extension of the Two Airlines Agreement contained changes, some of them significant and some routine.

Those with implications for Ansett included: that ATI was to publish accounts dealing with its airline interests; an as yet undefined limit on foreign ownership of ATI

Ansett's major new fleet acquisition during the 1970s was the stretched Boeing 727-200, which became the airline's primary workhorse until well into the 1980s. The first of an initial batch of six 727-277s arrived in February 1973. VH-RMZ – pictured here – was the last of that group, delivered in November 1974. (Geoff Wilkes)

was to be implemented; TAA would be able to more effectively compete with Ansett and could go into business ventures with road transport and accommodation operators; some reductions in parallel scheduling of air services was proposed; and there was encouragement for the airlines to introduce lower 'tourist promotion' fares. Some of these changes were implemented and others not.

A change of government in late 1972 saw Labor briefly take over from the Liberal party which had been in power for 17 years but this had little effect on the Two Airline Policy. Regardless of the details and who was in power, it was here to stay for the foreseeable future and remained the dominant influence on the industry throughout the 1970s.

Fleet Changes

Just as the entry to service of the Vickers Viscount and Lockheed Electra turboprops had signalled the end of the use of piston engined airliners on Australia's major domestic routes, so did the introduction of jets – Boeing

727s in 1964 and Douglas DC-9s in 1967 – mark the end for the turboprops.

In Ansett's case the Viscounts were the first to go with the majority of the remaining fleet removed from service in 1968-69. The last Ansett Viscount service was flown in August 1970 and the Electra was retired from passenger operations in May 1971, just one month before both Ansett and TAA moved their Melbourne operations from the now wholly inadequate Essendon Airport to the new Tullamarine facility.

This wasn't the end of Ansett's association with the Electra, however, as all three were converted to L.188AF freighters during 1972 for use by the airline's expanding air freight business. A fourth Electra freighter – which had originally been built for American Airlines – was acquired in 1975 and remained in service for three years. The original Ansett trio of Electras kept flying as freighters with the airline until early 1984.

By the end of 1971 Ansett's mainline fleet comprised six Boeing 727-100s and 12 Douglas DC-9s. Six Fokker F28 jets were operated on regional services by MMA while about two dozen F27 Friendships were spread throughout the regional subsidiaries along with other smaller tyres. Two Convair CV-440s were retained for operation by Airlines of South Australia until May 1973, 11 years after the last of the others had been disposed of by Ansett-ANA.

Twelve DC-3s remained (mostly operating in New Guinea) as did a single DC-4 freighter plus three Carvair conversions. The DC-4 would be out of service by 1973 and

Another significant purchase was the Fokker F28 Fellowship, Australia's first intrastate jet airliner. MMA launched services between Perth and Port Hedland in September 1969 with an F28-1000 leased from Fokker, the first of the airline's own F28s arrived June 1970.

Ansett took delivery of 12 727-277s between February 1973 and September 1980, these later augmented by four long range models. Pictured here (top to bottom) are: VH-RMX (delivered July 1974), VH-RMN (May 1979) and VH-RMK in December 1976. (Jim Thorn & Rob Finlayson)

Ansett received its first of 12 Douglas DC-9-31s in April 1967, with deliveries continuing until November 1971. The earlier aircraft eventually received the new colour scheme. VH-CZK was Ansett's penultimate DC-9, delivered in July 1971. (Terence Ellis)

the last Carvairs in January 1974, while the final Ansett DC-3 to remain in service (VH-MMF) was retired in December 1974.

Another 1974 retiree was the Sandringham flying boat in September when the building of an airstrip on Lord Howe Island made Ansett Flying Boat Services and its aircraft redundant.

Enter The Workhorse

The next major fleet acquisition for both Ansett and TAA was the Boeing 727-200, a stretched and higher capacity version of the original 727-100 which had entered service with the Australian airlines in 1964. The 727-200 went on to become the primary fleet workhorse of both airlines over many years.

Boeing first approached Ansett-ANA and TAA about the 727-200 in July 1965 when a sales team visited

Australia. At that stage the new model was just one month away from being formally launched (the first aircraft flew in July 1967) but it was not entirely suitable for Australian operations in its original form.

It was able to carry 145 passengers in a typical two class arrangement (about 30 more than the 727-100) or up to 189 maximum, but at the expense of range. Subsequent development of the 727-200 Advanced (available from 1972) offered more powerful engines, increased operating weights and much improved payload-range performance. It was this version that the airlines ordered in December 1970 – initially four each – but formal approval for the purchase was not announced by the Federal Government until February 1972.

In the meantime, discussions had been conducted between Boeing and the Australian aerospace industry on

Ansett-MAL was renamed Ansett Airlines of Papua New Guinea in June 1968 and continued operating under that name until it was absorbed into Air Niugini in November 1973. Fokker F27-600 VH-FNM had previously been part of the Ansett-MAL fleet and was photographed at Sydney in April 1973 before being taken into the general Ansett fleet. (Geoff Wilkes)

After being withdrawn from passenger service, all three of Ansett's Lockheed Electras were converted to L.188AF freighters in 1972 and continued flying in that form for over a decade. A fourth Electra freighter was added to the fleet in 1975. The L.188AF was capable of carrying a payload of over 15 tonnes either palletised (as here) or bulk.

the subject of the local manufacture of some components for all 727s, not just the Australian ones. In January 1971 Boeing invited bids for the manufacture of wing ribs, rudders and elevators over a three year period.

Two months later Hawker de Havilland was announced the winner of a $1,564,000 contract to build an initial 50 shipsets of ribs and rudders. The company became the sole source of supply for these items. A separate contract worth $846,062 and covering 50 elevators was also awarded to HDH which in turn subcontracted work out to the Government Aircraft Factories (GAF) and the Commonwealth Aircraft Corporation (CAC). Further contracts were subsequently awarded while CAC also supplied galleys for the Australian aircraft.

A fall in traffic growth in 1972 resulted in Ansett and TAA both deferring delivery of their first 727-200s for a few months until early 1973. Ansett's first aircraft (VH-RMU) was delivered to the airline in the USA during November 1972 and immediately leased to United Airlines for use on a National Aeronautics and Space Administration (NASA) contract. The aircraft arrived in Australia on 19 February 1973 and entered revenue service seven days later.

Ansett's initial four 727-277s were delivered between then and July 1974, these followed by two more in November 1974, plus 'top up' orders for another six delivered in 1976 (1), 1978 (1), 1979 (2) and 1980 (2). An additional four long range models were delivered in 1981, these ordered in March 1980 as part of a $400m contract placed by Ansett's new owners (TNT and News Corp) which also included 12 737-200s and five 767-200s. This is discussed in the next chapter.

The arrival of the 727-200 triggered the gradual withdrawal of the 727-100 fleet over the remainder of the decade. The first to go were the convertible 727-77C VH-RMY (after only six years' service) and the purely passenger VH-RMR in June 1976. The remaining three passenger 727-77s followed in 1978-79 with only the convertible VH-RMS surviving into the new decade. It flew the last Ansett 727-100 revenue service on 29 January 1980 between Adelaide and Melbourne.

Signs of Change

The very fabric of Ansett Transport Industries changed forever on 21 March 1972 when large road transport company Thomas Nationwide Transport (TNT) under the chairmanship of Sir Peter Abeles gained 23.5% of its shareholding through the acquisition of shares previously owned by W R Carpenter Holdings Ltd and Boral Ltd. It was the beginning of the battle for control of the company which would eventually lead to it being jointly owned by TNT and Rupert Murdoch's News Corporation.

TNT wanted to make a bid for Ansett as part of Peter Abeles' plans to broaden his company's business base and eventually expand it into the global market. Two weeks after the Carpenters/Boral shares acquisition Sir Peter announced he wanted to go further by purchasing all the other ATI shares it did not own itself.

Sir Peter's actions caused ructions in the whole industry and to some in government even threatened the future of the Two Airline Policy. Committees were established, reports written, editorials published and complaints lodged by other businesses – especially in the road transport industry – who thought they would be disadvantaged by a TNT takeover of Ansett.

Aircraft types taken out of Ansett service during the 1970s included the Lockheed Electra (above left) in May 1971 (although it continued as a freighter) and the Vickers Viscount (above right) in August 1970. (Terence Ellis)

Reg Ansett was of course extremely unhappy about this encroachment on the affairs of his company by the ambitious but also extremely successful Sir Peter Abeles, who represented the 'new way' of business – thinking globally, acting aggressively with the demeanour of the entrepreneur and completely unafraid of the conservative business 'establishment' that had set the rules of the game for many years.

Ansett looked for help in his efforts to keep 'his' company out of the hands of the predator Abeles, but there had been a shift in attitude towards the man once regarded as the quintessential 'Aussie battler' by many. Many of the newspaper editorials reflected the growing feeling that Reg Ansett and his business had received enough favours from government already, especially through the protection offered by the Two Airline Policy.

In *Finance Week*, Max Newton wrote: 'His whole business is built on government favours of one kind or another.... Reg has taken the traditions of political patronage as the path to profit to even greater heights than yet attained....'

Sir Peter Abeles was politically astute with many friends in the right places, but so was Reg Ansett. He had learnt nearly 40 years earlier that it was much better to have the politicians on your side than against you. His nemesis in the early days of Ansett Roadways in the 1930s – then Victorian Attorney-General Robert Menzies

– has become a great ally in the 1950s when as Prime Minister he presided over Ansett's takeover of the doomed ANA and ensured the Two Airline Policy worked very much in Ansett's favour.

As for more local politics, Ansett had no greater 'mate' in 1972 than Victorian Premier Henry Bolte. This friendship was long standing and close, the pair regularly seen at the races together, a passion they shared.

It was now time for Henry Bolte to prove just what a good friend to Reg Ansett he was. In April 1972 the Victorian Parliament enacted the Select Committee (Ansett Transport Industries) Bill which denied ATI's other shareholders the right to dispose of their interests until after 30 November 1972. It could be strongly argued that this draconian legislation was unconstitutional but it was allowed to go through.

Further, legislation which prohibited any company registered in Victoria being taken over by a company registered in another state was invoked. TNT was registered in New South Wales, so that was that. Once again, the legality of this was extremely questionable and it was to no-one's great surprise that on his retirement from politics in 1973 Henry Bolte was appointed to the Ansett board.

TNT withdrew its offer to ATI's other shareholders on 27 April 1972 and for the moment restricted its interest

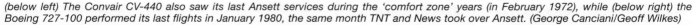

(below left) The Convair CV-440 also saw its last Ansett services during the 'comfort zone' years (in February 1972), while (below right) the Boeing 727-100 performed its last flights in January 1980, the same month TNT and News took over Ansett. (George Canciani/Geoff Wilkes)

to the original 23.5%. After some negotiation, it was agreed that Sir Peter and one other TNT representative would be allowed to join the ATI board but TNT's voting power would be restricted to 10%. This limitation was also to be applied to any other new shareholder and the appropriate changes to ATI's Memorandum and Articles of Association were approved by the Melbourne Stock Exchange in October 1972.

It had been an extraordinary series of events in Australian corporate history and although temporarily 'saving' Ansett, it marked the beginning of the end for the old regime at the company. When a further battle for control of Ansett by TNT, News Corp and the Bell Group erupted later in the decade there would be no benevolent politicians to help Reg Ansett out because his protagonists – Peter Abeles, Rupert Murdoch and Robert Holmes a Court – individually and collectively had considerably more political clout than 'RM'.

Seeing Out The '70s

Having survived – for the moment – the attentions of Sir Peter Abeles his takeover threats, Ansett Transport Industries was able to carry on the business of doing business relatively unmolested for most of the rest of the decade. Growth continued as did the acquisition of further non aviation interests including the purchase of a 50% shareholding in the Diners Club Australian franchise in 1974; more hotels were built; a 50% interest in pen and cigarette lighter manufacturer Biro Bic (Australia) was acquired in 1976; and Avis Rent-A-Car became a wholly owned ATI subsidiary in 1978. Not so successful was the 1976 purchase of a minority interest in finance company Associated Securities Ltd which collapsed two years later and caused ATI considerable financial distress (see breakout box 'The ASL Disaster').

In 1973 Ansett introduced its innovative Ansamatic (a contraction of 'Ansett' and 'automatic') computerised reservations system. A similar reservations system for ATI's hotels (called 'Ansotel') was introduced in 1977. These and Ansett's other computer systems introduced in the 1970s are discussed in the 'Ansett's Computers' breakout box.

The growth of Ansett Transport Industry's airline interests during the 1970s can be seen by comparing its operating statistics in 1977 with 1972. The figures include regional subsidiaries and have some apparent anomalies including a substantial drop in fleet numbers, the number of ports served, kilometres flown and the length of the unduplicated route network.

These reflect a certain amount of fleet rationalisation brought about by the introduction of generally larger jet aircraft, the retirement of older types, the ending of services in Papua New Guinea and the demise of Ansett Flying Boat Services. A decade earlier in 1966 Ansett-ANA and its subsidiaries had 120 aircraft of 21 different types of aircraft in its fleet; by 1977 this had reduced to 57 aircraft of just seven types.

Ansett's vital statistics for 1977 were (with 1972 in parenthesis): passengers carried 4,857,498 (3,794,778); average load factor 62.2% (62.2%); number of ports served 92 (157); total kilometres flown 66.861 million (74.157 million); unduplicated route network 63,440km (75,122km); available seating capacity 3,761 (3,277); freight and mail carried 73,812 tonnes (69,480 tonnes); passenger revenues $256.845m ($132.538m); freight and mail revenues $35.331m ($25.505m); total revenues $292.176m ($158.043m).

Sir Reginald Ansett, 13 February 1909 to 23 December 1981.

THE ASL DISASTER

As part of its ever increasing diversity into non aviation activities, Ansett Transport Industries in 1976 purchased a 30% interest in major Australian finance company Associated Securities Ltd (ASL) from the Royal Bank of Scotland. ATI's stake in the company later increased to 48.4%.

ASL operated in the consumer and industrial credit markets and was successful in both, returning useful profits. Buoyed by its core business success, it then decided to go into the speculative property business by buying large areas of land on the outskirts of the major cities, the idea being to develop them into housing estates.

Even though the anticipated housing boom in these areas would eventually come, unfortunately for ASL it was not when the company decided to enter the market. ASL somehow managed to achieve the impossible – it lost heavily on real estate investment.

The problem was that a housing slump hit the cities in the late 1970s, leaving ASL with substantial holdings on which it owed a very large amount of money and with little prospect of short term income.

It proved too much for ASL to absorb and the company was soon in serious trouble, desperately needing an influx of cash. Attempts to find new equity investors or a financial institution prepared to bail the company out failed, and in February 1979 ASL was placed in the hands of the liquidators.

ATI was forced to write off $20,000,000 in losses as a result of the fiasco which had seen both it and ASL overreach themselves.

International Aspirations

In October 1978 the Federal Government released details of its revised international aviation policy and although it contained the necessary policies to ensure Qantas would remain Australia's sole international carrier until 1981, it did promote discussion between the relevant ministers on the subject of Ansett and TAA undertaking some international flights under certain circumstances.

Two years earlier, the Tasmanian Government had proposed a service between the state and New Zealand and in November 1978 Qantas, Ansett and TAA were approached to discuss the proposal. In July 1980 Ansett and TAA were granted approval to operate Hobart-Christchurch services, Ansett's inaugural 'Southern Connection' flight on the route occurring on 3 December 1980 using Boeing 727-277 VH-RML.

TAA's first service on the same route was three days later and both airlines had to use Qantas flight numbers in order to comply with the laws governing international services as they then stood. Ansett operated the Hobart-Christchurch service on a weekly basis until March 1982.

Before the New Zealand services began, Ansett had on 18 April 1980 caused something of a ruckus among the legislators when it operated a charter flight from Townsville to Singapore via Darwin as a direct challenge to the Qantas monopoly as Australia's sole designated international carrier. The problem was that Qantas retained the rights to all international routes whether or not it was inclined to use them, which left several routes unserviced.

The flight to Singapore (using a 727-200) resulted from dissatisfaction with Qantas by the Queensland Tourist and Travel Corporation and was organised with its support. It was successful but also a one-off because applications by Ansett to develop the service into a regular scheduled one were refused. Nevertheless, the point had been made and many started asking why Qantas' monopoly should prevent others from operating on routes

The future of Ansett – Sir Peter Abeles of TNT Ltd and Rupert Murdoch of News Corporation Limited. By the first two weeks of the 1980s, their companies would own Ansett Transport Industries.

the designated flag carrier was not interested in servicing itself.

By the time of the Townsville-Singapore flight Ansett had new owners and a new approach to the way it would do business. It was the dawn of a new era not only for Ansett but for the Australian airline industry as a whole, an era that would see wholesale changes over the next decade.

The Australian National Airways name was removed in November 1968 when Ansett-ANA became Ansett Airlines of Australia, complete with a new livery including the famous stylised 'A' on the tail. (John Vogel)

Despite their age and attempts to replace them, 18 DC-3s belonging to Ansett airlines soldiered on into the 1970s, a handful in Papua New Guinea until as late as 1973-74. Airlines of NSW's VH-ANR was retired in July 1972, its final flight this special trip for enthusiasts over the south coast of the aircraft's home state. (Eric Allen)

ANSETT'S COMPUTERS

With computers now an integral part of our daily lives we think nothing of the power available even in the most basic machines. The functions of the airlines have long been computerised but there was a time only one-and-a-half generations ago when most administrative, stock, sales and logistical tasks had to be performed manually.

The early computers were monsters, big enough to fill a room and with power that couldn't come within light years of approaching today's cheapest home computers and laptops. There was a telling statistic that became available in the early 1990s when car manufacturer BMW released its then new 3-Series models. Its engine management system alone had more computing power within it than was available for the Apollo 11 moonlanding mission in 1969!

Ansett installed its first computer for accounting purposes in 1967. Since then, it has introduced a variety of systems for various functions associated with the running of its airlines and other businesses. Some of them are summarised below:

Ansamatic: Introduced 1973, an IBM based computer reservations system which was continually upgraded over the years.

Ansarite: Ansett became the first Australian airline to introduce computerised ticketing in 1976 with 'Ansarite' which could issue a printed ticket immediately a purchase was confirmed.

Ansaboard: A departure control system allowing passengers to get their seat allocations at a number of check-in points in the airport terminal. It also allowed multi-sector check-in and seat allocation and could automatically calculate the total average weight distribution on the aircraft based on standard weight allowances for men, women and children.

At the time of departure, Ansaboard calculated and printed the aircraft trim documents which showed the loaded weight of the aircraft and the amount of fuel on board. It also provided flight attendants with printed information on any passengers who might need special attention and sent information on passengers and cargo distribution to all the down route airports.

Ansotel: Introduced in 1977 and a real time hotels reservations systems linking about 500 establishments and allowing instant access to booking, tariff and hotel facilities information. Ansotel was based on the system used by British Airways and allowed customers to make single or multiple bookings.

Ansaquik: A comprehensive information database covering a wide variety of subjects including accommodation, time zones, weather reports, school holiday dates, public holidays, recreation facilities, tourist attractions, international airline connections and a myriad of other items.

Ansacare: A reservations system dedicated to the travel needs of disabled passengers; introduced 1982.

Ansamman: A parts/maintenance management system which provided instant appraisal of a quarter of a million aircraft parts to be serviced. Engineers in the workshop could make instant checks on spare parts stocks and reorder as necessary.

Ansarec: A system which controlled all the parts and components of the aircraft fleet, automatically tallying service hours and advising when service checks were due. At 250 hours before the due service date, Ansarec produced the worksheet necessary for the service and gave further reminders until action was taken and the component changed or overhauled. With systems like this in place it makes the inspection oversights which occurred with Ansett's Boeing 767 fleet in late 2000/early 2001 even more difficult to comprehend.

Ansavue: Introduced in 1971 with the opening of Melbourne's Tullamarine Airport, Ansavue was a computer controlled flight arrivals and departures information display for use in the airport terminals. When introduced it was the only colour display of its type in the world.

Ansatrace: Baggage which remained unclaimed throughout the network at the end of each day was recorded in the Ansatrace computer system, allowing any port trying to trace misplaced baggage access to the information.

Ansafads: The computer system which allowed the catering department to prepare sufficient meals for passengers. Information was provided to the caterers four times a day.

Ansafids: A flight monitoring system which allowed staff working in the airline's Central Operations control area to keep track of aircraft movements and therefore delays or changes to schedules. This allowed constant updates of arrivals and departure times to be issued.

FLEET SUMMARY – October 1975

Combined fleet (Ansett/ANSW/ASA/MMA): 6 Boeing 727-100; 6 Boeing 727-200; 12 Douglas DC-9-30; 5 Fokker F28 Fellowship; 4 Lockheed L.188AF Electra; 20 Fokker F27 Friendship; 2 DHC Twin Otter; 1 Sikorsky S-61N; 1 Bell JetRanger. On order: 2 Boeing 727-200; 4 Fokker F27-500 Friendship.

FLEET SUMMARY – June 1977

Ansett Airlines Of Australia: 3 Boeing 727-100; 7 Boeing 727-200; 12 Douglas DC-9-30; 12 Fokker F27 Friendship; 4 Lockheed L.188af Electra; 2 Sikorsky S-61n.
Airlines of New South Wales: 8 Fokker F27 Friendship.
Airlines of South Australia: 3 Fokker F27 Friendship.
MacRobertson Miller Airline Services: 5 Fokker F28 Fellowship; 1 DHC Twin Otter.

CHAPTER NINE

ANSETT – FULL STOP

By the early months of 1979, Ansett Transport Industries was in a slightly strange situation. On the face of it, things were rolling along as they had been for most of the past decade, but there were problems. The Associated Securities Ltd debacle (see previous chapter) had not only damaged the company's bottom line to a very substantial extent but also its image through the negative publicity which followed.

When the finance and investment company collapsed it took with it a large number of small investors, the 'mums and dads' who always suffer the most when a company like ASL fails. In addition, there was growing concern that Reg Ansett's 'old school' style of conservative management was becoming less appropriate for the times, when much more aggressive and higher risk management styles were coming to the fore. We were, after all, on the verge of the 1980s, the 'greed is good' decade.

Ansett's airlines accounted for just over half of ATI's total worth at the time and comprised the mainline Ansett Airlines of Australia plus regional subsidiaries Ansett Airlines of NSW, Ansett Airlines of South Australia and MacRobertson Miller Airlines. The huge diversity of the ATI group still existed in the form of hotels, resorts, road transport, television, insurance, general aviation, manufacturing, Avis Rent-A-Car, travel agents and numerous other activities.

The combined aircraft fleet comprised three Boeing 727-100s (with two of them about to be retired), nine 727-200s, 12 Douglas DC-9s, five Fokker F28-1000s, 26 Fokker F27s and four Lockheed Electra freighters. The airline was valued at just over $200,000,000.

The operating environment was healthy for Australia's two domestic airlines which between them carried 2,664,000 passengers in the January-March 1979 quarter, an increase of 2.3% over the previous year. The total number of domestic passengers carried for the full year (including regional operations) to the end of March 1979 reached a new high of 10,546,000 (up 5.6%) while freight carriage also grew by a similar rate.

There was an interesting new market segment which had been introduced in September 1978 – standby fares. These reduced rate fares were available – as their name implies – on a standby basis which meant that passengers had to hope there were seats still available on their flight at the time of departure. By the end of March 1979 the airlines between them were selling an average 4,400 standby tickets each week, 40% more than three months earlier.

Overall, the market was shared fairly evenly between Ansett and TAA with neither gaining any significant advantage over the other. With available capacity highly regulated this is not surprising and the market split would remain largely balanced until the end of the 1980s.

By now, TNT's interest in ATI had dropped from the 23.5% acquired in 1972 to 13.8%, but things were about to move in a very big way. At 69 years of age, Reg Ansett was about to embark on yet another battle to save his company, but this time he would be overwhelmed. TNT, the Bell Group, Ampol, Sir Reginald Ansett and his

(left) Ansett announced its largest ever order to date in March 1980, a $400m contract covering five Boeing 767-200s, four 727-200LRs and 12 737-200s. The 737s were delivered between June 1981 and June 1982, with VH-CZX the last of them. (right) Ringing the changes. A DC-9 and two 727-200s in the old livery at Melbourne with the new markings displayed by 727-277 VH-CZN. The new colour scheme was introduced in April 1981. The last DC-9 service was flown in June 1982, VH-CZL in the foreground was withdrawn six months before that. (Brian Chidlow & Rob Finlayson)

Boeing 727-277 VH-RMP on the ramp at Coolangatta in November 1980 with service vehicles in attendance. VH-RMP was only two months old at the time and was one of two new 'standard' 727-200s delivered in 1980, ahead of four 727-200LRs in 1981. (Geoff Wilkes)

'Friends of ATI' would be the major players, joined later by Rupert Murdoch's News Ltd.

The Battle for Ansett

The battle for control of ATI began in April 1979 when Western Australia's Bell Group – which already had considerable road transport interests and other activities – purchased 5.34% of ATI's shares. The Bell Group was headed by Robert Holmes à Court, a man who would figure prominently on the Australian business scene during the 1980s. In early July 1979 ATI's shares were valued at around $1.20 each; over the course of the next four months this would more than double as the contest played out.

The game of 'Monopoly with real money' started in earnest on 28 June 1979 when TNT began a relatively quiet push to increase its stake in ATI from the 13.8% held at the time. On 4 July, 150,000 ATI shares were traded at $1.22 each, these purchased by Bell and raising speculation that it and Holmes à Court were instigating a takeover of the company. He and Reg Ansett met and assurances were given that Bell wished to acquire no more than a 20% interest in ATI. This placated Reg Ansett, who saw an ally in Holmes à Court and a possible successor to take over control of ATI.

From then, large numbers of ATI shares were traded as owners of relatively small parcels took advantage of the increasing price. By the end of the first week of August they were around $1.80 each and the major shareholders were reckoned to be Bell (12.5%), TNT (19%), Ampol Petroleum (which had also been buying, 10% and rising) and Reg Ansett and his allies at just under 10% after indulging in a buying spree to help out.

This stopped Bell's purchasing program but the 'Friends of ATI' group didn't stop there. In mid August they purchased 20% of Ampol's own shares in what was a clever counter-attack engineered by Reg Ansett. The old dog wasn't quite finished with yet!

This move had the desired effect and ended Ampol's continued acquisition of ATI shares when on 15 August the oil company announced it would settle for the 20% it then held. TNT held a similar figure. In effect, a truce was called and it appeared Reg Ansett had once again been able to save his company from an unwanted takeover.

But then another major player entered the game and changed the whole scenario – News Corporation Ltd.

The Fourth Player

After a month of relative quiet, it was revealed on September 22 that News had acquired 4% of ATI at a price of $1.82 per share. Rupert Murdoch's interest in Ansett was not its airlines, hotels or any other travel and transport related businesses but its two television stations, ATV-0 in Melbourne and TVQ-0 in Brisbane with the former regarded as the prize catch. News was looking to make a big investment in the Australian television industry and only two months earlier had taken control of Channel 10 in Sydney.

News kept on buying ATI shares, pushing the share price up to $2.25 by the end of October. Concerned about this new and very powerful force in the battle for ATI and ongoing concerns about TNT, Reg Ansett took action, attempting to shore up his position by offering a deal to Robert Holmes à Court because he realised the shareholding owned by the Bell Group could hold the balance of power if News continued its thrust.

The basis of the plan was that Holmes à Court would succeed Reg Ansett as ATI's chief executive, Bell Brothers Holdings Ltd (which controlled the transport interests of the Bell Group) would have its activities merged into ATI and Holmes à Court would purchase the shareholding owned by TNT, News and Ampol. Both Peter Abeles and Rupert Murdoch were in general agreement with the plan but over the next month it began to unravel.

It was the ATI board which pulled the plug on 29 November 1979, citing the substantial financial commitment it would soon be facing to re-equip Ansett Airlines of Australia with widebodied aircraft and the fact that the deal was 'not in the best interests of shareholders'. There was also a bit of pride involved for Reg Ansett. It has been suggested that when it came down to it, he found it impossible to willingly hand control over to anyone and then go quietly away to retire.

There was also the fact that by then, Ansett had heard of meetings between the other three and had sensed a conspiracy. Holmes à Court, Abeles and Murdoch had been doing a little planning of their own and had met at Murdoch's property at Yass, near Canberra. At that meeting, Murdoch had sought the first right of refusal to purchase the Melbourne television station from whoever ended up with control of ATI.

To put all this into some kind of perspective, the primary motives of these three powerful businessmen *at that moment* must be remembered: Murdoch's was the acquisition of ATV-0 (media was the family business, after all), Abeles wanted to acquire a substantial portion of ATI as part of his global expansion plans for TNT, and Holmes à Court realised that his ATI shareholding was the key to the whole exercise and would be sought after. It therefore had the potential to deliver a quick and substantial profit.

After ATI's announcement that it would not proceed with the Bell deal things moved quickly. Holmes à Court sold his ATI shares to News for $2.50 each (and made an $11m profit) and then News purchased Ampol's shareholding bringing its total interest in ATI up to 47%. On 14 December 1979 News achieved its target shareholding of 50% and announced it would not go beyond that.

TNT was also on the move, the ATI board lifting the shareholding restrictions which had been imposed seven years earlier. TNT offered $2.25 per share and on 11 January 1980 the ATI board recommended that remaining small shareholders should accept TNT's offer. This was quickly done and by mid January Ansett Transport Industries was jointly owned by TNT and News Ltd.

Sir Peter Abeles and Rupert Murdoch were appointed joint managing directors of Ansett Transport Industries on 22 January 1980. Reg Ansett remained chairman until his death in December 1981 despite having sold his personal shares in ATI, but his role was now largely symbolic. The whole affair was desperately disappointing for Ansett, who had finally lost control over the airline he had established 44 years earlier.

As for the running of Ansett and its airlines, Rupert Murdoch took a back seat role to the flamboyant, cigar smoking former Hungarian 'truckie' Peter Abeles who very much became the 'hands on' public face of the new Ansett and the man responsible for fleet re-equipment and other major decisions. Abeles led the company with passion and flair in a way which created the impression he was loving every minute of it....

The Fokker F27 Friendship continued to be the mainstay of Australian regional operations throughout much of the 1980s, Airlines of NSW and its successor not operating its final F27 service until March 1988, although a couple of aircraft temporarily returned a few months later. Pictured here are (top to bottom): F27-500 VH-FCF of Airlines of NSW at Maroochydore in April 1980 in unavoidable 'Sunshine' holiday scheme; Airlines of NSW F27-500 VH-FCB at Coonabarabran in November 1980 still wearing the Ansett 'Alpha' scheme; and F27-500 VH-FCC of Air New South Wales at Moree in February 1982. (Geoff Wilkes)

A New Broom

There is no question that the TNT-News takeover of Ansett rejuvenated it, especially over the first decade when considerable amounts were spent on fleet upgrades and other acquisitions. Regional subsidiaries and affiliates were reorganised and rebranded (sometimes more than once); others were added to the stable and new initiatives such as the Ansett Golden Wing Club for business travellers were established. As the 1980s progressed there was an ever more pressing need to become better organised and more efficient as

VH-CZM, the first of Ansett's 12 Boeing 737-277s, delivered in June 1981. The 737-200 had a short life in Ansett service – by early 1987 all had been replaced by the larger, quieter and more fuel efficient 737-300.

deregulation of the Australian domestic airline industry became a matter of 'when', not 'if'.

One of the first jobs for Ansett's new owners was to instigate a fleet renewal program and what turned into a massive buying spree over the next few years began on 17 March 1980 when the airline's largest ever aircraft order was placed with Boeing, a $400m contract covering 12 737-200s, four 727-200LRs and five widebody twin aisle 767-200s. Attracting enormous publicity, the order showed that TNT-News meant business and were serious about revamping the airline in all its aspects in order to face the challenges that lay ahead.

The order raised a few eyebrows in financial circles as the deal that had been done with Boeing appeared to be very generous to Ansett. Of the total value of the order, $248m was provided by the US Export-Import Bank and this was approved in principle at the end of February

1980. The loan was at 'unusually low interest rates' according to the financial press and in May a US Senate Inquiry into its details was instigated. Australian Government approval for the purchase was given in August 1980 but it wasn't until April 1981 and following several investigations that final approval for the loan was given by the directors of the Import-Export Bank.

The four new 727-200LRs were the latest expression of the 'Advanced' 727 models which had been available to the market over the previous decade and took advantage of more powerful engines and increased weight options which allowed a full passenger load to be carried nonstop across the Australian continent (Sydney-Perth, for example) against the prevailing westerly winds. These were often of jetstream force and could produce headwinds of up to 100 knots (185km/h). TAA also ordered this version.

The Boeing 727-200LR was operationally significant for both Ansett and TAA as it could carry a full load of passengers east-west across Australia (Sydney-Perth, for example) against the prevailing and sometime very strong headwinds. Ansett's four 727-277LRs were delivered in June and July 1981; this is VH-ANF at Coolangatta in February 1985. (Geoff Wilkes)

(left) July 1981 was a significant month in the history of Australian domestic airline operations due to the arrival in Australia of TAA's first Airbus A300. Not only was the A300 Australia's first domestic widebody airliner, it also marked the first time TAA and Ansett had ordered different mainline equipment since the Two Airline Policy had been in place. (right) Ansett's widebody era began in June 1983 with the delivery of the first of five Boeing 767-277s. Due to union, these 767s were the only ones in the world fitted with a flight engineer's station, although this was removed years later. The first 767 delivery was delayed by seven months partly due to the crewing dispute and partly at Ansett's request to avoid a significant increase in capacity at the time of a downturn in traffic. VH-RMG was the fourth of the order, delivered in August 1983. (SW Collection & Geoff Wilkes)

The 727-200LRs were the first of the new order to arrive, VH-ANA delivered on 14 June 1981 and entering service (initially between Melbourne and Brisbane) on 20 June. The first Sydney-Perth service was flown on 29 June and all four had been delivered by the end of July.

Ansett's last early model 727-100 had meanwhile been retired in late January 1980, VH-RMS operating Adelaide to Melbourne for the last time on the 29th of that month, but in April 1981 Ansett announced it was going to undertake a $9 million interior refit of the 12 original 727-200 fleet plus repaint them in the airline's new livery. This was the biggest such undertaking in Australia thus far and the first refurbished aircraft returned to service in June.

The 737-200s were ordered to replace the similar number of DC-9s then in service and delivery of the first aircraft (VH-CZM) on 20 June 1981 occurred two months after the company's branding and livery was given a substantial revamp. Gone was the now familiar predominantly red livery with the stylised 'A' tail markings and in its place came an overall white scheme with a Southern Cross and Star of Federation tail logo. Gone, too was the trading name Ansett Airlines of Australia and in its place came simply the word 'Ansett.' – complete with the full stop.

Services with the 737-200 began on 1 July 1981 on a flight between Melbourne and Coolangatta. Seven of the 12 aircraft on order had been delivered by the end of 1981 with the remaining five following during the first half of 1982. Withdrawal of the DC-9 fleet began immediately the 737-200 entered service and was completed in June 1982 when VH-CZA operated the type's last revenue flight with Ansett when it flew from Launceston to Melbourne.

767 Ructions

Ansett's 767 order was important in the overall context of Australia's Two Airline Policy as it represented the first significant separation of equipment purchased by Ansett and TAA for main trunk route operations since the policy had come into full force 22 years earlier. TAA had ordered the Airbus A300 widebody in December 1979 and put the first aircraft into service in July 1981. The timing was unfortunate as the A300s arrived when the market was in one of its cyclical downturn periods and TAA found itself with an overcapacity problem. Ansett was potentially facing the same problem with its 767s.

(left) Airlines of South Australia could trace its origins back to 1927 and Guinea Airways which was taken over by Ansett in 1959. ASA ceased operations in June 1986 due to cost pressures with most of its routes taken over by Kendell Airlines. F27-600 VH-FNR was one of three Friendships in ASA's fleet at the end, this aircraft subsequently finding its way to Sweden where it was operated on freight services by Malmo Aviation on behalf of TNT. (right) The Fokker F28 played a significant role in the development of jet services to Australian rural and regional centres, 18 of them eventually seeing service with Ansett and several of its subsidiaries. F28-1000 VH-FKD was one of the first (delivered November 1970) and is seen here nearly 13 years later at Brisbane in Air New South Wales' 'canary' colour scheme. (Geoff Wilkes)

(left) The famous press conference held by Sir Peter Abeles at the Paris Airshow on 2 June 1985, where Ansett's joint managing director announced he was 'in a buying mood'. At this briefing, the Airbus A320 order was revealed and then it was off to lunch with Boeing! Less than three weeks later an order for 737-300s was also announced. (right) As MacRobertson Miller Airlines, Airlines of Western Australia (as it was renamed in 1981) was the pioneer Fokker F28 operator in Australia and eventually flew ten at various times from 1970. F28-1000 VH-FKG was purchased second hand in 1981 and went on to fly with Ansett WA, as the airline was again renamed in 1984.

The 767 order was not without its problems for Ansett, and once again the main cause was the aircrew union which decided to make life difficult by demanding the new Boeing have a flightdeck crew of three – two pilots and a flight engineer – even though the aircraft was specifically designed to have a cockpit crew of two with no flight engineer.

Once again, Ansett surrendered to the union's pressure. As a result, the initial five 767s were built with a flight engineer's station installed at considerable manufacturing and operating cost and were the only 767s in the world so equipped. Inside, Ansett's 767s were initially configured to carry 201 passengers (48 first class and 153 economy), giving the airline a mainline fleet sized in increments of approximately 50 seats starting with the 737-200 (about 100 seats) and progressing through the 727-200 (150) and finally the 767 with its 200 seats.

The whole issue of flightdeck crewing, the role of the flight engineer, and the general influence of the new technology cockpits which made the engineer unnecessary came to a head in late 1984 when both Ansett and TAA suffered strike action by the engineers which grounded their

Ansett Air Freight. While they're promising, we're delivering.

Everyone promises to deliver your parcel door-to-door overnight, just like Ansett Air Freight. But not everyone has the amazing ability to pick up and fly your parcel.

Ansett Air Freight has its own fleet of trucks and planes that make sure a parcel gets

where it's going. It's a service that runs 24 hours, every day. A service that ensures your parcel's safe passage anywhere in Australia.

So while everyone else is still trying to figure out how to get it there, we've probably already delivered it.

727s, 767s and A300s, albeit only for a few hours in the case of Ansett's 727s and 767s.

Sir Peter Abeles quelled the strike on behalf of Ansett by issuing a written promise that engineers would be used on any aircraft with more than 120 seats and would be guaranteed employment with the airline.

This was a big promise to make and also a potentially dangerous one, given the direction in which airliner flightcrew requirements was obviously heading. As it had done before with the DC-9, TAA resisted the temptation to make any promises and paid the price, finding the bulk of its fleet grounded for longer and suffering a substantial loss of business in the very busy period immediately before Christmas.

The delivery of Ansett's first 767-277 was delayed by seven months, partly due to the crewing dispute and partly at the airline's request so as to avoid the overcapacity problem. The first one (VH-RMD) arrived in Australia on 10 June 1983 (by which time the downturn was starting to reverse) and operated its first revenue service between Melbourne and Sydney on 27 June. Two others (VH-RME/F) had been delivered by then followed by VH-RMG in August 1983 and VH-RMH in September 1984.

(left) The 'fake Ansett' BAe 146-200 again, this time photographed at a damp Hatfield in May 1985 while being used as a trials aircraft. Note the aircraft now has Ansett WA titles and the registration G-WAUS. (right) Atmospheric night shot of a real Ansett WA BAe 146-200, in this case VH-JJP, the first one delivered in April 1985. (Eric Allen & BAe)

Not quite what it seems. Although Ansett and its subsidiaries eventually had 23 BAe 146s of various models, this -200 was not one of them. Carrying 'Air WA' markings and the Class B British registration G-5-146, this aircraft was painted up in Ansett colours for publicity purposes in August 1984 and appeared at that year's Farnborough Air Show with the new registration G-WAUS (for West Australian). The name Air WA was never used, Ansett WA adopted by the time the airline's first 146 was delivered in April 1985. This particular 146-200 (the eighth off the line) did eventually end up in Australia, with National Jet Systems in 1991, but never with Ansett. (BAe)

After evaluating the aircraft in service, TNT ordered three 146-200QT ('Quiet Trader') freighters for its expanding European air express business of which G-TNTA was the first, handed over in May 1987. Sir Peter Abeles was sufficiently impressed with the aircraft to place a 'commitment' for up to 72 BAe 146s, most of them freighters, in July 1987. The agreement prompted British Aerospace to open a second 146 production line at Woodford near Manchester, but in the end TNT took only 23 aircraft.

(left) Some Fokker F27s were painted in Ansett's new colours after April 1981, but most carried their regional airline liveries. F27-600 VH-FNO was one which did sport the new scheme for a time. (right) The Fokker 50 was a re-engined and modernised development of the ubiquitous F27 Friendship and Ansett was the launch customer, placing an initial order for 10 in February 1985. Twenty-two were eventually purchased by the group, most through US based partner Corsair which made the aircraft available for lease. Only 10 made it to Australia for service with Ansett, Air NSW, Ansett Express and Skywest from September 1987. VH-FNH was the seventh of the batch, delivered in February 1988. (Ansett & Geoff Wilkes)

Four additional second hand 767-200s were subsequently acquired from Britannia Airways and LAN-Chile in 1994-96. These were fitted with the standard two crew cockpit and Ansett's original five aircraft were 'deconverted' to the configuration they should have been in the first place after even the unions realised the flight engineer's day was past.

The nearly two years gap between TAA introducing its widebody Airbus A300s to service and the arrival of the first 767s caused some marketing problems for Ansett which it tackled aggressively. Advertising campaigns designed to denigrate TAA's A300s were launched with themes like 'Why Catch A Bus When You Can Fly a Boeing' predominating. Some ads hinted at passenger inconvenience caused by the A300's twin aisle arrangement, these conveniently forgetting that Ansett's forthcoming 767s would have the same configuration. When the 767s were delivered, the ads naturally emphasised the advantages of this layout!

The Ansett Air Show

Ansett's ordering spree continued into the 1980s with several significant purchases that would establish the airline's main fleet throughout the 1990s until its demise. It was an extraordinary time with orders placed for the Airbus A320, Boeing 737-300, BAe 146 and Fokker 50 in rapid succession as Sir Peter Abeles sought to find aircraft that would carry the airline through the inevitable deregulation of the Australian domestic market and beyond. The subsequent fleet mix – which included the Boeing 727 until 1997 and the 767 – inspired the derisive description 'Ansett Air Show' as Ansett's hangars filled with too many different types, according to most observers.

The fun started at the Paris Air Show in June 1985 – the month after the Australian Government announced its 'Independent Review of Economic Regulation of Domestic Aviation' – when Sir Peter Abeles announced a $US380m order for eight of the new and as yet unflown Airbus A320 airliners, the world's first with full fly-by-wire flight controls.

Three weeks later, 12 of the quieter and less thirsty second generation Boeing 737-300s were ordered at a cost of $500m to replace the 737-200s which had only entered service in 1981. These were smaller than the A320 (110 versus 140 seats) and available two years ear-

The Lockheed Electra's quarter century of Ansett and Australian service finally ended in early 1984 with the retirement of the last two L.188AF freighters. VH-RMC flew the last service of all, operating Cairns-Brisbane-Melbourne over the night of 31 January-1 February 1984. The aircraft had originally been delivered new to Ansett-ANA in February 1960 and was converted to a freighter in 1972. (Peter Barr)

Ansett Air Freight was formed as a separate company within Ansett Transport Industries in 1980. Three Electra freighters formed the basis of its fleet, joined in 1983 by Boeing 727-277 VH-RMF which was taken off passenger duties. The aircraft was converted to full freighter configuration the following year with a large cargo door. (Julian Green/Keith Myers)

lier. The stretched 737-400 with about the same passenger capacity as the A320 was ignored as it would not be available until after the A320, leaving Ansett with two different narrowbody aircraft types to fill its future trunk route needs. In addition, the Boeing 727-200 with about the same seating capacity as the A320 would remain in service for some time.

TAA – which would be rebranded and reorganised as Australian Airlines in August 1986 – also placed options on A320s but eventually settled for a mix of 737-300s and -400s to fill its narrowbody needs.

Another important but perhaps less newsworthy order was announced by Ansett in February 1985, covering an initial ten of the new Fokker 50 regional turboprops as the aircraft's launch customer. The group's total acquisition of the Fokker 50 increased to 22 aircraft through Seattle based partner company Corsair which made the aircraft available for lease to other operators.

A modernised and re-engined version of the venerable F27 Friendship which had served Australia so well for so long, the Fokker 50 didn't sit quite as comfortably within the fleet as the F27 had done but nevertheless remained in service until the end with West Australian subsidiary Skywest after having also flown with Ansett NSW/Ansett Express.

Deliveries of the Fokker 50 began in September 1987 and services were inaugurated by Air NSW two months

You can't have the best airline in the world without the best people.
Ansett.

later. Fourteen eventually appeared on the Ansett fleet list of which four never flew with Ansett – two were immediately leased out and two others were leased back to Fokker (then resold to the manufacturer) as soon as they were delivered.

Air NSW operated its last official Fokker F27 service (Brisbane-Coolangatta-Newcastle-Sydney) on 18 March 1988 after 29 years with the airline and its predecessors. Several F27s were temporarily returned to service in July when the airline's new Fokker 50 fleet was grounded after a spate of power losses which occurred in moist air. The final F27s in service with any Ansett airline flew with Eastwest with the last four withdrawn in November and December 1990.

The orders kept on coming as Ansett and Sir Peter Abeles continued their expansion into new areas. Substantial additional orders for the Boeing 737 and other types were placed for leasing subsidiary Ansett World Worldwide Aviation Services (AWAS) which had been established in 1986 and quickly became a major player on the world stage, and for TNT, which signed a 'commitment' for up to 72 BAe 146 freighters for its expanding European air express business. The 146 in both passenger and freighter forms was also ordered for Ansett and the TNT contract encouraged British Aerospace to open a second assembly line at the old Avro works in Manchester.

(left) The end of an era for the Whitsunday Islands in September 1984 when Ansett launches jet services to Hamilton Island and simultaneously ends the Sikorsky S-61N helicopter service from Proserpine to the Whitsundays resorts after nearly two decades. (right) The first of Ansett's initial batch of 12 Boeing 737-377s was delivered in August 1986 and entered service the following month. Ansett eventually operated 31 737-300s including seven temporarily leased during the 1989 pilots' dispute and the more recent 767 groundings. At the end, 24 were in service as the airline's most numerous type. (Jim Thorn/Boeing)

The last major type to enter service with Ansett's mainline operation was the highly advanced, fly-by-wire Airbus A320. Deliveries began in November 1988, Ansett being the first customer for the longer range -200 model. Ansett received 20 A320s over the years, all of which remained in service when the airline collapsed in September 2001. The A320 was the only type used when Ansett's administrators restarted the airline shortly afterwards. (Cameron Hadlow)

The first Ansett BAe 146-200 (VH-JJP) arrived in Australia on 26 April 1985 ahead of four more that would fly with Ansett WA. Twenty-three 146s of various models would eventually operate with Ansett and its subsidiaries including Ansett WA, Eastwest, Ansett New Zealand and Ansett Air Freight.

New Fleet Into Service

Ansett's first Boeing 737-377 (VH-CZA) was delivered on 22 August 1986 and entered service on the Melbourne-Sydney run on 15 September. All 12 were in service by January 1987 by which time another four had been ordered. Ansett eventually operated 35 737-300s including short term charters and leases and had 24 in service in September 2001 when the airline collapsed. All 12 of the still relatively new and low time 737-200s were withdrawn from service between September 1986 and January 1987 and sold to America West, in which Ansett would soon acquire a 20% stake.

The first A320 (VH-HYB) arrived in Australia on 26 November 1988, Ansett applying the marketing name 'Skystar' to this new generation of high technology air-

liner. Once again there were crewing issues to resolve, Peter Abeles' promise of four years earlier that Ansett aircraft with more than 120 seats would have a flight engineer coming back to haunt him.

Once again the AFAP began making noises insisting that a flight engineer's station be included. In the case of the very high technology, glass cockpit, highly computerised and fly-by-wire A320 this demand was even more ludicrous than it had been with the DC-9 and 767. To incorporate a flight engineer's station was completely impractical from a design point of view and operationally unnecessary.

The issue was eventually sorted out, helped by a late 1986 ruling by the Arbitration Commission which dismissed submissions by the Australian Federation of Air Pilots and the Australian Airline Flight Engineers Association that the A320 and other new generation airliners should have an engineer's station installed.

This and other union matters involving flight attendants, pilots and ground engineers resulted in the A320's entry to service being delayed until 2 January 1989 when VH-HYB flew from Melbourne to Sydney. The airline had

Ansett finally got into the New Zealand domestic market on a more or less permanent basis in October 1986 when it purchased a half share in Newmans Air, this increasing to full ownership in February 1988. Now operating as Ansett New Zealand, the airline's initial jet equipment was a quartet of elderly Boeing 737-100s (including the first production aircraft) leased from Ansett Worldwide Aviation Services, followed by two leased 737-200s. (Rob Finlayson & Ansett New Zealand)

Ansett New Zealand's long association with the BAe 146 began in July 1989 with the delivery of two -200s in July 1989. (BAe)

received three aircraft by then and eventually operated 20, the last of them delivered in December 1997.

Onwards and Upwards

The second half of the 1980s saw the Ansett group continue to expand its interests in many areas with new airline, air freight and leasing operations added to the company's portfolio, along with the reorganisation or takeover of existing ones. The result was another phase of 'empire building' not dissimilar to that instigated by Reg Ansett in the years following his gaining control of Australian National Airways in October 1957.

AWAS: The leasing of aircraft to the airlines had been an increasingly prevalent part of the industry since the end of the 1970s, largely driven by deregulation of the US industry in 1978 which inspired many new operators to enter the business. Most of these preferred to obtain their fleets through leasing rather than purchasing because it reduced the capital investment required by a substantial amount and had other cashflow benefits for them.

Eager to tap into this growing market and to further expand Sir Peter Abeles' global aspirations, TNT and News set about establishing an airliner leasing, purchasing,

training, maintenance and management company. Sir Peter announced the company's intentions at the Paris Air Show in June 1985.

Ansett Worldwide Aviation Services was formally launched in March 1986, initially offering Boeing 737-300s, Fokker 50s (in association with Corsair) and some of the 72 BAe 146s TNT had 'committed' to buy. Boeing allocated the customer designation suffix '3A' to aircraft ordered by AWAS, resulting in designations such as 737-33A and 757-23A. The first AWAS placement was a 737-300 to partially owned Ansett subsidiary America West in November 1986.

AWAS rapidly became a major player on the world airliner leasing scene and by early 1992 had 30 aircraft leased out and another 100 on order. By 1995 this had increased to 122 Boeing 737s, 757s, 767s and McDonnell Douglas MD-80s in service with a customer base of more than 20 operators including Air France, China Northern, British Midland, Alitalia, Ansett, America West, TWA, Continental, Garuda and Varig.

AWAS continued to grow from there and had more than 160 aircraft placed with airlines by 1998, but in April 2000 the company was sold to US based leasing

(left) ZK-NZA City of Queenstown, Ansett New Zealand's first BAe 146-200. This aircraft was transferred to Ansett WA in September 1992. (right) Ansett took over Skywest Holdings in July 1987, which had in turn acquired East-West Airlines four years earlier. Operating a network in Western Australia, Skywest flew four BAe Jetstream 31s. (Bill Lines & Stewart Wilson)

Ansett gained control of East-West Airlines when it took over Skywest Holdings in July 1987, inheriting a fleet of seven Fokker F27s and six F28 jets in the process. F28-4000 VH-EWC was one of them, this remaining with Ansett until 1997. (Julian Green)

firm MSDW Aircraft Holdings. The slightly revised name Ansett Worldwide was applied by the new owners in order to maintain continuity.

Aeropelican: Established in 1971, small NSW regional carrier Aeropelican Inter-City Commuter Air Service (which flew a single route between Newcastle and Sydney using DHC Twin Otters) became part of Ansett in July 1981 when 80% of owner Masling Commuter Services was purchased by TNT-News subsidiary Bodas Pty Ltd. Masling had itself acquired Aeropelican a year earlier. It was renamed Aeropelican Air Services in 1982 and remained an Ansett subsidiary until the collapse. Aeropelican was sold to the IAP Group in March 2002.

Ansett Air Freight: Nicknamed 'Wombat Airlines' (because they operated primarily at night) and previously the Air Cargo division of the airline, Ansett Air Freight was established as a separate and specialist division of Ansett Transport Industries in July 1980 using the three former Ansett-ANA Lockheed Electras which had been converted to freighters in 1972. These remained in service until 1983-84. The Electras were joined in April 1983 by Ansett Boeing 727-200 VH-RMX which was converted to full freighter configuration by Hayes International in the USA later in the year.

4401 550 916

Ansett New Zealand passenger ticket.

Another five 727 freighters were leased from various sources over the years but the permanent Ansett Air Freight fleet added a pair of BAe 146-200QTs which were delivered in 1989, these remaining with the carrier until the September 2001 collapse. Ansett Air Freight's operating name was changed to Ansett Australia Cargo (AAC) in June 1999.

Two 727-200Fs were in service by September 2001 along with two Horizon Airlines Hawker Siddeley HS.748s operated under contract on behalf of AAC plus a Fokker F27 Friendship under contract from Independent Air Freighters. Ansett Australia Cargo's operations were suspended on 13 September 2001 but limited services resumed on 8 October before ceasing permanently on 4 March 2002.

Ansett New Zealand: After two previous short lived attempts to break into the New Zealand domestic market, ATI appeared to have finally succeeded in October 1986 when it established Ansett New Zealand after acquiring a 50% interest in Newmans Air. The airline had begun operations in February 1985 as an offshoot of the well established Newmans tour company.

ATI's half share in the airline had only become possible two months earlier after the New Zealand Government passed the Air Services Licensing Amendment Bill which

(left) Airlines of Northern Australia was established as an ATI subsidiary in 1981 and was later renamed Ansett NT. It usually operated only a single Fokker F28-1000 (VH-FKF) but ceased operations in 1991 after losing its only profitable route (Darwin-Ayer's Rock) to regular Ansett Boeing 737 services. (right) Fokker F27-200 VH-MMO (formerly VH-FNF) was leased to Airlines of Northern Australia by fellow Ansett subsidiary Airlines of Western Australia for a time. This rare shot of the aircraft was taken at Coolangatta in October 1983, well away from the airline's normal area of operation! (Bill Lines & Geoff Wilkes)

raised the foreign ownership limit from 24.9% to 50%. The other owners of Ansett New Zealand when it was first established were Brierley Investments (27.5%) and Newmans (22.5%). Another change to the legislation in February 1988 allowed ATI to gain full control of the airline.

Ansett NZ began operations on 1 February 1987, flying its first trunk route service between Christchurch and Auckland with one of the two DHC Dash 8s previously used by Newmans. Four very early Boeing 737-100s were put into service during the course of the year (and remained on strength until 1989-90) by which time the BAe 146 was taking over as the airline's main jet equipment. The airline eventually operated a total of 12 BAe 146s of various models (up to 10 at a time) along with four Dash 8s.

Ansett NZ was a constant financial drain on its parent company's coffers, losing money consistently and in large amounts. By mid 1990 its losses were estimated at $NZ3,000,000 per month. The situation wasn't helped by the adverse publicity generated by the fatal crash of a Dash 8 on approach to Palmerston North in June 1995 and ongoing problems with the pilots' union which seemed determined to worsen the airline's precarious financial position with its demands.

The ownership of Ansett NZ changed in October 1996 when TNT sold its half share of Ansett to Air New Zealand. As part of the deal, News Ltd assumed 100% ownership of Ansett NZ by purchasing TNT's 50%. In June 2000, Air New Zealand purchased News Ltd's interest in Ansett and assumed full ownership. News had previously announced it was selling its 100% interest in Ansett NZ to a consortium of investors.

This occurred in September 2000, the new operating company called South Pacific Airlines but operating as Qantas New Zealand under a franchise agreement. The new operator's fleet of Dash 8s and BAe 146s remained as before with the aircraft still owned by Ansett. Qantas New Zealand only lasted until April 2001 before collapsing.

Airlines of Northern Australia/Air NT: Airlines of Northern Australia was established as a division of Ansett Transport Industries (Operations) Pty Ltd in April 1981 after the routes previously allocated to Northern Airlines (formerly Connair) were handed over to Ansett following a Northern Territory Government request for Ansett to fly these 'essential services'. The routes were Darwin-Katherine-Tennant Creek-Alice Springs and Darwin-Gove, with Darwin-Ayer's Rock subsequently added.

Airlines of Northern Australia normally operated a single Fokker F28 plus the occasional BAe 146 leased from Ansett WA as required. It was renamed Ansett NT in August 1985 but ceased operations in May 1991 after losing its primary money making route (Darwin-Ayer's Rock) to regular Ansett Boeing 737 flights. The airline's Darwin-Katherine-Tennant Creek-Alice Springs 'milk run' was unprofitable and in effect subsidised by the other service.

Eastwest Airlines: In July 1987 Ansett (through the TNT-News subsidiary Bodas Pty Ltd) took over Perth based Skywest Holdings (see

Wombat Airlines. Closeup of the wombat logo which appeared on most of Ansett Air Freight's aircraft, in this case BAe 146-200QT VH-JJY. Why? Because like the Australian marsupial, AAF operated almost exclusively at night! (Bill Lines)

below) which four years earlier had acquired the former New South Wales intrastate operator East-West Airlines. East-West and Skywest had joined forces largely in an attempt to break away from the constraints imposed by the Two Airline Policy on interstate routes.

East-West began operations from the NSW country town of Tamworth in June 1947, originally as the Anson Holding Co, the name reflecting its initial aircraft equipment. It was changed to East-West Airlines in July 1947. The airline operated local services and gradually expanded to become the state's second major intrastate operator in the 1960s, sharing the fully regulated market with Ansett owned Airlines of NSW.

East-West was taken over by a group headed by industry veteran Bryan Grey (who had worked for Ansett and Air Niugini and would later start Australia's first post deregulation startup, Compass Airlines) in August 1982, the airline now wanting to become the country's third interstate carrier and setting about challenging the legalities of the Two Airline Policy. The Skywest Holdings merger took place in December 1983 and several court challenges to the Two Airline Policy were mounted over the next three years.

One of them challenged the Independent Air Fares Committee on the subject of discounts and was withdrawn after the government agreed to review the policy. There was also a late 1985 High Court challenge to the legality of the Two Airline Policy as a whole. At that time East-West's fleet comprised Fokker F28 jets and F27 turboprops and there were plans to import some Boeing

Ansett Air Freight's two BAe 146-200QTs were delivered in May and June 1989 and operated in TNT Express colours. This shot taken at Perth in May 1989 shows VH-JJY in company with Boeing 707-330C freighter VH-HTC. This previously belonged to Hong Kong based Transcorp in which ATI held a majority interest. The 707 was sold in late 1990 but others were leased from time to time. (Wally Civitico)

Ansett won management contracts from several South Pacific airlines in the 1980s and also took a 40% interest in Air Vanuatu. The deals included the supply of aircraft and crews, examples being (top to bottom): 727-277 VH-RMN in Cook Islands International colours; DC-9-31 VH-CZD of Air Vanuatu; and Boeing 767-277 VH-RMD in Ansett colours but with 'Cook Island International' added on the forward fuselage. (Geoff Wilkes/SW Collection)

737s. As it was, some interstate routes were flown and the regulations got around by making a 'technical stop' on the way, for example Sydney-Melbourne via Albury.

Skywest Holdings announced a partial float of East-West in February 1987, several months of negotiation finally resulting in TNT-News purchasing the company in July 1987, just two weeks after the Perron Group had taken control. East-West Airlines, Skywest Airlines and charter subsidiary Skywest Aviation came with the deal.

Ansett's takeover of East-West/Skywest was in doubt for a time after a November 1987 decision by the Trade Practices Commission that the acquisitions were anti competitive due to the ownership of Skywest and associations with regional operators Kendell and Lloyd Aviation.

The TPC ordered Ansett to sell its East-West routes in Western Australia and also withdraw from the Skywest commuter network in the state and sell the airline side of Skywest's operations. Ansett could retain Skywest's general aviation and charter activities including the lucrative Coastwatch contract operated on behalf of Australian Customs.

Attempts were made to comply with the ruling by disposing of the appropriate assets but without success, the TPC reversing its decision a year later and allowing Ansett to continue ownership of all aspects of the East-West and Skywest businesses. By then, Lloyd had also become part of the Ansett stable and Kendell would be a wholly owned subsidiary in 1990.

With the purchase of East-West came new options for the Ansett network on the east coast of Australia. The airline was restyled as 'Eastwest' and developed into the 'tourist' arm of the Ansett network, serving ports such as Queensland's Gold Coast using a fleet of eight newly ordered BAe 146-300s plus some of the existing F27s and F28s.

Eastwest was given a fresh image in a bid to attract the younger tourist market but it didn't work very well and the airline failed to make money in the newly deregulated world of Australian skies. Boeing 727s were taken from the Ansett fleet and provided to Eastwest from early 1992 but this in combination with a more upmarket image failed to improve its fortunes and operations ceased in October 1993. Eastwest's fleet and route network were absorbed into the mainstream Ansett system. Eastwest's 727s were fitted with 164 seats.

Lloyd Aviation: TNT-News subsidiary Bodas Pty Ltd purchased a major shareholding in Adelaide based Lloyd Aviation Jet Charter on 7 August 1988. The company's assets included South Australian and Queensland regional operators Lloyd Airlines (Lloydair) and various charter activities.

Lloyd Airlines began scheduled services in South Australia in November 1985 and operations in Queensland began on some former Air Queensland routes in June 1987, with part of its services an 'on-carriage' deal with Ansett. Lloyd Airlines' Queensland operations were sold to Queensland Pacific Airlines in December 1988 and the South Australian part of the business ceased operations in September 1990.

Skywest: The entity known as Skywest Airlines was established in 1980 as the result of the gradual amalgamation of a number of West Australian airline and charter operators including Nor'West Air Taxis, Trans West Air Charter, Trans West Airlines, Murchison Air Charter, Jet Charter, Stillwell Airlines and others.

As noted above, Skywest Holdings was sold to News-TNT subsidiary Bodas Pty Ltd in July 1987, the deal including Skywest Airlines, charter division Skywest Aviation and East-West Airlines, which had merged with Skywest in December 1983. As an Ansett subsidiary, Skywest Airlines continued to operate its fleet of four BAe Jetstream 31s, these supplemented and eventually replaced by Fokker 50s.

Skywest Airlines remained part of the Ansett group until its collapse in September 2001 and was sold to Airline Investments Limited, a consortium of West Australian businessmen, in December 2001.

Transcorp: Ansett Transport Industries acquired a 51% interest in Hong Kong owned but Perth based freight carrier Transcorp in December 1985. The company had been established four months earlier and used a wet leased Boeing 707-320C on services between Asia and Australia. Operations continued only until October 1988 when Transcorp went into liquidation and the Boeing 707 was taken over by Ansett Air Freight, operating in TNT colours mainly on flights within Australia. The aircraft remained in service with AAF until December 1990.

America West: Ansett (through its owners TNT and News) took an initial 20% stake worth $US31.8 million in Phoenix, Arizona based America West in June 1987. The deal involved several related transactions including with Ansett Worldwide Aviation Services which leased it Boeing 737-300s and with Ansett New Zealand to which it sold 737-100s. America West also purchased Ansett's fleet of 12 737-200s when they were retired from service.

America West went into Chapter 11 bankruptcy protection in early 1991, Ansett increasing its stake in the airline to 26% in April of that year through a debt-for-equity swap. It emerged from Chapter 11 in August 1994 but Ansett's interest in the airline was disposed of shortly afterwards.

Other Activities

The general business of running the various existing Ansett airlines and other businesses continued during the 1980s while new operations were being established. In Australia, some of the regional subsidiaries were reorganised and renamed; business class was introduced; ATI's Whitsunday Islands interests were expanded to include half ownership of the airport on Hamilton Island plus taking over the operating lease of South Molle; the very successful Golden Wing Club for business travellers was introduced; and management contracts were established with South Pacific operators Air Vanuatu (of which Ansett owned 40%), Polynesian Airlines and Cook Islands International.

On the Australian domestic scene the move towards deregulation of the industry came closer as the decade wore on, culminating in October 1987 when the Federal Government announced it was giving three years' notice that the Airlines Agreement Act and its subsequent amendments would be terminated. From 1 November 1990, the Two Airline Policy would cease to exist and a fully deregulated operating environment would take its place.

The News-TNT takeover of Ansett Transport Industries in January 1980 signalled major changes for the group – a new management style, new livery and name for the airline and new equipment including the widebody Boeing 767. (Julian Green)

FLEET SUMMARY – April 1986

Ansett: 5 Boeing 767-200; 11 Boeing 727-200; 1 Boeing 727-200F; 12 Boeing 737-200; 2 Fokker F27-200 Friendship; 3 Fokker F27-400 Friendship; 2 Sikorsky S-61N. On order: 8 Airbus A320-200; 12 Boeing 737-300; 6 (optioned) BAe 146-200; 22 Fokker 50 (shared between Ansett, AWAS, Air NSW etc).
Air NSW: 3 Fokker F28-1000 Fellowship; 1 Fokker F27-200 Friendship; 1 Fokker F27-400 Friendship; 5 Fokker F27-500 Friendship.
Airlines of South Australia: 2 Fokker F27-200 Friendship; 1 Fokker F27-600 Friendship (ASA ceased operations June 1986).
Ansett NT: 1 Fokker F28-1000 Fellowship; 1 BAe 146-200 (leased from Ansett WA).
Ansett WA: 2 BAe 146-200; 3 Fokker F28-1000 Fellowship; 2 Fokker F28-4000 Fellowship.
Ansett Worldwide Aviation Services: 2 Boeing 727-200; 3 Boeing 737-200; 1 Fokker F27-500 Friendship. On order: 12 Boeing 747-300; 6 McDonnell Douglas MD-83 (plus six options); 9 (options) Airbus A320-200; 22 Fokker 50 (shared between AWAS, Ansett, Air NSW etc).
Transcorp Airways: 1 Boeing 707-330C.
Aeropelican: 4 DHC Twin Otter.

FLEET SUMMARY – March 1989

Ansett: 5 Boeing 767-200; 9 Boeing 727-200; 5 Airbus A320-200; 16 Boeing 737-300; 5 Fokker 50; 1 Fokker F27-200 Friendship; 2 Fokker F27-400 Friendship. On order: 3 Airbus A320-200.
Air NSW: 3 Fokker F28-1000 Fellowship; 5 Fokker 50.
Ansett Air Freight: 1 Boeing 707-320C; 1 Boeing 727-200F. On order: 2 BAe 146-200QT.
Ansett New Zealand: 4 Boeing 737-100; 1 Boeing 737-200; 2 DHC Dash 8-100. On order: 2 BAe 146-200; 5 BAe 146-300.
Ansett NT: 1 Fokker F28-1000 Fellowship (plus Ansett WA aircraft as required).
Ansett WA: 4 BAe 146-200; 1 Fokker F28-4000 Fellowship; 4 Fokker F28-1000 Fellowship. On order: 1 BAe 146-200.
Ansett Worldwide Aviation Services: Leased aircraft in service: 21 Boeing 737-200; 3 Boeing 757-200; 6 McDonnell Douglas MD-83. On order: 20 Boeing 737-300; 5 Boeing 737-500; 25 Boeing 757-200; 6 Airbus A320-200 (options); 12 McDonnell Douglas MD-83 (plus 12 options); 36 BAe 146-200 (options).
East-West Airlines: 5 Fokker F28-4000 Fellowship; 2 Fokker F27-3000 Fellowship; 7 Fokker F27-500 Friendship.
Aeropelican Air Services: 4 DHC Twin Otter 300.
Lloyd Aviation: 1 Embraer EMB.110P1 Bandeirante; 1 Cessna 402C.
Skywest Airlines: 4 BAe Jetstream 31, 4 Cessna 310R.

FLEET SUMMARY – April 1983

Ansett: 15 Boeing 727-200; 12 Boeing 737-200; 1 Fokker F27-400 Friendship.
Ansett Air Freight: 1 Boeing 727-200F; 3 Lockheed L.188AF Electra.
Air New South Wales: 6 Fokker F27-500 Friendship.
Airlines of Northern Australia: 1 Fokker F28-1000 Fellowship; 1 Fokker F27-200 Friendship.
Airlines of South Australia: 4 Fokker F27-200 Friendship.
Airlines of Western Australia: 7 Fokker F28-1000 Fellowship; 1 Fokker F28-4000 Fellowship; 1 Fokker F27-400 Friendship.
Aeropelican: 4 DHC Twin Otter.

Year	Ansett	TAA
1983	4.289m	4.296m
1984	4.583m	4.446m
1985	4.796m	4.806m
1986	5.060m	5.104m
1987	5.626m	5.301m
1988	6.116m	6.123m

Ansett and TAA (Australian Airlines from August 1986) continued to largely share the domestic market throughout the 1980s as the following six year comparison of revenue passengers carried shows. As can be seen from the figures it was pretty much split 50/50 most of the time with both airlines scoring a slight advantage from time to time.

The table shows the number of passengers in millions and indicates 42.5% growth from the total 8.585 million passengers carried in 1983 to the 12.239 million of 1988.

These were impressive figures, especially in terms of the amount of growth recorded in a relatively short time, but from 1990 it would become more difficult as the 'big two' had to face the prospect of competition from new airlines which were certain to introduce fares much lower than the public had become used to. It would be a whole new ball game for Ansett and Australian, and the game had to be played without the cosy protection of the Two Airline Policy.

THE NAME GAME

The names of the Ansett holding company, the main airline itself and the various subsidiary airlines changed several times over the decades, reflecting constant changes in company structure, ownership and marketing strategies. The following summarises those changes for a quick reference; for more detail on these and the complete Ansett family tree, see the schematic diagrams at the end of the book. The evolution of the main airline's operating name is:

Ansett Airways Pty Ltd: The original privately owned company established in January 1936.

Ansett Airways Ltd: April 1937; adjusted name when the airline became a publicly listed company.

Ansett Airways Pty Ltd: May 1946; returned to private company status as a subsidiary of the newly established Ansett Transport Industries .

Ansett-ANA: October 1957 with the ATI takeover of Australian National Airways.

Ansett Airlines of Australia: November 1968; the ANA connection is dropped.

Ansett.: April 1981; name adopted by new owners TNT and News Ltd, complete with full stop.

Ansett Australia.: October 1990; once again with the full stop.

Ansett Australia: July 1994; new and final livery, full stop deleted from title.

As for the holding company, Ansett Airways Pty Ltd and Ansett Airways Ltd were used as above until May 1946.

Ansett Transport Industries Ltd: May 1946; public company controlling all of Ansett's interests including the airlines, although these subsequently came under the umbrella of Ansett Transport Industries (Operations) Pty Ltd, a wholly owned subsidiary of ATI.

Ansett Australia Holdings Ltd: August 1994; replaced Ansett Transport Industries Ltd, while at the same time Ansett Australia Limited replaced Ansett Transport Industries (Operations) Pty Ltd as the airlines' umbrella organisation.

Ansett Holdings Ltd: June 1995; replaced Ansett Australia Holdings Ltd.

Many of the regional airline subsidiaries also had their names changed to suit ownership and marketing needs. These are:

Aeropelican Inter-City Commuter Air Service: Acquired by TNT-News July 1981; renamed Aeropelican Air Services 1982.

Airlines of Northern Australia: Began operations April 1981; renamed Ansett NT August 1985; ceased operations May 1991.

Barrier Reef Airways: Absorbed into Ansett Flying Boat Services May 1952 but retained name until March 1953; AFBS ceased operations September 1974.

Butler Air Transport: Acquired by ATI February 1958; renamed Airlines of NSW (December 1959); Ansett Airlines of NSW (June 1968); Air New South Wales (June 1981); Air NSW (May 1985); Ansett NSW (March 1990); Ansett Express (November 1990); absorbed into Ansett Australia October 1993.

East-West Airlines: Acquired by ATI July 1987, slightly renamed as Eastwest Airlines; absorbed into Ansett Australia October 1993.

Guinea Airways: Acquired by ATI from July 1959; renamed Airlines of South Australia (December 1959); Ansett Airlines of South Australia (November 1968); Airlines of South Australia (July 1981); ceased operations June 1986.

Hazelton Airlines: Acquired by Ansett Holdings March 2001; name retained.

Kendell Airlines: Acquired by TNT-News June 1990; name retained.

MacRobertson Miller Airlines (MMA): Majority shareholding acquired by ATI August 1955; MacRobertson Miller Airline Services (June 1969); Airlines of Western Australia (July 1981); Ansett WA (November 1984); absorbed into Ansett Australia July 1993.

Mandated Airlines Ltd (MAL): Acquired by ATI January 1961 and renamed Ansett-MAL; new name Ansett Airlines of Papua New Guinea June 1968; absorbed into Air Niugini November 1973.

Newmans Air: 50% interest acquired by ATI December 1986 (later 100%); renamed Ansett New Zealand; company sold March 2000 but retained name; ceased operations September 2000.

Papuan Airlines (Patair): Acquired by ATI July 1970; renamed Ansett (P&NG) Ltd 1972; absorbed into Air Niugini November 1973.

Queensland Airlines: Acquired (with Butler) by ATI February 1958; retained name until absorbed into Ansett-ANA December 1966.

Skywest Airlines: Acquired by TNT-News July 1987; name retained.

CHAPTER TEN

BRAVE NEW WORLD

The Australian domestic airline industry took the first step in being changed forever on 7 May 1985 when the Minister for Aviation (Peter Morris) announced a comprehensive review of the Two Airline Policy by commissioning its Independent Review of Economic Regulation of Domestic Aviation, or the 'May report' after its chairman, Mr Thomas May. The review took submissions from the airlines, state governments, unions, travel organisations, the public and other interested parties.

The report was published in January 1987 and was generally critical of the Two Airline Policy, saying it did not serve the travelling public well. This was borne out by the majority of submissions from the public, of which, according to the report: '.... the overwhelming majority were critical of the present regulatory arrangements.... a significant proportion of the population believes that the policy works to the consumer's disadvantage.... there is widespread dissatisfaction with the Two Airline Policy; in particular, this dissatisfaction involves perceptions of restricted competition, high fare levels and parallel services.'

Of interest is the fact that the review also found that on the trunk network Ansett Airlines 'has a competitive advantage over Australian Airlines because of the support it receives from the Ansett regional airlines and the other interests of the Ansett group.'

Perhaps this goes some way to explaining Ansett's early lack of enthusiasm for the concept of deregulation. In late 1985 Sir Peter Abeles made an apparently contradictory statement about the situation, saying 'we, [himself and Rupert Murdoch] would prefer a deregulated free market in aviation.... but believe the Two Airlines Policy was the best solution to Australia's unique situation.'

The report presented five options for consideration by the government, ranging from maintaining the *status quo* to full deregulation of the industry. Given the overwhelming public support for full deregulation, the decision was perhaps inevitable and on 7 October 1987 it was announced that from 1 November 1990, Australian domestic airline operations would be deregulated.

No longer would fares, fleets and schedules be determined by regulation. The airlines could now set their own agenda and make their own progress based on their own commercial decisions. The new rules meant that anyone with the financial and infrastructure wherewithal could start an airline and compete in the Australian domestic market against the 'big two'.

The Airbus A320 assumed greater importance within the Ansett fleet during the 1990s. By the end of 1995, 14 had been delivered with another six to follow over the next two years. VH-HYJ arrived in January 1991. (Julian Green)

(left) The pilots' dispute caused major disruption to the Australian domestic airline industry for several months from August 1989. Both Ansett and Australian Airlines had to wet lease foreign aircraft to help fill the void. One of them was Boeing 737-33A G-PATE, owned by AWAS and leased from Paramount Airways between November 1989 and May 1990 with temporary Ansett markings. (right) A night scene at Melbourne Airport in October 1991 with a 767-200 being serviced between flights and a 737-300 in the background. By this stage Ansett Australia had its original five 767-200s, 13 737-300s, 13 A320s and four 727-200LRs operating its mainline routes. (Geoff Wilkes/Bill Lines)

The decision meant that government would withdraw from the detailed economic regulation over aircraft imports, capacity, air fares and routes but would continue to control safety and security matters; consumer protection would be provided through the Trade Practices Act and Prices Surveillance Authority; access to terminal facilities for new operators would be assured; and action to strengthen the competitive position of Australian Airlines would be taken.

As a sidelight to the main provisions of termination of the Airlines Agreement Act, the Australian Airlines (Conversion to Public Company) Bill was introduced to parliament in December 1987, this setting up the operator for future privatisation, although for the moment all the shares would be held by the Commonwealth Government.

By the time the decision was made, Ansett had softened its attitude to deregulation, sensing its inevitability. The airline had been taking action to shore up its position in the second half of the 1980s by the acquisition of East-West Airlines, Skywest and Lloydair to create an even more substantial network of regional feeders. Kendell Airlines was added to the portfolio in 1990. This vital aspect of modern airline operations was one area where Ansett held a substantial advantage over Australian at the time.

Ansett greeted the new era with a change in livery and logo. Gone was Ansett. (full stop), replaced with Ansett Australia. (also with full stop) from October 1990 along with a new Australian flag logo on the tails of the airline's fleet.

TAA had also reinvented itself as Australian Airlines from August 1986 ahead of major changes. Many of these were to do with the coming of deregulation but others were part of the greater overall plan, when the government owned carrier would

merge with the also government owned Qantas to create a very substantial force in both the domestic and international markets.

Qantas eventually took over Australian in September 1992 and the Australian Airlines name disappeared, ahead of the planned privatisation of the combined operation. The public float of 75% of Qantas was successfully launched in July 1995, the remaining 25% already having been sold to British Airways.

Under the terms of the Qantas Sale Act, total foreign ownership was limited to 49%; any single foreign airline could not hold more than 25% of the shares; foreign airlines as a group could not hold more than 35%; substantial foreign shareholders could not appoint more than one-third of the company's directors; two-thirds of the directors and the chairman must be Australian citizens; and the airline's head office had to be located in Australia.

Qantas challenged these limitations in 2002 claiming they restricted the airline's access to global equity capital and imposed an artificial ceiling on its share capital. In August 2002 the government decided not to change the Act.

The year leading to deregulation was interesting and underscored the relatively comfortable existence enjoyed by both Ansett and TAA/Australian under the Two Airline Policy. Suddenly, a few more discount air fares became available – albeit usually with restrictive conditions attached – as both airlines sought to gain an advantage over the other.

When the first post deregulation startup – the low fare Compass Airlines – began operations in December 1990 a price war was immediately triggered with the major airlines starting to offer fares which were only a fraction of what was previously charged. The idea, of course, was to squeeze out Compass wher-

(left) Even though Ansett had taken over East-West Airlines in July 1987, some of the carrier's aircraft remained in their old colours for a considerable time afterwards. F28-4000 VH-EWC carried the East-West scheme into 1991 with 'Ansett' titles applied. (right) Ansett Express was established in November 1990 out of Ansett NSW with a 'hub bypassing' philosophy with more direct flights between ports. Its main base was moved from Sydney to Brisbane and a fleet of nine Fokker F28s and seven Fokker 50s used. F28-4000s VH-EWA and VH-FKO were photographed at Melbourne in February 1993, eight months before Ansett Express was absorbed into the main airline operation. (Rob Finlayson/Geoff Wilkes)

ever possible, although it was impossible to get executives from either Ansett or Australian to admit that.

The deep discounts offered by Compass and the major airlines stimulated new traffic as people who could not afford to fly before were now able to. But this was to prove Compass' undoing because it ended up being forced to sell tickets for less than they cost, with inevitable results.

Compass failed in December 1991 largely for that and other reasons including the fact that it had the wrong aircraft in service. The widebody Airbus A300s it leased were simply too large for the market. A larger fleet of smaller airliners of 737/A320/MD-80 size was needed so that higher frequencies and greater scheduling flexibility could be offered.

A second new cut price operator launched services in August 1992. Southern Cross Airlines also traded as Compass, the management hoping to cash in on the goodwill it thought the name had with the general public. 'Compass II' – as it was dubbed – only lasted seven months before it also failed under a cloud of financial impropriety, this later proven and resulting in a jail sentence for its chairman.

So far, deregulation of the Australian domestic airline system had been a disappointment with two new airlines starting and both failing quickly. It would be another seven years before further attempts would be made to take on the 'Big Two'.

Australia in the meantime reverted to another Two Airline System, but this time an unofficial one and largely by default. The question as to whether or not the local domestic market was large enough to support more than two trunk route carriers was starting to be asked, and it still is.

The Pilots' Dispute

Both Ansett and Australian had to endure one of the most disruptive events in the history of the local airline industry before deregulation was introduced – a pilots' dispute which started in August 1989 and lasted several months.

Once again, the Australian Federation of Airline Pilots (AFAP) was behind the dispute in yet another example of it trying to bludgeon the airlines. Once again, the AFAP assumed it would get its way with minimal resistance as it and its predecessor – the Australian Air Pilots Association – always had during its 43 years history. It was simply a matter of estimating how many days it would take the airlines to cave in to its demands.

What happened was very different, this dispute proving to be not only the AFAP's most destructive yet, but also its death knell because this time the airlines held firm with the support of the Federal Government under Prime Minister Bob Hawke.

Ostensibly, the dispute was over a massive pay claim but the real reason was consolidation of the union's power in the forthcoming deregulated era. What the AFAP didn't properly appreciate was the fact that it was not just taking on the airlines per se, but in the case of Ansett its owners, two of the world's most powerful and influential businessmen in Peter Abeles and Rupert Murdoch. For the Australian Government, there was considerable vested interest in the ongoing viability of Australian Airlines, bearing in mind its Qantas merger plans and subsequent privatisation.

Even the Australian Council of Trade Unions (ACTU) had advised the AFAP not to embark on its

The revamped Eastwest Airlines was promoted as Ansett's 'leisure' carrier after its acquisition in 1987, initially with a fleet of Fokker F27s and F28s. A fleet upgrade began in August 1990 with the arrival of the first of eventually eight BAe 146-300s. (BAe)

(left) Former East-West Fokker F28-3000 VH-EWF in full Ansett Express titles at Launceston in August 1991. This aircraft had been leased from Denmark's Cimber Air since 1987 but was purchased by Ansett in late 1993. (right) Fokker F28-1000 VH-FKE of Ansett WA at Paraburdoo in April 1991. This aircraft spent more than two decades of its life in Western Australia, having been delivered to MacRobertson Miller Airlines in 1971. The Ansett WA name disappeared in July 1993 when the operation was absorbed into Ansett Australia. (Geoff Wilkes)

planned strategy and failure to heed that advice resulted in the union receiving no support from Australia's premier trade union body. The ACTU warned that the AFAP would have to accept the consequences of being outside the normal (and legal) wages and arbitration system.

Six days into the dispute, the AFAP dramatically demonstrated its poor and tactically inept leadership when it convinced its 1,647 members to resign en masse, leaving the country with in effect no domestic air services. This action at a stroke lost the union any remaining support it may have had from the government and the public and forced the airlines to bring in foreign aircraft and their crews to help restore a semblance of service.

At least the dispute occurred during the northern hemisphere 'off' season, so there were aircraft and crews available. Even the RAAF chipped in, flying passengers in C-130 Hercules and HS.748 transports and doing its public image no harm at all as a result.

It took nearly seven months for the dispute to finally resolve itself, in which time the airlines suffered massive revenue drops and many areas of the nation's economy which depend on reliable air services to survive had to cut down by putting off staff.

AFAP Destroyed

At the end of the day, the AFAP completely failed in its aims and was beaten into submission with little or no remaining power base, no sympathy from the industry, government or public and no credibility whatsoever with any of them.

In practical terms the dispute was all but over by late March 1990 following the virtual unconditional surrender of the AFAP in order to be allowed back into the national wage fixing system. A ruling by the Industrial Relations Commission (IRC) brought an 'official' end to the dispute. The AFAP's decision to accept wage guidelines, abide by the IRC's findings and lift a ban on AFAP members seeking work with the airlines in effect made a complete mockery of its campaign and emphasised the fact that the whole affair was ill conceived in the first place and poorly led by the AFAP's senior people. The decision by the pilots to resign en masse was a serious tactical blunder.

In a decision handed down by the IRC's deputy president, Professor Keith Hancock, total responsibility for the crisis was laid at the AFAP's door. The IRC did, however, agree in principle to allow the AFAP to re-enter the

(left) Leasing rather than purchasing aircraft became an increasingly important part of the fleet acquisition programs of many airlines during the 1990s. Ansett was no exception, this Boeing 737-33A (VH-CZX) one of eight 737s leased from Ansett Worldwide Aviation Services from 1993. CZX was delivered to Ansett in February 1994 after five years' service with Euroberlin. (right) Boeing 727-277 VH-RMN was leased to Polynesian Airlines between April 1987 and April 1992 as part of the management contract Ansett held with the South Pacific operator. This shot was taken at a wet Melbourne Airport in February 1990. (Geoff Wilkes)

wages system, albeit with some reservations and conditions. The IRC hearings basically comprised a series of backdowns by the AFAP along with the conditions of re-entry to the wages system.

These included abiding by any subsequent IRC decision about award variations or variations covering the hiring of pilots subject only to its right under the Industrial Relations Act; desisting from any action other than through the IRC to prevent or discourage pilots from gaining employment in accordance with the awards; advising its members that they should not harass or intimidate working pilots (this was an ongoing and very nasty problem throughout the dispute); and neither organise nor support pickets in relation to matters which had been in dispute since the previous August.

These conditions were agreed to by the AFAP along with the major concession that it would not seek a return to work based on the pilot's previous seniority. The last point more than any other sums up the AFAP's complete capitulation, as this had previously been a major point of contention which prevented negotiations from progressing.

The IRC used some harsh words in its decision. It referred to the Federation's 'sophistry' in its arguments on employment bans and harassment of so-called 'scab' pilots – in other words it found the AFAP had lied.

Continuing harassment of working pilots had done little to raise the union's credibility with the general public. Police reports of violence against working pilots had included acts of physical abuse and damage to property more akin to the actions of thugs than a disciplined group of specialists operating in a highly technical profession.

Whilst the AFAP distanced itself from these events, it was still seen by the IRC as being the union's membership which was responsible for the problem. It summed up the situation by saying: 'Much of the unhappiness of the past seven months has stemmed from a conviction held within the Federation that its members were special – that the normal processes of industrial relations were inappropriate for them.'

The financial damage the dispute did to the industry is well illustrated by the passenger traffic figures recorded by Ansett and Australian in 1989-90. Between them they carried 8.507 million passengers during the 12 months to the end of March 1990, a 30.5% reduction on the previous year's combined total of 12.241 million. Of that reduced figure, Ansett claimed 48.2% of the market, its lowest for some years.

The bottom line also suffered, Ansett recording a gross, pre tax profit of just $2.58 million in the 1989-90 financial year compared with $67.33 million in 1988-89. Not all of this was attributable to the dispute as some of Ansett's subsidiaries continued to perform badly, notably Eastwest and Ansett New Zealand. Eastwest lost $7.22 million over the 12 months despite strong traffic growth (this in itself indicating fundamental and serious problems) and Ansett NZ lost $NZ29.3 million.

The real tragedy of the dispute lay in the damage it caused to the people directly involved and those associated with them. Careers were at best disrupted and at worst destroyed, as were friendships and professional associations. Many of the pilots involved had little choice but to look for work overseas and endure the disruption to family life that entails.

The British Aerospace 146 regional jetliner had become an increasingly important part of the Ansett fleet since the second half of the 1980s and by late 1991 more than 20 were in service with Ansett Australia, Eastwest, Ansett Air Freight and Ansett New Zealand. Shown here (top to bottom) are Ansett Australia BAe 146-200 VH-JJQ at Perth in 1994 (this one of the original pair delivered to Ansett WA in 1985); Ansett Air Freight BAe 146-200QT freighter VH-JJZ (complete with 'wombat' logo on nose) at Melbourne in March 1994; and BAe 146-300 VH-EWL at Sydney in November 1993, in Ansett Australia colours following the closure of Eastwest. Note the small but defiant 'Eastwest' logo just behind the forward door. Boeing 767-277 VH-RMF is in the background. (Rob Finlayson/Brian Wilkes/Geoff Wilkes)

It can be argued that the pilots whose lives and careers were disrupted had only themselves to blame because they chose to endorse their union's actions, but at the end of the day, everybody lost out.

Going Downhill?

There has always been considerable discussion trying to identify the moment that Ansett's descent into eventual oblivion occurred.

(left) A fundamental change to the Australian airline industry occurred in September 1992 when Qantas and Australian Airlines (formerly TAA) merged, creating a very substantial domestic and international carrier. The next step was privatisation in 1995. The Australian Airlines fleet was gradually repainted in Qantas colours, as illustrated by Airbus A300B4-200 VH-TAA. (right) Realising the importance of regional 'feed' to the mainline operation, Ansett added to its portfolio of regional airline subsidiaries in June 1990 with the acquisition of Wagga based Kendell Airlines. Kendell operated Fairchild Metros and Saab 340s, some of the latter seen here at Melbourne in January 1995 displaying a variety of liveries. (Rob Finlayson)

Some suggest it was the pilots' dispute which started the slide; others blame deregulation of the industry and removal of the Two Airline Policy's protection; and there is also a case to suggest the real damage started when it became apparent in the early 1990s that both TNT and News Corp were not as interested in Ansett as they had once been.

Both TNT and News were having their own problems in the early 1990s when the latest 'down' part of the economic cycle hit. This time the worldwide downturn was more marked than usual due to the effects of the Gulf War, and both Peter Abeles and Rupert Murdoch were facing difficult times. TNT had lost nearly $400m between 1990 and 1992.

Speculation that both TNT and News were considering selling at least a part of their interest in Ansett began in early 1991, and at the time it was thought that News was the most likely candidate to bail out first. The speculation grew during the course of 1991 when problems arose with several operations. Eastwest and Ansett NZ both continued to lose heavily while America West – in which TNT-News held a 26% share – went into Chapter 11 Bankruptcy protection.

Overall, analysts estimated Ansett's 1990-91 loss at around $50m and considered the company needed a $200m capital injection. This amount of money was not easily available from the company's owners at the time. Then there was the question of Ansett's debt level, estimated at $2.5 billion at the end of 1991, although $200 million of that was repaid in early 1992.

It is really from this point that Ansett began to lose its way as it was more often than not unprofitable over the next few years and its domestic market share continued to gradually decline. Management restructures, the sale of non core assets, staff redundancies and wage deals became more common as the decade progressed, all this at a time when the global airline industry was going through further major changes.

Ansett Transport Industries lost $92.1 million in the 1991-92 financial year but still commanded a 46.3% share of the Australian domestic market, ahead of Australian Airlines (41.0%), Ansett subsidiary Eastwest (5.7%) and the short lived startup Compass (7.0%). This was the final reporting period before Australian Airlines and Qantas merged. Two years later Ansett was capturing 56% of the total Australian domestic market and 52.5% of the routes it contested with Qantas.

In an attempt to bolster the fortunes of the Eastwest 'leisure' airline operation, Ansett introduced the Boeing 727-200 to the Eastwest fleet in January 1992 on the important Sydney-Coolangatta route. Taken from the mainline Ansett fleet, three 727s were repainted in Eastwest colours but reverted to standard in 1993 when the heavily losing operation was shut down.

Changes at the Top

Two significant events in Ansett's corporate history occurred in 1992 when Rupert Murdoch and Sir Peter Abeles stood down as joint chairmen and chief executives of ATI. News Corp CEO Ken Cowley took over as chairman and TNT CEO David Mortimer as deputy chairman. Sir Peter stated at the time that he would continue working to rejuvenate Ansett's financial fortunes but ill health forced him to resign most of his positions with both TNT and Ansett shortly afterwards.

The time was ripe for a 'changing of the guard' and some progress was made with Ansett. A strong indication that a sale was looming appeared in 1993 when for the first time since becoming a private company under TNT-News Control, ATI's full results for the 1992-93 financial year were published. As a private company there was no obligation to do this but the figures showed a profit of $59.5m before tax and abnormals compared with a $91.2m loss the previous year. Even though the net result was a deficit of $181.2m after foreign exchange losses were taken into account, publishing the operating profit was seen as a message to potential buyers that the business was viable.

These encouraging figures were reinforced by a good result in the 1993-94 financial year when Ansett Australia Holdings recorded its best ever gross profit of $209.2 million or $139.9 million after tax. One constant drain on the company's cashflow had meanwhile been removed from the equation in mid 1993 when Eastwest was finally recognised as being a bad idea and shut down.

The 1994-95 financial year started the slide downwards. Although the company made a net profit of $51 million, this was substantially less than the previous year and included a second half loss of $13 million. From then, Ansett's bottom line would be red more often than black.

Of significance is the fact that by the fourth quarter of 1994 Ansett's share of the domestic market had dropped to 50.5% and would steadily decline from there. By the end of September 2000 it was down to just 41.5%. Also interesting was executive chairman Ken Cowley's July 1994 statement during a television interview that he would like to see Ansett floated in 'eighteen months to two years'. He also revealed that both TNT and News had looked at selling some of their interest in Ansett over the past few years.

The 1990s was the era of commercial agreements between individual airlines, codesharing and the eventual establishment of large global alliances formally linking a number of airlines and their frequent flyer rewards programs.

Ansett and Australian simultaneously launched their frequent flyer 'loyalty' programs in August 1991, these initially offering either consumer goods or flights in exchange for accumulated points. Subsequent modification to the schemes removed

BAe-ANSETT FLYING COLLEGE

Drawing on experience gained from the jointly owned British Aerospace/British Airways Flying College at Prestwick, Scotland, BAe and Ansett decided to a establish a similar facility in Australia, intended to attract the professional end of the flying training market and focusing on airline customers.

Located at Tamworth NSW, what would be called the BAe-Ansett Flying College was formally launched in December 1990 and up and running a year later. Plans were in place to open the college for several years before it finally did, but the cyclical nature of the airline business plus the 1989 Australian pilots' dispute and other factors caused delays.

The facility offered an extensive flying and ground training syllabus intended to take students up to a standard where they graduate with a Commercial Pilots Licence with multi engine and instrument ratings. Modern 'live in' facilities and classrooms equipped with state-of-the-art computer based training aids were built for the college which was capable of accepting 16 new cadet pilots each month with a maximum 224 in residence at any one time.

The college's initial fleet comprised 12 Pacific Aerospace CT-4B Airtrainers, 24 Socata TB 10 Tobagos and nine Piper Senecas with the aerobatic CT-4 used for basic training up to the first 50 hours of the student's course. Each student spent a minimum 200 hours in the air of which 50 were on the CT-4, 105 on the Tobago and 45 on the Seneca. The complete course lasted 60 weeks and some 1170 hours were spent in the classroom plus 100 in simulators.

The college made some history shortly after its establishment when it was awarded the Australian Defence Force's flight screening contract, the first time this important task had been entrusted to a civilian organisation.

The college was subsequently renamed the Australian Air Academy and Ansett sold its half share to BAe in August 1996, after which the title British Aerospace Flight Training was adopted.

The inaugural Eastwest 'Gold Coast Highflyer' Boeing 727 service to Coolangatta was on 18 January 1992 using VH-ANE. As the passengers disembarked they no doubt took notice of the advertising on the aircraft and immediately rushed to the Conrad Jupiters casino in order to lose some money! (Geoff Wilkes)

lines and Lufthansa and eventually adding several other major carriers to its books including Singapore Airlines.

Frequent flyer schemes quickly became hugely successful all over the world with hundreds of millions joining. But their popularity also created some potential long term problems for airlines because each point earned represented a new entry in the 'liabilities' column of the ledger. With literally billions of unclaimed points on their books, airline financial managers around the world must be in dread of the day they are all called in!

the 'free set of steak knives' elements and concentrated on free flights, upgrades and other more travel related rewards. Partnerships were gradually built up with credit card companies, hotel chains and other organisations from which members could build up their points tallies without ever having actually flown with the host airline.

The announcement of codeshare agreements on various routes became an almost daily occurrence all over the world for several years until it seemed that every operator was in some way hooked up with someone else. Ansett was no exception, having put in place codeshare and/or frequent flyer program agreements with international carriers Lufthansa, United, Northwest, Alitalia, All Nippon, Garuda, Singapore, Swissair, Austrian and Malaysian by early 1993. Ansett also had a codeshare arrangement with British Airways for a while, but this lapsed when BA bought into Qantas.

Others were later added and it all culminated in March 1999 when Ansett was admitted to the Star Alliance as a full member, this group led by United Air-

Fleet Moves

The types of aircraft in Ansett's fleet had largely been established by 1990 with the Boeing 767, 727, 737 and Airbus A320 taking care of the trunk routes and the Fokker F28 and BAe 146 operating the major regional routes, the latter with Ansett WA but also Eastwest and Ansett New Zealand.

Ansett Air Freight had taken delivery of two BAe 146-200QT freighters in 1989 and its fleet had been supplemented from early 1989 through an agreement with Ipec to use its Argosy and DC-9 freighters under contract, the DC-9s subsequently operated by Independent Air Freighters on Ansett's behalf. AAF also leased several Douglas DC-8 freighters between 1989 and 1995, with only one in service at any time.

The Fokker 50 fleet of ten aircraft had all been delivered by early 1989 and flew with Ansett Express (the former Ansett NSW/Air NSW) before being allocated to

Eastwest Boeing 727-277 VH-RMN awaits takeoff clearance at Sydney in December 1992 while A320 VH-HYB comes in to land. (Julian Green)

(left) A general view of part of the Ansett domestic terminal and tarmac area at Sydney in 1993 showing two former Eastwest BAe 146-300s and a 727-200 still in Eastwest livery. By then, the Eastwest operation had ceased to exist. (right) Boeing 747-300 VH-INH was the second aircraft to enter service with Ansett International, operating its inaugural service from Sydney to Hong Kong on 10 September 1994. (Geoff Wilkes/John Vogel)

Skywest which also continued to operate its four BAe Jetstream 31s until 1999. Kendell had a mixed fleet of Saab 340s and Fairchild Metros while Aeropelican continued using its DHC Twin Otters.

By early 1995 Ansett's mainline fleet comprised six Boeing 767-200s, five 727-200s, 20 Boeing 737-300s and 12 Airbus A320s. On order were one 737-300 and five A320s.

As for non core activities, there started to be some disposal of subsidiary non airline companies in the first half of the 1990s, a trend which would continue throughout the remainder of the decade as Ansett's financial position gradually worsened and new owners took over.

Onto The World Stage

The Australian Government's 'One Nation' statement of February 1992 contained some significant and fundamental changes to aviation policy including allowing Qantas to fly on domestic routes (this allowing for the forthcoming merger with Australian Airlines); the start of negotiations with New Zealand for the establishment of an 'open skies' agreement between the two nations; and approval for Australian carriers other than Qantas to fly internationally.

Ansett Australia Flight Ticket.

Please note important information inside front cover.

Legislation was passed allowing the newly established International Air Services Commission (IASC) to award Australia's international air service capacity entitlements, these calculated in combination with the provisions various bilateral air services agreements negotiated with different countries. Applications for international capacity were assessed according to this and other criteria including tourism, trade and consumer benefits.

Ansett made its first application for international capacity – to Malaysia – in September 1992 and by early 1993 had added Indonesia, Singapore, Hong Kong and Japan to the list. In September 1993 Ansett Australia introduced its first international services when it began flying from Darwin, Melbourne, Perth and Sydney to Bali using aircraft from the domestic fleet. Darwin-Bali flights were added in March 1994 but these were just a precursor to the launch of the airline's dedicated international operation later in the year.

Ansett International's initial fleet comprised two Boeing 747-300s leased from Singapore Airlines, this being the source of all the 747s operated by the airline over the

The launch of Ansett International coincided with a new colour scheme and logo, the last one used by the airline. Ansett International represented a major undertaking and big step forward for the Ansett group. Two Boeing 747-312s were leased from Singapore Airlines as AI's initial equipment, VH-INJ operating the inaugural service between Sydney and Osaka on 4 September 1994. (Julian Green)

Despite Ansett's new livery being introduced in the second half of 1994, it took a while to repaint the entire fleet. Airbus A320 VH-HYL was photographed a year later still in the previous colour scheme. (Keith Anderson)

next seven years. In all, nine leased SIA 747-300s and four 747-400s (from August 1999) flew with Ansett International, normally two or three at a time. A 767-300ER was added in March 1996.

Ansett International's first 747-300 (VH-INJ) arrived in Australia on 29 August 1994, welcomed at Sydney by Prime Minister Paul Keating. VH-INH arrived the following month. After conducting a scheduled domestic Sydney-Perth flight on 31 August, VH-INJ launched Ansett International services on 4 September when it departed Sydney for Osaka in Japan.

The first Sydney-Hong Kong service was flown by VH-INH on 10 September and Kuala Lumpur, Taipei, Auckland, Jakarta, Seoul, Shanghai and Nadi were subsequently added to the network.

The new airline attracted some unwanted publicity just six weeks after it launched operations when VH-INH landed at Sydney with its nosewheel still retracted. The aircraft suffered damage to its underside and was out of service for nearly two months while repairs were made. There were no injuries as a result of the incident, caused by a mechanical problem.

The crew detected an 'unsafe' gear indication when it was selected down during the approach to Sydney. Actions taken to rectify the fault satisfied the captain that the undercarriage was down and properly locked, but it

The BAe-Ansett Flying College's initial equipment included 12 new production PAC CT-4B Airtrainers, these used for the first 50 flying hours of each student's training. (Stewart Wilson)

wasn't until the mainwheels were on the ground that the crew became aware (via the control tower) that the nosewheel leg was still retracted. Ansett International had to lease aircraft from Qantas and Malaysia Airlines to fill the capacity gap while VH-INH was being repaired.

Despite this, Ansett International quickly established a positive reputation for providing a high level of service – its 747s were dubbed 'Spaceships' by the marketing people to promote generous legroom in both classes – but the airline was a consistent money loser. It suffered badly at the hands of the Asian economic crisis of 1997-98 and was forced to drop several routes as the Asian market dramatically collapsed.

Ansett International was never able to properly develop due to financial constraints within the Ansett organisation. It was certainly unlucky to be hit by the Asian economic crisis when it was and as this market was its sole area of operation, the effects are obvious. Like the rest of the company, Ansett International needed a big influx of money and some proper direction, and this could really only be provided by a new owner with the best of connections in the global airline industry.

Ansett International also attracted the attention of the Foreign Investment Review Board shortly after its formation and in order to meet its requirements, 51% of the airline had to be sold to Australian institutional investors to ensure majority Australian ownership. This was achieved in late 1996.

The End Of ATI

The launch of Ansett International brought with it a new livery – Ansett's last – featuring a stylised gold 'A', the Southern Cross and the Federation Star, plus an advertising campaign based around the slogan 'One of the World's Great Airlines'.

This seemed to be the case as Ansett was collecting a regular flow of awards from the travel industry and others including 'Best Airline' in the inaugural Australian Federation of Travel Agents Australian Excellence Awards. In addition, the airline's package tour company, Ansett Holidays, was named best domestic tour operator at the same awards.

Ansett New Zealand standardised on a fleet of BAe 146s and Dash 8s in the 1990s but remained a substantial drain on its owners' bottom line throughout its existence. (Gerard Williamson/Peter Clark)

The domestic operation was still known as Ansett Australia but with the new livery and graphics, while the holding company underwent changes which saw the demise of one of Australia's best known company names – Ansett Transport Industries.

Established in May 1946 by Reg Ansett as the umbrella organisation for his rapidly diversifying and growing interests, the Ansett Transport Industries name survived the TNT-News takeover of 1980 and was retained until August 1994 when Ansett Australia Holdings Ltd was created in its place.

At the same time, Ansett Australia Limited replaced Ansett Transport industries (Operations) Pty Ltd as the division under which all of the company's airlines operated. Another change to the holding company's name was introduced in June 1995 when it became simply Ansett Holdings Ltd.

Ansett greeted the new decade and the arrival of industry deregulation in Australia with a new corporate livery based on the Australian flag, and a revised name – Ansett Australia. Introduced in October 1990, the new colour scheme is modelled by Boeing 737-377 VH-CZN in January 1991. (Cameron Hadlow)

FLEET SUMMARY – March 1995

Ansett Australia: 6 Boeing 767-200; 5 Boeing 727-200; 12 Airbus A320-200; 20 Boeing 737-300; 6 BAe 146-200; 5 BAe 146-300; 3 Fokker F28-1000 Fellowship; 2 Fokker F28-3000 Fellowship; 7 Fokker F28-4000 Fellowship; 6 Fokker 50. On order: 1 Boeing 747-300; 1 Boeing 767-200; 1 Boeing 737-300; 5 Airbus A320-200; 1 BAe 146-200.
Ansett International: 2 Boeing 747-300.
Ansett Air Freight: 1 Douglas DC-8-62F; 1 Boeing 727-200F; 2 BAe 146-200QT.
Ansett New Zealand: 1 BAe 146-200; 1 BAe 146-200QC; 8 BAe 146-300; 2 DHC Dash 8-100. On order: 1 DHC Dash 8-100.
Ansett Worldwide Aviation Services: Leased aircraft in service: 62 Boeing 737-300; 9 Boeing 737-500; 25 Boeing 757-200; 20 Boeing 767-200/300; 6 McDonnell Douglas MD-83.
Aeropelican Air Services: 4 DHC Twin Otter 300.
Kendell Airlines: 6 Saab 340A; 7 Fairchild Metro 23. On order: 3 Saab 340B.
Skywest Airlines: 3 Fokker 50; 4 BAe Jetstream 31.

FLEET SUMMARY – March 1992

Ansett Australia: 5 Boeing 767-200; 3 Boeing 727-200; 11 Airbus A320-200; 16 Boeing 737-300. On order: 1 Airbus A320-200 (delivery April 1992); 10 Airbus A321-100.
Ansett Air Freight: 1 Boeing 727-200F; 2 BAe 146-200QT.
Ansett Express: 5 Fokker F28-4000 Fellowship; 2 Fokker F28-3000 Fellowship; 2 Fokker F28-1000 Fellowship; 4 Fokker 50.
Ansett New Zealand: 6 BAe 146-300; 1 BAe 146-200QC; 1 BAe 146-200; 2 DHC Dash 8-100; 1 Fokker F27-600 Friendship.
Ansett WA: 5 BAe 146-200; 2 Fokker F28-4000 Fellowship; 3 Fokker F28-1000 Fellowship.
Ansett Worldwide Aviation Services: Leased aircraft in service: 2 Airbus A300-600; 37 Boeing 737-300; 9 Boeing 737-500; 13 Boeing 757-200; 4 Boeing 767-200; 1 Boeing 767-300; 6 McDonnell Douglas MD-83. On order: 2 Boeing 737-300; 5 Boeing 757-200 (plus 20 options); 2 Boeing 767-300 (plus 7 options); 6 Airbus A300-600R (plus 4 options); 12 McDonnell Douglas MD-83.
Eastwest Airlines: 1 Boeing 727-200; 7 BAe 146-300.
Aeropelican: 4 DHC Twin Otter 300.
Kendell Airlines: 6 Saab 340A; 7 Fairchild Metro II; 2 Fairchild Metro 23; 1 Fairchild Merlin IV.
Skywest Airlines: 4 BAe Jetstream 31.

CHAPTER ELEVEN

A FOREIGN AFFAIR

The period between 1995 and 2000 was an extraordinary one for Ansett, witnessing a declining financial position; attempts at restructuring the business to improve efficiency through the disposal of non core assets and reducing employee numbers; the introduction of the airline's frequent flyer program and then its revamped Global Rewards scheme in association with international partners; membership of the global Star Alliance; and the takeover of the airline by Air New Zealand in two stages.

The alarm bells regarding Ansett's financial position had begun ringing earlier in the decade, many industry analysts noting the group's potentially difficult cash situation. In April 1993, brokering house McIntosh Baring issued a report that estimated Ansett Transport Industries' net value at between zero and $300 million (based on assets worth $2.6-2.9 billion) and predicted the company would need substantial cash injections in the short and medium term.

The McIntosh Baring report predicted a $3 million operating loss for the 1992-93 financial year – despite first half earnings of $40 million – before taking into account predicted foreign exchange losses of $50-74 million. The report anticipated profits in 1993-94 but highlighted difficulties in reducing debt and finding a third equity partner to join current co-owners News Corporation Limited and TNT.

Ansett's actual results for 1992-93 were a gross operating profit of $59.5 million and a net deficit of $181.2 million after the foreign exchange losses were taken into account. In 1993-94 ATI recorded its highest ever gross profit of $209.2 million and by mid 1994 held 56% of the overall Australian domestic market and 52.5% of the markets it contested with Qantas. By the end of 1994 Ansett's overall share had dropped to 50.5% and continued to consistently decline after that as Qantas aggressively and successfully chased market share through adding 767 capacity.

Why, when on the face of it the 1993-94 financial year showed an ostensibly strong result?

The McIntosh Baring report provides part of the answer, stating that Ansett's three main problems were a weak balance sheet, underperforming assets and an expensive and inappropriate fleet, the latter an issue which would continually resurface over the next few years and after Ansett's collapse in 2001.

McIntosh Baring noted that the sale of assets such as Ansett New Zealand, Diners Club and the resorts could raise $200-300 million, but this would be insufficient to properly restore the balance sheet. An equity contribution of more than $100 million from the current owners was needed, followed by an additional cash injection of $150-200 million for a 25-30% stake in the company.

On top of that, the report suggested a public listing to raise a further $200-300 million. It also noted that Ansett would need to find an outside partner to invest in its planned international operation or to provide aircraft for it. Ansett International was launched in September 1994 and quickly became a further drain on resources.

The possibility that major changes would be made to Ansett's ownership and financial structure was confirmed in mid 1994 when the executive chairman of what was now Ansett Australia Holdings Ltd, Ken Cowley, stated in a television interview that he would like to see Ansett floated in '18 months to two years'. Mr Cowley also confirmed what many observers already suspected – that both TNT and News had looked at selling their interest in Ansett over the past few years.

Rearranging the Deck Chairs

The first hard news that part of Ansett would be sold emerged in May 1995 when it was revealed that talks between News and Air New Zealand had been going on since October the previous year with a view to the New Zealand flag carrier purchasing News' 50% shareholding in Ansett Australia Holdings.

A new logo and new Ansett Australia typeface from late 1994, but much bigger changes than mere decoration were just around the corner. (Rob Finlayson)

Ansett International quickly built up an excellent reputation for passenger service and comfort, particularly in the Asian market, but it was a consistent money loser. This was certainly not helped by the Asian economic crisis of 1997-98. Here, one of AI's Boeing 747-300s turns onto finals at the old Hong Kong Airport. (Rob Finlayson)

The talks broke down in July 1995, Air NZ's final offer before discussions ended covering a one third share of Ansett, but this was rejected by both News and TNT. As a result, News announced it would retain its 50% interest in the slightly renamed (again) Ansett Holdings Ltd 'for the long term'.

The decision to call off negotiations followed months of discussions during which it seemed that agreement was close several times. The price for a half share was reportedly put at between $400 million and $600 million, but News became frustrated by Air NZ's delays in agreeing to a figure. An important influence of Air NZ's reluctance to settle was due to the fact that Australia would not guarantee the granting of the international 'beyond rights' promised in the government's 'One Nation' policy statement of $2\frac{1}{2}$ years earlier. This contained a pledge to introduce a deregulated, 'open skies' Australia-New Zealand aviation market but the Australian Government partially reneged on its commitment, limiting the number of international ex Australia flights available to New Zealand carriers.

Publicly at least, TNT welcomed news of the talks ending, issuing a statement which said, 'With the uncertainty that has prevailed during the negotiation process, the resolution of shareholding issues will ensure both shareholders can now provide maximum attention to the further growth of Ansett as Australia's leading domestic airline.'

Ansett executive chairman Ken Cowley circulated a staff memo at the time announcing the decision to end negotiations with Air NZ and to state, 'It is fair to say that market conditions, particularly in the Australian domestic market, are very tough and we face difficult challenges in the coming months.' Mr Cowley was correct. Ansett had been steadily losing market share to Qantas over the previous few months and it was down to 48% by mid 1995. As for Qantas, it would only get stronger following its shares float and full privatisation in July 1995.

Despite the breakdown of talks, Air NZ considered the issue to be still open and announced its intention to continue pursuing an equity stake in Ansett. It didn't take long for talks between Air NZ and News to start again – in September 1995 – Ken Cowley this time saying, 'I'm going to continue to work hard to get some sort of link between Air New Zealand and Ansett.... we're not worried about our investment.... but we do need to reduce our exposure over the next five years and I hope we'll be able to do that.'

TNT Bails Out

At this stage it appeared certain that if one of Ansett's half owners did sell out (to Air New Zealand or anyone else) it would News. But all that changed in November 1995 when it was revealed that talks between Air New Zealand and TNT were being held.

(left) One of Ansett International's original pair of Boeing 747-312s leased from Singapore Airlines (VH-INH) at Sydney in February 1995. (right) Ansett acquired four additional Boeing 767-200s to boost domestic capacity in the mid 1990s. VH-RMK was the first of three 767-204s obtained from Britannia Airways and delivered in November 1994. The arrival of these 767s with standard two crew cockpits led to the removal of the flight engineer's station in Ansett's original five 767-200s. (Geoff Wilkes)

(left) Backing Ansett New Zealand's fleet of BAe 146 jets was a number of DHC Dash 8s including Dash 8-102 ZK-NEU snapped at Palmerston North in February 1996. Eight months earlier, sister aircraft ZK-NEY was lost in a fatal accident on approach to the airport in bad weather. (right) Ansett International added to its fleet in March 1996 with the delivery of Boeing 767-324ER VH-BZF, leased from GE Capital. (Peter Clark & Steve Allsop)

Early reports indicated that Air NZ would initially purchase half of TNT's holding in Ansett (or 25% of the company) for an estimated $A150-200 million and retain an option to purchase the remaining TNT interest within three years.

In December 1995 it was confirmed that Air NZ would purchase TNT's Ansett shares in two stages. The plan was for Air NZ to acquire half of TNT's shareholding initially for $200 million and the remainder for $225 million by February 1998. At the same time it was announced that Ansett had disposed of its own relatively small stake in TNT, 23 million shares worth about $44m.

The decision produced some potential problems. The New Zealand Government was concerned about Air NZ acquiring a half share in its only domestic competitor (Ansett New Zealand) and the effect that could have on competition, while the Australian Government was seeking a ruling on whether an Ansett half owned by Air New Zealand interests was a foreign owned or foreign controlled company as defined under the Air Navigation Act. The key to this was deciding whether or not Ansett's other shareholder (News) was regarded as foreign.

If foreign investment in an Australian international operator exceeded 49%, Ansett's status as an international carrier could be changed on the basis that it was no longer a substantially Australian owned and controlled company.

The New Zealand Commerce Commission (NZCC) issued its objections to the plan in February 1996, using the Ansett New Zealand situation as its main concern on competition grounds with New Zealand's two domestic airlines owned by the same organisation. To add to the complications, there was also the fact that Qantas owned 19.9% of Air New Zealand at that stage.

The NZCC ruled that Air NZ and Ansett Holdings would become 'associated persons' as defined by Section 47 of the NZ Commerce Act. Under the act, 'associated persons' are deemed able, either directly or indirectly, to exert a substantial degree of influence over the activities of the other. The result, according to the

Ansett New Zealand built up its fleet of BAe 146s to a peak of 10 aircraft including several former Eastwest -100s. This pair was photographed at Queenstown in July 1998 on the occasion of the first Queenstown-Auckland direct service thanks to a runway extension at the South Island tourist centre. (Peter Clark)

Commission, would be a monopoly on New Zealand domestic routes and therefore result in higher fares and reduced service standards.

This problem was eventually circumvented by News agreeing to purchase a 100% interest in Ansett New Zealand, satisfying both the NZCC's anti competition concerns and the needs of TNT and Air NZ. As a result, the NZCC approved Air NZ's purchase of TNT's Ansett shareholding in June 1996 on condition that the News takeover of Ansett NZ be consummated within one working day of the TNT/Air NZ agreement being completed.

Both Air NZ and Ansett expressed satisfaction with the NZCC's approval of the deal. On the acquisition of Ansett NZ by News, Air NZ managing director Jim McCrae said there was no problem and that his airline 'never had

Skywest retired its last three Jetstream 31s in March 1999 after 15 years' service. Skywest's Jetstreams were the hardest worked in the world in times of flying hours and cycles. (Les Bushell)

an interest in this operation and has always expected to see a high level of competition continue in the New Zealand domestic airline market. Our interest has always been to achieve a meaningful stake in Ansett Australia's domestic and international operations.'

The other major part of the puzzle which still remained unsolved was the fate of Ansett International.

This was resolved later in the year when the Australian Foreign Investment Review Board (FIRB) ruled the carrier would exceed foreign ownership limitations with Air New Zealand involved and therefore risk compromising its bilateral air service agreement rights. As a result, 51% of Ansett International was sold off to an institutional investor consortium – International Airline Investment Holdings – led by insurance giant AMP and including County NatWest. As for Qantas, it disposed of its 19.9% interest in Air New Zealand in March 1997.

The FIRB delayed its decision on Ansett International for several months, this in turn causing a postponement of the TNT/Air NZ deal's completion. In the meantime, some adjustments to the detail of the purchase were made. Air NZ would still end up with 50% of Ansett by acquiring TNT's shareholding, but it would now be done in a single move rather than the previously planned two parts. Under the revised agreement, Air NZ would pay a total $A475 million for half of Ansett, $325 million to TNT and a further $150m in the form of a capital injection. News also agreed to a $50m capital injection, recognising – like

The Boeing 737-300 remained the most numerous aircraft in the Ansett fleet until the September 2001 collapse, by which time 24 were in service. VH-CZF – one of the original batch of 12 built in 1986 – is shown here departing Sydney Airport in November 1997. (Trent Jones)

The Fokker F28 was phased out of Ansett service in December 1999, F28-4000 VH-FKI flying a Mount Newman-Perth service. This shot captures sister aircraft VH-FKJ at Perth in September 1995 in company with Skywest Fokker 50 VH-FNG. (David Daw)

everyone else – that the airline was in desperate need of some cash.

Another provision included in the deal was that TNT could be paid an additional $75 million if News decided to sell its share in Ansett before June 2003. TNT could also qualify for profit sharing payments should Ansett achieve certain targets.

On 1 October 1996 and following final shareholder and regulatory approval, Air New Zealand formally acquired TNT's 50% share of Ansett Australia Holdings. A new and relatively short era for the airline that had launched operations more than 60 years earlier in rural Victoria had begun. With the new ownership situation came a change at the top for Ansett Holdings, former Cathay Pacific managing director Rod Eddington taking over from Ken Cowley as the group's executive chairman. Mr Cowley remained as a director of the airline.

Starting On A High

The new era started on a high note with the announcement in January 1997 that Ansett had been appointed official carrier for the Sydney 2000 Olympics, its successful bid consortium including international carriers Air New Zealand, Lufthansa, Malaysia Airlines, South African Airways, Thai Airways International and United Airlines.

As the official carrier, Ansett and its partners would carry members of the Australian Olympic Committee, the Games organising committee, many of the competing athletes and others travelling on Olympics business before and during the event. Ansett subsidiary Traveland was appointed the official Olympics travel agent and the deal promised substantial new business for the airline.

On the other hand there was Qantas, which was not the official Olympic carrier but to some appeared to be behaving as if it was. Many people consider Qantas did Ansett's potential Olympics promotional and business opportunities considerable damage – especially overseas – when it later launched a series of advertising campaigns which at least created the impression that Qantas was involved in the Olympics.

The advertisements used high profile athletes and took advantage of Qantas' own high profile on the local and international markets, whereas Ansett was comparatively unknown overseas. The advertisements never stated anything to directly suggest that Qantas was the official Olympics carrier but they certainly created an impression that might have allowed viewers and readers of them to come to that conclusion.

In that sense the Qantas campaign was very successful and certainly had an effect on Ansett's Olympics business, although the extent of this is impossible to quantify. As for Ansett, it later claimed it was happy with the extra business generated by the Olympics, with a figure of $300 million mentioned by some.

Pointer to the Future

In May 1997 it was announced that a major international airline alliance had been established. The Star Alliance initially comprised United, Lufthansa, Thai International, SAS and Air Canada, these subsequently joined by Varig, Mexicana, All Nippon Airways, Air New Zealand, Ansett and Singapore Airlines.

Between them, the five founding airlines served 584 international destinations including 340 in the USA. By 2000 this had grown to over 720 destinations in 110 countries through extensive codeshare agreements. Frequent Flyer programs were co-ordinated, as were check-in, airport operations, purchasing, marketing, cargo, information technology and promotional activities.

It was the way of the future, the Star and other alliances offering their member airlines considerable benefits through what was in effect a giant cooperative operating on a global scale. Star was the second of these major alliances to be established (Atlantic Excellence/Qualiflyer with Delta, Swissair, Sabena and Austrian Airlines had been the first in June 1996) and was followed by others including 'oneworld' (British Airways, American, Qantas, Cathay Pacific, Canadian International etc) from September 1998. Star and oneworld quickly became the 'big two' and most influential.

What might have been. A nicely symbolic shot of a Singapore Airlines 747 nosing up to an Ansett terminal. At one stage it looked as if the deal had been done, but..... (Geoff Klouth)

Associated but independent designated carriers provided feed for Ansett airlines including Queensland's Flight West, New Zealand's Tranzair, and Ansett New Zealand Regional, which resulted from a merger between Tranzair and Northern Commuter Airlines. (Andrew Eyre/Greg Hore/Gary Hollier)

For Ansett, involvement with Star was still nearly two years away. In June 1997 it, Ansett International, Air New Zealand and Singapore Airlines (SIA) announced plans to establish the Asia-Pacific region's largest airline commercial alliance. Initial plans revolved around the carriers codesharing on each other's flights, integrating networks and scheduling, co-operating on product development promotion and marketing, frequent flyer scheme co-operation, and combining information technology and cargo operations resources.

The plan needed regulatory approval, this forthcoming (from the Australian Competition and Consumer Commission) in June 1998. The association with SIA added some credence to industry rumours that it had been considering a possible investment in Ansett.

The agreement gave SIA its long desired albeit indirect entrée to the Australian domestic market (it had lost out to British Airways in its bid for 25% of Qantas a few years earlier), and at the Memorandum of Understanding signing ceremony, SIA deputy chairman and chief executive Dr Cheong Choong noted the alliance 'gives Singapore confidence to further expand into Australia'.

For Ansett, SIA was regarded as a 'natural partner' according to Rod Eddington, who also noted that the tie-up with SIA – on top of the links with 'bedrock partner' Air New Zealand – provided good opportunities for Australia's second largest airline to reduce costs and increase revenues in its bid to return to profitability.

Despite the rumours, the alliance did not involve SIA taking an equity stake in Ansett at that time, but most industry analysts continued to believe that SIA retained the desire to buy into the Australian airline, something that would prove to be the case a couple of years later.

As for the new alliance, it existed in its original form only until March 1999 when both Ansett and Air New Zealand were admitted to the Star Alliance as full members after having been afforded 'observer' status the previous July. SIA followed shortly afterwards.

Disposing of Assets

Meanwhile, Air New Zealand and News had to take some action to ensure that Ansett had a future at all. An injection of capital was required, fleet replacement was looming as an issue in the not too distant future, revenues had to be increased and costs had to be reduced.

The disposal of non core assets became a feature of Ansett Holdings' activities over the next few years, businesses given the chop including bus and coach body builder Ansair, road transport company Ansett-Ridgeways, general aviation firm Pacific Aviation, the company's half share in the Australian Air Academy (formerly BAe-Ansett Flying College) to co-owner British Aerospace, Skywest's charter operation (the airline business was retained) and in May 1998 its Whitsunday Islands resorts, one of Ansett's longest established activities and a favourite of Reg Ansett.

Ansett sold its 100% interest in Hayman Island and its half share in Hamilton Island Airport to the BT Hotel Group for a total of $94m. BT already has a majority share of Hamilton Island plus a minority interest in the airport. Hayman's sale price was a bargain basement $61.5m – the resort cost over $300m to develop. The sale of Hamilton Island Airport ended Ansett's exclusive rights to the facility, while the disposal of Hayman would have broken Reg Ansett's heart had he still been alive.

The Australian domestic airline industry changed again in mid 2000 when low cost operators Impulse and Virgin Blue launched operations. Both created new traffic but also took business away from Ansett. Impulse disappeared into Qantas in 2001 but following the collapse of Ansett, Virgin Blue remains the only mainline competitor to the much larger 'flying kangaroo'. (Tim Dath/Gerard Williamson)

More disposals followed – the 68% stake in Diners Club Australia (to Diners Club International); wholly owned subsidiary Transport Industries Insurance (which had been established in 1960 as a captive insurer to manage Ansett's requirements and became a general insurer in 1975, offering travel and general insurance); the door-to-door express road freight business to TNT; and the catering arm to Gate Gourmet, part of Swissair's SAir Group. Ansett Air Freight was renamed Ansett Australia Cargo in July 1999.

In April 2000, Ansett Worldwide Aviation Services (AWAS) was sold to US based aircraft lessor MSDW Aircraft Holdings. The new merged entity was renamed Ansett Worldwide in July 2001 but despite the name retained no association with the airline or its owners. AWAS had been one of News-TNT's success stories having started in March 1986 with 12 Boeing

Former Eastwest BAe 146-300 VH-EWI on short finals for Sydney Airport in June 1999. By then, Ansett still had 11 146s in the Ansett Australia fleet plus two freighters and another 10 operating with Ansett New Zealand. (Craig Murray)

737-300s and six McDonnell Douglas MD-83s on its books. By the time it was sold, AWAS managed a fleet of over 160 aircraft serving with airlines around the world.

Reducing the Workforce

Ansett's restructuring and cost cutting program started to get serious in 1998 with the announcement in April that 15 corporate retail offices would be closed within two months – six in Queensland, five in Western Australia, two in Melbourne's central business district, one in Launceston and one in Alice Springs. Eighty-nine jobs were affected.

Ansett also launched a voluntary redundancy scheme in early 1998 as part of its ongoing attempts to cut costs and improve efficiency and profitability. Reducing its workforce was considered an important part of this

As part of Ansett's 'Great Business Plan' announced in September 1999, the regional subsidiaries were given many less profitable routes previously served by the main airline. Kendell Airlines was a major part of this strategy and received the first of 11 Bombardier CRJ200 regional jets in September 1999. (Rob Finlayson)

pany more efficient and increase profitability to 10% of revenue. The plan resulted from the airline's Business Review Program, conducted with consultants Bain & Co, executive management, and some 60 senior managers over the previous 10 months, this intended to identify short term cost savings, review Ansett's internal processes and develop long term operating strategies. It was planned that most of the changes would be implemented over a three year period 'in an agreed order of priority designed to accelerate the major benefits', according to Rod Eddington.

As part of the review, the airline's route network came under scrutiny and it was discovered that although most trunk and major routes had been performing profitably, leisure routes and regional services to smaller centres in eastern Australia had been losing money. It was therefore decided to withdraw or reduce services to a number of centres in Queensland, New South Wales, Tasmania and the ACT (Canberra) and hand these over to wholly owned regional subsidiary Kendell Airlines.

Between November 1999 and July 2001 Ansett would pull out of the Adelaide-Canberra, Melbourne-Launceston, Brisbane-Canberra, Brisbane-Rockhampton, Brisbane-Mackay, Sydney-Coffs Harbour and Sydney-Ballina routes; reduce services to Canberra from Melbourne and Sydney; and reduce Melbourne-Hobart services to one daily return flight.

To replace these reduced services, the Great Business Plan allowed for Kendell to acquire 12 Bombardier CRJ200 or Embraer ERJ-145 50 seat regional jetliners, configured in a single class and allowing a boost of frequencies between the affected ports. It was decided that the new jets would be maintained at Kendell's Wagga Wagga base and their introduction would allow Ansett to dispose of two Boeing 737-300s and four former Eastwest BAe 146-300s.

Fleet rationalisation was also on the agenda but without any decisions being reached. Mr Eddington acknowledged that Ansett needed to have either the Boeing 737 or Airbus A320 in its fleet (but not both) but said a decision was not an immediate priority as the current fleets were still relatively young. He suggested that any

process. The airline said at the time that it hoped that jobs held by people genuinely interested in taking a redundancy package would be made available to other staff if and when the positions were vacated.

About 1,000 employees quickly indicated an interest in the plan, although the airline could offer no guarantees that packages would be offered to all who applied for them as skill shortages in certain areas had to be avoided.

Ansett announced no specific target for the number of jobs it wanted to axe but 'at least several hundred' was mentioned. The sting in the tail was that Ansett made no secret of the fact that compulsory redundancies would have to be introduced if the number of voluntary departures was insufficient.

According to human resources director Trevor Martin: 'Compulsory redundancies are a last resort. If positions become redundant, we will try to redeploy people, if that is what they want. Knowing where there are other people willing to take voluntary redundancy will increase the opportunities for redeployment'. In addition, new recruitment procedures were introduced to ensure that vacant positions were filled from within the company wherever possible.

The question of employee numbers was always a difficult one at Ansett over its last few years. By mid 1998 the overall number employed by Ansett Holdings (including all subsidiaries) was about 16,100, some 1,800 fewer than two years earlier and largely as a result of the sale of subsidiaries. Productivity – based on revenue generated per employee – had increased by 18.3% to $217,403 over the same period, but this was considered by most to be still too low.

More jobs were cut over the next couple of years as further assets were sold off, but by the time of Ansett's collapse in September 2001 most analysts considered that its workforce of about 15,000 was at least 20% too high for its market share. By then, Ansett held only 40% of the Australian domestic market.

The Great Business Plan

In September 1998 Ansett launched its vision for the future – the Great Business Plan – intended to make the com-

The selling of non core assets was a large part of Ansett's business plan in the second half of the 1990s. Among the disposals was Reg Ansett's favourite – the Hayman Island resort – and Ansett's half share in neighbouring Hamilton Island Airport. (David Neafsey)

such decision may be about 12 months away. Three years later when Ansett collapsed both types were still in the fleet with the number of 737s increased and the 20 A320s which were in service in 1998 retained.

As for Ansett International, it was in a difficult position. The commercial alliance agreement between Ansett, Air New Zealand and Singapore Airlines signed the previous year seemed to limit AI's options and there was also the fact that in 1998 the Asian financial crisis was in full swing. This had forced the withdrawal of AI from several routes and contributed to the airline losing $57 million in the 1997-98 financial year whereas Ansett Holdings overall recorded a before tax operating profit of $59.8 million. As this figure represented only 1.7% of revenues, Ansett had a long way to go to reach the target 10%.

At first, it appeared as if the Great Business Plan's initiatives were having a positive effect with Ansett recording considerably improved profits for the 1998-99 financial year. Ansett Australia reported a before tax operating profit of $163m, including a $15.9m profit by the regionals and a much reduced loss of just under $10m by Ansett International. As for parent company Ansett Holdings Ltd, its before tax profit was $200.4m including $52.8m worth of abnormals mainly involving the sale of non core assets. In addition, Ansett Australia staff numbers fell by 450 to 11,920.

For the Staff and Friends of Ansett Australia

News

JUNE 1999 No. 2000

New Level 3 Management Announced

MEB MAR 00 DILBERT Manager Information Technology ANSETTAUSTRALIA

MEB MAR 00 MR BEAN Manager Strategy and Direction ANSETTAUSTRALIA

MEB MAR 00 RONALD Manager Inflight Catering ANSETTAUSTRALIA

MEB MAR 00 M LEWINSKY Manager Corporate Affairs ANSETTAUSTRALIA

MEB MAR 00 C SKASE Manager Finance ANSETTAUSTRALIA

MEB MAR 00 KENNY Manager Health and Safety ANSETTAUSTRALIA

Needless to say, not everyone within Ansett was completely enamoured with management, as this very unofficial staff newsletter shows. In case the reproduction is too difficult to read, the new Level 3 Managers were: Dilbert (Information Technology), Mr Bean (Strategy and Direction), Ronald Mac (Inflight Catering), M Lewinsky (Corporate Affairs), C Skase (Finance), and Kenny (Health and Safety).

As a consequence of the Great Business Plan's increased emphasis on regional operations and the need for improved feed to the main airline, Ansett and leading New South Wales based regional carrier Hazelton Airlines in April 1999 signed a five year agreement under which Hazelton would be the sole preferred NSW carrier for Ansett other than on routes also operated by the main airline and Kendell.

Hazelton operated a fleet of eight Saab 340s and four Fairchild Metros at the time and flew to 17 centres in NSW (including Sydney) plus Coolangatta, Brisbane and Traralgon/Morwell. Ansett also secured first right of refusal on 20% of Hazelton's shares, this option taken up in October 2000 and precipitating a protracted and sometimes bitter battle for full control of the airline between Ansett and Qantas, both of which realised its importance. Ansett eventually prevailed and by March 2001 had acquired over 90% of Hazelton's shareholding.

Fleet Moves

In October 1998, Ansett regional subsidiary Kendell Airlines ordered 12 Bombardier CRJ200 regional jets and placed options on 12 more, confirming the plans announced in the Great Business Plan that would see a major expansion of Kendell's fleet and route network, taking over many services previously operated by Ansett Australia.

The first CRJ200 (VH-KJF) was delivered to the company's Wagga Wagga base on 30 September 1999 with the remaining 11 of the order arriving between December 1999 and June 2001. It is generally considered that the CRJs didn't quite work for Ansett and Kendell and when Ansett collapsed the regional jets were not returned to service when Kendell resumed flying while under administration.

In a mid 2001 interview with *Australian Aviation* magazine, then Air New Zealand/Ansett chief executive Gary Toomey confirmed there were problems with the aircraft: 'The CRJs have not been as successful as people might have anticipated... there are still issues about integrating them into the fleet and some of the issues revolve around us having to use expensive contract pilots because the conversion of some of the Kendell pilots from the Saabs didn't go as well as they had planned.

'Whether those aircraft are the right aircraft for some of the key markets that they operate now has put a question mark in my mind, particularly on some of the more lucrative routes. On the Canberra-Brisbane route for example, we are putting back some [BAe] 146s onto the service three times a day because they provide a two class configuration for the high yield government traffic which is a requirement they have.'

As for the mainline fleet, Ansett took delivery of two more Airbus A320s (an additional four aircraft were already on order) and two Boeing 767-200s for domestic services in the second half of the 1990s, one 767-300 for Ansett International (March 1996) and two 737-300s. All were leased. The domestic orders were intended to allow Ansett to retire its remaining Boeing 727s and Fokker F28s while in August 1999 Ansett International received its first Boeing 747-400, leased from Singapore Airlines. A second 747-400 from the same source followed the next month.

Retirees included the Fokker 50 which flew its last service with Ansett Australia on 30 August 1996, the occasion also marking the final time a propeller driven aircraft flew a 'proper' Ansett service. The type was retained for use by regional subsidiary Skywest. Australia's

Ansett Air Freight was renamed Ansett Air Cargo in June 1999, at the same time its door-to-door express road freight business was sold to TNT. BAe 146-200QT VH-JJZ reflects the revised title. (Rob Finlayson)

first regional jetliner – the Fokker F28 – was also withdrawn from service in December 1999 after 30 years, as was the last of Skywest's four hard-worked BAe Jetstream 31s in March 1999, the highest timed Jetstreams in the world at that stage.

The most significant aircraft type to be withdrawn from service was undoubtedly the Boeing 727, the first jet airliner to operate domestic services in Australia. Ansett announced the sale of its last six Boeing 727-200s in December 1996 – five passenger aircraft and a freighter – to Tennessee based Intrepid Aviation. Four departed for the USA almost immediately, leaving two in service until April 1997. After 33 years, the Boeing 727 finally bowed out of Ansett service on 23 April 1997 when 727-200LR VH-ANB flew the type's last commercial sector from Hobart to Melbourne.

Ansett operated a total of 28 727s over the years (including short term leases) and the type's final act in the airline's service occurred on 26 April 1997 when five special flights over Melbourne were put on for staff and enthusiasts using 727-200LRs VH-ANA and ANB.

Monopoly With Real Money

The 12 months period from January 1999 was remarkable, even by the often confusing and uncertain standards of the airline industry generally and some of the region's operators in particular. For a while it seemed that just about everyone was looking at purchasing an interest in everyone else: Singapore Airlines in Ansett and Air NZ, Air NZ in Ansett, Qantas in Air NZ, Ansett employees in their own airline, and so on.

It all started in January 1999 when after months of speculation, Singapore Airlines confirmed it was looking at acquiring a 25% equity stake in Ansett and therefore access to the Australian domestic market. Things began to look as if they were definitely going somewhere on 29 March 1999 – just

20
FLYING TO THE FUTURE

The 2Oth
Ansett Australia
Travel & Transport
Writers Seminar

Hayman Island
Great Barrier Reef
August 27-29 1995

Another Ansett institution to go during the cost cutting 1990s was the Travel & Transport Writers' Seminar, a great favourite of everyone and an event which created much positive PR for Ansett. The 20th seminar was the penultimate one.

one day after Ansett and Air New Zealand were admitted into the Star Alliance as full members – when Singapore Airlines announced it had offered to purchase News Ltd's 50% holding in Ansett Australia for $A500m.

News of the offer was greeted with enthusiasm by most observers, who agreed that SIA was capable of providing Ansett with the capital injection it needed as well as proper representation on the world stage. For a time it appeared that consummating the deal was certain, but as existing half owner Air New Zealand had pre-emptive rights to the first option on Ansett, providing its bid at least matched SIA's. Despite this small uncertainty, it looked as if the SIA deal would go ahead. After all, even if Air New Zealand had the wherewithal to buy the other half of Ansett, few were convinced its resources were sufficient to make the necessary ongoing investment in the Australian based carrier.

Comparisons between Air New Zealand and Ansett at the time are interesting. By 1999 Air NZ was carrying 6.5 million passengers per annum (Ansett 13.5 million); Air NZ had 76 aircraft in its fleet and conducted 470 daily departures (Ansett 102 and 540); Air NZ had 9,200 employees (Ansett 14,900 – so much for plans to reduce staff numbers!); and Air NZ's total revenue in the 1998-99 financial year was $US1.8 billion (Ansett $US2.3 billion). In other words, Ansett was a bigger operation.

The deal between Ansett and SIA that everyone thought was a 'done thing' began to collapse in June 1999 when discussions were discontinued on News Ltd's behest due to uncertainties created by Air NZ's position on its pre-emptive rights. Air NZ's board had approved the sale to SIA but major shareholder Brierley Investments Limited (BIL) increased its stake in the airline and then attempted to get SIA to buy Ansett through Air NZ directly or through BIL in order to turn a quick profit. The result was an unsatisfactory situation for SIA and an impasse.

The situation had another negative effect for SIA – the timing of its plan to join the Star Alliance. The two events were linked because SIA wanted to finalise the Ansett deal before being admitted to Star as a full member.

A statement on the matter was issued: 'News Limited today expressed its disappointment that Singapore Airlines and Air New Zealand had not yet resolved issues between them concerning Ansett Australia. Chairman and chief executive Mr Rupert Murdoch said that News Limited had therefore discontinued discussions about the future of the company's 50% stake in Ansett. We have faith that Singapore Airlines and Air New Zealand will be able to reach agreement on how they wish to proceed. Once this occurs, News is prepared to renew discussions with them.'

SIA issued its own statement, expressing its disappointment with News' decision to withdraw its offer to sell to SIA: 'In a joint statement issued on 29 March 1999, SIA and News Ltd announced that an understanding on the sale had been reached, and the transaction was expected to be finalised in the second half of 1999. Air New Zealand has the pre-emptive right to match any offer to buy News' stake. SIA met with Air New Zealand several times to discuss their waiver of this right. As News has now decided to withdraw its offer to sell, the question of the waiver no longer applies....'

Most observers agreed that those involved had more to lose than gain if the situation remained at stalemate – News would be left with half an airline, a non core business that required substantial investment in the near future; SIA would lose access to the Australian domestic market; Air NZ would lose expansion opportunities; BIL would waste the investment it made in purchasing additional Air NZ shares in the hope of deriving a quick profit; and Ansett itself would be deprived of the investment it so badly needed.

Upping The Ante

The situation remained static over the next few months until October 1999 when the asking price for News Ltd's half share in Ansett suddenly increased substantially. The price had been $A500 million, but since then Ansett had announced a $148.9 million profit for the 1998-99 financial and seen the positive effects of the Great Business Plan restructuring manifest themselves through the balance

sheet. The result was that the price for half of Ansett was possibly twice as much and News appeared to be in no hurry to sell – at least until the price was right. The true motivation for withdrawal of the earlier sale offer to SIA suddenly became clearer.

When asked what the price might now be, Rupert Murdoch replied: 'It would have to be a great deal more. If you take a multiple of Qantas or Air NZ itself then the price would be doubled' – to one billion dollars. Industry analysts immediately suggested this was optimistic and the true value of half of Ansett now was probably closer to $700 million.

The situation was further complicated in December 1999 when it was announced that Ansett Australia's employees had put together a plan to buy the 50% of Ansett owned by News Ltd. The plan had the broad support and backing of the major unions associated with the airline and would be funded through a mixture of debt and equity with shares vested in the employees over time through a mechanism linked to future remuneration and productivity gains. The Ansett Employee Buyout Steering Committee was working with Deutsche Bank and New York based investment bank Klein and Co on the planned purchase, with a price of around $500m discussed.

Committee spokesman Captain Gavin Springs said the buyout 'would be good for the airline, beneficial to shareholders and great for the country as it will restore a significant level of Australian ownership in an important corporate icon. We expect Air New Zealand will find it more attractive to partner with employees rather than a rival airline.... we believe the revitalisation that would result from employee ownership and participation would give Ansett added competitive strength when challenging new entrants in the Australian market....'

A Done Deal

Unfortunately for them, the Ansett buyout group didn't get very far, because on 18 February 2000, Air New Zealand announced it had exercised its pre-emptive rights and would purchase News Ltd's 50% of Ansett Holdings for around $A680m. Industry reaction was at best subdued, many analysts predicting problems and ruing the opportunity Ansett may have missed by not being taken over by the larger, cashed up, prestigious and more dynamic Singapore Airlines.

There was considerable (mainly private) discussion among those involved in the industry about Air New Zealand's seemingly 'get Ansett at all costs' attitude, about how to the observer it seemed that Air NZ's desire to control Ansett fully had become almost obsessional. There was general agreement that the price had been too high (especially for Air NZ) and that anyway, there was no way the carrier was going to be able to give Ansett the ongoing financial support it so desperately needed.

There were a few more things that had to happen before the Ansett-Air New Zealand deal was finally consummated. Some confusion was caused in March 2000 when it was

The All Blacks front row may have had plenty of muscle but did Air New Zealand have sufficient power to help Ansett get the shove on the opposing pack? As most expected, the answer was 'no'. (SW Collection)

ANSETT'S ALLIANCES 1992-99

Date	Airline	Notes
Oct 1992	United Airlines	Codeshare on Ansett domestic flights, frequent flyer program (FFP) participation, reciprocal lounge access; Olympics Alliance partner from 1997.
Oct 1994	Malaysia Airlines	Codesharing via Melbourne and Sydney to Adelaide, Cairns, Canberra, Hobart and Gold Coast; Olympics Alliance partner from Jan 1997.
Nov 1995	Virgin Atlantic	Marketing agreement and joint fares between UK and Australia via Hong Kong.
Nov 1995	Eva Air	Codesharing on Taipei-Sydney and Taipei-Brisbane routes, seat allocation on some Ansett domestic routes.
April 1996	KLM	Intercontinental route partner, codesharing between Sydney, Brisbane, Melbourne, Canberra, Adelaide and Cairns; through check-in and FFP co-operation.
Jan 1997	Lufthansa	Olympic Alliance partner; connecting service from Frankfurt via Singapore to Melbourne, Sydney and Brisbane; shared passenger lounges in Melbourne, Sydney and Brisbane; reciprocal FFPs.
Jan 1997	South African	Olympics Alliance partner; reciprocal FFP participation.
Jan 1997	Thai International	Olympics Alliance partner; reciprocal FFP participation.
June 1998	Air NZ/SIA	Asia-Pacific region alliance covering joint marketing, promotion, codesharing, reciprocal FFPs, rationalised ground services, integrated schedules and joint cargo services. Reciprocal domestic codeshares on most Ansett/Air NZ domestic flights.
March 1999	Star Alliance	Admitted as full member with United, Lufthansa, Air Canada, Thai International, SAS, Varig and Air NZ.
March 1999	All Nippon Airways	FFP co-operation and codeshare agreement on Osaka-Sydney route.

revealed that Qantas was looking at purchasing the 47% of Air New Zealand owned by Brierley Investments, this having the potential to create all sorts of problems if it happened.

If Qantas was able to acquire a stake in Air NZ, then it (Air NZ) would have to dispose of Ansett on competition grounds, but even if that happened, both the Australian and New Zealand competition watchdogs would be concerned about the conglomerate that would be created. For example, the two airlines between them controlled 80% of the trans-Tasman market.

The key to the eventual outcome was Brierley Investments, which needed cash to eliminate debt estimated at around $1.3 billion and wanted to divest its B-class shares in Air NZ, these representing 16.7% of the airline. However, Singapore Airlines also had been discussing buying these and other shares to give it 25% of Air NZ, but was rebuffed.

A Qantas investment in Air NZ was at the time potentially problematic – in the administrative and regulatory sense – especially in view of the ongoing Ansett-News-Air NZ-SIA saga. The industry was spared that situation developing, because in April Singapore Airlines acquired an 8.3% stake in Air New Zealand and a few days later increased that shareholding to 25%, the maximum allowed by New Zealand's foreign ownership laws.

Less complicated was the announcement in March 2000 that News was selling its 100% interest in Ansett New Zealand to a group of investors which included Australian bush clothing manufacturer R M Williams. The deal was completed the following September, Ansett New Zealand becoming Tasman Pacific Airlines and operating as Qantas New Zealand under a franchise agreement. The former Ansett NZ fleet of BAe 146s and

Dash 8s was retained, these aircraft still owned by Ansett. The airline survived only until April 2001 before collapsing, forcing Qantas to operate NZ domestic services in its own right.

Finally, on 23 June 2000, Air New Zealand's acquisition of News' shareholding in Ansett was formally completed following finalisation of the necessary regulatory details. Ansett's future path was now set, but it would prove to be a short one.

FLEET SUMMARY – March 1998

Ansett Australia: 10 Boeing 767-200; 20 Airbus A320-200; 21 Boeing 737-300; 7 BAe 146-200; 4 BAe 146-300; 2 Fokker F28-4000 Fellowship. Stored awaiting disposal: 2 Fokker F28-3000; 1 Fokker F28-4000.

Ansett International: 3 Boeing 747-300; 1 Boeing 767-300ER.

Ansett Air Freight: 1 Boeing 727-200F; 2 BAe 146-200QT; 1 Fokker F27-600QC (Independent Air Freighters contract).

Ansett New Zealand: 1 BAe 146-200QC; 9 BAe 146-300; 4 DHC Dash 8-100.

Ansett Worldwide Aviation Services: Delivered for leasing: 74 Boeing 737-300; 11 Boeing 737-500; 21 Boeing 757-200; 4 Boeing 757-200PF; 4 Boeing 767-200ER; 21 Boeing 767-300ER; 8 Airbus A300-600R; 18 McDonnell Douglas MD-83.

Aeropelican Air Services: 4 DHC Twin Otter 300.

Kendell Airlines: 8 Saab 340A; 8 Saab 340B; 5 Fairchild Metro 23. On order: 12 Bombardier CRJ200.

Skywest Airlines: 5 Fokker 50; 3 BAe Jetstream 31.

THE ANSETT OLYMPICS

In January 1997, Ansett was selected as the official carrier for the Sydney 2000 Olympics, it and its partner airlines hoping to cash in on the world's second largest sporting event. Some of Ansett's aircraft carried special colour schemes to celebrate the occasion.

Boeing 747-312 VH-INJ at Sydney in July 1999. (Craig Murray)

Airbus A320 VH-HYB appeared at the Australian International Airshow at Avalon in February 1997 wearing an Olympics scheme and announcing the official carrier appointment to the world. (Paul Sadler)

Boeing 747-312 VH-INJ again, from the starboard side. (Richard Hall)

Ansett was used as the Olympic torch relay airline as the flame travelled across Australia. Airbus A320 VH-HYN was one of the aircraft used. (Rob Finlayson)

Boeing 747-412 VH-ANA at Sydney in August 1999. (Mike McHugh)

Ansett International's Boeing 767-324ER VH-BZF was also used in the Olympic torch relay. (Rob Finlayson)

Boeing 737-33A VH-CZT with Olympics mascots Syd, Millie and Ollie prominent. (Paul Merritt)

The carnival is over: A320 VH-HYB looks a little forlorn in primer after its Olympics livery was removed at Ansett's Melbourne maintenance base in December 2000. A standard colour scheme would soon be applied. (Brian Wilkes)

CHAPTER TWELVE

TURNING TO DUST

When Qantas deputy chief executive and chief financial officer Gary Toomey resigned these positions in September 2000 to take over as the Air New Zealand/Ansett group's managing director and chief executive, he obviously thought it was a smart move, a logical next step in his hitherto successful career.

They say that timing is everything, and in Gary Toomey's case it was just about as bad as it can be. After a short break, the highly regarded Toomey joined Air NZ-Ansett in December 2000, just in time for the events which would see Ansett's problems on the front pages of the newspapers and as the lead stories of television news and current affairs programs. It was a nightmare for Toomey, his fellow employees and the airline itself. The situation was not of his making, but the new CEO suddenly found himself in the position of having to deal with a series of crises and then oversee the demise of Ansett.

A chartered accountant by profession, 45 years old Toomey was seen by many as one of the rising (relatively)

young stars of the Australian corporate world. He had joined Qantas in 1993 after a brief stint as the chief financial officer of biscuit maker Arnott but prior to that had been Australian Airlines' chief financial officer for five years between 1987 and 1992. Previously he had been company secretary to several firms.

The period between late December 2000 and early May 2001 was a time filled with a litany of errors unbefitting not only an operator which had been claiming in its advertising to be 'one of the world's great airlines', but also an Australian airline industry which has long prided itself on its vigilance regarding matters of air safety.

Ansett's nightmare – at least as far as the public was aware – began with the discovery two days before Christmas 2000 that scheduled inspections (25,000 cycles) of its 767s were overdue by a very wide margin, claimed by the airline to be as a result of an error by a single person in its maintenance department. This resulted in the grounding of the fleet while inspections were carried out.

The 767 fleet was grounded twice between late Dec 2000 and April-May 2001 while the problems caused by inadequacies in Ansett's maintenance and inspection standards and systems were sorted out. The situation also focused attention on CASA's own system of checks. (Paul Merritt)

The Civil Aviation Safety Authority (CASA) then launched an investigation into Ansett's maintenance procedures and practices, but more was to come. Hairline cracks were discovered in the horizontal tail surfaces of some of the 767s, an incorrect leading edge slat was found fitted to one aircraft, and in April, it was revealed that an Alert Service Bulletin issued by Boeing and covering inspections of early model 767 engine mounting pylons for cracks had been 'overlooked' for more than a year.

CASA upgraded the Advisory Service Bulletin to a compulsory Airworthiness Directive and expanded its audit of Ansett's activities. Inspections resulting from this found cracks in the pylons of three Ansett 767s.

The crunch came on 12 April 2001 when it discovered that an Ansett 767 had flown eight sectors with an incorrectly stowed and therefore inoperative emergency exit slide. This was a 'no go' defect and the last straw for CASA, which grounded Ansett's entire fleet of ten 767s – representing one-third of the airline's capacity – on the day before the busy Easter holiday period.

Even worse for Ansett was the threat by CASA to issue a Show Cause Notice as to why its Air Operators Certificate should not be withdrawn unless the airline could prove that major changes and reforms could be quickly implemented. Ansett was able to do this to CASA's

767s on the ground at Tullamarine. Both groundings occurred at extremely busy times – the Christmas period and Easter. (Paul Merritt)

satisfaction and the 'show cause' was not issued, but an enormous amount of damage was done to Ansett's public and corporate image in the meantime. Each 767's maintenance paperwork was audited by CASA and the aircraft then physically inspected before being allowed back into the air.

A Tale Of Woe

Ansett's run of woes began on 23 December 2000 when CASA grounded seven of the airline's 767-200s after it was discovered that the aircraft had not undergone mandatory structural inspections which in some cases should have been carried out a considerable time earlier. The aircraft were out of service for a short time while general safety inspections were performed, the Civil Aviation Safety Authority allowing them back into the air under certain conditions and before the missed checks had been carried out.

Ansett issued a statement to an incredulous industry that publicly blamed the error on a single technical officer who allegedly received a Service Bulletin from Boeing two years earlier notifying the airline that the 767s

needed to undergo the inspection on reaching 25,000 cycles. Ansett says the officer somehow took the figure as being 50,000 cycles and filed the bulletin, thinking it would be some time before it would apply.

The error was noticed by Ansett engineers on one aircraft they were working on. Further checks revealed another six 767s had exceeded the 25,000 cycles mark. CASA launched an investigation into Ansett's quality assurance systems following this and other incidents which subsequently occurred in rapid succession.

The groundings occurred at the Christmas peak, causing delays and disruptions to some Ansett services.

On 2 March 2000, Boeing issued an Alert Service Bulletin (No 767-57A0070 Revision 1) covering inspections of early model 767-200 aircraft for fatigue cracks in the engine mounting pylon pitch load fittings. Boeing recommended the inspections be performed within 180 days. An Alert is the highest level of Service Bulletin issued by Boeing, and although compliance is not compulsory (as it is with an Airworthiness Directive), any airline not doing so could be regarded as at best foolish and at worst derelict in its duty of care to passengers.

The bulletin applied to 767-200s up to number 101 off the line. Ansett's original five 767s were numbers 24, 28, 32, 35 and 100 delivered between March 1983 and September 1984. In addition, a former Britannia Airways aircraft (number 79, built in early 1984) was in the fleet along with some later models.

In December 2000 it was discovered that Ansett had 'overlooked' the engine pylon inspections covered by the Boeing Alert Service Bulletin, although this did not enter the public domain until April 2001. Ansett consulted CASA and Boeing as to the best way of making up the inspections and the end of April was the deadline given to complete them.

The nightmare rolled on into the first days of 2001 when hairline cracks were found in the horizontal tail surfaces of one of the 767s undergoing the delayed 25,000 cycles check and although the cracks presented no immediate safety problem, the resulting publicity further damaged Ansett's image in the eyes of the travelling public.

The situation for Ansett worsened later in January when it was discovered that a 767-300 had been incorrectly fitted with a leading edge slat from a 767-200. Although the slats are of the same size and work on both models, the 767-300's is strengthened and is technically a different part. The error was discovered shortly before the aircraft was due to leave Melbourne for Hong Kong.

Outside help had to be brought in to fill the capacity gap left by the grounded Ansett 767s. Air Canada 767-300 C-FTCA (in Canadian livery) was one of the aircraft temporarily leased by Ansett, between April and July 2001. (Tim Dath)

At this point CASA announced it was expanding its investigation into Ansett to include the latest incident and to discover if the mix-up was 'indicative of wider, systemic problems at Ansett that had not been understood fully by CASA or the airline.'

Also in January, the Australian Transport Safety Bureau announced it was conducting its own enquiry into Ansett and also 'CASA's systems for compliance, including procedures for delegating responsibilities to airlines for regulatory compliance.'

CASA ordered changes to procedures within Ansett in February, forcing the airline to record in detail its handling of recommendations by aircraft manufacturers for changes to maintenance and inspection procedures. Details were required to be provided when manufacturers' recommendations were acted upon and a full technical justification recorded when they were not. Until then, only those recommendations that had been adopted were fully documented. CASA said the changes would allow it to carry out safety audits more effectively.

CASA's initial investigations into Ansett revealed shortcomings in the airline's maintenance systems in a number of areas with a major audit of its maintenance activities planned to be carried out in early March. In the meantime there was some good news for Ansett as the 767-200s affected by the original problem had now met all the necessary inspection requirements and were clear to resume normal operations.

More Problems

Things settled down a bit for Ansett for a month or so after that very difficult period, and there was a feeling that perhaps the worst was over. Unfortunately, the worst was still to come.

On 10 April 2001 inspections of seven Ansett 767-200s covered by the Boeing engine pylon Service Bulletin of March 2000 revealed that three aircraft had cracks in the pylons which required grounding and repair. A fourth 767 was quickly repaired and returned to service.

CASA criticised Boeing for failing to recognise the seriousness of the pylons problem and says the manufacturer should have ordered Ansett to conduct the inspections. As noted earlier, a Service Bulletin does not require a mandatory inspection or fix, it is legally only an advisory notice. An Airworthiness Directive issued by the relevant authority (in this case the US Federal Aviation Administration) does require compulsory compliance. In Australia, most US ADs are automatically issued locally.

In response to the situation which had developed at Ansett, CASA upgraded the Boeing Service Bulletin to Airworthiness Directive status and another three 767s were immediately grounded for inspection.

Not flying means not producing income, and as we were soon to discover, Ansett desperately needed healthy cashflow. Ansett 767s on the ground at Melbourne. (Paul Merritt)

Another aircraft leased in during the April-May 2001 767 groundings was Polynesian Airlines' 737-300 5W-ILF. (Trent Jones)

Ansett did not help its own case when a senior executive, said at least twice at a media conference that the Service Bulletin was received by the airline only 'a couple of months ago' and then 'just before Christmas'. What he meant was that the bulletin was only *discovered* by Ansett 'just before Christmas', a rather different situation. CASA immediately applied new conditions to Ansett operations and threatened to withdraw approvals for the airline's maintenance organisation to carry out certain work on its own aircraft.

The situation deteriorated even further on 12 April when the Australian Transport Safety Bureau (ATSB) revealed that the airline had flown a 767 with an incorrectly stowed and therefore inoperative emergency exit slide on eight sectors before the fault was discovered. This unserviceability is one with which an airliner cannot legally fly, and the implications were serious.

For CASA this was the final straw, and the Authority grounded Ansett's entire fleet of ten Boeing 767s, saying the aircraft would not be able to fly again until CASA was satisfied they all met relevant safety standards. CASA announced it would undertake safety checks on all the 767s, inspecting the aircraft and auditing recent maintenance work. The checks would begin over the Easter weekend.

For Ansett the grounding could not have come at a worse time; the Thursday before Good Friday, one of the busiest days of the year for Australia's domestic airlines. One-third of the airline's capacity was out of service.

Even worse, part of CASA's action on the grounding of the 767s was that Ansett would be issued a notice on April 20 giving it 14 days to 'show cause' why its Air Operators Certificate and Certificate of Approval should not be withdrawn.

CASA said the notice was based on a pattern of ongoing structural, management and personnel problems. Ansett would be required to prove to CASA that major changes to these areas can be quickly implemented and would also have to prepare detailed proposals covering reforms to its maintenance systems.

CASA Director of Aviation Safety, Mick Toller, said it was clear there has been a lack of proper control over the planning of maintenance, over the control of critical documents and the execution of maintenance..... 'CASA

could no longer accept Ansett's assurances that the safety of 767s could be maintained.'

Ansett initially claimed the first inspected 767 would be returning to service within a couple of days, but the reality was that the process took much longer due to the detailed examinations undertaken. Checking of the paperwork for each aircraft itself took several days and then there was the physical inspection of the aircraft. At the same time, Ansett suspended four of its ground staff pending an investigation into the emergency slide problem. The unions warned Ansett against using these people as scapegoats for the airline's problems.

On 15 April, CASA gave Ansett approval to charter six aircraft from overseas operators in order to help relieve the capacity shortage caused by the 767 grounding. Air New Zealand provided a 767-300 and 747-400, Singapore Airlines a 747-400, Air Canada a 767-300 and Emirates two 777s. Most of these aircraft were available on a temporary full time basis but the 777s were used only during downtime between scheduled international flights. CASA approval was needed to ensure the flightcrews of the aircraft had the required knowledge of Australian domestic aviation rules. In the first days of the grounding, Ansett had also chartered aircraft from local operators including Qantas.

The following day, talks were held between Gary Toomey and CASA, these described as 'productive'. According to Mr Toomey: 'A range of issues was discussed.... and the outcome was an agreement between CASA and Ansett to work together between now and Friday [the 'show cause' deadline] to reach mutual agreement on the structure of the engineering organisations within Ansett; and the internal control systems relating to the planning and implementation of Airworthiness Directives and Service Bulletins.'

Singapore Airlines (at that time a 25% shareholder in Air New Zealand) agreed to provide technical assistance in addition to Ansett's own resources in compiling the data required by CASA. SIA was also supplying a 747-400 for use on Ansett's domestic routes while the 767s were grounded.

On 18 April, the physical inspection of the first 767 to have its paperwork checked started and Ansett's management began a busy two day period during which they had to convince CASA that the airline did not deserve to

Big brother lends a helping hand. Ansett International 747-400 VH-ANA on domestic duties during the 767 groundings, this photo taken on 16 April 2001. (Craig Murray)

have its Air Operators Certificate withdrawn. They were successful, because on 20 April – deadline day – CASA announced that Ansett would not be issued with a formal Show Cause Notice following the regulator's acceptance of the airline's detailed plans for improvement across its maintenance and operational areas.

Ansett had undertaken to perform a wide ranging review of its maintenance division including staff, training and spares management; introduce better maintenance planning and control measures; introduce a system that properly tracks documentation; implement quality control in all areas through a special new unit to ensure work meets the desired standards; introduce a safety education campaign for all staff; ensure all 767 Service Bulletins are complied with unless permission is received from CASA not to do so; provide a strong and ongoing commitment to apprenticeships; bring in additional resources from Boeing for specific aircraft repair planning issues; and introduce a new risk management review process. An important structural change was the moving of maintenance control from the engineering organisation to the airline itself.

The first of the grounded 767s returned to service on 20 April after its paperwork and physical inspections were completed and passengers on the Melbourne to Sydney flight were handed a bottle of champagne by Gary Toomey as they boarded the aircraft. A telling fact was that hardly any of the 169 passengers knew they were on a 767, let alone the first one back in service after the groundings – until masses of television film crews began pointing cameras at them! It was observed that the media people were desperately trying to find someone who was scared about getting on the aircraft, and was prepared to say so....

Also interesting to note is the fact that inspections of the first 767 revealed only very minor problems including chipped paint, a misplaced fire extinguisher and too many magazines on board! All the affected 767s were back in service by early May.

Winning Hearts and Minds

Even though the administrative battle to keep Ansett flying appeared to have been won, there was still the issue of restoring public confidence in the airline.

After all, for much of the previous five months Ansett had never been far away from the headlines and for all the wrong reasons. The airline's financial health had also come under increasing scrutiny during this period and although most industry observers knew that things weren't quite as they should be, many were taken by surprise when the true extent of the damage was later revealed.

As for the passengers, many had already transferred their allegiances to Qantas or Virgin Blue because they were unsure that Ansett was going to be able to deliver them to their destinations safely, or even at all if the airline went under.

Ansett's PR people were therefore working overtime to try to alleviate such fears but they had some difficulties to face on the way. It wasn't all sweetness, light and champagne for Ansett on the day the first 767 was returned to service because it was revealed that one aircraft was found to have an undercarriage component in place which should have been replaced 2° months earlier. This naturally attracted widespread media coverage and probably scared a few more passengers away.

Worse was to come for the Ansett PR crew on 21 April when photographs of the 767s' cracked pylons appeared in the daily press under headlines like 'On A Wing And A Prayer'. The photographs were supplied to CASA by Ansett and the airline did not expect to see them plastered all over the front page of the newspapers. Questions were asked: were they leaked to the press by CASA? And if so, who authorised the leak?

On 27 April, Air New Zealand-Ansett chairman Sir Selwyn Cushing and chief executive Gary Toomey held a media conference to update activities within the group. Among the issues covered were confirmation that [by then] three 767s were back in service; the exercise had cost the airline $NZ5.2m (about $A4.1m) to date; on time performance during the groundings had averaged 89% (better than the same period of 2000); 'no shows' and cancellations were no different to usual; forward bookings remained strong; and that no issues of safety significance had been identified in the 767s inspected to date.

It was also announced that Ansett was selling its seven early model 767-200s to GECAS, General Electric's aircraft leasing arm, for a reported $350m. In return, Ansett would

A hugely successful recovery and confidence building campaign? Absolutely not!

lease more modern and larger 767-300s from GECAS, albeit still second hand aircraft. The first 767-200 would be disposed of within 12 months and the fleet progressively replaced through to 2004. Three of Air New Zealand's 767-200s would also be sold as part of the deal, this being as much as anything intended to show the public that measures were being put in place to fix the problems.

Ansett launched a $20m advertising campaign in early May, a 'touchy-feely' affair designed to reassure airline travellers that it was safe, friendly, secure and here to stay. In the television commercials, several famous faces were shown cheerfully checking in, boarding and leaving Ansett flights. The catchcry 'absolutely' was used as the campaign's hook, employees being told to use the word 'absolutely' when dealing with the public where they might have previously answered a question with a simple yes.

The campaign failed to convince a generally sceptical public because it wanted – and needed – hard answers to hard questions, not fluffy hyperbole. Ansett claimed the campaign was successful, but not too many agreed with that.

Speaking to *Australian Aviation* magazine a month after the 767 grounding crisis had been resolved, Gary Toomey commented on its effect on the airline in terms that were an excellent example of how to say 'absolutely' nothing in 143 words: 'In terms of market share or in financial terms very little [impact]. But in terms of long term branding it is a little harder to claim that it has had no impact and I'm sure that it has brought the Ansett brand into focus in a way which we would have preferred not to have happened. Having said that, the outcome of it all is that the repurchasing intent of Ansett passengers has actually doubled from about 26 to 58 per cent. So I think that is interesting.

'What it really highlights though is that nothing has really changed in our strategy and that is that we need to re-equip, we need to grow our capacity, we need to have new products, so I think it just brings those objectives into focus more and more by having a high profile about what's happened.'

CASA In The Hot Seat

It was not only Ansett's procedures which came under scrutiny during this period, but also those of the regulatory body, the Civil Aviation Safety Authority. It was interesting to observe how the emphasis of the critics gradually moved from Ansett to CASA as the drama unfolded, and it's not too difficult to see why. Over the previous few years, CASA had gone out of its way to tell the industry and the Australian public how it had been introducing all these new systems which check on operators so as to ensure they were providing air travellers with the safest possible airlines.

Yet Ansett's serious error in missing the 25,000 cycles check, its 'overlooking' of the pylon cracks Service Bulletin and other problems all got through the CASA net. If this is providing proper oversight of the industry in order to protect the safety of Australia's airline passengers, observed many, then something was obviously very wrong.

When the missed inspection situation arose in late December 2000, the Australian Transport Safety Bureau announced it would undertake its own investigation into not only Ansett's procedures, but also 'CASA's systems for compliance, including procedures for delegating responsibilities to airlines for regulatory compliance.'

CASA was not happy with this and the issue came to something of a head in early May 2001 at a Senate Committee hearing covering the ATSB's investigations. There has always been tension between CASA and the independent ATSB (and the Bureau of Air Safety Investigation – BASI – before that) and this came to the fore at the hearing. CASA

By June 2001 Ansett's grounded 767s had returned to service. This is 767-277 VH-RMH on approach to Melbourne Airport in that month. (Brian Wilkes)

resisted the ATSB's attempts to get unlimited access to documents and staff, Director of Aviation Safety Mick Toller describing the details of the investigation as 'woolly' and accusing the ATSB of conducting a 'fishing expedition.'

The fact that these two organisations were arguing with each other was in itself a serious concern as they are supposed to represent different parts of a common philosophy – achieving a high level of air safety – rather than being enemies and rivals.

CASA's credibility suffered another setback in April 2001 when an internal audit report criticising the organisation was leaked. The report claimed CASA had failed to fix problems identified by the Auditor-General two years earlier and might have misled the Senate about the pace of reforms. It went on: 'The industry's level of compliance with safety legislation is no longer being actively measured by CASA.... if the safety regulator does not have this information, the industry has already achieved self regulation.'

CASA quickly dismissed the report as an unfinished draft which had not been presented to its director or the board and was flawed in several areas. This may well be true, but the leaking of the report provided ammunition for the many who agreed with the thrust of its content.

One other issue that CASA failed to satisfactorily explain is how photographs of the cracks on Ansett 767 pylons ended up in the mass media in April 2001. The photographs were supplied by Ansett at CASA's request but were leaked, Mick Toller saying 'I believe that they may have come from the Authority, and if they did I believe that's inappropriate.' That was big of him!

'Inappropriate' is understating the situation somewhat as it was a complete breach of trust and unprofessional behaviour of the worst kind. If the photographs were leaked by CASA (who else could it have been?), the leak must have been authorised by somebody for reasons unknown. And that somebody was most probably a senior person. If this is true, then CASA should have had a lot of explaining to do, not only to Ansett but to the industry and the public.

That Ansett had serious problems in managing its maintenance programs is an inescapable fact. If this was the result of cost and staff cuts then the airline needed to completely reassess itself and its future. Either way, serious mistakes were made which would have resulted in the withdrawal of its Air Operators Certificate had it been a small airline operating local services – and this was not without precedent in the period leading up to the crisis. Of course, four months later, in September 2001, the full extent of Ansett's and Air New Zealand's financial problems was revealed and suddenly things which had occurred over the previous year gained some perspective.

As for CASA, it's difficult to find that organisation blameless because its self-proclaimed close scrutiny of commercial air transport operation failed to detect at least two serious mistakes by one of Australia's major airlines.

FLEET SUMMARY – March 2001

Ansett Australia: 9 Boeing 767-200; 20 Airbus A320-200; 23 Boeing 737-300; 7 BAe 146-200; 3 BAe 146-300. On order: 1 Boeing 737-300. Stored awaiting disposal: 4 Fokker F28-4000 Fellowship.

Ansett International: 2 Boeing 747-400; 1 Boeing 767-300ER.

Ansett Australia Cargo: 2 Boeing 727-200F; 2 BAe 146-200QT; 2 BAe HS.748-2B (Horizon Airlines contract); 1 Fokker F27-600QC Friendship (Independent Air Freighters contract).

Aeropelican Air Services: 4 DHC Twin Otter 300.

Hazelton Airlines: 2 Saab 340A; 7 Saab 340B; 2 Fairchild Metro 23.

Kendell Airlines: 9 Bombardier CRJ200; 8 Saab 340A; 8 Saab 340B; 7 Fairchild Metro 23. On order: 3 Bombardier CRJ200.

Skywest Airlines: 5 Fokker 50.

CHAPTER THIRTEEN

END GAME – ABSOLUTELY

To many in the industry, the Air New Zealand takeover of Ansett was doomed from the start. Very few people in the know considered it was a marriage made in heaven because they realised that between them, there simply wasn't the financial clout necessary to solve the problems of either operator. Both needed a substantial injection of cash but neither had the capability of providing it.

In terms of revenues generated, Ansett was 32nd in the world and Air New Zealand 39th. Combined, their ranking increased to a much more respectable 20th, but there was much more to the success of an airline than just the number of dollars it generated. There was yield and therefore profitability, the prospects of ongoing profitability, controlled costs, a suitable fleet, an appropriate number of employees, and the necessary management skills to ensure ongoing growth and profitability.

Many were unconvinced of Air New Zealand's expertise in these areas – or even that appropriate due diligence had been performed before the Ansett purchase – and those doubts were to prove justified. That Ansett was left to flounder without effective leadership is an unfortunate truth that applied over the airline's final year of existence.

Former Ansett chief executive Rod Eddington had once famously described the company as 'a great airline but a poor business'. His Great Business Plan of 1997 and other initiatives had begun to produce results by the time Air New Zealand took over full control, but it was unable to capitalise.

Changing Circumstances

When Air New Zealand took full control of Ansett in June 2000, the Australian domestic scene was again in a state of change. Just two weeks earlier, New South Wales regional operator Impulse Airlines had expanded onto the trunk routes (initially Sydney-Melbourne), offering low fares and using Boeing 717s. In August, Sir Richard Branson's Virgin Blue launched operations on Australian trunk routes with a fleet of Boeing 737s. Initial services were on the Brisbane-Sydney route but the low fare airline's network quickly expanded.

These were the first new entrants into the market since the collapse of the second Compass Airlines seven years earlier. In the intervening period Australia had once again been a 'two airline' nation, albeit a deregulated one.

The early morning gloom greets A320 VH-HYI as it completes the final Ansett revenue flight on 5 March 2002 after operating overnight from Perth to Sydney. (Paul Sadler)

Impulse and Virgin Blue had an immediate effect on the market, their low fares attracting thousands of new passengers and taking some away from Qantas and Ansett. Curiously, it was Ansett that seemed to suffer most from inroads made by the new entrants and this in combination with the Boeing 767 grounding disasters Ansett suffered in 2001 had caused the airline considerable damage. By mid 2001 its share of the Australian domestic market had dropped to just over 40%.

Impulse would last only until May 2001 when it was absorbed into Qantas, originally as a separate entity before being purchased outright. It was a strange set of circumstances. Impulse had always claimed it was making money but few believed it. When the announcement of the Qantas deal was made, it was then said that Impulse was going broke. Either way, Qantas ended up controlling what was a potentially annoying competitor and Impulse's owners came out it with a healthy amount of money in their pockets.

As for Virgin Blue, its influence was always going to be considerable if only because of its founder, flamboyant British businessman Sir Richard Branson. The master of the publicity stunt, Sir Richard was also an astute operator who knew how to make things work. There was always the feeling that Virgin Blue was not going to be a fly-by-night venture and that it would pose a real, long term challenge to Ansett and Qantas. But little did even Sir Richard know how important to the Australian airline scene Virgin Blue would shortly become.

Ansett Australia posted an operating profit of $96.7 million for the 1999-2000 financial year, the last reporting period before the Air New Zealand takeover. This was down 40.5% on the previous 12 months but within that, Ansett International turned around to record an $8.1 million profit. On the other hand, the regionals' combined profit dropped by two-thirds to $5.2 million. Overall, Ansett Holdings reported a before tax profit of $121.7 million (down 36.6%) while new parent Air NZ posted an after tax loss of $NZ600 million after taking substantial abnormals into account.

In December 2000 Qantas deputy chief executive and chief financial officer Gary Toomey was appointed the new managing director and chief executive officer of the Air NZ-Ansett group, just in time for the 767 maintenance problems and groundings to start and Ansett's major problems to publicly emerge. For Mr Toomey the timing was as bad as it could be, because even though none of the blame could be attributed to him, in effect he presided over the demise of Ansett and the almost fatal illness of Air New Zealand.

In February 2001, the Air NZ-Ansett Group announced its first financial results since integration. It was disappointing – a net profit of just $NZ3.8 million for the six months to December 2000 and then only after a large tax credit was taken into account.

Trouble Brewing

By May 2001, rumours abounded about Air New Zealand's financial position and speculation about changes of ownership were rife throughout the industry. Qantas and Singapore Airlines were at the forefront of takeover attempts and both made offers. Qantas' was rejected in June and both it and SIA were stymied by the New Zealand Government's dithering on the issue of raising foreign ownership limits from the existing level of 25%. Air NZ's share price plummeted as news of its financial position leaked out and SIA later withdrew its offer.

There was some press speculation at the time that Ansett Australia might record a massive $A400 million loss in the 2000-2001 financial year, although some analysts were less pessimistic, predicting a $NZ200 million (about $A170m at the time) operating loss for the Air NZ-Ansett group as a whole.

Gary Toomey was quick to deny the speculation was correct, telling aviation journalists at a June luncheon briefing that, 'Despite the doom and gloom scenarios of some ill-informed commentators, Ansett's losses this year haven't suddenly ballooned and will be nowhere near the $400 million figure bandied about.'

The skipper of VH-HYI – Captain Geoff McDonald – faces the media after arriving in Sydney in command of the final Ansett service. It was an emotional day for Ansett staff, the public and the entire Australian aviation industry because a long and significant era had come to an irreversible close. (Paul Sadler)

According to some analysts, the possibility of a big loss at Air New Zealand gave more impetus to the proposed deal involving Qantas taking 49% of the airline, which in turn would sell off Ansett to Singapore Airlines. The general situation prompted further calls for the foreign ownership limit of 25% in Air NZ be lifted. At the time, it was being suggested by New Zealand Government sources that an increase to 35% was 'more than possible' and that even 49% was a possibility given the 'right' deal.

What constituted the 'right' deal was never revealed because the New Zealand Government under Prime Minister Helen Clark procrastinated on the issue and the moment was lost – with devastating (and expensive) consequences for both Air NZ and Ansett.

The situation was further complicated by Brierley Investments' 30% holding of Air NZ's 'A' shares, these reserved for New Zealand investors. Singapore Airlines had 24.9% in 'B' shares (for everyone else) and by the middle of the year was looking to dispose of them.

Qantas had earlier issued a brief press release confirming it was seeking to buy a stake in Air New Zealand, who would then sell Ansett to Singapore Airlines. The ramifications of this were interesting – whether or not the deal went ahead – and there were some who were suspicious that Qantas might just be indulging in a little tactical play to divert Air NZ-Ansett's attention from its main tasks of returning to profit, regaining lost Australian domestic market share and repairing its damaged brand name and reputation.

Assuming Qantas was genuine in its desire to acquire some of Air NZ, there were significant advantages for

More traditional sendoffs from airport firefighters on 4 March at Adelaide (top) and Hobart. (Robert Wiseman/Theo Van Loon)

the carrier. Cost savings could be gained through fleet commonality, efficiencies of scale, route and schedules rationalisation, common spares holdings and so on. It would also confirm Qantas' status as the pre-eminent Australasian airline group.

For Ansett and Singapore Airlines there were the same benefits that existed before Air NZ spoiled the party and insisted on exercising its pre-emptive rights over Ansett's ownership – Ansett would have the advantage of being owned by a cashed up, profitable and successful parent; and SIA would gain direct access to the Australian domestic market.

Parochial Issues

But the New Zealand Government made it quite clear that Air NZ was not going to be handed over to Qantas on a plate, Deputy Prime Minister Jim Anderton saying: '... on the face of it, the idea of selling our national airline to anyone would be an anathema to the Alliance [his political party] and we would have to be confronted with an unassailable case for doing so...'

This blinkered approach ended up costing Air NZ dearly, and there was also the small matter that apparently it was quite alright for New Zealanders to take over or have a substantial interest in Australian airlines, but not the other way around!

The ineptitude of the New Zealand Government is further revealed when it is recognised that at the time, Air New Zealand was largely foreign owned anyway, by Singaporean interests. Singapore Airlines had 24.9% and Brierley Investments Limited 30%. BIL was originally a New Zealand based company traded on the NZ stock exchange, but in 2000 it relocated to Singapore with its shares listed on the Singapore exchange.

To circumvent foreign ownership restrictions, BIL's stake in Air NZ was held via a New Zealand

registered trust with independent directors, BIL New Zealand Assets Ltd. which controlled its 'A' class shares for New Zealand investors.

The approach shown by Air New Zealand when it pushed through its purchase of the News Ltd's half of Ansett had led to poor decisions being made, and now the New Zealand Government was being guilty of the same thing.

On the day of Ansett's collapse – 14 September – New Zealand Prime Minister Helen Clark found her aircraft blockaded at Melbourne by angry Ansett airport ramp workers who parked plant and equipment around it. She was forced to make alternative arrangements using an RNZAF Orion which seriously inconvenienced her and her entourage.

Under normal circumstances this would be regarded as a serious breach of protocol. After all, here was a nation's leader being in effect put under siege by the inhabitants of a foreign country. But in this case, there weren't too many Australians who didn't find the episode quite funny. Mrs Clark later accused us of 'kiwi beshing.'

The whole issue of airline ownership and who owns what was confirmed as being largely a matter of national pride according to a survey of Australians and New Zealanders conducted during the ANZ/Qantas/SIA/Ansett ownership squabbles. About 65,000 people were asked how they felt about the ownership issues facing these airlines: SIA increasing its stake in Air NZ, SIA buying Ansett and Qantas taking a substantial shareholding in Air NZ.

It was found that Australians generally disliked the notion of SIA buying Ansett and New Zealanders were very strongly against Qantas taking a slice of Air NZ as they were 'sick of business going offshore to Australia'. Conversely, Australians were highly supportive of Qantas buying some of Air NZ.

New Zealanders were divided as to whether or not SIA should increase its Air

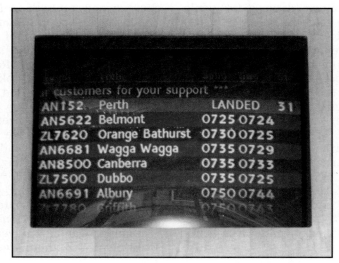

Death notice. The arrivals board at Ansett's Sydney terminal on 5 March 2002 – AN152 from Perth has landed. (Jim Thorn)

Despite its worsening financial and operational problems, Ansett continued its sometimes acrimonious battle with Qantas to gain control of regional carrier Hazelton Airlines. This was finally achieved in March 2001 but the relationship proved to be a short lived one. (Lance Higgerson)

NZ shareholding, with many concerned about loss of identity. Many, however, agreed that SIA would help Air NZ become more competitive. Interestingly, many Australians' objections to SIA buying Ansett were based a dislike of this 'Australian icon' becoming foreign owned, but at the same time they were forgetting that it already was!

But at the end of the day, it was the hip pocket that dictated how the respondents felt about it all. Most said that ownership would not influence their decision on which airline they used – that came down simply to the cost of fares and the cheapest would get their business.

Last Chance

By August 2001, it was nearly all over for Air NZ-Ansett, the company haemorrhaging money at an alarming rate. The penultimate roll of the dice occurred during that month when it was revealed that the group had offered $250 million to take over Virgin Blue, an offer very publicly rejected by Sir Richard Branson when a piece of paper purporting to be a

cheque for that amount was torn up – in front of the television cameras, of course!

In a revealing article subsequently published in the Christchurch newspaper *The Press*, some details of Gary Toomey's battle to keep the group afloat during its period of crisis were revealed.

According to the article, Mr Toomey took no fewer than 16 plans to the Air New Zealand board and the one selected was buying Virgin Blue. The idea was to expand Air NZ's own low cost operation – Freedom Air – into the Australian market by using Virgin Blue's network and therefore establishing a low cost airline in both countries.

The catch was that Air NZ shareholder Singapore Airlines had agreed to help pay for Ansett's desperately needed fleet upgrade only if the Virgin Blue deal went through. Six months of negotiations followed but by the time Sir Richard Branson turned down the offer in August it was too late. Crucially, there was no contingency plan in place.

Ansett had taken steps to introduce more modern Boeing 767s to replace the earlier models which had been so troublesome in 2001. Newer 767-300ERs were leased in but only one of them – VH-BZL leased from Air Canada – was able to enter service before the September 2001 collapse, and then only for a month. (Rob Finlayson)

Boeing 767-300ER VH-BZI was also leased from Air Canada and painted in Ansett colours arrived in Australia immediately before the September 2001 collapse and therefore didn't enter service. Another Air Canada 767-300ER – VH-BZM – suffered the same fate. (Brian Wilkes)

The length of time negotiations between Air NZ-Ansett and Virgin Blue wasn't realised by most when they broke down. It was later revealed that in April 2001, Gary Toomey had set up a deal with Sir Richard Branson to purchase Virgin Blue for $US120 million but a disagreement with Air NZ shareholder Singapore Airlines had delayed closure. The idea was to run Virgin Blue as a low cost and separate brand within the Ansett operation on certain routes, the result being a substantial reduction in costs on those routes and a boost in overall market share to nearly 50%.

As time dragged on, Virgin Blue started becoming profitable, which made Sir Richard less inclined to sell, assuming he was in the first place. He would also have been fully aware of Ansett's desperate situation and sensed an opportunity for Virgin Blue to grow more quickly if Ansett dropped out of the market. The disappearance of Impulse into Qantas would also have been a factor.

In a September 2002 interview, Gary Toomey said he believed the failure of the Virgin Blue deal was a major contributory factor to Ansett's collapse: 'Basically, Ansett without Virgin was pretty much not a goer in its own right.'

By the end, Mr Toomey had already cut $120 million from Ansett's costs and had identified a further $500 million in savings. These included slashing 3,000 jobs in Australia (helping reduce Ansett's staff numbers to the level it really should have been at anyway), reducing pilots' pay and moving administration of the airline's frequent flyer program from Australia to New Zealand.

A new fleet plan was also drawn up encompassing the acquisition of 19 aircraft for Ansett (mainly newer 767-300s and five additional 747s for Ansett International) plus five more aircraft for Air New Zealand and three for Freedom Air. Disposal of the older 767-200s which had caused so many problems in 2001 was a central part of the plan, which revolved around the Virgin Blue purchase and the SIA input which would follow.

Unfortunately, neither the Virgin Blue purchase nor any input from Singapore Airlines became available. Virgin Blue had already rejected the takeover offer (very few people believed Air NZ could afford it anyway) and SIA withdrew its shares purchase offer on 6 September.

Air NZ's very last roll of the dice occurred on 10 September when Air NZ offered Ansett to Qantas for a token $1, that offer rejected by the Australian carrier two days later.

Black September

The date of Qantas' rejection of Air NZ's offer to take over Ansett was 12 September 2001, one of the blackest days in the entire history of aviation. While it was the 12th in Australia and Ansett was collapsing, it was the 11th in the USA, the day terrorists hijacked four airliners and flew two of them into the twin towers of the World Trade Centre in New York and one into the Pentagon in Washington DC with devastating effect including the loss of over 3,000 lives. The fourth airliner came down before it could reach its target thanks to the efforts of the passengers on board.

In Australia and New Zealand the general populace was reeling from these events but those in the airline industry had to deal with a double blow, especially those involved with Ansett. On that day, Air New Zealand suspended trading of its shares – the value of which had plummeted – and placed Ansett into voluntary administration with Price-WaterhouseCoopers.

One day later, Air New Zealand announced a staggering $NZ1.425 billion (about $A1.13bn) loss for the 2000-2001 financial year including a $NZ1.321 billion write-down of Ansett. In other words, Air New Zealand had divested itself of any further responsibility for its subsidiary. Ansett's domestic operations made a loss of $NZ165.4 million before interest and tax and Ansett International lost $NZ22.8 million.

The two Air Canada 767-300ERs which arrived too late to enter service with Ansett await their next assignment at Melbourne in early October 2001. (Paul Daw)

Does this picture sum up Ansett's last couple of years? A lack of motive power results in nothing happening. After all, like A320 VH-HYL, the kiwi is a flightless bird! (Howard Geary)

It was estimated that Ansett had dropped more than $A60 million over the previous two months or so, which raised many questions including how was it possible for the airline to lose that much in such a short time when it was operating with very healthy domestic load factors of an average 74%? This should have been a profitable number and there were mumblings about asset stripping of Ansett by Air NZ, centralised treasury functions and swept bank accounts.

This was angrily denied by Air NZ, which specifically mentioned and refuted claims that it had put $200 million of its aviation fuel bills through Ansett's accounts; took Ansett engines and spares to New Zealand; and cleared out Ansett's bank accounts in the last few weeks before the administrators were called in.

The role of Air NZ's directors came under the scrutiny of the Australian Securities and Investment Commission (ASIC), which launched an investigation to determine whether Ansett had continued to trade while insolvent – a breach of directors' duties – and other irregularities including adequacy of disclosure as to Ansett's true financial position before it collapsed.

In July 2002 came the result of these investigations, and they left a bitter taste in the mouths of many. ASIC decided not to initiate action against Air New Zealand and its former directors in the wake of the Ansett collapse. Despite a belief that Air NZ may have engaged in 'misleading and deceptive' conduct under Section 52 of the Trade Practices Act, ASIC decided not to proceed because it would be too expensive, logistically difficult and risky.

Legal advice had suggested that ASIC would need to pursue many individual actions rather than a single large one on behalf of creditors. Of these, only a small number of those (who bought Air NZ shares during the period in question) would have any chance of proving they lost money as a direct result of Air NZ's actions, according to the advice.

Documentation subsequently released by the New Zealand Government under the Official Information Act revealed that it pressured the Australian Government not to support legal action against Air New Zealand in the period immediately after Ansett's collapse.

A letter from the New Zealand Deputy Prime Minister to his Australian counterpart – dated September 14, the day Ansett was grounded – warned that taking action against Air NZ could compromise a rescue package for the airline and could 'prejudice rather than progress the interests of those with financial claims against the company'. The letter urged the Australian Government to indulge in its 'best endeavours to encourage a calm response to the financial difficulties facing all parties.'

The Australian Government did not seriously consider complying with the request, nor to a later one in which Air NZ asked that an ASIC inquiry into the airline be dropped as part of the $150m cash settlement against any financial claims Ansett may have had against Air NZ.

Air NZ returned to majority state ownership following the October 2001 announcement that the New Zealand Government would provide desperately needed recapitalisation to the tune of $NZ885 million. Air NZ requested a further $NZ700 million from its government a month later but this was rejected. It did, however subsequently make an extra $NZ150 million available to the airline should it be needed.

Just another unsecured creditor – the author's Global Rewards membership card, after September 2001 nothing but another worthless piece of plastic.

Also revealed – inadvertently, as it turned out – was documentation which stated that an estimated $NZ1.705 billion capital injection was needed to achieve a 65% debt to equity ratio, and that the $NZ670 million shortfall between that figure and the amount provided by the government would have to be attained by a combination of cost cutting, non core asset sales and revenue growth. At first glance the document seemed to imply that the

(left) Lost and forlorn. The check-in counter at Adelaide Airport on 4 March 2002. That last day must have been unbelievably difficult for the staff who were still working and those who thought they were going to have a job with the Tesna version of Ansett. *(right)* Five A320s were used by 'Ansett Mk.2' to launch services on 29 October 2001 and by the time it all ended on 4 March 2002, 16 had been returned to service at various times. Passenger loads were generally poor, however, and the temporary operation was losing around $6m each week. (Robert Wiseman & Theo Van Loon)

sum needed to be saved in the current year if Air NZ was to remain viable, but the airline's company secretary stated it was actually over a longer period of time.

In 2002 it was announced that 13 former directors of Ansett and its travel subsidiary Traveland (including former Air NZ chief executive Gary Toomey) were being sued by the Travel Compensation Fund, a body established to compensate travellers who purchased tour packages through Traveland before it and owner Ansett collapsed. The action had not been heard by the NSW Supreme Court at the time of writing and represents 11,356 claims for compensation worth $17.25 million from Traveland clients. There are allegations that deposits held by Traveland were systematically put into Ansett's coffers and then transferred to Air NZ.

Blame Game

At the time Ansett was cast adrift by Air New Zealand, its acting chairman, Dr Jim Farmer, almost unbelievably said that 'we don't have any obligation to those [Ansett] employees'. Equally incredibly, Dr Farmer laid blame for the 2000-2001 financial result at the door of major shareholders Singapore Airlines and Brierley Investments but earlier he had blamed previous Ansett owners TNT and News for the airline's troubles. After the collapse it was the turn of the New Zealand and Australian Governments, fuel prices, the Australian dollar relative weakness against the US dollar and Australian domestic competition to be blamed.

It seems that everyone was at fault except the Air New Zealand-Ansett board of directors. The more astute observers knew better.

Shortly after the collapse it was also revealed that Air New Zealand had paid its senior executives bonuses. It was reported in *The Australian* newspaper that Dr Farmer justi-

fied the move with the following quite extraordinary statement: 'The decision to award bonuses was... in recognition not of the financial performance of the company, which of course has not been good, but in recognition of the quite extraordinary effort made by senior management to try and deal with company's problems'. Paying bonuses for failure... a novel concept and one which Ansett's out of work employees might have had something to say about!

The end came on 14 September with the most devastating news of all – PriceWaterhouseCoopers' Peter Hedge shut Ansett down. It had run out of cash and needed $170 million just to keep flying for two more days. Major bills had fallen due and there was simply no alternative. The airline was losing about $1.3 million each day and its debt was estimated at up to $2.8 billion.

In his statement on the issue, Mr Hedge said: 'After due consideration of the issues involved, and examination of daily operating costs, it is with regret that it has been necessary to suspend immediately all flight operations of Ansett Australia, Ansett International, Hazelton Airlines, Kendell Airlines, Skywest Airlines and Aeropelican. It is important to clarify that this action, to cease flight operations, is due to the lack of necessary cash or facilities to fund the operations.

'I am acutely aware, as is the Ansett management team, of the impact this regrettable action will have on employees, customers, suppliers and many regional centres, cities and towns across Australia. However, after considering the immediate financial position of the company, the level of daily losses being incurred, and in the absence of any immediate viable solution, it was decided there was no other option.'

In an instant, some 15,000 people lost their jobs (not to mention the tens of thousands

All over Australia, the final Ansett departures on 4 March 2002 were marked by get-togethers of workers past and present. In Perth, flight attendants dressed in uniforms from over the years gather around pilot Michael McCaul. (Greg Wood)

A scene repeated at several locations around Australia in early March 2002 – the traditional ceremonial spraying by airport firefighters of an Ansett aircraft as it either departs from or arrives at a particular airport for the last time. In this case the place is Melbourne on 5 March after flying from Sydney following completion of the final Ansett revenue flight earlier in the day. The aircraft is Airbus A320 VH-HYI and it had flown overnight from Perth to Sydney on 4-5 March as flight number AN152. (Paul Merritt)

of other jobs in associated industries which suddenly came under threat), 32 regional centres lost their air services and the Australian airline transport system lost 40% of its capacity.

Qantas – which suddenly commanded more than 85% of the Australian domestic market – and Virgin Blue moved quickly to offer assistance to help out. Qantas offered free flights to stranded Ansett passengers and discount fares for people holding now worthless Ansett tickets. The airline also moved to provide interim services to the regional centres around Australia that were without air services in association with QantasLink.

Virgin Blue – which only had nine aircraft in its fleet at the time and a limited network – also did what it could to help by also offering discounts to Ansett ticket holders and putting on additional flights out of normal operating

hours. Both airlines opened registers for Ansett staff seeking employment.

Mark Squared

PriceWaterhouseCoopers' tenure as Ansett's administrator lasted only five days. On September 17 it was announced that Mark Mentha and Mark Korda of Andersens would take over, the change engineered largely by the Australian Council of Trade Unions (ACTU) secretary Greg Combet.

The official reason given was that a conflict of interests existed as PriceWaterhouseCoopers was also advising the Air New Zealand board on the Ansett matter. PWC always denied there was a clash of interests – and they were probably correct – but the ACTU wanted a change to administrators who were more inclined to try to get the airline up and running again and try to sell it as a going concern.

Ansett workers returning their uniforms used them to decorate terminals in various cities, many with some kind of message written on them. Some of those messages were less than flattering: this pair says 'Thanks for Nothing Fox (Bill) & Lew (Ben) Liars', and 'The usual Suspects – Howard, Anderson, Dixon, Toomey, Fox, Lew – RIP Ansett'. (Paul Sadler)

A grounded Ansett would be just about impossible to sell, especially in the wake of the downturn that had hit the industry in 2001 and the double blow of the September 11 terrorist attacks. The airline industry worldwide was in crisis with fleets and staff being radically cut and enormous losses recorded. There was probably no worse time in the history of aviation to try to sell a broke airline.

For the ACTU there was an obvious interest in Ansett getting back into the air and continuing operations after being sold – most of the airline's employees were unionists and therefore the union movement had an obligation to look after their welfare as much as was possible. There was also the cynic's view that in these days of declining union membership and therefore power, the loss of several thousand members was not good.

The 'Two Marks' – as they were quickly dubbed by the media (or 'M″' – 'Mark Squared' by the more intellectual members of the Fifth Estate) – became national celebrities as they worked their way through the enormous task of sorting Ansett out.

They had been friends for 20 years and had worked together for some time. The fact that they were able to quickly get the airline back into the air – albeit on a much reduced scale – shortly after taking over endeared them to the public and to Ansett's employees. That they were able to come within an ace of selling Ansett further enhanced their reputations and the failure to do so was not blamed on them.

Korda and Mentha already had good business reputations before they were appointed Ansett's administrators. They had previously been involved in sorting out several high profile corporate insolvencies including Bob Ansett's Budget Rent-a-Car, music retailer Brash's, Bradmill and home builder Jennings Industries.

Kick Starting Ansett

On 27 September, just 13 days after it had been grounded, the two Marks made the announcement many in the industry had considered to be impossible – Ansett would fly again under the 'Kick-Start' or 'Ansett Mk.II' program. The relaunch of the airline would be very limited but it was a start and gave the administrators a much better chance of selling Ansett as a going concern.

Two days later – on 29 September – Ansett Mk.II began flying 'no frills' services between Sydney and Melbourne, initially with five Airbus A320s. Apart from some charters conducted during the Federal Election campaign by a couple of BAe 146s, the A320 was the only aircraft used by the new, interim Ansett.

Brisbane, Perth and Adelaide were subsequently added to the network and 16 of Ansett's 20 A320s returned to service, although not necessarily at the same time. The response from the public was disappointing as passenger loads were generally mediocre despite the Federal Government guaranteeing fares protection until 31 January 2002 and the introduction of $99 one-way fares between Melbourne and Sydney. There was an early boost in traffic thanks to the AFL football finals, but on the whole, passenger loadings were less than expected.

Ansett Mk.II was able to generate a 7% share of the overall Australian domestic market by mid October 2001 and the airline was claiming 20% of the passenger traffic on routes it contested. By then, 12 A320s were in service and about 1,100 people re-employed.

Dead Ansett aeroplanes No 1 (top to bottom): 767s and a 737 at Melbourne in May 2002; BAe 146s at Essendon in February 2002; A320 at Melbourne. (Gerard Williamson/Brian Wilkes)

Ansett's regional subsidiaries were also able to restart operations ahead of active attempts to sell them and were in fact in the air again before the main airline. All except Hazelton were under the administration of Korda and Mentha, Hazelton not because Andersen had been its auditor and there was the possibility of the perception of a clash of interests.

Aeropelican resumed operations on 21 September and by the end of the month was flying 20 weekly return flights on its only route between Sydney and Newcastle/Belmont. Previously, the frequency had been 79 weekly return flights. On 7 March 2002 it was announced that Aeropelican was to be sold to the Sydney based IAP Group, the southern hemisphere's largest supplier of airliner spare parts and owner of Horizon Airlines. The sale was completed on 26 April.

Hazelton Airlines had only been taken over by Ansett Holdings in March 2001 after a protracted battle with Qantas and quickly found itself embroiled in its new owner's problems. Like every other Ansett regional subsidiary, Hazelton was grounded on 14 September but resumed limited operations seven days later with

Sydney-Orange-Griffith and Sydney-Dubbo-Broken Hill services. Sydney-Canberra was added later in the month.

Once it became part of the Ansett fold, Hazelton had started working with Kendell Airlines on the issue of rationalising their routes and it seemed logical to attempt to sell both of them as a combined operation. An advantage was that their turboprop fleets complimented each other, comprising Saab 340s and Fairchild Metros.

Kendell Airlines also quickly resumed services and was soon operating on most of the routes it had been serving before the Ansett collapse. A big difference was that none of the relatively new Bombardier CRJ200s were returned to service, these remaining firmly on the ground before being returned to their lessors. The oldest CRJ was only two years old and the youngest three months but the type had not been as successful in service as was hoped.

In May 2002, the Australiawide consortium – led by former ANstaff consortium advisor Michael Jones – was named as preferred tenderer to purchase both Hazelton and Kendell. It was revealed at the same time that Kendell had lost about $10 million since it restarted operations. The sale was scheduled to be finalised in the first week of June but after some delays due to contractual and administrative issues needing to be resolved, the contract was finally signed on 28 June. Some more delays resulted in settlement finally occurring in late July and the new airline began operations as Regional Express (Rex) on August 6.

Skywest Airlines was the first of the Ansett regionals to be sold. It had resumed limited services on 23 September 2001 using one of its five Fokker 50s. On 14 December it was announced that Skywest was to be sold to Airline Investments Limited (AIL), a consortium of West Australian businessmen, for $6.5 million. The airline subsequently signed reservations, ground handling, co-branding and cargo handling agreements with Tesna for the new Ansett, but the collapse of that deal left Skywest to fend on its own without a direct passenger feed from a major domestic carrier.

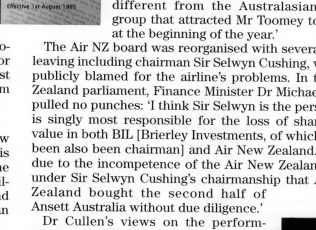

Money Matters

On October 3 2001 it was announced that Air New Zealand would revert to majority state ownership, this the only way out of the financial hole it was in. The airline would be recapitalised to the tune of $NZ885 million (about $A725m) in the form of a two phase loan and equity investment. This left the NZ Government with an 83% interest in the airline.

In addition, Air NZ agreed to pay the Ansett administrators $A150 million to settle any financial claims Ansett may have against its former parent. Approved by the Australian Federal Court on 12 October, the money cleared the way for the process of staff redundancies to begin as $35 million of it would go towards worker entitlements and the remainder as working capital to fund Ansett Mk.II operations until a buyer was found.

An additional $195 million loan was made available by the Australian Government to cover worker entitlements.

Under an agreement with the Federal Government, Ansett employees who took voluntary redundancy would receive four weeks' pay with the remainder of their entitlements funded (indirectly) by a $10 levy on domestic airline tickets. At the time of writing in late September 2002 this levy was still in place but there was talk that the Federal Government was looking at winding it down.

The first phase of Air NZ's recapitalisation program involved a NZ Government loan to the company of $NZ300 million, payment of the $A150 million Ansett claim and the balance of the government loan used as working capital. The loan carried interest at the 90 day bank bill rate of the time plus 4.3% (a total of around 9.3%) and would fall due when the loan was repaid.

The second phase of the program was conducted in December 2001 and January 2002 and involved Air NZ repaying the $NZ300 million loan and interest by way of issuing new convertible preference shares to the NZ Government; the investment of a further $NZ585 million in new ordinary shares; and the combining of existing Class A and Class B shares into a single class of ordinary shares nominally valued at just $NZ0.26 each.

No further investment was sought from Brierley, Singapore Airlines or other existing shareholders and the new capitalisation saw their shareholding in Air NZ diluted substantially from 25% to just 4.3% in the case of SIA and from 30% to 5.2% for Brierley.

Chief executive Gary Toomey resigned on 9 October 'by mutual agreement'. Acting chairman Dr Jim Farmer described Mr Toomey's resignation as 'a sad moment for us, but we agree the circumstances in which the company finds itself are quite different from the Australasian airline group that attracted Mr Toomey to join us at the beginning of the year.'

The Air NZ board was reorganised with several others leaving including chairman Sir Selwyn Cushing, who was publicly blamed for the airline's problems. In the New Zealand parliament, Finance Minister Dr Michael Cullen pulled no punches: 'I think Sir Selwyn is the person who is singly most responsible for the loss of shareholder value in both BIL [Brierley Investments, of which he had been also been chairman] and Air New Zealand... it was due to the incompetence of the Air New Zealand board under Sir Selwyn Cushing's chairmanship that Air New Zealand bought the second half of Ansett Australia without due diligence.'

Dr Cullen's views on the performance of Air NZ's directors was to some extent echoed almost a year later by new chairman Jim Palmer when Qantas was once again looking to take a substantial stake in the airline. Discussing Air NZ's options on the matter, Mr Palmer noted the 'major failure of previous strategy.'

The Price of Loyalty

One of the side issues to come out of investigations into Ansett's liabilities was that associated with its Global Rewards frequent flyer scheme. It was revealed that the numbers involved were staggering with Ansett's total liability in this area valued at about $1.1 billion, a commitment it is doubtful the airline could have met. Each one of the 2.7 million Global Rewards members was an unsecured creditor.

At the time of Ansett's failure there were about 70 billion points spread among the Global Rewards members, sufficient for 4.1 million return economy class flights between Sydney and Melbourne, 2.3 million between Sydney and Auckland, 580,000 business class Sydney-Kong return flights, or 270,000 first class return flights between Sydney and London.

Overall, Ansett's major creditors were owed more than some $2.6 billion, including $730 million in employee entitlements.

Enter Tesna

The revitalised Ansett's prospects took a turn for the better in mid October when two consortia announced bids to acquire the airline. The first – on 15 October – was from ANstaff, an Ansett staff syndicate led by the Ansett Pilots' Association and former chief executive Graeme McMahon.

It was soon realised that this plan was probably unrealistic as the harsh truth of the enormous amounts of money necessary to relaunch Ansett became known – the bid was withdrawn the following month – but on 19 October another, more plausible bid came from the 'Tesna' syndicate led by high profile businessmen Solomon Lew (the former head of Coles Myer) and Lindsay Fox, founder of the extremely successful Linfox transport and logistics company. Like Sir Peter Abeles before him, Lindsay Fox started as a 'simple truckie' and built up his business from there. Tesna, of course, was Ansett spelled backwards minus one of the 'ts'.

The bid involved $3.6 billion for the acquisition of Ansett's mainline assets of which $270 million would be for the purchase of the Ansett assets necessary to restart the airline. Tesna said it would lease 29 new Airbus A320s, re-employ 4,000 Ansett workers, take over the liability of workers' entitlements for re-employed staff and finance the new aircraft. A deadline of 31 January 2002 was set for finalisation of the deal.

On 8 November Ansett Australia's administrators accepted the Tesna bid, the sale involving the acquisition of most Ansett mainline assets including terminals, maintenance facilities and 16 existing Airbus A320s pending the arrival of the planned new fleet. The new Ansett would be a full service, two class carrier operating on domestic trunk and leisure routes.

It was an ambitious plan but there were some big issues to face before it could be turned into reality. One of them was resolving the status of the $195 million

Australian Government loan originally intended to cover worker entitlements, along with obtaining creditor approval of the deal, and the status of the substantial liabilities including the Global Rewards frequent flyer scheme.

It was proposed that Fox and Lew would put $400 million of their own money into Ansett, take over $300 million in employee entitlements, borrow $400 million for working capital, and finance the 29 new A319/320/321 family aircraft which would eventually replace the existing A320s.

Ansett's administrators would then liquidate the remainder of the airline including its other aircraft, using the proceeds and the funds from Fox and Lew to repay Ansett's creditors, which at that stage were estimated to be getting about 20 cents in the dollar.

A very significant part of the Tesna business plan – and a major factor in its ultimate undoing – was a heavy dependence on direct and indirect financial support from the Australian taxpayer.

Among its requests – the guarantee of loans; ensuring the airline was given at least a 50% share of government travel business; being given monopolies on certain routes; accelerated depreciation allowances; fast tracking of the airline's air operator's certificate approval; exemption of non mainline airports (ie Essendon and Avalon – both of which Linfox had an interest in from cross ownership restrictions); relief from withholding tax on aircraft lease payments for five years; guarantee of entitlements to transferring employees for five years; underwriting a 65% load factor for 12 months; and the completely ludicrous one of having Qantas' domestic market share capped at 65-70%.

This was a very substantial wish list which would be largely funded by the nation's taxpayers. It should have been clear at the time that without that support it was unlikely that Tesna would be able to make a go of the new Ansett. When asked on a television program why Tesna should get taxpayer funding, Mark Mentha replied: '[Virgin Blue owner] Richard Branson is a foreign millionaire, these people are Australians, they're putting substantial money at risk and I think they deserve the support of Australia. And if the Federal Government and the State Governments give that support I think we'll have a very viable airline in Ansett and competition in the skies long term.'

But the Federal Government remained unmoved, Prime Minister, John Howard saying in mid November: 'We are not going to provide an equity injection and we're not going to behave in a way that gives Ansett an unfair advantage over its rivals.' It has to be said that most Australians – both in and outside the airline industry – agreed with the Prime Minister.

Meanwhile, the government continued to underwrite tickets sold on Ansett until January 31,

provide subsidies to Ansett's regional affiliates, provide the $195 million loan to cover early redundancies, extend its staff entitlement guarantees should Tesna's Ansett collapse, ensure Ansett had access to landing slots at Sydney, and protect its international rights.

Tesna's plan was formally accepted by the administrators on 8 November and the syndicate appeared to be on track to launch the new Ansett as scheduled on 1 February 2002. The airline had been taking bookings and planned to initially operate 751 flights per week between the major capital cities using the 16 leased Ansett A320s. Canberra was to be quickly added to the network and by mid 2002 the fleet was planned to total 30 aircraft.

The overall issues facing the Australian airline industry and Ansett's revival in particular became more complicated later in November when the Lang (now Patrick) Corporation announced plans to inject $300m into Virgin Blue and to take majority control of the airline. It also said it would be attempting to gazump the Tesna bid for Ansett, even though the administrators had already announced Ansett would go to that syndicate. At the time it was thought that the Lang/Virgin deal going ahead was dependent on the success of the Ansett bid.

Lang's bid and business plan was very different from Tesna's and would have resulted in an airline duopoly. It basically involved purchasing Ansett's infrastructure such as airport terminals and maintenance facilities. About 1,500 former Ansett staff would be hired for the recapitalised Virgin Blue but Ansett itself would disappear. It was really the Sydney terminal that Lang was after but its bid was never a serious contender and everyone knew it including those involved. Patrick Corp went on to buy a half share in Virgin Blue for $260 million in March 2002 and three months later it was announced that Virgin Blue had agreed to purchase the former Ansett jet base facility at Melbourne Airport.

Singapore Airlines was also involved in the sale process at the invitation of the administrators. It did not submit an offer but provided consultancy services and prepared a business plan for the mainline airline.

The Tesna Deal

The key terms of the deal struck between Ansett's administrators and Tesna included the transfer of the following assets to the consortium:
• All of Ansett's mainline assets.
• The leases to Ansett's domestic terminals at Sydney, Melbourne, Brisbane, Perth, Coolangatta, Cairns, Townsville, Rockhampton, Adelaide, Hobart, Darwin, Alice Springs and Canberra.
• The jet base and maintenance base at Melbourne-Tullamarine Airport (the land only and not the engineering business).
• The flight simulator centre, data centre and associated car parks at Tullamarine.

• The hangar and flight kitchen at Sydney Airport.
• The flight kitchen, ground service equipment (GSE), cargo building and engineering building at Brisbane.
• The flight kitchen at Cairns.
• The international cargo building and flight catering building at Perth.
• The GSE building at Darwin.
• All plant and equipment relating to the mainline airline.
• All intangible assets relating to the airline including the 'Ansett' brand name.
• Call centres sufficient to meet Tesna's requirements.
• Certain supply contracts and other agreements selected by Tesna.
• An amount of cash representing the value of forward ticket bookings as at the transfer date.
• Fuel stocks.

• Non aircraft consumables including spare parts for all vehicles and plant and equipment transferred to Tesna.
• The head office site at 501 Swanston Street Melbourne plus other office buildings in the Swanston and Franklin Streets precinct.
• All business records and information relating to the mainline airline and other information necessary for the maintenance of the Airline Operating Certificate and other regulatory compliance obligations.

Assets specifically excluded from the sale agreement included:
• All aircraft including the freighters used in the domestic cargo business and all leased aircraft.
• Plant and equipment relating to aircraft.
• Aircraft rotables, spares (including spare engines) or consumables.
• The engineering business.
• Any interest of the Ansett Group in any real property (whether freehold or leasehold) not specifically identified.

The administrators did not sell to Tesna any cash at the bank, debtors or proceeds of the $150 million settlement with Air New Zealand. Tesna would make offers to employ about 4,000 Ansett workers and assume responsibility for employee entitlements based on a new enterprise bargaining agreement to be negotiated with the ACTU and relevant unions.

The total purchase price of the sale was $514 million of which Tesna would pay Ansett $270 million cash and assume liabilities and obligations, these comprising employee entitlements payable by the administrators of up to $244 million. The purchase price would be adjusted at completion for accruals, pre-payments and fuel stocks. The completion date was agreed to be 31 January 2002, at which time the risks and benefits of ownership would transfer to Tesna.

Other features of the sale agreement included provision to ensure that Tesna had a fleet of at least 16 Airbus A320s at completion; Tesna would purchase from Ansett maintenance services for its A320s for a period of two years; Ansett would provide information technology services for Tesna at cost for two years;

and Tesna's backers would provide $400 million for the leasing of 20 new A320s on 'reasonable terms and conditions.'

All that was needed now was approval from Ansett's creditors to go ahead with the deal, this to be put to them at a meeting on 29 January.

Tesna had meanwhile been chasing outside investment in the new Ansett and on 18 December announced the involvement of financier and Ryanair chairman David Bonderman and former America West chief executive Bill Franke as equity partners. Bonderman's Fort Worth based Texas Pacific Group (TPG) had a long history of bailing out struggling airlines including recapitalising Continental in 1992 and America West two years later. Due diligence on Ansett was partly conducted but the numbers didn't come close to stacking up – according to one insider – and Tesna's possible financial backers disappeared form the scene without a word.

With hindsight, it was probably at this point that Tesna's plans were doomed, especially in combination with the lack of taxpayer support via the Federal Government. Things kept progressing, however. Deals were done with suppliers and many of the other services organisations necessary to any airline, the million-and-one other details were being worked on, former BMI (British Midland) executive James Hogan was appointed the new Ansett's chief executive, and so on. On the face of it was still full steam ahead.

A Very Big Job

Ansett's administrators released their first report on the Ansett group on 16 January 2002, this weighty document well illustrating the extent of the job the two Marks had to do. It outlined the various options for the airline's future that would shortly be put to the creditors (liquidate now, continue the administration, execute a Deed of Company Arrangement etc), plus the administrators' strategies, finances, and the general state of the nation.

Among the figures was an unaudited before tax operating loss of $263.7 million for the 2000-2001 financial year and after tax loss of $378.3 million. Both of these figures were rather larger than had been stated in Air New Zealand's annual report for that period.

The administrators noted the major challenges faced by Ansett as being: an extremely competitive Australian aviation market; sustained high fuel prices; low exchange rates; the Ansett Group's high cost structure; the age and complexity of the Ansett fleet leading to higher maintenance and operating costs; scheduling complexity and greater operational down time; management issues and work practices; a substantial holding of spare engines; rotables and consumables due to the diversification of the fleet; and the temporary cessation of operations during Easter 2001. In other words, just about all of the basics as they apply to a successful airline operation were wrong.

Excluding Hazelton Airlines (which was not under the two Marks' administration), Ansett controlled a total of 133 aircraft when it was grounded of which 49 were owned, 45 were under finance and 39 were under operating leases. Those of the mainline fleet which were owned outright were the older Boeing 767-200s, the BAe

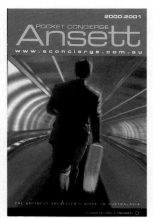

146s and Fokker F28s, the latter having already been retired from service. All the others (767-300s, 737s and A320s) were either under finance or leased, as were Ansett International's two 747-400s and one 767-300.

The administrators noted that 'there was significant uncertainty immediately after our appointment about the number of aircraft that were owned, owned but financed and not owned but subject to operating leases. Considerable investigation was therefore required to confirm the ownership and financing of the aircraft fleet. A substantial amount of the documentation was held by Air New Zealand, which assisted in the process.'

Of interest was the extent of the administrators' effort in dealing with the complexities of Ansett's situation. Since mid September 2001 there had been 80 people working full time on the project along with 120 part timers at a cost of nearly $11 million by mid December. The administrators were keen to point out that the hourly rate they were charging – which ranged from $89 for support people up to $359 for partners – was 35% below the rate normally charged by the firm.

At the other end of the scale, by the time the administrators' report was released, it was estimated that creditors could expect a return of only five cents in the dollar, even if the Tesna deal went through.

End of the Line

The creditors' meeting of 29 January approved the sale of Ansett to Tesna and also agreed to a new deadline for completion due to the mountain of legal paperwork of Himalayan proportions that still had to be processed. The new deadline was set at 28 February, and although this was going to cost about $24 million in ongoing losses – Ansett Mk.II was dropping about $6 million a week at that stage – there was little choice but to agree to the delay.

For some, alarm bells were already starting to go off regarding Tesna's commitment and these fears were backed up during February by several events – a reduction in the planned number of employees from 4,000 to 3,000 (the latter actually a more realistic figure for the planned operation's early stages); the ongoing massive losses; the realisation that Ansett Mk.II was attracting only a modest customer base (load factors were typically down at around 35%); attempts by Tesna to reduce its $270 million initial outlay; and the poorly received announcement of the proposed frequent flyer scheme on 19 February. The scheme was greeted less than enthusiastically because it did nothing to encourage previous Global Rewards members who had lost all their points to rejoin.

The longer finalisation of the deal was delayed, the less chance there was of success as with every passing day more passengers went to Qantas or Virgin Blue.

As Air New Zealand had done, Tesna turned to Sir Richard Branson in what with hindsight can be seen as the last roll of the dice to save the new Ansett. With the government refusing to commit taxpayers' money to the project and potential investors Bonderman and Franke walking away, it had become clear that it was going to be mainly Lindsay Fox's and Solomon Lew's money on the line and the chances of losing it were steadily increasing.

The pair flew to England to talk to Branson about a Virgin Blue/Ansett merger. While in Europe, they signed a Memorandum of Understanding with Airbus to lease 30 A320/321s plus 10 options.

The talks with Sir Richard Branson were made public on 11 February, their idea coming from the realisation that Virgin Blue was probably the greatest impediment to Ansett's chances of success and had to be either removed from the equation – which was impossible – or at least brought into the team.

As he had with Ansett five months earlier, Branson realised the desperation of Tesna's position and made it clear that if a merger happened, the airline would be run by him as a Virgin operation with Fox and Lew mere equity partners. Branson knew this would be unacceptable to them, as indeed it was.

Outwardly, it was all still happening and even the administrators genuinely believed until the last that the deal would go through. Qantas chief executive Geoff Dixon must have had a sixth sense about the whole thing. At a 21 February press conference announcing his airline's half year profit, he predicted there would only be two major airlines operating in Australia by the end of the year.

Then the bombshell. On 27 February – the day before the deadline for completion – the two Marks had to announce to the world that the Tesna deal was off, that Ansett would not be revived, that it would be shut down permanently at midnight on 4 March and its assets liquidated. 'As administrators', said Mark Korda, 'we are ready, willing and able to complete the deal', obviously still holding out some hope that a miracle would occur. It didn't, and the hopes and dreams of thousands were shattered.

Lindsay Fox and Solomon Lew held a brief press conference later in the day and tried to lay blame for the failure of the deal on the government and even the administrators. They were far from convincing. After that, not a word from them or any of their close associates on the subject.

The final Ansett flights were operated on 4 March, the very last revenue service to touch down flight number AN152 which arrived at Sydney at 6.42am on the 5th after operating the overnight 'red eye' service from Perth. It had departed the Western Australia capital at about 11.45pm the previous night and the aircraft involved was Airbus A320 VH-HYI.

And that was the end of 66 years, two weeks and one day of Australian aviation history.

Aftermath

The two Marks then had to set about disposing of Ansett's assets. They issued their second report on 15 March, in which they strongly recommended that the administration be continued and that deeds of company arrangements be executed.

Their reasoning was that if the Ansett companies were immediately wound up, certain leases on key assets – including the airport terminals – may be ended and lessors may exercise rights of buy back. This was tested in the High Court when Canberra Airport's owners tried to take over the Ansett terminal there, but it was ruled that this couldn't happen when a company is in administration.

The report stated that based on the various assumptions made, the possible return to priority creditors is potentially 100% but any return to unsecured creditors was unlikely. It was noted that many variables could significantly effect this including the realisation of asset values (especially aircraft, engines and spares); ongoing costs; and the resolution of contingencies.

Another creditors' meeting in Melbourne on March 27 voted in favour of the recommendations made by administrators to execute deeds of company arrangements for each Ansett company and therefore continue the administration for another six months.

Creditor support meant that negotiations with airport owners and other parties for the sale of Ansett's terminals, regional subsidiary Kendell Airlines, the airline's maintenance and engineering operation, the Ansett Simulator Centre and Ansett International Cargo could continue as 'going concerns'. These operations still employed 1,452 people.

Some groups were opposed to continuing the administration and wanted the company's remaining assets liquidated. Among them was the Global Rewards Action Group (representing some former Ansett frequent flyer scheme members), lessors and airports.

The deeds of company arrangements prevented airports from using buy-back clauses to automatically take over the airline's domestic terminal leases at a loosely defined 'market value'. The Federal Government – which was a creditor for $90m in taxes and other debts – supported the vote in favour of continued administration.

A further administrators' report was issued in mid September 2002. This noted that in the 12 months since Ansett's collapse some $630 million had been raised from the sale of assets and another $98.1 million was subject to settlement.

Assets sold included Ansett's interest in the domestic terminals at Sydney, Melbourne, Brisbane, Adelaide, Perth, Canberra, Launceston and Hobart; the airline's interests in various regional airports; freehold property including land, buildings, the Melbourne headquarters and a number of special purpose facilities; subsidiaries Skywest, Aeropelican, Kendell, Hazelton and Ansett International Cargo Handling; office furniture, fittings and IT equipment through auction; vehicles, trucks, tugs and airport ground service vehicles; and surplus engineering equipment not required for maintenance of the remaining aircraft fleet. In addition, 78 aircraft had been sold, leased or returned to lessors.

Yet to be sold were: 43 aircraft including 767-200s, A320s and BAe 146s; simulators, engines, spares and rotables; remaining property interests; a collection of more than 5,000 pieces of memorabilia; and possibly the most important item of all – the Ansett Australia brand and other trademarks and brand names owned by Ansett.

FLEET SUMMARY – 14 September 2001

Ansett Australia: 3 Boeing 767-300ER (only 1 in service); 9 Boeing 767-200; 20 Airbus A320-200; 24 Boeing 737-300; 7 BAe 146-200; 3 BAe 146-300. Stored awaiting disposal: 4 BAe 146-300; 4 Fokker F28-4000 Fellowship.

Ansett International: 2 Boeing 747-400; 1 Boeing 767-300ER.

Ansett Australia Cargo: 2 Boeing 727-200F; 2 BAe 146-200QT; 2 BAe HS.748-2B (Horizon Airlines contract); 1 Fokker F27-600QC (Independent Air Freighters contract).

Aeropelican Air Services: 4 DHC Twin Otter 300.

Hazelton Airlines: 2 Saab 340A; 7 Saab 340B; 2 Fairchild Metro 23.

Kendell Airlines: 11 Bombardier CRJ200; 7 Saab 340A; 8 Saab 340B; 7 Fairchild Metro 23.

Skywest Airlines: 5 Fokker 50.

The following table notes the disposal and/or dispersal of Ansett Australia's and Ansett Intern
It notes the final scheduled commercial services flown (including dates and flight numb

Abbreviations: AW – Ansett Worldwide; ILFC – International Lease Fir

Type	Regn	Notes/Disposal
Airbus A320-211	VH-HYA	lsd from AW; last serv 4/3/02 AN405 Sydney-Melbourne; to Willmington Trust (USA) 3/02; stored Mojave.
Airbus A320-211	VH-HYB	lsd from AW; last serv 1/3/02 AN9 Sydney-Melbourne; to Willmington Trust (USA) 3/02; stored Mojave.
Airbus A320-211	VH-HYC	lsd from SAL; last serv 4/3/02 AN287 Brisbane-Sydney; stored Melbourne; to Marshall Aerospace (UK) 7/02.
Airbus A320-211	VH-HYD	last serv 4/3/02 AN259 Sydney-Perth; stored Melbourne.
Airbus A320-211	VH-HYE	lsd from SAL; last serv 4/3/02 AN286 Sydney-Brisbane; stored Melbourne; to Marshall Aerospace (UK) 8/02.
Airbus A320-211	VH-HYF	lsd from SAL; last serv 4/3/02 AN35 Adelaide-Melbourne; stored Melbourne; to Marshall Aerospace (UK) 8/02.
Airbus A320-211	VH-HYG	lsd from SAL; last serv 4/3/02 AN144 Melbourne-Brisbane; stored Melbourne; to Marshall Aerospace (UK) 8/02.
Airbus A320-211	VH-HYH	last serv 4/3/02 AN211 Brisbane-Sydney; stored Melbourne.
Airbus A320-211	VH-HYI	last serv 4-5/3/02 AN152 Perth-Sydney (last Ansett sched flight); stored Melbourne; to Lufthansa Maintenance (Berlin) 7/02.
Airbus A320-211	VH-HYJ	last serv 4/3/02 AN355 Melb-Adl; stored Melb; to Lufthansa Maintenance (Berlin) 8/02.
Airbus A320-211	VH-HYK	lsd from AW; last serv 4/3/02 AN276 Sydney-Brisbane; stored Melbourne; to Lufthansa Maintenance (Berlin).
Airbus A320-211	VH-HYL	lsd from AW; last serv 11/11/01 AN757 Sydney-Melbourne; stored Melbourne; to Lufthansa Maintenance (Berlin) 8/02.
Airbus A320-211	VH-HYN	lsd from ILFC; last serv 4/3/02 AN91 Sydney-Melb; returned to ILFC (USA) 4/02.
Airbus A320-211	VH-HYO	lsd from ILFC; last serv 4/3/02 AN185 Melbourne-Perth; to USA for storage.
Airbus A320-211	VH-HYQ	last serv 4-5/3/02 AN170 Perth-Melbourne; stored Melbourne.
Airbus A320-211	VH-HYR	in Canada for maintenance 9/01; stored Air Canada, Winnipeg.
Airbus A320-211	VH-HYS	last serv 13/9/01 AN174 Perth-Sydney; stored Melbourne.
Airbus A320-211	VH-HYT	last serv 4/3/02 AN85 Sydney-Melbourne; to France 3/02.
Airbus A320-211	VH-HYX	lsd from GATX Capital; last serv 13/9/01 AN191 Melbourne-Adelaide; to France 5/02.
Airbus A320-211	VH-HYY	lsd from GATX Capital; last serv 13/9/01 AN220 Perth-Brisbane; to Air Malta 2/02.
BAe 146-200	VH-JJP	last sched serv 13/9/01 AN347 Perth-Pt Hedland; subsequent charters; stored Melb.
BAe 146-200	VH-JJQ	in Brisbane for maintenance 9/01; reduced to components 6/02.
BAe 146-200	VH-JJS	last serv 13/9/01 AN393 Broome-Perth; to Hawker Pacific 6/02.
BAe 146-200	VH-JJT	last serv 13/9/01 AN329 Karratha-Perth; regist to Trident Jet 4/02.
BAe 146-200	VH-JJU	last serv 13/9/01 AN335 Newman-Perth; stored Melbourne.
BAe 146-200	VH-JJW	last sched serv 13/9/01 AN367 Ayers Rock-Perth; subsequent charters; stored Melb.
BAe 146-200	VH-JJX	in Townsville for maintenance 9/01; stored there.
BAe 146-300	VH-EWM	last serv 13/9/01 AN159 Cairns-Brisbane; stored Brisbane then Melbourne.
BAe 146-300	VH-EWR	last sched serv 14/9/01 AN976 Cbr-Bris; subsequent charters; stored Bris then Melb.
BAe 146-200	VH-EWS	in Brisbane for maintenance 9/01; stored Brisbane then Melbourne.

POSAL

ainline fleet of Boeing 737s, 747s, 767s, Airbus A320s and BAe 146s after the airline's collapse.
quent sale (if applicable) and status as at late September 2002 if still in Ansett's hands.

oration; lsd – leased; SAL – Singapore Aircraft Leasing; serv – service.

Type	Regn	Notes/Disposal
Boeing 737-377	VH-CZA	in Christchurch NZ for maintenance 9/01, stored there
Boeing 737-377	VH-CZB	last serv 13/9/01 AN140 Sydney-Brisbane; stored Melbourne.
Boeing 737-377	VH-CZC	in Auckland NZ for maintenance 9/01, stored there.
Boeing 737-377	VH-CZD	in Brisbane for maintenance 9/01, dismantled there 6-7/02.
Boeing 737-377	VH-CZE	last serv 14/9/01 AN118 Hobart-Sydney; to Channel Express 6/02.
Boeing 737-377	VH-CZF	last serv 13/9/01 AN357 Kalgoorlie-Perth; stored Melbourne.
Boeing 737-377	VH-CZG	last serv 13/9/01 AN182 Adelaide-Melbourne; to Channel Express 6/02.
Boeing 737-377	VH-CZH	last serv 13/9/01 AN96 Adelaide-Melbourne; to Channel Express 5/02.
Boeing 737-377	VH-CZI	last serv 13/9/01 AN59 Sydney-Melbourne; to Channel Express 9/02.
Boeing 737-377	VH-CZJ	last serv 14/9/01 AN200 Canberra-Sydney; stored Melbourne.
Boeing 737-377	VH-CZK	last serv 13/9/01 AN142 Sydney-Brisbane; stored Melbourne.
Boeing 737-377	VH-CZL	last serv 14/9/01 AD1493 Lake Argyle-Perth charter; stored Melbourne.
Boeing 737-377	VH-CZM	last serv 14/9/01 AN227 Cairns-Sydney; stored Melb; to Regionair (Singapore) 9/02.
Boeing 737-377	VH-CZN	in Melbourne for maintenance 9/01; stored there.
Boeing 737-377	VH-CZO	last serv 14/9/01 AN7 Darwin-Sydney; stored Melb; to Regionair (Singapore) 10/02.
Boeing 737-377	VH-CZP	last serv 14/9/01 AN165 Cbr-Melb, stored Melb; registered in Seychelle Islands 9/02.
Boeing 737-33A	VH-CZQ	last serv 13/9/01 AN188 Perth-Adelaide; lsd to Virgin Blue 10/01.
Boeing 737-33A	VH-CZR	last serv 13/9/01 AN40 Melbourne-Sydney; to Qantas NZ 10/01.
Boeing 737-33A	VH-CZS	last serv 14/9/01 AN123 Townsville-Brisbane; to Qantas NZ 11/01.
Boeing 737-33A	VH-CZT	last serv 13/9/01 AN917 Melbourne-Adelaide; stored Melbourne; to Brazil 10/02.
Boeing 737-33A	VH-CZU	last serv 13/9/01 AN175 Brisbane-Melbourne; to Qantas NZ 10/01.
Boeing 737-33A	VH-CZV	last serv 13/9/01 AN110 Melbourne-Sydney; stored Melbourne.
Boeing 737-33A	VH-CZW	last serv 13/9/01 AN99 Melbourne-Adelaide; stored Melbourne.
Boeing 737-33A	VH-CZX	last serv 14/9/01 AN15 Coolangatta-Sydney; stored Melbourne.
Boeing 747-412	VH-ANA	last serv 14/9/01 AN888 Hong Kong-Sydney; returned to SIA 11/01.
Boeing 747-314	VH-ANB	last serv 14/9/01 AN882 Kansai-Brisbane; returned to SIA 11/01.
Boeing 767-277	VH-RMD	last serv 13/9/01 AN51 Sydney-Melbourne; stored.
Boeing 767-277	VH-RME	in maintenance Melbourne 9/01; stored.
Boeing 767-277	VH-RMF	in maintenance Melbourne 9/01; stored; to Kras Air (Russia) 10/02.
Boeing 767-277	VH-RMG	last serv 14/9/01 AN216 Perth-Sydney; stored Melbourne.
Boeing 767-277	VH-RMH	last serv 14/9/01 AN218 Perth-Melbourne; stored.
Boeing 767-204	VH-RMK	last serv 13/9/01 AN159 Brisbane-Sydney; stored Melbourne.
Boeing 767-204	VH-RML	last serv 13/9/01 AN183 Sydney-Melbourne; stored.
Boeing 767-216ER	VH-RMM	lsd from GATX Capital; last serv 13/9/01 AN56 Melb-Sydney; returned to USA 1/02.
Boeing 767-204	VH-RMO	lsd from AWAS; last serv 13/9/01 AN55 Sydney-Melbourne; stored Mojave.
Boeing 767-324ER	VH-BZF	lsd from GE Capital; last serv 13/9/01 AN53 Sydney-Melbourne; to Dublin 12/01.
Boeing 767-35HER	VH-BZL	lsd from Air Canada; last serv 13/9/01 AN155 Bris-Syd; returned to Canada 11/01.

Dead Ansett aeroplanes No 2 (top to bottom): 737s at Melbourne; CRJs at Melbourne in December 2002; 737, A320 and 767 at Melbourne in December 2001. (Paul Daw).

CHAPTER FOURTEEN

THE ANSETT FLEET

Guilty as Charged or Just Maligned?

There had been some criticism of Ansett Australia's fleet makeup over the last decade or so of its life, some justified, some perhaps not. Former Ansett Fleet Development Manager – Commercial, Mark Brownley, takes a look at the issue and provides a report card on the aircraft as well as examining some of the general philosophies that apply to fleet procurement and management.

★   ★   ★

When one of the many Ansett creditors stepped off the aircraft in Sydney in early October 2001 after the airline's collapse, hungry to reclaim a dormant Boeing 767 that had been in the failed airline's care for a good five years, they did so because the administrator had made an informed decision to return to the sky with a no frills startup initially using five Airbus A320s.

Informed because the A320 is a good airliner and would have been a worthy reincarnate to enable Ansett Mk.II to take to the sky. It's very flexible, mission capable, economical in terms of both trip and unit costs and replete with 140 plus seats, profitable to boot.

When the dust finally settled on the Ansett stable of airliners three weeks earlier, the BAe 146 had finally got it comeuppance (some federal election charters aside); 747s and 767s were out; and the ubiquitous 737 was gone too. In an environment of survival of the fittest only the A320 made the grade because it was a smart aircraft for Australia with its long linear network. It was one of the smarter legacies of the Sir Peter Abeles years that withstood the test of time.

The A320 would go on to vindicate Abeles' leap of faith in evolving Airbus technology and design economics and can eat up routes like Melbourne-Brisbane, Sydney-Perth, Adelaide-Perth, Melbourne-Perth, Adelaide-Darwin, Darwin-Perth and establish regional routes such as Perth-Denpasar (Bali).

Paradoxically, the A320 is only one of many astute fleet choices made by Peter Abeles over the years but instead of upgrading as aircraft technology and economics evolved, Ansett made a habit of collecting types, each superseded marque serving as a millstone to weigh heavily on profits, efficiency and operational flexibility.

The Ansett fleet was maligned for years by management, commentators, fleet planners, even casual observers and enthusiasts, mainly because of the explosion in types resulting from the consolidation of regional airlines under the Ansett Australia banner, contributing orphan types – 727, 146, F28 – to what would became a mutant parent.

At one point in time in the 1990s nine types populated the fleet. And as a fleet it is true that it failed the airline, its shareholders and customers. But to blame the fleet for the demise of Ansett is to overstate the significance of fleet decisions in the fight for survival.

Costs could still have been managed down assiduously (Rule No 1 – unit costs must not rise); on time performance pursued (Rule 2 – high-yielding business travellers value certainty); maintenance processes re-engineered (Rule 3 – heavy maintenance overruns increase costs and deny revenue opportunities); enterprise agreements restructured (Rule 4 – don't give away anything of value without receiving something of value in return); crew establishment levels tested (Rule 5 – a cost efficient establishment and reserve); workforce numbers reduced (Rule 6 – right size, don't oversize); turnaround times reduced (Rule 7 – more time in the air means more revenue opportunities and a broader base over which to spread fixed costs); procurement practices revised (Rule 8 – spending less is better than spending more).

Managing the business and not the operation could have bought time; time enough to right size and right type the fleet.

But if you were going to sheet home blame, the line was a long one. Rightly or wrongly, everything and everyone from the fleet to the Foreign Investment Review Board, competition policy to Gary Toomey, Air New Zealand to executive management, News Corp and Sir Peter Abeles, the Federal Government and, of course, Geoff Dixon and Qantas, all came in for their share of criticism.

However, if you take a closer look at the usual suspects, you'd have to believe that human factors were entirely to blame. But were they? After all, if an airline is anything, it's the archetypal fusion of human factors and technology.

But what about the pressurised, pressed aluminium tubes that cost hundreds of millions to operate and billions to replace? Interestingly, from the Ansett case study emerges the missing link between human factors and technology that is worthy of exploration – Sir Peter Abeles.

Boeing 747 – 'No problems here; an astute choice for routes to Asia'. 747-300 VH-INJ in Sydney 2000 markings departs Sydney Airport in August 1997. (Trent Jones)

Boeing 727 – 'There was no room in competitive Australian skies for the ubiquitous three holer once Australian Airlines pensioned off its 727s in the early 1990s'. VH-ANA was one of the last two Ansett 727s in service, retired in April 1997. The graphics on the forward fuselage mark the occasion. (Paul Merritt)

Boeing 737 – 'It's difficult not to make money with a 737.... [but] the airline needed to choose either Boeing or Airbus. Instead, it wanted to have its cake and eat it too. That was a big mistake'. This is 737-33A VH-CZV at Brisbane. (Rob Finlayson)

Boeing 767 – 'The 767 was designed for US transcontinental flying, not hour-twenty sectors like Melbourne-Sydney and Sydney-Brisbane.... this notwithstanding, the 767 was a sensible choice for one of the world's most heavily supplied air routes'. Ansett's plans to replace its ageing 767-200s with larger and newer 767-300s was getting underway when the airline failed. (Paul Merritt)

BAe 146 – 'Much maligned and deservedly so.... a dog of an aeroplane that suffered interminably from engine reliability problems'. BAe 146-300 VH-EWR was originally delivered to Eastwest in 1991. (Alan Scoot)

Sir Peter was the transport entrepreneur who presided over Ansett from 1979 until 1992 and was personally responsible for the procurement of a majority of key Ansett fleet types (767, A320, 737, BAe 146 and Fokker 50) still in service when the airline went belly up.

If anyone was to be held to account, surely the man who bought aircraft with the same deference as the family car had a case to answer. By examining the motivation for these purchases and the selection criteria applied, it goes some way to unlocking the secret to one of Australian aviation's more pressing conundrums – in the end, what role did the Ansett fleet play?

The Type Equation

When it comes to fleet mix, less is more. Ansett simply had too many fleet types. A Boeing widebody and Airbus narrowbody were all that was required for the mix to work. Instead, in terms of aircraft types, management in the airline's latter years had to make a combination of 747s, 767s, A320s, 727s, 737s, BAe 146s, F28s and F50s mesh. In a densely populated, hub-and-spoke environment such as the USA, multiple fleet types can make sense, provided the population of each type can reach critical mass. That is, the formation and operation of mini airlines with aircraft selected and operating almost exclusively on sector lengths for which they were designed.

However, Ansett could never hope to achieve these economies of scale in critical areas such as spares and inventory, aircrew establishment and training, maintenance and engineering, by maintaining fleets numbering fewer than 10 units. The 767, 747, 146, F28 and F50 fleets were all on the wrong side of the magic number, 20 or more. Against that criterion, only the A320 and 737 could hope to pass muster.

In the final analysis, the numbers wouldn't stack. They couldn't. Ansett suffered from too few of too many types. However, contrary to popular belief, rationalisation, consolidation and right typing, while necessary, was not sufficient. The shareholders' decision to ignore the pleas from generations of planners and customers did not consign Ansett to the grave.

The fleet would never prove profitable when Ansett claimed less than 40% of the market, a malaise into which the business slid irretrievably. A high cost, multi-fleet proposition like Ansett needed volume to stay alive. If nobody wants to fly you, not even an all 737-300 fleet

will save your life. That's the job of management and marketing, not the fleet. Re-equipment wouldn't have guaranteed survival, but it would have bought Ansett a reprieve, a stay of execution. After all, on a fully allocated basis older aircraft are always cheaper to operate than new ones.

In some ways then, Ansett's ageing fleet was actually a blessing in disguise when cashflow was tight and profits just a memory. If they had just re-equipped, it would have been parlous indeed. Now that the airline has gone, a review of the rationale, the capability and the deployment of the fleet reveals much about the role of the technology in the airline's demise. It will show, as those in the know would appreciate, that the fleet, while not beyond reproach, is not the poisoned chalice that ended competition in Australian skies.

Let's take a look at the report card:

Boeing 747: No problems here. An astute choice for routes to Asia. A credible, four engined statement that implied safety and comfort, attributes that rate highly on utility scales for traffic of Asian origin. The 747's economics were no doubt underpinned by sharp deals cut with Singapore Airlines.

Boeing 767: The 767 was designed for US transcontinental flying, not hour-twenty sectors like Melbourne-Sydney and Sydney-Brisbane. High bypass ratio engines such as the CF6-80A do not take kindly to high cycle patterns of operation, the very same that Qantas and Ansett relied on these workhorses to sustain. This notwithstanding, the 767 was a sensible choice for one of the world's most heavily supplied air routes, Melbourne-Sydney ranking as high as third and Sydney-Brisbane not far behind.

However, the economics of route density (the number of trips and the yield per trip) plus sophisticated revenue management means that a profitable operation can be sustained on the back of a 211 seat widebody with an 8-10 hour endurance which would otherwise have to operate long haul to make any real money.

Despite its age, the 767 remained the right solution for the 'Golden Triangle' that is Melbourne-Sydney-Brisbane. Ansett's biggest mistake was to acquiesce to industrial demands when the 767 was ordered and fit its original five aircraft with a flight engineer station that boosted trip flightcrew costs significantly. These 767s were unique in having a three crew cockpit and were changed back to the intended two crew arrangement only a few years before Ansett's demise.

Otherwise, the logical migration from the 767-200 to the -300, foreshadowed as early as 1996 and just getting underway when the airline folded, would have had it on the right track.

Boeing 727: There was no room in competitive Australian skies for the ubiquitous three holer once Australian Airlines pensioned off its 727s in the early 1990s. However, as late as April 1997, Ansett was still pushing 149 seats through the air with three Pratt & Whitney JT8D gas guzzlers. That's a lot of tin. In addition to fuel, its oversize design meant higher air navigation charges and unit costs disproportionately higher than its 143 seat A320 stablemate.

Fokker F28 – 'A grab bag of expensive to run, outdated, Stage 2 airliners that nobody wanted. Their use by date had long since passed and Ansett couldn't give them away'. In its time, the F28 Fellowship created an important piece of Australian airline history when it became the nation's first regional jet airliner. (Bill MacRae)

A great aeroplane for its time, the 727 overstayed its welcome at Ansett. On airline balance sheets, nostalgia is costly.

Airbus A320: The case for the A320 is proven – economical, flexible, modular, mission capable, very respectable trip costs in the 140-150 seat category and sensational unit economics the world over. It was and remained the mainstay of the fleet despite the popularity of and affection for the 737. In the latter years, Ansett's fleet planners rightly favoured the A320 over the 737 as every one of the 29 additional seats could be supplied at a lower unit cost. And since the A320s initially numbered fewer than the 737s, each A320 could be added to the fleet with a disproportionate increase in efficiency.

As administrators, Mark Mentha and Mark Korda earned their stripes as rookie fleet planners with their decision to keep the A320 flying.

Boeing 737: It's difficult not to make money with the 737. The airliner that has sold more than any other model in the history of commercial aviation, it was the aircraft of choice before the A320 arrived on the scene but still remains very competitive in the 114-143 seat category. Economical, reliable and always a standout asset class for investors, the expansion of the 737 fleet in later years enabled Ansett to mine non-stop opportunities such as Perth-Darwin and increase frequency between established city pairs such as Melbourne-Adelaide and Melbourne-Brisbane.

But in the highly competitive fleet category, for the purposes of simplicity and in the interests of cost-effective capacity, the airline needed to choose either Airbus

Fokker 50 – 'Actually not a bad airliner [but] yet another type'. The successor to the famed F27 Friendship didn't have the same level of acceptance in Australia as its predecessor, but after flying with Air NSW/Ansett Express and other subsidiaries, found a niche with Skywest in Western Australia. Ten Fokker 50s were delivered to Ansett from late 1987. (Keith Anderson)

Airbus A320 – 'Economical, flexible, modular, mission capable.... sensational unit economics the world over'. A320-211 VH-HYO was delivered to Ansett in 1995. (Airbus)

or Boeing. Instead, it wanted to have its cake and eat it too. This was a big mistake.

BAe 146-200/300: Much maligned and deservedly so. A dog of an aeroplane that suffered interminably from engine reliability problems. Although the engineers eventually made it work, the question is at what cost? The Lycoming ALF502 evolved from a helicopter engine and never easily made the transition to fixed wing applications. They were fiddly, labour intensive and not sufficiently robust for high cycle operations.

The stretched 146-300 was never going to work. Its 93 seats could not be delivered economically to the market and the aircraft's capabilities were extremely limited – it couldn't fly 'hot and high' so was quarantined to more temperate climates on the east coast. Unfortunately, Ansett deployed it on the important Sydney-Coolangatta sector while the competition ran 737s.

Inventories, licenses and maintenance had to be duplicated across the country to support siblings that could not co-exist. But even within the 146-200 fleet all was not in order. Different tanking configurations caused operating weights to vary and constrain scheduling and operational flexibility. Passengers soon tired of diversions and the use of alternate airports!

Fokker F28-1000/3000/4000: A grab bag of expensive to run, outdated, Stage 2 airliners that nobody wanted. Their use by date had long since passed and Ansett couldn't give them away. After it was pulled

from Canberra and NSW, the F28 was consigned to WA where regional communities no doubt preferred noisy Rolls-Royce Spey jets to prop driven aircraft or no RPT at all. For Ansett the F28 it was just another type.

Fokker 50: Actually not a bad airliner – a complete rebuild of the F27 and more economical than most would appreciate – but initially operated Canberra-Sydney and in so doing going head-to-head with 737s. Rightly consigned to the west where it operated successfully with Skywest. Yet another type.

Although the fundamentals were in place at critical milestones in its evolution, the Ansett fleet couldn't make the transition to each new phase of competition. Sir Reginald Ansett and Sir Peter Abeles ensured that the hangars were full of the latest and greatest the planemakers had to offer. However, the business had to drag superseded types into progressively less forgiving market conditions and more demanding economic realms.

But in the final analysis, it didn't make the difference between success and failure. There were other more pressing business and commercial agenda that could have staved off administration (see the Rule Book above). After all, it is a conveniently overlooked fact that ageing airliners are cheaper to operate on a fully allocated basis than newer replacement types. Ironically, Ansett's fleet actually had something going for it, working in the interests of shareholders while they worried about the business!

ANSETT AIRCRAFT 1936-2002

Notes: This table attempts to list the 'airliner' type aircraft operated by Ansett Airways, Ansett-ANA, Ansett Airlines of Australia, Ansett and Ansett Australia over the years, including wholly and partially owned subsidiaries. Helicopters are also included.

The 'In Service' column reflects an individual aircraft's period of service only when with an Ansett airline and not in the case of previous owners which later became part of the Ansett family. For example, Hazelton Airlines' aircraft are listed from March 2001 (3/01) only, the date of the company's takeover by Ansett.

For the fleet current in 2001 it also reflects the period up to September 2001 when Ansett collapsed, except for some of the A320s which were used by 'Ansett Mk.II' up to early March 2002. The regional subsidiaries are also noted up until September 2001, although some of these also continued to operate under administration after that date. Light aircraft are generally excluded as are most of the very short term charters of other airlines' aircraft which were occasionally undertaken, although some of these are noted.

The aircraft are presented in alphabetical order by manufacturer. The 'Notes' column lists the aircraft's name (if any), the Ansett airline/s with which it flew and other points of interest.

Abbreviations: AAC – Ansett Australia Cargo; AAF – Ansett Air Freight; AANA – Ansett Airlines of Northern Australia; AAPNG – Ansett Airlines of Papua New Guinea; Air NZ – Air New Zealand; AFBS – Ansett Flying Boat Services; ALNA – Airlines of Northern Australia; ANA – Australian National Airways; ANSW – Airlines of NSW/Air NSW/Ansett NSW; ANZ – Ansett New Zealand; ASA – Airlines of SA; AWA – Airlines of WA/Ansett WA; ANT – Ansett NT; AWAS – Ansett Worldwide Aviation Services; BAT – Butler Air Transport; cvtd – converted; dbr – damaged beyond repair; del/deliv – delivered; EWA – East-West Airlines; lsd – leased; MAL – Mandated Airlines; MMA – MacRobertson Miller Airlines; ntu – not taken up; PAT – Papuan Air Transport (Patair); QAL – Queensland Airlines; regn – registration; SPANZ – South Pacific Airlines of New Zealand; TAA – Trans Australia Airlines; VAC – Victorian Air Coach; wfu – withdrawn from use; w/o – written off.

Type	Regn	In Service	Notes
Airbus A320-211	VH-HYA	12/88-3/02	A320 named 'Skystar' in Ansett service
Airbus A320-211	VH-HYB	11/88-3/02	
Airbus A320-211	VH-HYC	12/88-3/02	
Airbus A320-211	VH-HYD	3/89-3/02	
Airbus A320-211	VH-HYE	1/89-3/02	
Airbus A320-211	VH-HYF	2/89-3/02	
Airbus A320-211	VH-HYG	4/89-3/02	
Airbus A320-211	VH-HYH	5/89-3/02	
Airbus A320-211	VH-HYI	1/91-3/02	flew last Ansett service, Perth-Sydney 4-5/3/02
Airbus A320-211	VH-HYJ	1/91-3/02	
Airbus A320-211	VH-HYK	3/91-3/02	
Airbus A320-211	VH-HYL	4/92-11/01	
Airbus A320-211	VH-HYN	12/97-3/02	
Airbus A320-211	VH-HYO	9/95-3/02	
Airbus A320-211	VH-HYQ	9/96-3/02	
Airbus A320-211	VH-HYR	10/96-9/01	
Airbus A320-211	VH-HYS	11/96-9/01	
Airbus A320-211	VH-HYT	4/97-3/02	
Airbus A320-211	VH-HYX	7/96-9/01	ex Onur Air
Airbus A320-211	VH-HYY	6/96-9/01	ex Onur Air
Airbus A320-211	F-GHQK	-	deliv 10/91 but immediately sold to Air Inter
Airbus A320-211	F-GHQM	-	deliv 11/91 but immediately sold to Air Inter
Airspeed Envoy I	VH-UXM	10/36-8/45	dbr forced landing Hamilton-Essendon flight 8/45
Airspeed Ambassador 2	VH-BUI	2/58-8/58	Butler Air Transport
Airspeed Ambassador 2	VH-BUJ	2/58-8/58	Butler Air Transport
Airspeed Ambassador 2	VH-BUK	2/58-9/58	Butler Air Transport
Aviation Traders Carvair	VH-INJ	9/65-6/72	cvtd from DC-4 VH-INJ
Aviation Traders Carvair	VH-INK	11/65-1/74	cvtd from DC-4 VH-INK
Aviation Traders Carvair	VH-INM	7/68-1/74	cvtd from DC-4 VH-INM (last Carvair built)
BAe Jetstream 31	VH-ESW	7/87-3/99	Skywest
BAe Jetstream 31	VH-HSW	7/87-3/99	Skywest
BAe Jetstream 31	VH-JSW	7/87-3/99	Skywest
BAe Jetstream 31	VH-OSW	7/87-2/97	Skywest
BAe Jetstream 32EP	ZK-ECN	10/98-9/00	Ansett NZ, lsd from Air National
BAe Jetstream 32EP	ZK-ECP	7/99-9/00	Ansett NZ, lsd from Air National
BAe 146-200	VH-JJP	4/85-9/01	Ansett WA/Ansett
BAe 146-200	VH-JJQ	6/85-9/01	Ansett WA/Ansett
BAe 146-200	VH-JJS	10/88-9/01	Ansett WA/Ansett
BAe 146-200	VH-JJT	11/88-9/01	Ansett WA/Ansett
BAe 146-200	VH-JJW	8/89-9/01	Ansett WA/Ansett
BAe 146-200	ZK-NZA	7/89-9/01	Ansett NZ *City of Queenstown*, to Ansett WA 3/93 as VH-JJU, Ansett Australia 3/95
BAe 146-200	ZK-NZB	7/89-9/01	Ansett NZ, to Ansett WA 9/92 as VH-JJX, Ansett Australia 3/93
BAe 146-200QC	ZK-NZC	10/89-9/99	Ansett NZ *City of Manukau*
BAe 146-200QT	VH-JJY	5/89-9/01	Ansett Air Freight
BAe 146-200QT	VH-JJZ	6/89-9/01	Ansett Air Freight

Type	Regn	In Service	Notes
BAe 146-300	VH-EWI	8/90-2/00	Eastwest/Ansett
BAe 146-300	VH-EWJ	8/90-9/00	Eastwest/Ansett/Ansett NZ 2/95-9/00 as ZK-NZM *Queenstown*
BAe 146-300	VH-EWK	9/90-9/00	Eastwest/Ansett NZ 7/97-9/00 as ZK-NZL *City of Rotorua*
BAe 146-300	VH-EWL	10/90-9/00	Eastwest/Ansett/Ansett NZ 2/97-9/00 as ZK-NZN
BAe 146-300	VH-EWM	12/90-9/01	Eastwest/Ansett
BAe 146-300	VH-EWN	4/91-9/00	Eastwest/Ansett NZ 1/92-9/00 as ZK-NZK *City of Invercargill*
BAe 146-300	VH-EWR	6/91-9/01	Eastwest/Ansett/Ansett Express
BAe 146-300	VH-EWS	6/91-9/01	Eastwest/Ansett
BAe 146-300	ZK-NZF	12/89-12/99	Ansett NZ *City of Wellington*
BAe 146-300	ZK-NZG	12/89-9/00	Ansett NZ *City of Christchurch*
BAe 146-300	ZK-NZH	1/90-9/00	Ansett NZ *City of Auckland*
BAe 146-300	ZK-NZI	12/89-9/00	Ansett NZ *City of Dunedin*
BAe 146-300	ZK-NZJ	2/90-9/00	Ansett NZ *City of Nelson*
Bell 47G-3B-1	VH-ANG	10/66-3/68	Ansett-ANA Helicopter Division
Bell 47G-2	VH-FVS	1966	lsd from F V Sharpe (Bell Distributor)
Bell 47J-2A Ranger	VH-IND	3/65-3/68	
Bell 47J Ranger	VH-INE	10/59-3/68	
Bell 47J Ranger	VH-INF	6/60-3/68	
Bell 47G-3B-1	VH-INI	2/63-1/67	w/o Salamaua PNG 1/67
Bell 47J-2A Ranger	VH-INM	2/62-2/64	w/o Maydena Tas 2/64
Bell 47J Ranger	VH-INN	12/60-12/63	w/o Essendon Vic 12/63
Bell 47J Ranger	VH-INR	1/59-3/60	w/o Melton Weir Vic 3/60
Bell 47J-2 Ranger	VH-INV	3/63-3/68	
Bell 47J-2A Ranger	VH-INW	5/64-3/68	
Bell 47J-2 Ranger	VH-INZ	9/63-3/68	
Bell 47J-2A Ranger	VH-THH	1/69-2/69	chartered from TAA
Bell 206A JetRanger	VH-ANC	4/67-8/70	
Bell 206A JetRanger	VH-AND	1/70-2/80	cvtd to 206B
Boeing PB2B-2 Catalina*	VH-BRA	5/52-4/53	AFBS, ex Barrier Reef Airways *The Beachcomber*
Boeing 707-323C	3D-ASD	2/90	AAF, lsd from Air Swazi Cargo
Boeing 707-330C	VH-HTC	10/88-12/90	*Brisbane*, Transcorp/Ansett Air Freight
Boeing 707-338C	VH-EAB	4/73	Ansett-ANA, chartered from Qantas for Easter traffic
Boeing 707-338C	VH-EBV	4/73	Ansett-ANA, chartered from Qantas for Easter traffic
Boeing 707-338C	G-BDEA	1/88-2/88	AAF, chartered from Anglo Cargo, ex Qantas/BCal
Boeing 727-77	VH-RMD	8/65-3/79	Ansett-ANA/Ansett
Boeing 727-77	VH-RME	10/64-9/78	Ansett-ANA/Ansett
Boeing 727-77	VH-RMF	11/64-5/79	Ansett-ANA/Ansett
Boeing 727-77	VH-RMR	8/66-6/76	Ansett-ANA/Ansett
Boeing 727-77C	VH-RMS	10/69-1/80	Ansett/Ansett
Boeing 727-77C	VH-RMY	7/70-6/76	
Boeing 727-25F	VH-LAP	-	ex Easter/Bloodstock Air Services, deliv 4/84 for AAF but did not enter service, to Ansett Industries 11/84 and leased out
Boeing 727-277	VH-RMK	12/76-12/88	
Boeing 727-277	VH-RML	6/78-7/89	named *Southern Connection* 12/80 for Hobart-Christchurch service
Boeing 727-277	VH-RMM	1/79-5/89	
Boeing 727-277	VH-RMN	5/79-9/96	lsd Polynesian Airlines 4/87-4/92, lsd Eastwest 5/92-5/93
Boeing 727-277	VH-RMO	1/80-8/89	named *Spirit of North Queensland* 4/80 for trial Townsville-Singapore flight
Boeing 727-277	VH-RMP	9/80-8/88	
Boeing 727-277	VH-RMU	11/72-6/84	lsd NASA 12/72-3/73 and Wien Air Alaska 12/83-6/84
Boeing 727-277	VH-RMV	11/73-6/84	lsd Wien Air Alaska 12/83-6/84
Boeing 727-277	VH-RMW	4/74-6/84	lsd Wien Air Alaska 12/83-6/84
Boeing 727-277	VH-RMX	7/74-9/01	last passenger service 3/83, cvtd to 727-277F for Ansett Air Freight/Ansett Australia Cargo.
Boeing 727-277	VH-RMY	11/74-5/89	lsd Air Jamaica 10/85-10/86
Boeing 727-277	VH-RMZ	11/74-5/89	lsd TAA 1/84-12/84 as *Frank Hann*
Boeing 727-277LR	VH-ANA	6/81-4/97	Ansett, lsd Eastwest 1/92
Boeing 727-277LR	VH-ANB	7/81-4/97	4000th Boeing jetliner, Ansett, lsd Eastwest 1/92
Boeing 727-277LR	VH-ANE	6/81-1/97	Ansett, lsd Eastwest 1/92-2/94
Boeing 727-277LR	VH-ANF	7/81-12/96	Ansett, lsd Eastwest 1/92-12/93
Boeing 727-233F	N6809	3/99-2/00	AAF, sub-lsd from Kittyhawk Air Cargo
Boeing 727-233F	N6833	6/97-9/97	AAF, lsd from Aircraft Leasing Inc
Boeing 727-251	N852US	10/97-1/98	AAF, lsd from Aircraft Leasing Inc
Boeing 727-281F	VH-TXD	2/01-9/01	AAC, lsd from Transasian Air Express
Boeing 727-2J4F	VH-DHE	12/96-6/97	AAF, lsd from DHL
Boeing 737-130	ZK-NEA	2/87-2/90	Ansett NZ *City of Auckland*, ex Lufthansa (1st production 737), lsd from AWAS
Boeing 737-130	ZK-NEB	6/87-12/89	Ansett NZ *City of Wellington*, lsd from AWAS
Boeing 737-130	ZK-NEC	4/87-12/89	Ansett NZ *City of Christchurch*, lsd from AWAS
Boeing 737-112	ZK-NED	7/87-1/90	Ansett NZ *City of* Nelson, lsd from AWAS
Boeing 737-2A6	ZK-NEE	7/88-12/89	Ansett NZ, lsd from Corsair
Boeing 737-2U4	ZK-NEF	6/88-12/88	Ansett NZ, lsd from America West
Boeing 737-277	VH-CZM	6/81-9/86	lsd to Polynesian Airlines 12/84-1/85, lsd Polynesian/Air Vanuatu from 11/85
Boeing 737-277	VH-CZN	7/81-12/86	
Boeing 737-277	VH-CZO	8/81-11/86	
Boeing 737-277	VH-CZP	9/81-10/86	
Boeing 737-277	VH-CZQ	10/81-11/86	
Boeing 737-277	VH-CZR	11/81-2/87	
Boeing 737-277	VH-CZS	12/81-1/87	
Boeing 737-277	VH-CZT	2/82-11/86	
Boeing 737-277	VH-CZU	3/82-1/87	

Type	Regn	In Service	Notes
Boeing 737-277	VH-CZV	4/82-1/87	
Boeing 737-277	VH-CZW	6/82-11/86	
Boeing 737-277	VH-CZX	6/82-9/86	
Boeing 737-377	VH-CZA	8/86-9/01	
Boeing 737-377	VH-CZB	9/86-9/01	
Boeing 737-377	VH-CZC	9/86-9/01	
Boeing 737-377	VH-CZD	10/86-9/01	
Boeing 737-377	VH-CZE	10/86-9/01	
Boeing 737-377	VH-CZF	10/86-9/01	
Boeing 737-377	VH-CZG	11/86-9/01	
Boeing 737-377	VH-CZH	11/86-9/01	
Boeing 737-377	VH-CZI	12/86-9/01	
Boeing 737-377	VH-CZJ	12/86-9/01	
Boeing 737-377	VH-CZK	1/87-9/01	
Boeing 737-377	VH-CZL	1/87-9/01	
Boeing 737-377	VH-CZM	10/88-9/01	lsd to America West 10/89-9/91
Boeing 737-377	VH-CZN	10/88-9/01	
Boeing 737-377	VH-CZO	10/88-9/01	lsd to America West 10/89-4/90
Boeing 737-377	VH-CZP	11/88-9/01	lsd to America West 10/89-4/90
Boeing 737-33A	VH-CZQ	2/01-9/01	lsd from Ansett Worldwide
Boeing 737-33A	VH-CZR	5/01-9/01	lsd from Ansett Worldwide
Boeing 737-33A	VH-CZS	5/96-9/01	lsd from AWAS
Boeing 737-33A	VH-CZT	4/95-9/01	lsd from AWAS
Boeing 737-33A	VH-CZU	5/94-9/01	lsd from AWAS
Boeing 737-33A	VH-CZV	11/93-9/01	lsd from AWAS
Boeing 737-33A	VH-CZW	12/93-9/01	lsd from AWAS
Boeing 737-33A	VH-CZX	2/94-9/01	lsd from AWAS
Boeing 737-33A	N166AW	9/89-3/90	lsd from America West during pilots' dispute
Boeing 737-33A	N167AW	9/89-2/90	lsd from America West during pilots' dispute
Boeing 737-33A	N168AW	11/89-1/90	lsd from America West during pilots' dispute
Boeing 737-33A	G-PATE	11/89-5/90	Ansett/Eastwest, lsd from Paramount Airways during pilots' dispute
Boeing 737-3H9	YU-AND	11/89-1/90	lsd from JAT during pilots' dispute
Boeing 737-3H9	YU-ANJ	11/89-1/90	lsd from JAT during pilots' dispute
Boeing 737-3Q8	5W-ILF	4/01-5/01	lsd from Polynesian Airlines during 767 groundings
Boeing 737-3S3	5W-FAX	2/93-6/93	AAF, lsd from ILFC
Boeing 747-312	VH-INH	9/94-9/99	Ansett International, lsd from SIA
Boeing 747-312	VH-INJ	8/94-8/99	Ansett International, lsd from SIA
Boeing 747-312	VH-INK	11/95-12/98	Ansett International, lsd from SIA
Boeing 747-312	N121KG	6/95	Ansett International, lsd from SIA, also 7/96
Boeing 747-312	N122KH	3/97	Ansett International, lsd from SIA
Boeing 747-312	N123KG	9/96-10/96	Ansett International, lsd from SIA
Boeing 747-312	N123KJ	10/97-12/97	Ansett International, lsd from SIA
Boeing 747-312	N124KK	4/97-6/97	Ansett International, lsd from SIA
Boeing 747-312	N125KL	1/96-2/96	Ansett International, lsd from SIA
Boeing 747-412	VH-ANA	8/99-9/01	Ansett International, lsd from SIA
Boeing 747-412	VH-ANB	9/99-9/01	Ansett International, lsd from SIA
Boeing 747-412	9V-SMA	8/00	Ansett International, lsd from SIA
Boeing 747-412	9V-SMT	4/99	Ansett International, lsd from SIA
Boeing 747-412	9V-SPD	4/01	lsd from SIA during 767 groundings
Boeing 747-419	ZK-SUJ	4/01	lsd from Air NZ during 767 groundings
Boeing 767-284ER	VH-RMA	11/92-1/93	lsd from AWAS
Boeing 767-219ER	VH-RMC	6/97-6/98	lsd from Air NZ, Ansett International, lsd out to other operators from 6/98, returned to Air NZ 4/99
Boeing 767-277	VH-RMD	6/83-9/01	all 767-277s delivered with 3-crew cockpits
Boeing 767-277	VH-RME	6/83-9/01	
Boeing 767-277	VH-RMF	6/83-9/01	
Boeing 767-277	VH-RMG	8/83-9/01	
Boeing 767-277	VH-RMH	9/84-9/01	
Boeing 767-204	VH-RMK	11/94-9/01	ex Britannia Airways
Boeing 767-204	VH-RML	12/95-9/01	ex Britannia Airways
Boeing 767-216ER	VH-RMM	4/96-9/01	ex LAN-Chile
Boeing 767-204	VH-RMO	7/96-9/01	ex Britannia Airways
Boeing 767-219ER	ZK-NBA	4/01	lsd from Air NZ during 767 groundings
Boeing 767-319ER	ZK-NCK	4/01-5/01	lsd from Air NZ during 767 groundings
Boeing 767-375	C-FTCA	4/01-7/01	lsd from Air Canada during 767 groundings
Boeing 767-324ER	VH-BZF	3/96-9/01	Ansett International
Boeing 767-33AER	VH-BZI	—	lsd from Ansett Worldwide, del 9/01 did not enter service
Boeing 767-35HER	VH-BZL	8/01-9/01	lsd from Air Canada
Boeing 767-35HER	VH-BZM	—	lsd from Air Canada, del 9/01 did not enter service
Bombardier CRJ200	VH-KJF	9/99-9/01	Kendell *City of Launceston*
Bombardier CRJ200	VH-KJG	12/99-9/01	Kendell *City of Melbourne*
Bombardier CRJ200	VH-KJJ	1/00-9/01	Kendell *City of Hobart*
Bombardier CRJ200	VH-KJN	2/00-9/01	Kendell *City of Canberra*
Bombardier CRJ200	VH-KJQ	3/00-9/01	Kendell *City of Mackay*
Bombardier CRJ200	VH-KJS	6/00-9/01	Kendell *City of Rockhampton*
Bombardier CRJ200	VH-KJU	6/00-9/01	Kendell *City of Adelaide*
Bombardier CRJ200	VH-KJV	9/00-9/01	Kendell *City of Sydney*
Bombardier CRJ200	VH-KJX	2/01-9/01	Kendell, lsd to Eurowings from 4/01
Bombardier CRJ200	VH-KJY	3/01-9/01	Kendell

Type	Regn	In Service	Notes
Bombardier CRJ200	VH-KXJ	6/01-9/01	Kendell
Bristol Freighter Mk.31	VH-BFA	8/61-11/67	ex Pakistan AF, Ansett-ANA, to Ansett-MAL 5/64
Bristol Freighter Mk.31	VH-BFB	8/61-11/67	ex Pakistan AF, Ansett-ANA. to Ansett-MAL 5/64
Bristol Freighter Mk.21	VH-INJ	10/57-6/61	*Pokana*, ex ANA
Bristol Freighter Mk.21	VH-INK	10/57-58	*Kiopana*, ex ANA, 6th Freighter built
Bristol Freighter Mk.21	VH-INL	10/57-58	*Mannana*, ex ANA
Bristol Sycamore 3A	VH-INO	10/57-1/60	ex BEA/ANA *Yarrana*, Ansett-ANA Helicopter Division, w/o 1/60
Bristol Sycamore 4	VH-INQ	9/58-9/61	ex BEA, Helicopter Division, w/o 9/61
Consolidated Catalina	VH-BRI	10/59-7/62	PBY-5A, AFBS *The Golden Islander*, dbr Hayman Island 7/62
Convair CV-340-32	VH-BZD	8/54-3/59	ex Braniff, Ansett/Ansett-ANA
Convair CV-340-51A	VH-BZE	4/55-4/59	Ansett/Ansett-ANA
Convair CV-440-97	VH-BZF	6/57-2/72	Ansett/Ansett-ANA/ASA
Convair CV-340-36	VH-BZG	11/56-6/57	Ansett, lsd from Hawaiian Airlines
Convair CV-440-97	VH-BZH	9/57-5/62	Ansett/Ansett-ANA
Convair CV-440-97	VH-BZI	10/57-5/62	Ansett-ANA
Convair CV-440-97	VH-BZM	9/57-1/62	Ansett/Ansett-ANA
Convair CV-440-75	VH-BZN	11/57-2/72	Ansett-ANA/ASA
Convair CV-440-75	VH-BZO	12/57-11/59	Ansett-ANA
De Havilland Moth	VH-UNF	9/34-2/39	DH.60M, bought by Reg Ansett, tfrd to Ansett Airways 1936
DHC Caribou	VH-BFC	9/65-1/69	Ansett-MAL/AAPNG
DHC Twin Otter 100	VH-MMY	12/67-6/87	MMA *Yampi* 12/67-4/76, Aeropelican 4/76-6/87
DHC Twin Otter 300	VH-KZN	6/87-9/01	Aeropelican, ex Atlantis Airlines (USA)
DHC Twin Otter 300	VH-KZO	7/81-9/01	Aeropelican
DHC Twin Otter 300	VH-KZP	7/81-9/01	Aeropelican
DHC Twin Otter 300	VH-KZQ	7/81-9/01	Aeropelican
DHC Twin Otter 300	VH-PGS	12/69-11/73	AAPNG
DHC Twin Otter 300	VH-PGT	12/69-11/73	AAPNG
DHC Twin Otter 300	VH-PGU	6/70-10/78	Ansett/MMA
DHC Twin Otter 300	VH-USW	8/87-3/96	Skywest
DHC Twin Otter 300	VH-XFE	6/94-11/94	ex Flight West
DHC Twin Otter 300	VH-XSW	8/87-11/96	Skywest
DHC Dash 8-102	ZK-NES	4/96-9/00	Ansett NZ, lsd from Bombardier
DHC Dash 8-102	ZK-NET	10/95-9/00	Ansett NZ, lsd from Bombardier
DHC Dash 8-102	ZK-NEU	12/95-9/00	Ansett NZ, lsd from Bombardier
DHC Dash 8-102	VH-XFU	1/93-3/93	Ansett NZ, lsd from Flight West
DHC Dash 8-102	ZK-NEV	6/95-12/95	Ansett NZ, lsd from Flight West (same a/c as VH-XFU, above)
DHC Dash 8-102	ZK-NEW	3/95-2/96	Ansett NZ, lsd from Flight West
DHC Dash 8-102	ZK-NEY	12/86-6/95	Ansett NZ, w/o Palmerston North 6/95
DHC Dash 8-102	ZK-NEZ	12/96-9/00	Ansett NZ
DHC Dash 8-311B	ZK-NER	2/00-9/00	Ansett NZ, ex SA Express
DHC Dash 8-314B	ZK-NEQ	5/00-9/00	Ansett NZ, ex SA Express
Douglas DC-3	VH-AAU	2/58-2/67	QAL/Ansett-ANA/MAL
Douglas DC-3	VH-ABR	10/57-10/71	ex ANA *Kanana*, Ansett-ANA/ASA, preserved airworthy
Douglas DC-3	VH-AMJ	6/47-11/56	Ansett *Anselina*, later VH-RMJ/BZJ
Douglas DC-3	VH-AMK	6/46-10/58	*Anstratus*, Ansett/Ansett-ANA, later VH-RMK/BZK
Douglas DC-3	VH-AML	11/46-8/57	*Ansaga*, Ansett, later VH-RML/BZL
Douglas DC-3	VH-ANH	10/57-12/70	ex ANA *Tullana*, Ansett-ANA/VAC/ ANSW/Ansett
Douglas DC-3	VH-ANJ	10/57-11/68	ex ANA *Kadana*, Ansett-ANA/VAC/ANSW
Douglas DC-3	VH-ANM	12/58-5/66	ex ANA *Yannana*, QAL/Ansett-ANA/BAT/ANSW, to SPANZ 10/61-2/66 as ZK-CAW *George Bolt*
Douglas DC-3	VH-ANN	10/57-4/66	ex ANA *Ranana*, Guinea/Ansett-ANA/ASA/QAL
Douglas DC-3	VH-ANO	10/57-9/69	ex ANA *Tinana*, Ansett-ANA/VAC/Ansett
Douglas DC-3	VH-ANP	2/60-6/67	ex ANA *Boyana*, Guinea/Ansett-ANA/ASA/VAC
Douglas DC-3	VH-ANQ	10/57-11/67	ex ANA *Dromana*, Ansett-ANA/ANSW/VAC
Douglas DC-3	VH-ANR	10/57-7/72	ex ANA *Oana*, Ansett-ANA/ANSW
Douglas DC-3	VH-ANS	2/60-12/66	ex ANA *Moongana*, Guinea/Ansett-ANA/ASA/ANSW
Douglas DC-3	VH-ANT	10/57-11/68	ex ANA *Wandana*, Ansett-ANA/Ansett, cvtd to freighter 1958
Douglas DC-3	VH-ANV	10/57-2/71	ex ANA *Louana*, freighter, Ansett-ANA
Douglas DC-3	VH-ANW	2/60-10/71	ex ANA *Moogana*, Guinea/ASA/Ansett-ANA
Douglas DC-3	VH-ANX	10/57-3/72	ex ANA *Tarrana*, Ansett-ANA/ASA/Ansett/MMA
Douglas DC-3	VH-ANZ	10/57-2/70	ex ANA *Largana*, Ansett-ANA/ASA/ANSW/MMA
Douglas DC-3	VH-AOH	2/61-7/67	ex Butler *Darling Downs*, QAL/Ansett-ANA/ANSW/MAL
Douglas DC-3	VH-AOI	2/58-1/69	ex Butler *Warrana*, QAL/Ansett-ANA/ANSW/MAL
Douglas DC-3	VH-AVL	2/58-3/60	ex Guinea, QAL, to SPANZ 10/60-12/65 as ZK-BYD *Ernest Rutherford*
Douglas DC-3	VH-BDU	2/61-10/67	ex Butler, ANSW/MAL
Douglas DC-3	VH-BUR	5/60-1/66	ANSW, op for NSW Dept of Lands Aerial Survey Unit
Douglas DC-3	VH-BZA	7/48-1/56	Ansett *Anscirrus*, originally VH-RMA, crashed near Hobart 1/56
Douglas DC-3	VH-BZB	11/49-10/58	*Ansertes*, lsd to Guinea Air Traders 11/49-8/50
Douglas DC-3	VH-BZC	5/50-10/58	*Ansalanta*, Ansett
Douglas DC-3	VH-EWB	10/65-1/66	lsd from East-West by MMA
Douglas DC-3	VH-EWE	1965	lsd from East-West by Ansett-MAL
Douglas DC-3	VH-EWF	6/65-12/65	lsd from East-West by ASA
Douglas DC-3	VH-INB	2/60-12/67	ex ANA *Croana*, Guinea/ASA/ANSW/Ansett-ANA, reregist VH-GAL
Douglas DC-3	VH-INC	10/57-7/66	ex ANA *Pathana*, Ansett-ANA/ANSW
Douglas DC-3	VH-IND	10/57-12/60	ex ANA *Menana*, Ansett-ANA/BAT/ANSW, to SPANZ 12/60-12/65 as ZK-BYE *Jean Batten*
Douglas DC-3	VH-ING	10/57-1/67	ex ANA *Mukana*, Ansett-ANA/VAC/ANSW
Douglas DC-3	VH-INI	10/57-12/60	ex ANA VH-INA *Pengana*, reregist VH-INI Ansett-ANA/ANSW, crashed into sea off Sydney 12/60
Douglas DC-3	VH-MAB	6/61-11/73	ex MAL VH-MAM, Ansett-MAL/AAPNG

Type	Regn	In Service	Notes
Douglas DC-3	VH-MAC	1/61-6/67	ex MAL, Ansett-MAL
Douglas DC-3	VH-MAE	1/61-7/72	ex MAL VH-BFV, Ansett-MAL, w/o Wapenamanda NG 7/72
Douglas DC-3	VH-MAL	1/61-9/73	ex MAL, Ansett-MAL/AAPNG
Douglas DC-3	VH-MAN	1/61-11/73	ex MAL, Ansett-MAL/AAPNG
Douglas DC-3	VH-MAR	1/61-68	ex MAL, Ansett-MAL/AAPNG
Douglas DC-3	VH-MAS	2/61-4/67	ex MAL, Ansett-MAL
Douglas DC-3	VH-MAT	1/61-11/73	ex MAL, Ansett-MAL/AAPNG
Douglas DC-3	VH-MAV	1/61-7/69	ex MAL VH-MAH, Ansett-MAL/AAPNG
Douglas DC-3	VH-MMA	4/63-11/73	MMA *Ashburton*, AAPNG
Douglas DC-3	VH-MMD	4/63-11/73	MMA *Fitzroy*, AAPNG
Douglas DC-3	VH-MMF	4/63-12/74	MMA *Fortescue*, AAPNG
Douglas DC-3	VH-MMK	4/63-1/69	MMA *Kimberley*
Douglas DC-3	VH-MML	1/69-11/73	MMA *Lyndon*, AAPNG
Douglas DC-3	VH-MMM	4/63-1/69	MMA
Douglas DC-3	VH-MMO	4/63-5/69	MMA
Douglas DC-3	VH-MMT	4/65-10/69	MMA *Turner*
Douglas DC-3	VH-PNA	7/70-10/72	ex Patair *Mt Victoria*, AAPNG, used for JATO trials
Douglas DC-3	VH-PNB	7/70-4/72	ex Patair *Mt Albert Edward*, AAPNG, lsd by TAA from 6/71, w/o Madang 4/72
Douglas DC-3	VH-PNM	8/72-3/74	ex Patair *Mt Murray*, AAPNG
Douglas DC-3	VH-TAG	6/50-8/50	Ansett, lsd from TAA
Douglas DC-3	G-AMKE	12/61-2/62	lsd from Air Links by SPANZ
Douglas DC-3	ZK-AQU	7/65-8/65	lsd from NZNAC by SPANZ
Douglas DC-4-1009	VH-ANB	10/57-4/58	ex ANA *Lackrana*
Douglas DC-4-1009	VH-ANC	10/57-1/58	ex ANA *Warana*
Douglas DC-4-1009	VH-ANE	10/57-5/58	ex ANA *Arkana*
Douglas DC-4/C-54A	VH-ANF	10/57-8/67	ex ANA *Loongana*
Douglas DC-4-1009	VH-ANG	10/57-4/58	ex ANA *Palana*
Douglas DC-4-1009	VH-INJ	8/63-5/65	ex SAS/JAL, ANSW/ASA, cvtd to Carvair 1965
Douglas DC-4-1009	VH-INK	4/64-6/65	ex SAS/JAL, Ansett-ANA, cvtd to Carvair 1965
Douglas DC-4-1009	VH-INL	7/64-73	ex JAL, Ansett-ANA
Douglas DC-4/C-54E	VH-INM	3/65-2/68	ex JAL, Ansett-ANA, cvtd to Carvair 1968
Douglas DC-4/C-54A	VH-INX	10/57-12/70	ex ANA *Katana*, Ansett-ANA/MMA
Douglas DC-4/C-54A	VH-INY	10/57-3/58	ex ANA *Laxapana*
Douglas DC-4-1009	VH-INY	1/61-1/70	ex Qantas VH-EBL, cvtd to freighter 1967
Douglas DC-4/C-54A	VH-INZ	10/57-4/58	ex ANA *Ratmalana*
Douglas DC-4-1009	VH-TAB	1959	lsd from TAA, mixed passenger/freight
Douglas DC-4/C-54A	VH-TAC	11/69-1/70	lsd from TAA, freighter
Douglas DC-6	VH-INV	10/57-3/60	ex National/ANA *Nairana*
Douglas DC-6	VH-INW	10/57-3/60	ex National/ANA *Kurana*
Douglas DC-6B	VH-INA	11/63-9/66	ex United/US Overseas
Douglas DC-6B	VH-INH	10/57-3/67	ex ANA *Bungana*, lsd to TAA 2/60-8/66
Douglas DC-6B	VH-INS	10/57-7/66	ex ANA *Beltana*
Douglas DC-6B	VH-INT	10/57-12/66	ex ANA *Olympiana*
Douglas DC-6B	VH-INU	10/57-12/67	ex ANA *Kwinana*, lsd to TAA 2/60-8/66
Douglas DC-8-61F	N23UA	1/89	AAF, sub-lsd from Trans International
Douglas DC-8-61F	N813CK	1/89	AAF, sub-lsd from Trans International
Douglas DC-8-62F	N791AL	8/89-2/90	AAF, lsd from R T Leasing Inc
Douglas DC-8-62F	N1804	7/94-4/95	AAF, lsd from International Air Leases
Douglas DC-8-62F	N735PL	4/95	AAF, lsd from Air Transport Int'l
Douglas DC-8-62F	N51CX	11/95-12/95	AAF, lsd from GMD Inc
Douglas DC-8-71F	N872SJ	2/95-3/95	AAF, lsd from Guinness Peat Avn
Douglas DC-8-73F	N875SJ	2/95-3/95	AAF, lsd from Guinness Peat Avn
Douglas DC-9-31	VH-CZA	4/67-6/82	Ansett-ANA/Ansett
Douglas DC-9-31	VH-CZB	4/67-3/82	Ansett-ANA/Ansett
Douglas DC-9-31	VH-CZC	6/67-1/82	Ansett-ANA/Ansett
Douglas DC-9-31	VH-CZD	3/68-5/82	Ansett-ANA/Ansett, lsd Air Vanuatu 10/81-12/81
Douglas DC-9-31	VH-CZE	11/68-7/81	Ansett
Douglas DC-9-31	VH-CZF	7/69-6/82	lsd Air Vanuatu 9/81
Douglas DC-9-31	VH-CZG	2/70-1/82	
Douglas DC-9-31	VH-CZH	9/70-11/81	
Douglas DC-9-31	VH-CZI	2/71-6/81	
Douglas DC-9-31	VH-CZJ	4/71-8/81	
Douglas DC-9-31	VH-CZK	7/71-9/81	
Douglas DC-9-31	VH-CZL	11/71-12/81	
Fairchild Metro II	VH-BIF	6/90-6/93	Kendell, ex Air Queensland
Fairchild Metro II	VH-BIS	6/90-7/94	Kendell, ex Stillwell Aviation
Fairchild Metro II	VH-KDQ	6/90-8/95	Kendell *Progress of Albury/Wodonga*
Fairchild Metro II	VH-KDR	6/90-9/95	Kendell *City of Wagga Wagga*
Fairchild Metro II	VH-WGV	6/90-3/94	Kendell, ex Air Queensland
Fairchild Metro II	VH-WGX	6/90-4/94	Kendell, ex Air Queensland
Fairchild Metro II	VH-WGY	6/90-7/94	Kendell, ex Air Queensland
Fairchild Metro 23	VH-DMI	3/01-9/01	Hazelton
Fairchild Metro 23	VH-DMO	3/01-9/01	Hazelton
Fairchild Metro 23	VH-KAN	8/93-9/01	Kendell
Fairchild Metro 23	VH-KDJ	8/92-9/01	Kendell *City of Portland*
Fairchild Metro 23	VH-KDO	8/93-9/01	Kendell *Spirit of Coober Pedy*
Fairchild Metro 23	VH-KDT	9/92-9/01	Kendell *Spirit of Ceduna*
Fairchild Metro 23	VH-KED	3/94-9/01	Kendell *Spirit of King Island*
Fairchild Metro 23	VH-KEU	3/94-9/01	Kendell *Sunraysia Chaffey Trail*

Type	Regn	In Service	Notes
Fairchild Metro 23	VH-KEX	2/95-9/01	Kendell
Fairchild Merlin IV	VH-SWP	6/90-9/93	Kendell, ex Opal Air
Fokker F.XI Universal	VH-UTO	1/36-2/39	built 1928 in USA by Atlantic Aircraft Corp, w/o hangar fire Essendon 2/39
Fokker F27-500	VH-EWP	7/87-8/89	Eastwest *Norfolk Island*
Fokker F27-500	VH-EWU	7/87-11/90	Eastwest *City of Albury*
Fokker F27-500	VH-EWV	7/87-12/90	Eastwest *City of Tamworth*
Fokker F27-500	VH-EWW	7/87-12/90	Eastwest *City of Devonport*
Fokker F27-500	VH-EWX	7/87-11/90	Eastwest *Sunshine Coast*
Fokker F27-500	VH-EWY	7/87-8/90	Eastwest *City of Armidale*, lsd Ansett WA 9/89-2/90
Fokker F27-500	VH-EWZ	7/87-8/90	Eastwest *City of Port Macquarie*
Fokker F27-500	VH-FCA	12/75-12/88	ANSW/Ansett
Fokker F27-500	VH-FCB	1/76-1/88	ANSW/Ansett
Fokker F27-500	VH-FCC	6/76-12/88	ANSW/Ansett
Fokker F27-500	VH-FCD	6/76-11/87	ANSW/Ansett
Fokker F27-500	VH-FCE	6/77-11/86	ANSW
Fokker F27-500	VH-FCF	8/77-12/88	ANSW
Fokker F27-200	VH-FNA	10/59-7/76	Ansett-ANA/MMA/AAPNG
Fokker F27-200	VH-FNB	10/59-7/76	ANSW/Ansett/ASA
Fokker F27-200	VH-FNC	2/60-10/76	ANSW
Fokker F27-200	VH-FND	2/60-2/76	ANSW
Fokker F27-200	VH-FNE	2/60-3/71	QAL *Sir Henry Abel Smith*, Ansett-ANA/ANSW, dbr hangar fire Essendon 3/71
Fokker F27-200	VH-FNF	3/60-6/64	Ansett-ANA RMA *Ord*, lsd MMA as VH-MMO 6/64
Fokker F27-200	VH-FNG	3/61-7/76	ANSW/AAPNG, lsd Air Niugini from 11/73
Fokker F27-200	VH-FNH	7/61-3/65	Ansett-ANA, w/o Launceston 3/65
Fokker F27-200	VH-FNI	7/61-1/81	Ansett-ANA/ASA *City of Whyalla*/Ansett
Fokker F27-200	VH-FNJ	12/64-11/80	ANSW/ASA/Ansett
Fokker F27-200	VH-FNK	8/65-7/76	Ansett-ANA/ASA, lsd Air Niugini from 11/73
Fokker F27-200	VH-FNL	12/65-1/77	Ansett-ANA/MMA
Fokker F27-200	VH-FNM	1/66-10/85	Ansett-ANA/MAL/AAPNG/Ansett, lsd BPA/Air Qld from 10/80
Fokker F27-200	VH-FNN	3/66-7/76	Ansett-ANA *Bert Hinkler*/MAL/AAPNG, lsd Air Niugini from 11/73
Fokker F27-600	VH-FNO	8/66-7/89	Ansett-ANA/MMA/AANA/Ansett
Fokker F27-600	VH-FNP	8/66-1/87	ANSW/ASA *City of Whyalla* and *Sir Thomas Playford*/Ansett
Fokker F27-600	VH-FNQ	12/66-11/90	Ansett-ANA/Ansett, lsd Safe Air 12/89-5/90
Fokker F27-600	VH-FNR	1/67-11/93	Ansett-ANA/Ansett/ASA *Daisy Bates*, to Ansett Industries (Hong Kong) 8/88 as SE-KGC operated mainly by Malmo Aviation on TNT European freight runs
Fokker F27-600	VH-FNS	1/67-7/77	MAL/Ansett-ANA
Fokker F27-600	VH-FNT	3/67-3/87	Ansett-ANA/Ansett, sold to Air UK 3/87 but returned 7/90 and leased out
Fokker F27-400	VH-FNU	8/70-8/86	ex Air France, Ansett/ASA, lsd Air Pacific 5-9/84, lsd Air Qld 10/84-7/85 and 11-12/85
Fokker F27-200	VH-FNV	10/71-10/85	ex All Nippon, Ansett/ASA, lsd Air Qld from 1/82
Fokker F27-200	VH-FNW	11/71-10/85	ex All Nippon, Ansett/ASA, lsd Air Qld from 1/82
Fokker F27-300	VH-MMB	8/70-3/71	ex LTU/Sabena, for MMA
Fokker F27-200	VH-MMO	6/64-5/89	VH-FNF reregistered for MMA 6/64-5/69, then Ansett/ANSW/Air Qld
Fokker F27-200	VH-MMR	7/66-7/86	MMA RMA *Robe*/ANSW/ASA *Sir Hans Heyson*/Ansett
Fokker F27-200	VH-MMS	4/63-1/89	del to MMA 12/59, to Ansett 6/69, lsd ANSW 5/79-3/80
Fokker F27-100	VH-MMU	1/66-11/68	lsd by MMA from PAL as RMA *Mubahay* and *Malagasy*
Fokker F27-200	VH-MMV	3/68-7/88	MMA RMA *Victoria*/Ansett/ASA *Sir Douglas Mawson*/Ansett
Fokker F28-1000	VH-ATE	12/87-3/88	Ansett, ex Dept of Transport and Communications
Fokker F28-1000	VH-FKA	6/70-5/95	MMA *Pilbara II*/AWA/ANSW/Ansett Express/Ansett
Fokker F28-1000	VH-FKB	7/70-9/89	MMA *Kimberley*/AWA/ALNA/ANSW
Fokker F28-1000	VH-FKC	10/70-10/95	MMA *Arnhem Land*/AWA/ALNA/ANSW/Ansett
Fokker F28-1000	VH-FKD	11/70-4/94	ANSW/MMA *Goldfields*/AWA/ALNA/Ansett Express
Fokker F28-1000	VH-FKE	9/71-7/96	MMA *Gascoyne*/AWA/Ansett
Fokker F28-1000	VH-FKF	10/80-3/95	ex Martinair, Ansett/MMA *Greenough*/AWA/ANT
Fokker F28-1000	VH-FKG	4/81-11/89	ex TAT, MMA *Horrie Miller*/AWA
Fokker F28-1000	VH-MMJ	8/69-6/70	MMA *Pilbara*, lsd from Fokker
Fokker F28-3000	VH-EWF	8/87-7/95	Eastwest lsd from Cimber Air, ANSW/Ansett Express/Ansett (bought 12/93)
Fokker F28-3000	VH-EWG	8/87-7/96	Eastwest lsd from Cimber Air, AWA/ANSW/Ansett Express/Ansett (bought 12/93)
Fokker F28-4000	VH-EWA	8/87-7/96	Eastwest *Don Shand*/Ansett Express/Ansett
Fokker F28-4000	VH-EWB	8/87-11/96	Eastwest *George Harrison*/Ansett Express/Ansett
Fokker F28-4000	VH-EWC	8/87-3/97	Eastwest *Basil Brown*/Ansett Express/Ansett
Fokker F28-4000	VH-EWD	8/87-12/99	Eastwest/Ansett Express/Ansett
Fokker F28-4000	VH-FKI	7/82-12/99	MMA *Cyril Kleinig*/AWA/ALNA/Ansett
Fokker F28-4000	VH-FKJ	12/82-3/99	MMA *Goldfields*/AWA/Eastwest (as VH-EWH)/AWA (as VH-FKJ)
Fokker F28-4000	VH-FKO	7/90-11/97	ex Lloyd Aviation (VH-LAR), Ansett/Eastwest/Ansett Express/Ansett
Fokker 50	VH-FNA	9/87-2/02	Ansett/ANSW/Ansett Express/Skywest
Fokker 50	VH-FNB	10/87-2/02	Ansett/ANSW/Ansett Express/Skywest
Fokker 50	VH-FNC	11/87-8/96	Ansett/ANSW/Ansett Express/Skywest
Fokker 50	VH-FND	8/88-2/02	Ansett/Ansett Express/Skywest
Fokker 50	VH-FNE	12/87-1/97	Ansett/ANSW/Ansett Express/Skywest
Fokker 50	VH-FNF	1/88-2/96	Ansett/Skywest
Fokker 50	VH-FNG	1/88-12/95	Ansett/Skywest
Fokker 50	VH-FNH	2/88-2/02	Ansett/Ansett Express/Skywest
Fokker 50	VH-FNI	2/88-2/02	Ansett/Ansett Express/Skywest
Fokker 50	VH-FNJ	3/88-8/98	Ansett/ANSW/Ansett Express, lsd Austrian Air Services 3/93-10/94, Ansett/Skywest, lsd MAS 10/95-97, lsd Skyways 10/97
Fokker 50	VH-FNK	3/88-6/88	Ansett, immediately lsd Austrian Air Services 3/88-6/88
Fokker 50	VH-FNL	3/88-6/88	Ansett, immediately lsd Austrian Air Services 3/88-6/88
Fokker 50	VH-FNM	4/88-9/88	Ansett, immediately lsd and then sold back to Fokker
Fokker 50	PH-LMA	4/88-9/88	VH-FNN allocated but ntu, aircraft immediately lsd and then sold back to Fokker

Type	Regn	In Service	Notes
Lockheed L.10B Electra	VH-UZN	9/37-2/39	*Ansirius*, w/o hangar fire Essendon 2/39
Lockheed L.10B Electra	VH-UZO	8/37-1/51	*Ansertes*, airworthy in 2002
Lockheed L.10B Electra	VH-UZP	10/37-5/46	*Ansalanta*, w/o Parafield SA 5/46
Lockheed L.14 Electra	VH-ADT	1/43-44	lsd from W R Carpenter for USAAF charters
Lockheed L.188A Electra	VH-RMA	2/59-12/83	Ansett-ANA/Ansett/AAF, cvtd L.188AF 1972
Lockheed L.188A Electra	VH-RMB	4/59-1/84	Ansett-ANA/Ansett/AAF, cvtd L.188AF 1972
Lockheed L.188A Electra	VH-RMC	2/60-2/84	Ansett-ANA/Ansett/AAF, cvtd L.188AF 1972
Lockheed L.188AF Electra	VH-RMG	8/75-5/78	ex American Airlines/McCulloch Int'l for AAF
Mohawk 298 (Nord 262)	VH-HEI	2/91-3/91	Ansett Express, lsd from Queensland Pacific
Mohawk 298 (Nord 262)	VH-HIX	12/91	Ansett Express, lsd from Southern Pacific Regional
Mohawk 298 (Nord 262)	VH-HKS	4/91-2/93	Ansett Express, lsd from Southern Pacific Regional
Mohawk 298 (Nord 262)	VH-HKT	10/91-2/93	Ansett Express, lsd from Southern Pacific Regional
Piaggio P.166	VH-FSA	11/65	Ansett-ANA, lsd from Forrester Stephen
Piaggio P.166	VH-GOA	4/61-12/69	Ansett-MAL/AAPNG
Piaggio P.166	VH-GOB	6/61-1/71	Ansett-MAL/AAPNG
Piaggio P.166	VH-GOC	4/64-8/72	Ansett-MAL/AAPNG, rereg VH-BBG
Piaggio P.166	VH-GOE	5/64-3/70	Ansett-MAL/AAPNG
Piaggio P.166	VH-MMP	2/64-6/69	MMA *Pilbara*
Piaggio P.166	VH-PGA	7/64-3/68	Ansett-ANA/ANSW
Piaggio P.166B	VH-ASA	1/63-6/66	ASA/Ansett-ANA
Piaggio P.166B	VH-PQA	63-66	QAL/Ansett-ANA
Porterfield 35/70	VH-UVH	12/36-2/39	damaged hangar fire Essendon 2/39, later rebuilt
Saab 340A	VH-EKD	6/90-9/01	Kendell *City of Wagga Wagga*
Saab 340A	VH-EKT	6/90-9/01	Kendell *City of Burnie*, ex Air Limousin
Saab 340A	VH-KDB	12/91-9/01	Kendell, ex KLM CityHopper
Saab 340A	VH-KDI	6/90-9/01	Kendell *City of Whyalla*
Saab 340A	VH-KDK	6/90-9/01	Kendell *City of Mount Gambier*
Saab 340A	VH-KDP	6/90-9/01	Kendell *City of Broken Hill*
Saab 340A	VH-KEQ	1/97-9/01	Kendell, ex Air Midwest/Nusantra Saki
Saab 340A	VH-LPI	7/97-5/01	Kendell, lsd from Saab
Saab 340A	VH-ZLY	3/01-9/01	Hazelton, ex Crossair
Saab 340A	VH-ZLZ	3/01-9/01	Hazelton, ex Crossair
Saab 340B	VH-CMH	3/01-9/01	Hazelton
Saab 340B	VH-EKG	6/95-9/01	Kendell
Saab 340B	VH-EKH	7/95-9/01	Kendell
Saab 340B	VH-EKK	2/97-9/01	Kendell, ex Skyways AB
Saab 340B	VH-EKN	10/95-9/01	Kendell
Saab 340B	VH-EKX	9/96-9/01	Kendell, ex Aer Lingus Commuter/Northwest Airlink Express
Saab 340B	VH-KDR	7/96-9/01	Kendell, ex Skyways AB
Saab 340B	VH-KDV	9/96-9/01	Kendell, ex Skyways AB
Saab 340B	VH-KDQ	3/96-9/01	Kendell, ex Skyways AB
Saab 340B	VH-LIH	3/01-9/01	Hazelton
Saab 340B	VH-OLL	3/01-9/01	Hazelton
Saab 340B	VH-OLM	3/01-9/01	Hazelton
Saab 340B	VH-OLN	3/01-9/01	Hazelton
Saab 340B	VH-SBA	see notes	Skywest 4/94-12/94 lsd from Saab, Hazelton 3/01-9/01
Saab 340B	VH-TCH	3/01-9/01	Hazelton
Short Hythe	VH-AKP	1952-54	lsd by AFBS 8/52 and 12/52, to AFBS 5/53-3/54 *Tahiti Star*
Short Sandringham 4	VH-BRC	5/50-9/74	*Beachcomber*, ex TEAL
Short Sandringham 4	VH-BRD	3/51-10/52	*Princess of Cairns*, ex TEAL, w/o Brisbane River 10/52
Short Sandringham 4	VH-BRE	12/54-7/63	*Pacific Chieftain*, ex Qantas, w/o Lord Howe Island 07/63
Short Sunderland III	VH-BRF	9/64-8/74	*Islander*, ex RNZAF, cvtd to 'Sandringham'
Short Skyvan 3	VH-PNI	7/70-9/72	ex Patair, AAPNG *Mt Kumi-Kumi*, w/o Siluwe PNG 9/72
Short Skyvan 3	VH-PNJ	7/70-10/73	ex Patair, AAPNG *Mt Kari-Kari*
Sikorsky S-61N	VH-BRH	8/76-9/84	for Whitsunday Islands services
Sikorsky S-61N	VH-BRI	11/64-7/84	*Coral Islander*, for Whitsunday islands services
Sikorsky S-62A	VH-AND	5/67-8/67	for Bass Strait oil rigs contract, crashed 8/67
Sikorsky S-62A	VH-ANE	5/67-3/68	for Bass Strait oil rigs contract
Sud-Ouest Djinn	VH-INP	10/57-5/58	Ansett-ANA Helicopter Division, w/o 5/58
Vickers Viscount V.720	VH-TVC	3/60-11/61	lsd from TAA, crashed into Botany Bay NSW 11/61
Vickers Viscount V.720	VH-TVE	3/60-10/66	lsd from TAA
Vickers Viscount V.720	VH-TVF	3/60-4/67	lsd from TAA
Vickers Viscount V.720	VH-RMQ	10/62-12/68	ex TAA (VH-TVB), crashed Port Hedland WA 12/68
Vickers Viscount V.747	VH-RMO	9/58-12/68	ex Butler (VH-BAT), lsd to MMA 4/68-9/68
Vickers Viscount V.747	VH-RMP	9/58-3/69	ex Butler (VH-BUT), wfu by Ansett-ANA 9/67 then lsd to MMA 5/68-3/69
Vickers Viscount V.812	VH-RMK	9/60-8/69	ex Continental
Vickers Viscount V.818	VH-RML	2/62-12/69	ex Cubana
Vickers Viscount V.832	VH-RMG	3/59-8/69	
Vickers Viscount V.832	VH-RMH	4/59-8/70	
Vickers Viscount V.832	VH-RMI	4/59-9/66	crashed Winton Qld 9/66
Vickers Viscount V.832	VH-RMJ	5/59-2/70	

* VH-BRA is a WW2 Boeing built Catalina, hence its non Consolidated designation.

ANSETT FAMILY TREE
Including predecessors and with company logos, courtesy Fred Niven.

Glenn Alderton

ANSETT HISTORICAL FLOW CHART

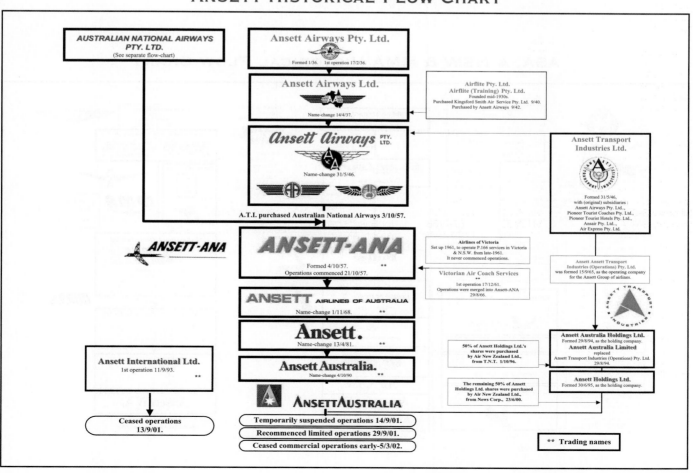

AUSTRALIAN NATIONAL AIRWAYS PTY. LTD.
(See separate flow-chart)

Ansett Airways Pty. Ltd.
Formed 1/36.   1st operation 17/2/36.

Ansett Airways Ltd.
Name-change 14/4/37.

Airflite Pty. Ltd.
Airflite (Training) Pty. Ltd.
Founded mid-1930s.
Purchased Kingsford Smith Air Service Pty. Ltd. 9/40.
Purchased by Ansett Airways 9/42.

Ansett Airways PTY. LTD.
Name-change 31/5/46.

Ansett Transport Industries Ltd.
Formed 31/5/46,
with (original) subsidiaries :
Ansett Airways Pty. Ltd.,
Pioneer Tourist Coaches Pty. Ltd.,
Pioneer Tourist Hotels Pty. Ltd.,
Ansair Pty. Ltd.,
Air Express Pty. Ltd.

A.T.I. purchased Australian National Airways 3/10/57.

ANSETT-ANA

ANSETT-ANA
Formed 4/10/57.   **
Operations commenced 21/10/57.

Airlines of Victoria
Set up 1961, to operate P.166 services in Victoria
& N.S.W. from late-1961.
It never commenced operations.

Victorian Air Coach Services   **
1st operation 17/12/61.
Operations were merged into Ansett-ANA
29/8/66.

Ansett Ansett Transport Industries (Operations) Pty. Ltd.
was formed 15/9/65, as the operating company
for the Ansett Group of airlines.

ANSETT AIRLINES OF AUSTRALIA
Name-change 1/11/68.   **

Ansett.
Name-change 13/4/81.   **

**50% of Ansett Holdings Ltd.'s
shares were purchased
by Air New Zealand Ltd.,
from T.N.T. 1/10/96.**

Ansett Australia Holdings Ltd.
Formed 29/8/94, as the holding company.
Ansett Australia Limited
replaced
Ansett Transport Industries (Operations) Pty. Ltd.
29/8/94.

Ansett International Ltd.
1st operation 11/9/93.   **

Ansett Australia.
Name-change 4/10/90   **

**The remaining 50% of Ansett
Holdings Ltd. shares were purchased
by Air New Zealand Ltd.,
from News Corp., 23/6/00.**

Ansett Holdings Ltd.
Formed 30/6/95, as the holding company.

AnsettAustralia

**Ceased operations
13/9/01.**

Temporarily suspended operations 14/9/01.
Recommenced limited operations 29/9/01.
Ceased commercial operations early-5/3/02.

**   ** Trading names**

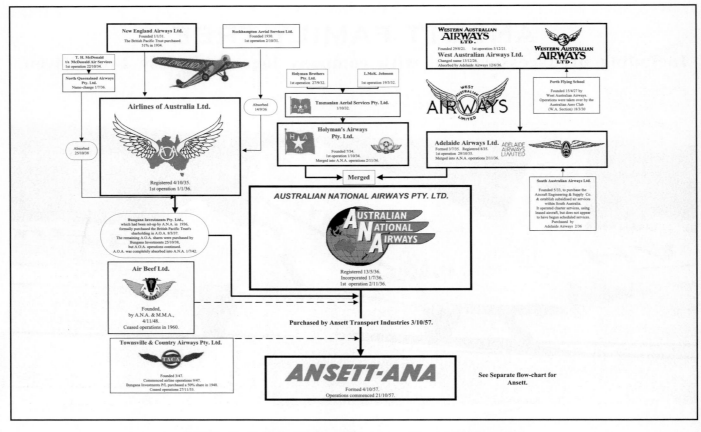

ANA & AOA Historical Flow Chart

ASA, A-NSW & MMA Historical Flow Chart

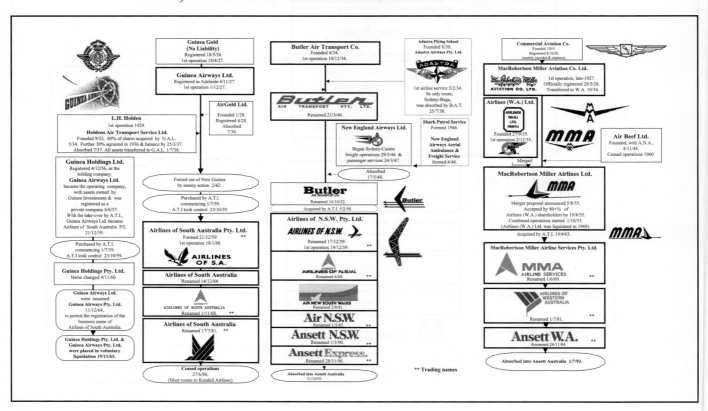

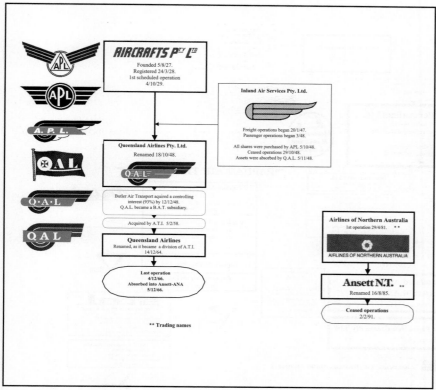

QAL & ANSETT NT HISTORICAL FLOW CHART

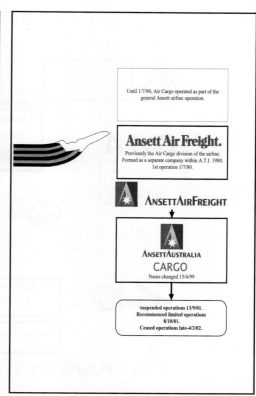

AAF & AAC HISTORICAL FLOW CHART

EWA, BRA & TOA HISTORICAL FLOW CHART

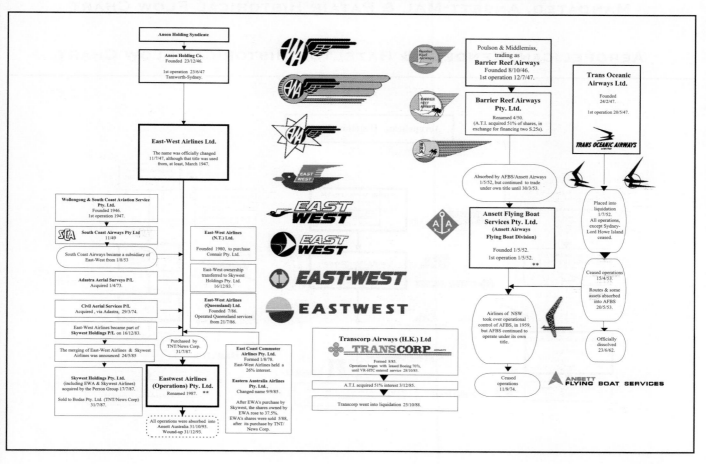

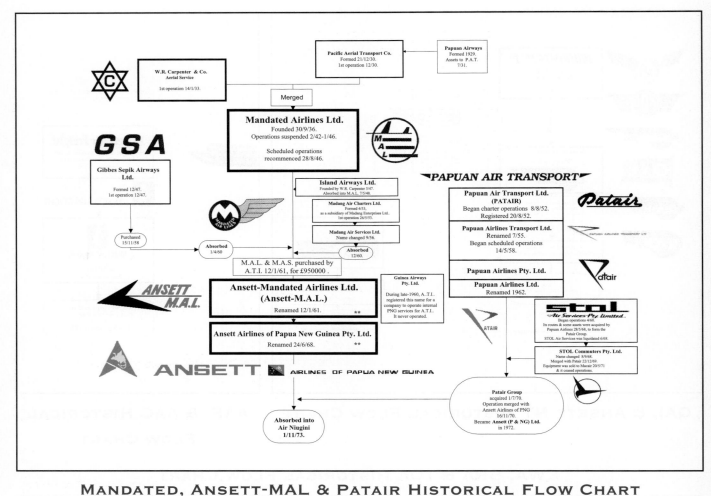

MANDATED, ANSETT-MAL & PATAIR HISTORICAL FLOW CHART

AEROPELICAN, KENDELL & HAZELTON HISTORICAL FLOW CHART

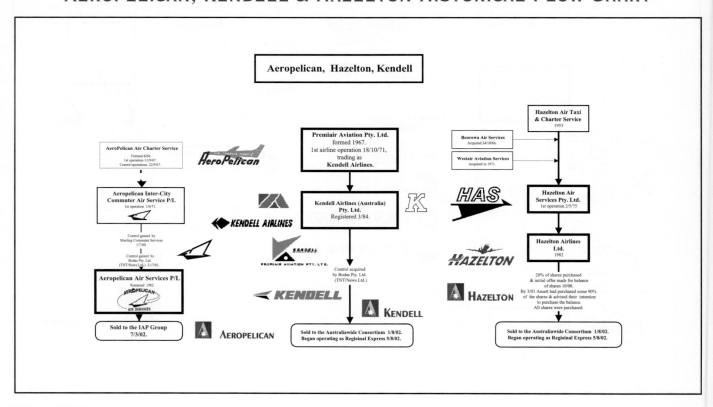

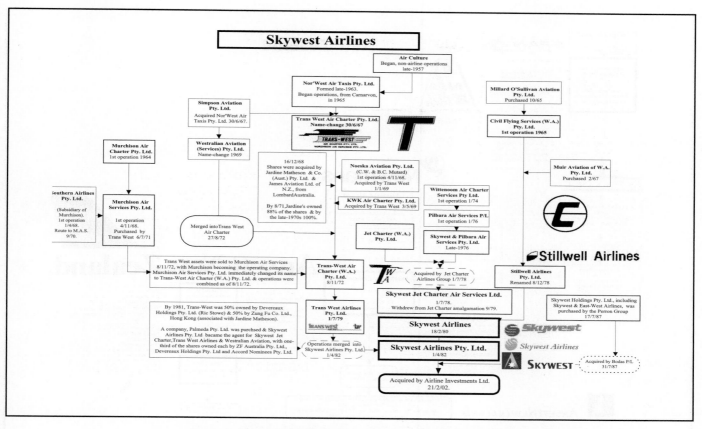

SKYWEST HISTORICAL FLOW CHART

CONNELLAN, CONNAIR, NORTHERN, LLOYD, PACIFIC AVIATION & SOUTHERN HISTORICAL FLOW CHART

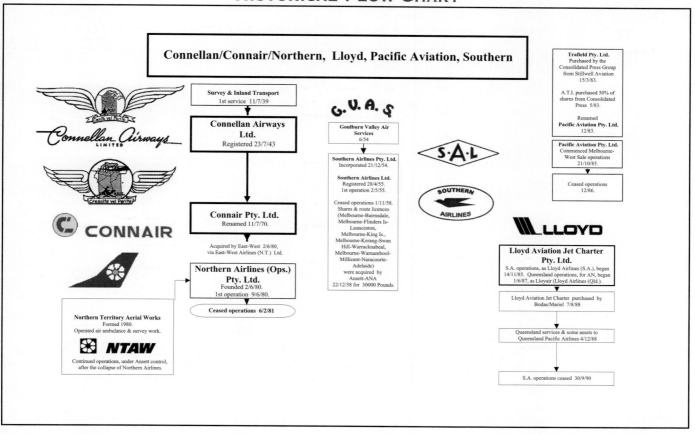

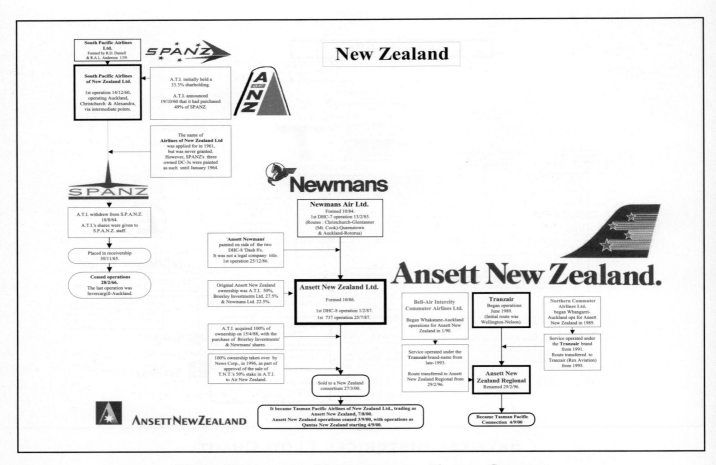

New Zealand

South Pacific Airlines Ltd.
Formed by R.D. Daniell
& R.A.L. Anderson 1/59.

South Pacific Airlines of New Zealand Ltd.

1st operation 14/12/60, operating Auckland, Christchurch & Alexandra, via intermediate points.

A.T.I. initially held a 33.3% sharholding.
A.T.I. announced 19/10/60 that it had purchased 49% of SPANZ.

The name of **Airlines of New Zealand Ltd** was applied for in 1961, but was never granted. However, SPANZ's three owned DC-3s were painted as such until January 1964.

Newmans

Newmans Air Ltd.
Formed 10/84.
1st DHC-7 operation 13/2/85.
(Routes : Christchurch-Glentanner (Mt. Cook)-Queenstown & Auckland-Rotorua)

A.T.I. withdrew from S.P.A.N.Z. 18/8/64.
A.T.I.'s shares were given to S.P.A.N.Z. staff.

Placed in receivership 30/11/65.

Ceased operations 28/2/66.
The last operation was Invercargill-Auckland.

'Ansett Newmans' painted on side of the two DHC-8 'Dash 8's.
It was not a legal company title.
1st operation 25/12/86.

Original Ansett New Zealand ownership was A.T.I. 50%, Brierley Investments Ltd. 27.5% & Newmans Ltd. 22.5%.

Ansett New Zealand Ltd.
Formed 10/86.
1st DHC-8 operation 1/2/87.
1st 737 operation 25/7/87.

Ansett New Zealand.

A.T.I. acquired 100% of ownership on 15/4/88, with the purchase of Brierley Investments' & Newmans' shares.

100% ownership taken over by News Corp., in 1996, as part of approval of the sale of T.N.T.'s 50% stake in A.T.I. to Air New Zealand.

Bell-Air Intercity Commuter Airlines Ltd.
Began Whakatane-Auckland operations for Ansett New Zealand in 1/90.

Service operated under the **Tranzair** brand-name from late-1993.
Route transferred to Ansett New Zealand Regional from 29/2/96.

Tranzair
Began operations June 1989.
(Initial route was Wellington-Nelson).

Northern Commuter Airlines Ltd.
began Whangarei-Auckland ops for Ansett New Zealand in 1989.

Service operated under the **Tranzair** brand from 1991.
Route transferred to Tranzair (Rex Aviation) from 1995.

Sold to a New Zealand consortium 27/3/00.

Ansett New Zealand Regional
Renamed 29/2/96.

It became Tasman Pacific Airlines of New Zealand Ltd., trading as Ansett New Zealand, 7/8/00.
Ansett New Zealand operations ceased 3/9/00, with operations as Qantas New Zealand starting 4/9/00.

Became Tasman Pacific Connection 4/9/00

ANSETTNEWZEALAND

NEW ZEALAND HISTORICAL FLOW CHART